Radical Transformations in Minority Religions

All religions undergo continuous change, but minority religions tend to be less anchored in their ways than mainstream, traditional religions. This volume examines radical transformations undergone by a variety of minority religions, including the Children of God/Family International; Gnosticism; Jediism; various manifestations of Paganism; LGBT Muslim groups; the Plymouth Brethren; Santa Muerte; and Satanism.

As with other books in the Routledge/Inform series, the contributors approach the subject from a wide range of perspectives: professional scholars include legal experts and sociologists specialising in new religious movements, but there are also chapters from those who have experienced a personal involvement. The volume is divided into four thematic parts that focus on different impetuses for radical change: interactions with society, technology and institutions, efforts at legitimation, and new revelations.

This book will be a useful source of information for social scientists, historians, theologians, and other scholars with an interest in social change, minority religions and 'cults'. It will also be of interest to a wider readership including lawyers, journalists, theologians and members of the general public.

Beth Singler is a digital anthropologist whose first book, *The Indigo Children: New Age Experimentation with Self and Science*, was the first ethnography of this primarily online community. Currently, as the Junior Research Fellow in Artificial Intelligence at Homerton College, University of Cambridge, Beth applies her anthropological approach to the stories we have about AI, digital discussions of its nature and impact, and online communities promoting apocalyptic, transhumanist, and future focussed accounts of AI.

Eileen Barker, FBA, OBE, is Professor Emeritus of Sociology with Special Reference to the Study of Religion at the London School of Economics. In 1988, with the support of the Home Office and the mainstream Churches, she founded INFORM, an educational charity, now based at King's College, London, which supplies information about alternative religions that is as objective and up-to-date as possible. She has over 400 publications, translated into 27 languages.

Routledge Inform Series on Minority Religions and Spiritual Movements

Series Editor Eileen Barker
London School of Economics and Political Science, UK

Inform is an independent charity that collects and disseminates accurate, balanced and up-to-date information about minority religious and spiritual movements.

The *Routledge Inform Series* addresses themes related to new religions, many of which have been the topics of Inform seminars. The series editorial board consists of internationally renowned scholars in the field.

Books in the series will attract both an academic and interested general readership, particularly in the areas of Religious Studies, and the Sociology of Religion and Theology.

Fiction, Invention, and Hyper-reality
From popular culture to religion
Edited by Carole M. Cusack and Pavol Kosnáč

New Religious Movements and Counselling
Academic, Professional and Personal Perspectives
Edited by Sarah Harvey, Silke Steidinger and James A. Beckford

Minority Religions in Europe and the Middle East
Mapping and Monitoring
Edited by George D. Chryssides

Minority Religions and Uncertainty
Edited by Kim Knott and Matthew Francis

Revisionism and Diversification in New Religious Movements
Edited by Eileen Barker

Reactions to the Law by Minority Religions
Edited by Eileen Barker and James T. Richardson

Radical Transformations in Minority Religions
Edited by Beth Singler and Eileen Barker

For more information about this series, please visit: www.routledge.com/religion/series/AINFORM

Radical Transformations
in Minority Religions

Edited by Beth Singler and
Eileen Barker

Routledge
Taylor & Francis Group

LONDON AND NEW YORK

First published 2022
by Routledge
2 Park Square, Milton Park, Abingdon, Oxon OX14 4RN

and by Routledge
605 Third Avenue, New York, NY 10158

Routledge is an imprint of the Taylor & Francis Group, an informa business

British Library Cataloguing-in-Publication Data
A catalogue record for this book is available from the British Library

Library of Congress Cataloging-in-Publication Data
A catalog record has been requested for this book

ISBN: 978-0-415-78670-6 (hbk)
ISBN: 978-1-032-11680-8 (pbk)
ISBN: 978-1-315-22680-4 (ebk)

DOI: 10.4324/9781315226804

Typeset in Sabon
by MPS Limited, Dehradun

This volume is dedicated to our husbands, Carl and Peter.

Contents

Figures

Fraternity had no lifestyle restrictions, received monthly lessons, paid annual dues and could attend most events. All staff were members of the fraternity and subscribers to the Pearls of Wisdom, the Church's weekly digest of ascended master teachings. Summit University was a three-month retreat and training programme. The mailing list included individuals who had attended an event or otherwise expressed interest. Not to scale   261

Contributors

Eileen Barker, FBA, OBE, is Professor Emeritus of Sociology with Special Reference to the Study of Religion at the London School of Economics. Since the early 1970s, she has been studying minority religions and the social reactions to which they give rise. In 1988, with the support of the Home Office and the mainstream Churches, she founded INFORM, an educational charity, now based at King's College, London, which supplies information about alternative religions that is as objective and up-to-date as possible. She has over 400 publications, translated into 27 languages.

Stefano Bigliardi is Associate Professor of Philosophy at AUI (Al Akhawayn University in Ifrane), Morocco. He specialises in the debate on religion and science.

Claire Borowik is a communication and grant-writing consultant for grassroots non-profits with an MA in Intercultural and International Communications. She served as the co-director of Worldwide Religious News Service (WWRN) from 1997 to 2017, providing religious news to the academic and legal communities, and has participated in numerous initiatives promoting religious diversity. Claire served as the director of international public affairs for the Family International from 2006 to 2010, and previously managed legal and media affairs for the organisation in South and North America for 14 years. She has authored numerous articles on the Family International and its evolution from a communalist movement to online religion.

André van der Braak is Professor of Buddhist Philosophy in Dialogue with Other World Views at the Faculty of Religion and Theology of the Vrije Universiteit Amsterdam, Netherlands. He published *Nietzsche and Zen: Self-overcoming without a Self* (2011) and *Reimagining Zen in a Secular Age* (2020), and co-edited *Religion and Social Cohesion: Western, Chinese and Intercultural Perspectives* (2015).

Frank Cranmer is an Honorary Research Fellow in the Centre for Law & Religion at Cardiff University and a Fellow of St Chad's College, Durham, UK. His particular interests are religion and human rights and religion and employment law. He blogs with David Pocklington at www.lawandreligionuk.com.

Andrew Dawson is Professor of Modern Religion and Head of the Department of Politics, Philosophy and Religion at Lancaster University, UK. Among Andrew's edited publications are *The Politics and Practice of Religious Diversity* (2016) and *Religion, Migration and Mobility* (2017).

Bernard Doherty is currently Course Director in the School of Theology and a Research Fellow for the Centre for Public and Contextual Theology at Charles Sturt University based at St Mark's National Theological Centre in Canberra, Australia. He is also an adjunct lecturer in the School of Law at the University of Notre Dame, Sydney and an Honorary Research Fellow at INFORM (Information Network Focus on Religious Movements) based at King's College, London.

Laura Dyason is a PhD student at the University of Sydney and former member of the Plymouth Brethren Christian Church. Her research is primarily focused on the experiences of second-generation members who leave the PBCC to join mainstream life as adults and explores the issues and personal complexities of leaving this community.

Shai Feraro is a Research Associate at the University of Haifa and Tel Hai College and serves as Secretary of the Israeli Association for the Study of Religions. He is the author of *Women and Gender Issues in British Paganism, 1945–1990* (2020) and has co-edited *Contemporary Alternative Spiritualities in Israel* (2016) and *Magic and Witchery in the Modern West* (2019).

Eugene V. Gallagher is the Rosemary Park Professor of Religious Studies emeritus at Connecticut College, USA. He is the author of *Reading and Writing Scripture in New Religious Movements* (2014), co-author of *The Religious Studies Skills Book* (2019), and co-author of *New Religions: Emerging Faiths and Religious Cultures in the Modern World* (2021).

Fabrizio Lorusso is a researcher and professor at the Ibero-American University of León (Mexico), Department of Social Sciences. His field of research is Human Rights, Neoliberalism and Social Movements in Latin America. He works with the collectives of families of the disappeared people in Mexico and published multiple essays and books about Mexican culture, recent history, and politics.

Stefano Morrone received his M.A. in Political Science from the University of Bologna. He is professionally active in Mexico as a documentary photographer. His work focuses on human rights, migration, and gender.

Erin Prophet is Visiting Assistant Professor in the Department of Religion, University of Florida. She focuses on the relationship between religion and medicine. Her dissertation examines on 19th-century religious responses to Darwin. She is the author of *Cults and New Religious Movements* (forthcoming).

David G. Robertson is Lecturer in Religious Studies at the Open University, co-founder of the Religious Studies Project, and co-editor of the journal *Implicit Religion*. His work applies critical theory to the study of alternative and emerging religions and to 'conspiracy theory' narratives. He is the author of *UFOs, the New Age and Conspiracy Theories: Millennial Conspiracism* (2016) and co-editor of *After World Religions: Reconstructing Religious Studies* (2016) and the *Handbook of Conspiracy Theories and Contemporary Religion* (2018).

Russell Sandberg is Professor of Law at Cardiff University where he specialises in Law and Religion, Legal History, Family Law and interdisciplinary approaches to law. He is author of *Law and Religion* (Cambridge, 2011) and *Religion, Law and Society* (Cambridge, 2014).

Karl E. H. Seigfried is Theology and Religious History Faculty at Cherry Hill Seminary and Adjunct Professor in Humanities at Illinois Institute of Technology, USA. While at University of Chicago Divinity School, he was President of Interfaith Dialogue and served on the Spiritual Life Council. He has written on Ásatrú for outlets as diverse as the BBC and the U.S. Department of Defense, and his work on mythology and religion has appeared in *Journal of the Oriental Institute, International Journal of Indic Religions, Pathways for Ecumenical and Interreligious Dialogue,* and *Sightings* of the Martin Marty Center for the Advanced Study of Religion. His website, *The Norse Mythology Blog*, has featured interviews with faith leaders, politicians, and scholars as well as the *Worldwide Heathen Census* providing the first global estimate of numbers of adherents to modern Germanic paganism.

Shanon Shah is the Director of Faith for the Climate, a UK-based network focusing on faith-based climate action, conducts research at Inform, and is the author of *The Making of a Gay Muslim: Religion, Sexuality and Identity in Malaysia and Britain* (2018). He is also Tutor in Interfaith Relations at the University of London's Divinity programme and previously lectured in religious studies at the University of Kent and King's College London.

Beth Singler is a digital anthropologist whose first book, *The Indigo Children: New Age Experimentation with Self and Science*, was the first ethnography of this primarily online community. Currently, as the Junior Research Fellow in Artificial Intelligence at Homerton College, University of Cambridge, Beth applies her anthropological approach to the stories we have about AI, digital discussions of its nature and impact, and online communities promoting apocalyptic, transhumanist, and future focussed accounts of AI.

Jonathan Woolley is an environmental anthropologist, currently on secondment to the UK Government's Policy Lab as an ethnographic researcher. Jonathan was awarded a PhD in March 2018 from the Department of Social Anthropology at the University of Cambridge, where his research formed part of the Cambridge Interdisciplinary Research on the Environment (CIRE) network. He is author of *Common Sense in Environmental Management: Thinking Through Land and Water*. He has been an active member of the Druidic community in the UK for several years and is one of the Order of Bards, Ovates, and Druids' Mount Haemus scholars.

1 Radical transformations in minority religions: reflections

Beth Singler

> She changes everything She touches and everything She touches, changes.
> Starhawk (1979: 67)

As an anthropologist, I try to be reflexive about how I engage with my field and my informants. I also try to think about how I first encountered that field and what my first apprehensions of it were. For instance, when it comes to new religious movements, most of my earliest encounters were with forms of Paganism. Specifically, I read the words above, from the Spiral Dance written by Starhawk the Pagan author, and they shaped both my understanding that there could even be such a thing as a *new religious movement,* as well as the importance of 'change' to them all.

I first came across these words in a reprint of Starhawk's 1979 book, *The Spiral Dance,* and then again in her 1993 novel inspired by the same ideas, *The Fifth Sacred Thing.* Years of interest in Pagan movements then led me to a dissertation on Wicca during my undergraduate degree, and then into research on digital spirituality, first as a postgraduate looking at the New Age Movement, New Religious Movements and the Internet, and then as a post-doctoral researcher specialising in the communities and conceptions of Artificial Intelligence. Change has also been a key aspect of my own life story, not only as I focussed on different topics in 'New Religious Studies' over the years but also as I had moved back into academia after working in the film industry in the UK.

Change then, I have always thought, is inherent to the nature of new religious movements. Even if we do not adopt change as a theistic concept as Starhawk and other Pagans might, change exists as soon as a new religious movement emerges or is founded. Change also occurs when an individual chooses to convert to a new religious movement and accept its tenets; a move which might also be seen as radical by friends and family or by their existing religious community. Change occurs when members leave movements for any number of reasons, or when the numbers leaving results in the end to the movement. Change is present when the new religious

DOI: 10.4324/9781315226804-1

movement receives new revelations from its source of spiritual knowledge and enacts them within the practices of that group. Change happens when societal pressures are exerted onto the new religious movement, and they chose either to become more insular or to engage with the outside world and become more open and accessible. Temporal change also brings new issues for new religious movements; founders age and die, new members are born or convert and bring with them the ideas and skills of different generations, and technology changes and advances and provides opportunities and threats.

In the previous volume on transformations in minority religions, my co-editor Eileen Barker wrote a comprehensive introduction to the volume and to the area that laid out definitions for 'new religious movement', as well as for 'revisionism' and 'diversification': types of change we might see within NRMs. 'New religious movement' is not a term without contention and is itself changeable in focus and meaning. Barker identifies the main aspects of an NRM as a religious group that is often predominantly first generation, involves a leadership with charismatic authority, and that expresses alternative beliefs to the mainstream religious views of the context. Although, with regard to demographics, Barker does also recognise that many contributions to that volume involve discussion of transformations taking place because of the influence of second and third generations–something that also came up in the contributions to this volume.

On the definition of 'new religious movement', debate about what constitutes a 'religion' has also taken note of the ideological aspect of naming (or not naming) something as a religion. Groups such as the Pagan Federation, Scientology, and some Jedi temples have attempted – some through legal means – to be identified as religions for the greater legitimacy that might bring (see Richardson and Barker 2020, also in this Inform/Routledge series). Whereas some other groups try very hard *not* to be labelled a 'religion' – as the word for them denotes rigid, unchanging, doctrine, and hierarchy and is contrary to how they perceive themselves. Personally, I have seen this response in some AI focussed movements, for instance the Turing Church, who prefer to call themselves 'un-religions' to denote that they are disrupting and exploiting, or 'hacking', traditional ideas, including religion itself, and putting their aspects to work often for transhumanist aims (Singler 2020). Even with these issues in mind, 'new religious movements' still works as a legitimate object of study, as well as a signifier of an academic objectivity that the increasingly pejorative 'cult' does not. Perhaps in the future, we will see change again in naming and in who sees themselves as new religious movements scholars.

When it comes to transformations *within* new religious movements, the terms 'revisionism' and 'diversification' highlight important structural and relational aspects of the process. Of the former, Barker explained it as 'a significant departure from an authoritative or generally accepted doctrine, theory, or practice' (Barker 2013, 2). As a 're-vision', a new way of seeing or a seeing again, revisionism could be applied to the creation of any new religious movement against the contemporary situation or context. Even within new religious movements such moments of revelation can in some cases lead to schismatic groups that claim to be entirely separate from their original movement. Revisionism can also involve reconsidering existing ideas and practices and can involve making a claim for a return to how things were meant to be at the foundation of the group. As explored in several chapters in this volume, revisionism can also occur to reform the new religious movement, to make it appear more in line with contemporary society, and thus more legitimate.

Barker's definition of 'diversification' in her introduction to the previous volume also introduced and highlighted the difference between horizontal and vertical diversification. While diversity exists between and within in all religious movements, deviation from existing tenets can lead to schism when individual believers 'select and lay weight on different aspects of any belief system' (Barker 2013, 6). This is a *horizontal* diversification. *Vertical* diversification – variations in beliefs between layers of a movement's vertical hierarchy – is also often found: 'It is quite common for an inner circle of elites to be privy to esoteric knowledge about which rank-and-file members are ignorant' (Barker 2013, 5). Barker uses the example of Scientology here, which is well known for staggering initiation into knowledge along the 'Bridge to Total Freedom', with higher levels, and deeper knowledge, accessible through paid-for courses. Knowledge of the ultimate aims and goals of the movement can also be limited to a select few. Transformations can come about when such knowledge is breached and disseminated, or when new pockets of dissent come up with their own alternative 'elite' knowledge. Freezone Scientology is an example of a schismatic formation that sees itself as expressing the openness of knowledge Scientology's founder intended (Lewis 2014).

The contributors to this volume have shared their elite, but unhidden, knowledge and research expertise to discuss modern movements. A wide variety of groups have been considered, including the Plymouth Brethren, ISKCON, Heathenry, Gnosticism, Druidry, and Jediism. We also have chapters from legal experts, as well as sociologists applying knowledge gained from studying new religious movements to other movements. In one case, we have a response to a chapter from members of the group discussed – the PBCC writing in response to Doherty and Dyason's chapter. Again, as in the previous volume, we are pleased to see the writers continuing in the spirit of the Inform seminars that have inspired these volumes, with non-polemical contributions that add to the scholarly body of work on new religious movements. 'Methodological agnosticism' is also their shared approach. Defined by Barker as an approach which,

> does not deny the truth or assert the falsity of non-empirical beliefs; it merely acknowledges that the social sciences have no techniques or

expertise with which they can judge or evaluate supernatural claims, although they will try to describe these and their consequences as accurately as possible. (Barker 2013, 11)

This volume is divided into four thematic parts that address different origins for radical transformations: interactions with society, technology and institutions, efforts at legitimation, and new revelations.

Interactions with society leading to radical change

Eileen Barker's chapter considers how minority religions change in response to cases of child sexual abuse within their communities. Her chapter places such radical transformations in a larger contemporary context that includes exposures of abuse and 'cover-ups' by other, more mainstream, groups such as established, traditional, religions. Barker's argument is that social or cultural structures within a movement can obscure abuses and obstruct change, but that that culture can itself be changed by individuals who choose to do something. Her primary cases of such change in the light of internal abuses are ISKCON (the International Society for Krishna Consciousness), the Children of God (later known as The Family International), and the Jesus Fellowship (at times known as the Jesus Army).

In his chapter on contemporary Heathenism, Karl Seigfried lays out the relations between different groups of Ásatrú, a reimagining of 'pre-Christian Germanic religion with an emphasis on medieval Icelandic texts'. The evolution of perspectives between these different groups lies in part upon their changing attitudes towards ancestry. For some groups, the emphasis on ancestry has led them into a more exclusive, even racist, stance against those outside their claimed ethnic origin. Seigfried examines three approaches to ancestry, some more inclusive than others, and lays out the development and changes within groups from the original sparks of inspiration that rebirthed the 'Viking' religion in the current era.

Writing as someone who directly experienced the changes in the EnlightenNext movement and the changeable, and sometimes volatile, nature of Andew Cohen himself, André Van Der Braak's chapter provides an account of internal vertical change within to a hierarchical system. Cohen is introduced as a product of the 'guru phenomenon' that began in the 1900s with the Victorian interest in, and translation of, the Indian traditions. Cohen is, however, a home-grown guru, and his revisions of the concept of 'Enlightenment' have echoes in the naming, structure, and fractures within his movement between its founding and its decline. 'Enlightenment', a translation of traditional Indian concepts and words seen in Hinduism and Buddhism, is put to use in Western consciousness movements to various ends, and Van Der Braak's chapter expounds on

Cohen's own 'Evolutionary Enlightenment' and how 'his various revisions of the notion of enlightenment also served to facilitate the legitimization of the increasing occurrence of several forms of verbal and physical violent behaviour within the community'. The chapter is a frank exploration of charismatic leadership and how it can fail its followers.

Jonathan Woolley's chapter pays attention to the role of newer rituals in ameliorating, or not, tensions between generational cohorts in British Druidry. While claiming sympathies with the druidism of millennia before, contemporary Druidry is actually much younger, and it is still changing its approach towards dealing with the newer generations that are either being born into the movement or finding their way there. Woolley's chapter unpicks the influence of classical tropes that have shaped current conceptions of these two generations – the wise old Druid, and the youthful apprentice figure – and uses ethnographic material to understand how these archetypes and evolving rituals based upon them have not fully dealt with intergenerational issues.

Technology and institutions

The Brazilian new religious movement of Santo Daime draws on a conflux of influences in its 'works', or rituals: 'the pragmatic supernaturalism of the popular Catholic, Amazonian-folk (caboclo) and Afro-Brazilian elements', according to Andrew Dawson's chapter on the evolution or 'progress' of such works. Dawson expounds on Santo Daime's dual foci: external regime and interior self-betterment. Both of which are centred on the ritualised consumption of ayahuasca. Changes in the movement have come about in part due to transnational diaspora and transcultural appropriation, with the Brazilian movement gaining followers internationally since the late 1980s. Becoming an international movement has drawn greater attention to the role of ayahuasca in the works and to legal implications, played out in various nations and states. Dawson lays out three primary transformations associated with Santo Daime's 'progressively transnational profile': repertorial diversity and eclecticism, organisational differentiation, and ritual reconfiguration.

Shai Feraro's chapter surveying two decades of British Paganism pays specific attention to the role played by publications in bringing about change after the foundation and growth of more hierarchical modes of Paganism, such as Gardnerian Wicca in the 1950s and 1960s. Feraro explores how such publications were not just a space for sharing material and information about events, but also a location for the rise and development of the feminist and ecological discourses that changed the wider Pagan milieu of the 1970s–1980s. Using the magazine *Wood and Water* as a case study, Feraro's chapter details the development of the burgeoning Pagan community in the UK and the tensions and changes that took place. The feminist turn in Paganism benefitted from such technologies, while also being a part of an ecological shift that critiqued technology and led to visible activism. Empowered by magical thinking, such activism sought to change the world.

My chapter considers what happens when an external force causes a change in the primary source material that an NRM has been using for its beliefs. In the case of the real-world Jedi, I discuss whether a change in ownership of the intellectual property that had initially inspired their movement – the Star Wars films and the Extended Universe founded upon them – has had any effect on the believers and their beliefs. Interviewing Jedi from various different temples and groups, I found that for many the 'canon' of the Star Wars Universe was merely starting point. But further, I argue that the nature of fandom itself encouraged a rhetoric of difference to the source material and indifference to its revision. Change, I show, was an integral part to the movement before the collapse in canon material and was present even before the Jedi came to the attention of the public through the 2001 UK Census.

Seeking legitimacy in the face of outside forces

Amongst the external forces that can bring about transformations in NRMs we must include legislative decisions, with their repercussions for legitimacy and even religious freedoms. Cranmer and Sandberg's chapter on this begins with the knotty problem of the Church of Scientology for whom the question of whether they are a legitimate religion, and as an entity capable of holding religious services, has played out in various cases around the world. Focussing on the UK legislature, this chapter also takes in cases brought under the the Human Rights Act 1998 and the Racial and Religious Hatred Act 2006. Cases wherein the rights to minority religious expression were discussed, and such groups have had to try to prove their legitimacy against fixed criteria. How minority movements shift and change under such measurement is of continuing relevance.

Bernard Doherty and Laura Dyason introduce us to a period of fourteen years in the existence of the Exclusive Brethren in Australia during which the group 'rebranded' as the Plymouth Brethren Christian Church (PBCC). This, they discuss, was a part of a larger change in the nature of the group as Bruce D. Hales took over after the passing of his father, John S. Hales. Changes this chapter describe include attempts at reconciliation with former members, political campaigning, charity work, a more open attitude to the adoption of technology, and allowing the movement's youth access to higher education. One important question raised in this chapter is whether to understand these changes as a rebranding for a veneer of legitimacy or as a more genuine revisionism (or neither), and Doherty and Dyason provide the views of former members who lived through this time of rapprochement and reform. This chapter is followed by a response from the PBCC themselves, providing an account of these changes from an insider perspective.

David Robertson's chapter on Samael Aun Weor's Universal Christian Gnostic Movement (UCGM) introduces us to a group founded in 1976 on the idea of the restoration of primitive Christian practice, but which has actually been moulded by influences from 19th-century Rosicrucian groups such as the Order Templis Orientalis (OTO). The OTO itself grew out of Freemasonry, sexual magic, and Western accounts of Tantra that were being brought over from India by curious Victorians. Robertson's chapter traces two aspects of the UGCM that became more and more distinct over time: a push towards legitimacy as a mainstream Christian movement and a parallel shift into New Age spirituality, at a time when the Internet was enabling the growth of such movements into countries wary of more dominant forms of Christianity. Diversification and change have come about for this movement as they have faced the external pressures of fitting into a changing context.

Shanon Shah applies ideas and frames from the study of new religious movements to the evolution of a British-based LGBT Muslim group in Chapter 13. Change in this instance comes about both because of external pressures from expectations of the Islamic response to homosexuality and because of internal tensions and relationships within the group itself. Shah's consideration through an NRM lens also allows him to illuminate the changes and innovations in theological thinking in the group; ideas that spring from the social context of the group and its relation to other Muslim groups and established belief. This approach may well be fruitful for considering radical transformations in other groups with ties to official religious thinking but with their own foci.

The role of new revelations in radical change

Claire Borowik's chapter examines the Family International, discussing a period after that discussed in Eileen Barker's chapter. She explains how, in 2010, this counter-cultural fringe movement faced a 'organisational overhaul'. This was a more comprehensive change than previous shifts of emphasis and structure. The official documents outlining the changes described this 'Reboot' as 'an expediency in order to meet new goals of evangelisation and membership expansion'. Prophecy declined in importance after the 'Reboot' in the light of increasing emphasis on the Bible, with the work of contemporary Protestant theologians coming to be used in the community. Previous 'unorthodox' sexual practices have also been occluded in the official texts as legitimacy is sought by the movement according to Borowik. Radical transformations have come about through a re-positioning of the movement in the mainstream and a change in perspective on prophecy.

For a chapter on the Saint of Death herself, it is perhaps not surprising that change in Chapter 15 comes about for the *Santa Muerte* movement in Tultitlán, Mexico, after the death of one of its leading figures. Stefano Bigliardi, Fabrizio Lorusso, and Stefano Morrone employ ethnographic methods to examine the communities and temple groups arising around *Santa Muerte* before and after the death of Jonathan Vargas, whose mother has continued to tell his spiritual story and to lead an international organisation, sharing *Santa Muerte* across the globe. What is happening with the group is proposed to be a 'religious mutation' by Bigliardi, Lorusso, and Morrone, a part of a wider shift in Latin America, producing new religious movements and altering existing social structures. *Santa Muerte*, in the examples of the two temples, is a reminder in its own focus of the temporal and changing nature of all things.

Eugene Gallagher (Chapter 16) explores how claims to transcendental authority in a changing movement are employed to legitimate decisions. His particular case-study, the Church of Satan and its offshoot the Temple of Set, expands on the use of revelation in particular and explores the role of charismatic authority. He points out a shift in claims; when the Church was founded by Anton Szandor LaVey there was no recall to supernatural intervention, instead he claimed 'insight' rather than 'intervention'. However,

> by basing his authority on insight rather than revelation and by portraying himself as the first among equals, LaVey left wide open the possibility that someone would claim equal if not superior authority. Just such a claim animated the first major schism within the Church of Satan.

Gallagher details the revisionism that came out of Michael Aquino's claims to revelation and his foundation of the Temple of Set as a more kemetic-focussed group.

Erin Prophet's chapter on the groups that evolved out of the I AM movement, such as the current Church Universal and Triumphant (CUT), examines the role of the 'messengers' in such groups influenced by Theosophical and New Thought ideas. In particular, she draws attention to the role of 'messengership' in CUT in expressing charismatic authority, legitimacy, and in responding to internal and external changes and pressures on the groups. Prophet writes from personal experience, as she was the daughter of the movement's founders, and she was in training to become a 'messenger' herself, for six years. This gives her direct knowledge with which to discuss how changes in levels of exclusivity, in responses to questions of evil and soteriology, and in understandings of personal responsibility have transformed these movements. She is clear that when revealed messages fail to meet contemporary expectations, we see either schism and change or steadfastness and decline.

Change and the academic

This volume comes seven years after the previous one, and many changes in the lives of its two co-editors explain why it took time to come into being. Eileen and I began discussing putting together a follow-up volume to *Revisionism and Diversification in New Religious Movements* when we were both speaking on panels at the International Association for the History of Religions (IAHR) conference in Erfurt in 2015. I was just a PhD student back then; it was in 2016 that I completed my PhD and started my first post-doc, moving onto a research project thinking about the questions raised by Artificial Intelligence. While I still applied frameworks from my PhD anthropological work on the New Age movement, as well as research done on new religious movements such as Jediism and Scientology, my day to day work was often shaped by the concerns of the principal investigators on the project. Likewise, Eileen found herself increasingly involved again with Inform after its funding changed and diminished, long after officially retiring in 2003 (she had worked without pay for Inform since founding it in 1988). While we pulled the volume together contributors dropped out, were replaced, and changed their proposed plans. None of this is offered as an excuse for the length of time this edited volume has taken, but in recognition of the role played by change in the development of the volume itself. Revelations and prophecy have perhaps not been of much influence, but certainly our own social situations, demographics, external pressures, technological needs and developments, and internal diversification and diversity have played a role in the life span of this project.

Even now, as I sit at my kitchen table writing this introduction to the volume, working from home and home-schooling my son during the tail end of the UK's first lockdown due to the coronavirus global pandemic, I am encountering changing circumstances. The world outside has become quieter in some ways as we have learnt to socially distance ourselves, while (rightfully) louder in others, as the Black Live Matter movement has responded vocally to yet more police violence and racism. These external events are a reminder to us of quite how much new religious movements are a product of their time, and how religion also plays a role in framing responses to radical changes in society. Lockdown has been for some, a moment of quiet, almost ascetic reflection. Others have loudly discussed their right not to be locked down or be-masked, pulling on versions of Christianity closer to national civic religion as they debate their freedoms. Religious movements still attempting to go ahead with large-scale religious rituals, such as funerals or large, charismatic, meetings, have been thwarted or experienced painful consequences. An increase in doing religion online has led to questions about how ritual and sacraments are done virtually, adding to an older discussion within religious groups that scholars who pay attention to digital religion have been observing for decades already. In all, religion is shaped by its age; change emerges as the world continues to change. This volume is a contribution to the study of specific new religious movements, as well as a contribution to our overall awareness of the nature and varieties of change itself.

Bibliography

Barker, Eileen. (2013). *Revisionism and Diversification in New Religious Movements* (Ashgate Inform Series on Minority Religions and Spiritual Movements), Farnham: Ashgate.

Lewis, James R. (2014). "Free Zone Scientology and Other Movement Milieus: A Preliminary Characterization." *Temenos-Nordic Journal of Comparative Religion*, 49(2), 255–276.

Richardson, J. and Barker, E. (eds) (2020). *Reactions to the Law by Minority Religions* (Routledge Inform Series on Minority Religions and Spiritual Movements), London: Routledge.

Singler, Beth. (2020). "'Blessed by the Algorithm': Theistic Conceptions of Artificial Intelligence in Online Discourse." *AI & Society*, 35, 945–955.

Starhawk. (1979). *The Spiral Dance: A Rebirth of the Ancient Religion of the Great Goddess*, San Francisco: Harper.

Starhawk. (1993). *The Fifth Sacred Thing*, New York: Bantam.

Part I

Internal forces leading to radical changes

2 What did they do about it? A sociological perspective on reactions to child sexual abuse in three new religions[1]

Eileen Barker

The only thing necessary for the triumph of evil is for good men to do nothing.[2]

Scores of books and articles have been written about the sexual abuse to which children and, to a slightly lesser degree, women have been subjected in some new religions (e.g. Anderson 2007; Baldasty 2005; Bogdan and Lewis 2014; Collective of Women 1997; Lewis and Melton 1994; Raine and Kent 2019; Willey and Kent 2017; Yeomans 2013). However, relatively little has been written on how such religions have undergone radical changes in the process of dealing with the abuse. This chapter explores ways in which three high-profile religions that emerged in the West in the late 1960s (ISKCON, the Children of God, and the Jesus Fellowship) cultivated social contexts that, for a specific period in their history, enabled and even encouraged child sexual abuse (CSA), which was first denied and/or covered up, then, in the face of growing evidence, acknowledged, resulting in radical changes in the culture and structure of the respective movements.

The events described in this chapter have taken place against the backdrop of a changing social scene and widespread public exposures of abuse and 'cover-ups' by other sections of contemporary society. These have included most of the traditional religions, the Roman Catholic Church being an obvious example,[3] but by no means the only one.[4] A 2020 World Health Organisation Report states that one in five women and one in 13 men report having been sexually abused as a child aged 0–17 years.[5] The enormity of the problem in England and Wales alone is indicated in the initial findings of the Independent Inquiry into Child Sexual Abuse, which, at the time of writing, has yet to produce its final report.[6]

Sexual abuse can be verbal or involve physical contact, when it can range from inappropriate touching to fondling or violence and rape. Various types of abuse, including sexual penetration of under-age children, have been perpetrated by adult members of all three of the religions discussed in this chapter. Such practices have resulted in children becoming confused,

DOI: 10.4324/9781315226804-2

imagining it is their fault and feeling guilty, not daring to tell anyone because they believe they will not be believed; they have suffered from the trauma well into, frequently throughout, adulthood; and their experiences may also contribute to disease and illness in later life (Kirkengen 2001). Furthermore, abuse can be traumatic not only for children who suffer from it themselves but also for those who witness it happening to their peers.

For over a century, social scientists have demonstrated the wide variety of ways in which social contexts need to be taken into account if one wants to understand the actions of individuals. Three important variables (and the relationship between them) are all likely to play a role in processes leading to any social action: the social structure,[7] the prevailing culture,[8] and the individuals involved.[9] Comparing the contexts within which CSA occurred in the three religions discussed here, it could be argued that it was predominantly for structural reasons that CSA (mainly of boys) took place in ISKCON, for cultural reasons that abuse (almost entirely of girls) occurred in the Children of God, and, although both the structure and culture permitted and indirectly enabled it, individual paedophiles were of particular significance in perpetrating CSA (of roughly equal numbers of girls and boys) in the Jesus Fellowship.

Evidence suggests that the overwhelming majority of individuals who joined the post-world War II new religions did so for idealistic reasons (Barker 1984; Melton 2004; Rochford 1985; Saxby 1998). They wanted to make the world a better place; all three religions were engaged in a range of 'good works',[10] and all three religions attracted 'good men and women';[11] and, perhaps above all, they wanted to dedicate their lives to following the precepts of good Christians or good devotees of Krishna. They were not all paedophiles.

This chapter does not attempt to address important questions about how the social situation contributed to individuals becoming the perpetrators who sexually abused children (Langone 2016); instead, it focusses on an equally important question: In what ways did the social context first impede 'good people' from doing anything to prevent 'the triumph of evil', and what contributions did some of these people eventually make towards radically changing that context? To answer these questions, this chapter will set the scene by briefly explaining the origins of these movements and the context of the abuse; it will then examine changes that were made at the institutional level and look at where the movements are now, ending with a comparative discussion of the changes and the people behind them.

Setting the scene

The International Society for Krishna Consciousness(ISKCON)

The International Society for Krisha Consciousness (ISKCON) is a movement within the tradition of Vaishnava Hinduism, its central scripture being the Bhagavad-Gita. Founded in New York City in 1966 by A. C.

Bhaktivedanta Swami Prabhupada (1896–1977), it then moved to California, rapidly becoming part of the then-flourishing counter-cultural hippie scene (Rochford 1985; Shinn 1987). Soon young men and women in Indian garb, dancing and chanting their *Hare Krishna* mantra in streets, airports, and other public venues became a familiar sight throughout North American and Western European cities as they reached out for converts while distributing literature and soliciting donations.

Devotees were expected to lead ascetic lives. In the early days, nearly all lived in ashrams associated with a temple, rising for 4 a.m. worship, study, and chanting. Meat, drugs, and alcohol were forbidden, and devotees were expected to remain celibate, except for purposes of procreation within marriage. In the early 1970s, Prabhupada, 'disgusted with this troublesome business of marriage', decided to stop sanctioning marriages (Rochford 1998a:49). Nonetheless, an increasing number of devotees were marrying,[12] and 'householder life' came to be considered a spiritual weakness by ISKCON's renunciate elite. Moreover, while children were initially portrayed as spiritually pure, by the mid-1980s they were perceived by some leaders to be little more than 'karmies' (non-religious outsiders) (Rochford 1998a:50). Rather than having children educated in secular public schools or becoming limited in their spiritual growth by 'the ropes of affection' between parent and child, Prabhupada directed they should be sent to ISKCON *gurukulas* (boarding schools) from the age of about four (Rochford 1998a:46). From the organisation's perspective, sending the children away would mean that both parents would be free for the all-important institutional objectives of full-time missionising and fundraising (Rochford 1998a:63). The first *gurukula*, opened in Dallas in 1971, was closed as unfit by State authorities in 1976 (Muster 2001:74–5); by 1980, however, 24 *gurukulas* had been opened in eighteen countries (Jagadish 1981:1).

ISKCON *gurukulas* followed a strict regime with detailed rules covering every aspect of the children's lives.[13] Teachers were immature and inexperienced, often selected only because they were the least successful at soliciting donations (Rochford 1998a:54). Men and women were segregated and, while sex education was not taught, the children learned that thoughts of sex were sinful; spiritual development was all-important (Muster 2001:75). There was little or no accountability or effective oversight of the schools and, although some were well-managed and caring, many children found themselves suffering physical, spiritual, emotional, and/or sexual abuse in *gurukulas* that have been likened to 'concentration camps' (Wolf 2004:341), orphanages, or 'total institutions' (Rochford 1998a:58). Letters to and from parents were intercepted and opportunities to go home to see one's family were rare. Those who suffered most were young boys, who were beaten and/or sexually abused on a regular basis by both teachers and older students.[14] Girls were less likely to be assaulted, but it was not uncommon for them to be married or betrothed at 13 to an older man (Rochford 1998a:64n.11; Wolf 2004:333), itself a form of abuse.

From the mid-1980s, reports of child abuse were emerging. By 1986, all ashram-based *gurukulas* in North America had closed, but children were still being sent to *gurukulas* in India and elsewhere (Rochford 2007:65). The extent of this abuse can be read in a submission on behalf of the Children of Krishna (introduced below) in their case against ISKCON. This document catalogues instances of children forced to live in filthy, over-crowded, and rat-infested conditions, suffering from malnutrition, denied access to medical care, being beaten and kicked into submission, and not infrequently subjected to rape, oral sex, intercourse, sexual fondling, and/or forced to practice or watch masturbation (Turley 2000:12–5).[15] One internal account makes the point that abuses perpetrated in the 1980s and 1990s were 'directly ISKCON-related, meaning that the accused was representing ISKCON at the time of the alleged incident or that the alleged abuse occurred on ISKCON property' (Wolf 2004:323). In 1993, a widely circulated document detailed the child molestation prevalent within the ISKCON leadership (PADA Prabhupada Anti-Defamation Association 1993).

The Children of God (CoG)

The Children of God (CoG), later known as The Family and now known as The Family International (TFI), was founded by David (Moses) Berg (1919–1994) around 1967 as part of the Jesus Movement then widespread on the West Coast of the USA. It was soon attracting negative attention as young adults 'suddenly disappeared' into the movement (Patrick and Dulack 1976). This did not prevent it spreading throughout the world, however, setting up thriving missionary homes in five continents. Following the example of the early Christians, members lived communally, and spent much of their time selling literature and witnessing to potential converts (Figure 2.1).

As well as publishing a vast amount of literature, the movement produced numerous videos that ranged from children's songs and stories to depictions of Armageddon (Bainbridge 2002; Barker 2016; Melton 2004: Van Zandt 1995). Membership peaked at approximately 10,000 (including children) around the turn of the century (Borowik 2018:65–6). Children were considered to be among the saved, and it was assumed they would continue missionising until the imminent arrival of the Endtime, initially expected to be around 1993 (Berg 1976:940; Chancellor 2000:24; Bainbridge 2002:60). Children were home-schooled, but not necessarily in the same home as their parents. From 1980 to 1986, Berg proclaimed that children would be considered adult members of the community at the age of 12, based on Old Testament tradition, and promoted marriages between teenagers, though this position would be reversed by 1991 (Chancellor 2000:131; Ward 1995a).

Originally, there had been a strict moral code of separation between men and women outside marriage, but soon Berg was urging his followers to reject what he considered the prudishness of mainstream Christianity and enjoy the God-given pleasures of sex[16] and, for a time, the only unambiguously forbidden sexual practice within the movement was male

Figure 2.1 The Children of God in London's West End, 1972 (Photograph Courtesy of The Family International).

homosexuality.[17] According to Berg, Jesus' commandments 'Thou shalt love the Lord thy God' and 'Thou shalt love thy neighbour as thyself' (Matthew 7:12; 22:37, 39) came to be understood as meaning that, under the 'Law of Love', members could extend their love to fellow humans by serving their sexual, as well as their purely spiritual or material needs. From 1973, Berg's partner, Karen Zerby (b.1946), known in the movement as Maria, and other women in his inner circle were having sexual relationships with potential converts and donors whom they met in bars and night-clubs (Barker 2016; Chancellor 2000; van Zandt 1991; Williams 1998). By 1976, the practice had become more widespread, with Berg encouraging (mostly female) disciples to adopt this new 'ministry' – and to complete detailed monthly 'Flirty Fishing' Witnessing Reports.[18] Not all members were willing to 'FF', however, and with the spread of sexually transmitted diseases a 1987 policy memo banned sexual contact with outsiders, except 'close and well-known friends' (Chancellor 2000:22).

More common than 'flirty fishing' was 'sharing', when communities would ensure that everyone could enjoy sexual love, even if they had no regular partner. It was not uncommon for sex to take place in front of children. Around the late 1970s, the 'Mo letters' described sexual exploration among children with explicit illustrations (Berg 1977, 1976, 1975, 1980),[19] and

CoG's child-rearing practices were detailed in a series of letters that followed the upbringing of Maria's son Ricky Rodriguez (1975–2005). These included graphic descriptions of how Ricky was initiated into sexual play.[20] Berg's daughter, Deborah, published a book claiming that her father had had an incestuous relationship with her (Davis 1984), and Berg's granddaughter, Merry (Mene) Berg (1972–2017), was to report numerous abuses she had endured during her childhood (Ward 1995a).[21] However, it was not only children in Berg's inner circle that experienced abuse; adult/child sexual encounters occurred in a number of communities between the late-1970s and late-1980s. Detailed accounts, often recollections by the now-adult children, can be found on former-member websites,[22] in books,[23] and in the Ward (1995a) judgement (see below).

It is important to note that, just as child abuse did not take place in all ISKCON *gurukulas*, by no means all children brought up in CoG homes were subjected to abuse (Jenkins 2008), and when authorities conducted raids in Australia, Argentina, France and Spain, they could find no proof that any of the over-500 children whom they took had been abused (Borowik 2018; Wright and Palmer 2016:73–98).

The Jesus Fellowship Church (JF)

The Jesus Fellowhip Church (JF), the Jesus Army, and New Creation Christian Community grew out of the Bugbrooke Baptist Chapel under its Pastor, Noel Stanton (1926–2009),[24] when, in 1969, its members were 'filled with the Holy Spirit'. The Church's beliefs were 'reformed, evangelical and charismatic'.[25] Over the ensuing years, JF spread throughout England, with the core members, known collectively as the New Creation Christian Community, living in communal houses and, from 1974, sharing 'the common purse' (Cooper and Farrant 1997; Saxby 1998). At its height around 2007, it had approximately 3,500 members in about 24 congregations around the UK (Kay 2007:157).

According to JF understanding of the New Testament, marriage was of central importance in the 'old creation':

> whereas the new creation commission is spiritual [...] the dynamic of the new creation is that of *spiritual reproduction* through people coming into new earth. (Stacey n.d.:48–9, italics in original)

Those who felt thus called committed themselves to a life of celibacy.[26] The Fellowship did, however, recognise that not all felt called, and marriage was of central importance for bringing up children 'in the fear of the Lord' (Stacey n.d.:52), with children generally being loved and welcomed as part of the community's future.

JF's many ventures have included a farm and several co-operative businesses; these provided employment for members, all of whom were paid the same wage. It also established seven walk-in Jesus Centres for immigrants

Figure 2.2 One of the Jesus Army's Fleet of Vans, 2014 (Photograph by Eileen Barker).

and others looking for laundry facilities, language tuition, literacy skills, legal advice, or just a chat with someone who would listen over a cup of tea.

Outreach played an important role in JF's recruitment methods (Figure 2.2). Brightly painted buses displaying *Jesus Army* in large letters could be found parked in the streets of London and other cities, inviting people to enter and hear the message. Unlike many new religions of the 1960s which disproportionately attracted young middle-class hippies or college students, JF embraced all-comers. It numbered several professionals such as doctors and teachers, but also focused on saving the socially and economically needy, offering accommodation and work for the homeless and unemployed – and this could involve welcoming drug and alcohol addicts and former prisoners into their communal homes. In 2004, JF initiated a prison rehabilitation scheme, rehoming men who had 'found Jesus' while in jail. This had resulted in the judiciary sanctioning some early releases, and both the Probation Service and the Police had approached JF for help on several occasions. Initially, there was little or no awareness of the risks involved in this open-door policy, and few checks or screening were conducted; newcomers were accepted into the community with ample opportunity to mix with the children.[27]

Perhaps inevitably, some of those whom JF had welcomed came to the attention of the police. In 1993, a multiple child murderer and rapist stayed on JF premises under an assumed name for over a month before he was detected. In 1996, another man with a history of sex offences against young boys worked (again under an assumed identity) as a groundsman and managed to abuse three young boys – a crime for which he was to receive a five-year sentence in 2010.[28] There was, moreover, a growing number of reports of additional incidents of CSA having occurred within the community by teenagers and adults, including a leader who was eventually sent to jail.[29] Allegations of sexual abuse were also brought against JF's founder, Noel Stanton.[30]

What did they do about it?

ISKCON

In 1970, Prabhupada had founded a Governing Body Commission (GBC) to act as ISKCON's managing authority after his death,[31] and in 1977, he selected eleven disciples (all but one being members of the GBC) to initiate new devotees on his behalf. Following his death, they (and the GBC) assumed they would become 'regular gurus', initiating their own disciples (Rochford 1998c:111). For a short period, things seemed to be going smoothly, but between 1980 and 1986, five of the 11 initial gurus were exposed for serious moral impropriety, including drug-trafficking, gun-running, and sexual abuse, and internal antagonisms were rife. By 1984, a devotee was to write: 'Dialogue in ISKCON has come to mean aggressive infighting. Fanaticism often replaces intelligent analysis. To discuss is to do battle' (Gelberg 1988:171).

It was within this climate that initial attempts to do anything about the abuse in the *gurukulas* went unheeded or suppressed by much of ISKCON's leadership. According to one former student who attended a *gurukula* between 1976 and 1986:

> When incidents of sexual abuse came to light they were ignored or hidden. *Gurukula* administrators often seemed more concerned with protecting the reputation of the schools and ISKCON than with the protection and welfare of the children. They usually treated sexual abuse as a "fall down" that could be rectified by better spiritual practice (*sadhana*). ... Perpetrators were simply counselled to practice better *sadhana* to reduce their sexual desires, and in some cases, they were not even removed from their position as teachers but simply quietly transferred to another school. (Deadwyler 2004:346)

In 1986 and 1987, two men in American ISKCON schools were convicted of CSA.[32] In January 1988, the mother of a 6-year-old student who had suffered CSA wrote to ISKCON's Minister of Education asking for action to be taken, but nothing happened and there is no evidence that it was discussed at the GBC.[33] Shortly thereafter, two journalists wrote a book exposing various crimes being perpetrated within ISKCON (Hubner and Gruson 1988), thereby drawing public attention to the situation.

Other parents, former members, and several senior devotees who were concerned about the situation were becoming increasingly vocal and eventually the GBC could no longer ignore the allegations (Rochford 1998a, 1998b), and in 1990, it passed 'Resolution 119', its first official policy on child abuse. This ordered that local governing authorities were to appoint two or three devotees to investigate all alleged cases of child abuse, which had to be reported to the local GBC secretary and ISKCON's International Office of Education. Furthermore, the alleged perpetrator had to be segregated from children and ISKCON projects according to the severity of the offence. Abused children were to get professional counselling and preventative programmes should be established (Bharata 1998:72).

Although the GBC had now accepted a moral obligation, it left responsibility for prevention, investigation, and prosecution to local ISKCON authorities who in practice had few resources, and the GBC supplied no practical means of enforcing the Resolution (Bharata 1998:72–3; Wolf 2004:331). While most of the schools set up Child Protection Teams, abuse continued, as did the complaints both within and without the movement. Then, at a 1996 North American GBC and Temple Presidents' meeting, ten now-adult devotees described their *gurukula* experiences, which had included severe physical abuse and homosexual rape at knifepoint (Bharata 1998:72–3). An immediate result was the foundation of an independent, grass-roots organisation, 'Children of Krishna Inc.', with $105,000 being pledged towards its mission to support, to further, and to protect children's educational, economic, emotional, and spiritual well-being.[34] Although not an official ISKCON organisation, Children of Krishna's board of directors consisted of ISKCON youth and some senior devotees, and it received donations from various other concerned devotees (Wolf 2004:331–2).

Next, the GBC created a Child Protection Task Force, consisting of leaders, second-generation devotees, and devotee professionals, including a lawyer and a social worker. The Task Force introduced further safeguarding proposals, and in 1998 it appointed Dr David Wolf as director of an international Child Protection Office (CPO).[35] The aims were (i) to care for victims of past child abuse; (ii) to respond to and resolve previous and present cases, accepting that ISKCON now had a policy of zero tolerance of child abuse, and every allegation must be investigated by trained devotees in co-operation with the State authorities; and (iii) to ensure preventative education and screening throughout ISKCON (Wolf 2004:332ff). Much of the Task Force's resolutions were fulfilled. A list of 200 people who allegedly inflicted child abuse in the 1970s and 1980s was compiled,[36] but there were problems when investigating allegations concerning abusers with 'friends in high places'. However, in 2001, the GBC amended the procedure for appeals against CPO decisions so that both the GBC and the ISKCON Justice Minister played less of a role (Wolf 2004:335–6).

Throughout the 1990s, several senior devotees unconnected with the *gurukulas* and appalled by the allegations were anxious to remedy the situation. Burke Rochford, a sociologist who had been studying the movement since the 1970s, was invited to write an article for the *ISKCON Communications Journal* in the hope this might help improve the situation.[37] This Rochford did, detailing abuse that had occurred between 1971 and 1986 (Rochford 1998a). The story made the front page of the *New York Times*.[38] The *Journal* also published an account of ISKCON's subsequent measures to deal with the problem (Bharata 1998), but media accounts frequently assumed Rochford's descriptions were on-going. The fact that the movement itself had published the exposé was, however, newsworthy and clearly indicated that at least some devotees were serious about remedying the situation (Rochford 1998b).

In 2000, 92 former *gurukula* students filed a US$400m claim for alleged sexual and emotional abuse.[39] Among the many physical and emotional abuses listed in the Petition was 'Sexual abuse including rape, oral sex, intercourse with children, sexual fondling of children, and masturbation with children".[40] The case was dismissed and refiled; then, in a negotiated settlement, it was agreed that ISKCON would ask all children who had suffered any abuse to report and claim compensation.[41] This resulted in over 400 additional claims. A $9.5 million settlement was eventually made in a bankruptcy court in favour of 535 victims, and several further millions of dollars were added when ISKCON sued its insurance companies to contribute to the settlement. The total for all settlements, including legal fees, was $15 million. Anuttama Dasa, a devotee who has played a key role in the processes of prevention and compensation, offered a public apology on behalf of ISKCON to all those who had suffered.[42]

Since then, ISKCON's Child Protection Teams have endeavoured to ensure that no unsupervised contact can take place between adults and children, and that preventative information and literature is widely distributed throughout the movement, with regular training sessions for both adults and children. It became strict policy that all allegations of child abuse should be reported to the civic authorities, with whom close cooperation was to take place, and any devotee found guilty of inappropriate behaviour with children faced expulsion. A 32-page Guidelines document, revised and ratified by the GBC, laid out the policy in detail.[43]

The Children of God

In 1986, several teenage girls reported to World Services (CoG's central staff organisation) that they had been subjected to inappropriate and uninvited sexual contact with adult males. Maria directed that an internal memorandum should be sent to all CoG members, stating: 'we do not agree with adults having sexual contact with children. [...] Adults should refrain from any sexual involvement with all underage children and minors' (Chancellor 2000:20). When the abuse persisted in some locations (Chancellor 2000:21), further memos were sent, stressing that adult sex with children aged under sixteen was an excommunicable offence (Chancellor 2000:20; Family 1992:5; Zerby 1989:112–5).

Then, in the early 1990s, an English woman went to court to fight for custody of her as-yet-unborn grandchild on the grounds that the child would be subjected to abuse if brought up within the movement. The case was long and fierce, with scores of witnesses testifying on both sides. In his summing up, Lord Justice Ward noted that, following the prohibition of child/adult sexual relations, there had been some rather limited apologies and minimal acceptance of responsibility from the leadership to those who had suffered, with, partly because of the court proceedings, 'a guarded document with guarded concessions' circulated in 1992 admitting to and apologising for mistakes of the past (Ward 1995a:108). Whilst awaiting the judgement, the movement had also published *The Love Charter*.[44] This contained strict guidelines covering community life, including details of with whom and at what age sex was permitted, stressing that there would be zero tolerance of CSA, and emphasising that this was an excommunicable offence (Family 1995:233–6).

In his initial judgement, Ward (1995a:291–5) stated that while he was persuaded The Family (as CoG was now known) had undergone considerable changes since the late 1980s, he needed to be convinced that the improvement was permanent. He asked the leadership to produce a written statement declaring the now-deceased Berg and his teachings had been responsible for CSA and that it now denounced Berg and his teachings on the subject, and guaranteed safeguards were in place to ensure the abuse would not recur. The leadership complied with this request (Amsterdam 1995a), and the mother was allowed to keep custody of her child, under a number of conditions, including regular access for the grandmother (Ward 1995b). Moreover, The Family set up a 'Ministry of Reconciliation' (Amsterdam 1995b:Appendix; Ward 1995b), offered further apologies to those who had been abused and, throughout the mid-1990s, made several attempts to reconcile with former member (Borowik 2018:24),[45] although such efforts rarely mollified those speaking out against the movement (Kent 2004:66–7). The current Child Protection Policy stresses that members are subject to the law regarding reporting crimes of child abuse to the appropriate authorities.[46]

From the 1990s, however, an increasing number of second-generation adults (SGAs) were leaving the movement (Chancellor 2000:242; McMillion 2002:14–5; Zerby 1993), some organising themselves through dedicated websites[47] and other media outlets,[48] and becoming active in the 'cult awareness movement' (Giambalvo et al. 2013:236; Kent 2004).

The Jesus Fellowship

JF had had a Child Protection policy from 1993, but in the wake of the incidents described above,[49] it expanded this in 2005. Then, in 2012, with an increasing awareness that previous and potential incidents of abuse needed to be dealt with, the 'Apostolic Group' (JF's senior leadership) undertook a major revision in consultation with the Churches' Child Protection Advisory Service (CCPAS),[50] resulting in a 49-page policy document (Haines et al. 2012).

Around the same time, there was a growing number of reports of Catholic and other Churches being sued for massive damages for covering up CSA.[51] As JF Community's assets were all in one big pot, advice was sought about public liability insurance for past and future allegations of abuse, and JF's legal advisors counselled it to discover the extent to which incidents might have occurred in the past. In accordance with this, and anxious to deal with the past and ensure that mistakes would not be repeated, a letter, and then further requests were circulated to the whole membership in 2013, asking for information from any source (including former members) concerning any real or suspected abuse to be sent in confidence to JF's leadership or the CCPAS. This resulted in 133 allegations of mistreatment of, mainly, women and through bullying, physical and/or sexual abuse, most of which were third-party, rather than personal accounts.

Initially, it appeared that the local police, in Northampton, UK, were interested in less than a dozen of the cases, and the Apostolic Group was anxious to deal with the allegations of bullying and to improve the position of women members. However, several more allegations were reported, bringing the total referrals of all kinds of abuse to just over 200. Furthermore, around that time, civil authorities in England were coming under attack by the media for not having investigated allegations about the CSA perpetrated by a well-known television personality, Jimmy Savile, with sufficient rigour.[52] By December 2014, the Northampton police had decided they would investigate all the JF cases and established 'Operation Lifeboat', an enquiry team of five police officers.[53] The majority of referrals were not taken further as they were not about criminal offences or were duplicate reports, and some cases were sent to police forces elsewhere. Eventually, eleven arrests were made by Operation Lifeboat for historic sexual and physical abuse, the majority of which resulted in sentences. Some JF leaders were suspended from duty, one for CSA, for which he was found guilty in court, and the others for allegations of inappropriate behaviour of a non-criminal nature. In 2015, the police recommended that an audit be carried out on the group's safeguarding procedures. JF commissioned the CCPAS to conduct this, which resulted in a comprehensive report with several suggestions for improvement (CCPAS 2015).

In July 2017, the five remaining members of the Apostolic Group stood down and were replaced by a national leadership team (NLT) to facilitate an independent investigation into allegations that the five might have previously failed to report or obstructed investigations into disclosures of historic abuse. The NTL commissioned a conflict management organisation (CMP)[54] to conduct the enquiry. At the time of writing, the full 800-page report has yet to be released, but a version of it was leaked to the BBC in 2020.[55] It was recommended that the five should be debarred from any senior leadership roles or safeguarding issues. Having been interviewed by the police under caution, they were eventually informed there was insufficient evidence to take the matter further.

In May 2018, the Jesus Fellowship Survivors' Association (JFSA)[56] was founded to give a voice and support to victims of abuse and to lobby on their behalf. Consisting mainly of those who had been brought up as children in JF but then left, by the end of 2019 it had 213 Facebook-group members and 34 members of a separate group confined to children raised in JF.

Then, in May 2019, the NLT proposed to the membership that the Constitution of the Jesus Fellowship Church should be revoked. The motion was passed; the Jesus Army would cease to exist; and the NLT would step down once the winding up of the central Church has been completed. Any remaining congregations were to become fully independent, responsible for every aspect of their functioning, including finance, staffing, and safeguarding.

Nothing stays the same, and, in the wake of their respective experiences of CSA, the three religions now face very different futures. Their current situations are now briefly sketched before moving onto a discussion of some similarities and differences in their responses, and how those responses relied on 'good people'.

Where are they now?

All religious movements that are new – insofar as they consist of first-generation converts – are almost bound to undergo some radical changes when a second generation is born (Barker 2017). None of the movements discussed above has been able to rely on the continuing commitment of the majority of its second-generation membership, many of whom became disillusioned with the movement for a variety of reasons, including the history of abuse that either they or their friends suffered during childhood (Barker 2012; Chancellor 2000:242; Van Eck Duymaer van Twist 2015; Wolf 2004:342).

ISKCON

ISKCON's adaptation has been the most successful so far as survival is concerned. Very few devotees now live in temples; most have formed their own nuclear families and have outside work. Furthermore, the membership no longer predominantly consists of Western hippies, but of congregations of Asian-origin families who attend festivals and other rituals in the temples

(Figure 2.3). These congregants, often with middle-class occupations, donate sufficient funds for the upkeep of the temples, where a small minority of devotees preserve the Vaishnava traditions taught by Prabhupada (Rasamandala 2020; Rochford 2007).

There are those who still view ISKCON as a cause for anxiety, largely because of the continued presence of some devotees known to have perpetrated abuse in the past.[57] An hour-long film by a concerned devotee, *Cost of Silence*, highlights ways in which potential and actual abuse could still haunt the movement.[58] One incident that remains a matter of concern occurred in 1990, when an eleven-year-old girl was inappropriately touched by an initiating guru who continues to be active within ISKCON.[59] This and other criticisms have elicited numerous official responses from ISKCON, which has responded by acknowledging the need for eternal vigilance and detailing the on-going efforts it makes to ensure the maximum possible safety for its children (Anuttama 2016).[60]

Despite its past reputation, however, ISKCON has become widely accepted as a representative of one of the main traditions of Hinduism in the West (Anuttama 2017; Rasamandala 2020). The Oxford Centre for Hindu Studies, founded in 1997 by an ISKCON devotee, is a now a Recognised Independent Centre of the University of Oxford;[61] and the BBC regularly

Figure 2.3 Festival at ISKCON's Bhaktivedanta Manor, UK, 2012 (Photograph by Eileen Barker).

calling on an ISKCON devotee, Akhandadhi das, to deliver its 'Thought for the Day'.[62]

Children of God

The Family International, as the Children of God are now known, underwent several radical changes following the London custody case. These culminated in the 2010 'Reboot', when the communities were disbanded and members had to accept responsibilities for themselves, rather than relying on the movement for financial and other support (Borowik 2018; Borowik's chapter in this volume; Shepherd and Shepherd 2013). There was a gradual fall in the numbers working for World Services (Shepherd and Shepherd 2010), and eventually Maria and her husband, Peter Amsterdam (b.1951), were left to supervise the movement with the assistance of a small handful of volunteers. Although some people chose to go on living communally, witnessing and carrying out charitable work,[63] most broke away, taking outside paid employment for the first time for many years. Membership has continued to fall, with many not really knowing whether they still consider themselves a member, yet possibly staying in touch through Facebook, chat groups and other social media (Borowik 2018). But there is little in the way of any structure to receive new members. To all intents and purposes, TFI has become a virtual community of approximately 1,500 members (Barker 2016; Borowik's chapter in this volume).

Jesus Fellowship

The Jesus Fellowship Church, having formally ceased to exist in May 2019, left some of its affiliated organisations, such as individual Jesus Centres, surviving under their own governance. Many, if not most, erstwhile members now lead their separate lives, possibly attending a nearby evangelical church. Another similarity can be noted here: whilst in their early days, both CoG and JF were likely to stress how different they were from contemporary manifestations of Christianity, they are now more likely to identify themselves as Christians. ISKCON devotees have always stressed they were within the Hindu tradition, but only recently have they been more widely accepted as such by outsiders.

At the time of writing, there remain several unresolved issues. Former community members, who had donated all their money and never owned property, were given modest leaving packages to enable them to establish new homes. JFSA continues to offer a wide range of support to victims of abuse. Lawyers for the JF Trust, the JFSA and the insurers continue to discuss details of the distribution of the Fellowship's assets (of, reportedly, £50 million)[64] between past and current members,[65] with ongoing group claims for those harmed under the age of 21[66] and for former community members.[67]

The final section of this chapter compares some of the similarities and differences between the three religions' changing structures and cultures and how 'good people' eventually played a part in combatting CSA.

Contextualising 'the triumph of evil'

In the early years of the post-war 'cult scare', when the majority of new religions consisted of youthful converts, a frequent accusation was that they brainwashed their membership (Barker 1984), thereby justifying the practice of illegally kidnapping members of movements in order to 'deprogramme' them (Bromley and Richardson 1983). By the 1990s, deprogramming had all but disappeared in the West (Giambalvo et al. 2013), but there was a new cause for public concern: Child sexual abuse. This phenomenon should not be viewed in isolation, however. Perhaps for the first time in history, the treatment of children was becoming widely viewed as a serious social issue, not only for new religions but also for established religions and other sectors throughout society (Radford et al. 2011:89).[68]

According to the historian Philip Jenkins, 'clergy sexual abuse [received] virtually no attention from media or policymakers before about 1984–1985, yet [became] a major focus of public concern within a few years' (1996:3). This being so, one could argue that the abuse, so widely reported in new religions with young children growing up in the West around that time, might not have been noticed in an earlier period – and it might not have happened today to the extent that it did then, now that new child protection and reporting laws have been introduced, and safeguarding has become more institutionally established in the culture of the wider society.

But it is not only the institutions of the external society to which we must look. Jenkins (1996:3–4) makes another pertinent point:

> Although 'paedophile priests' are disturbed and dangerous individuals, they could not wreak the harm they do were it not for the institutional context that ignores or connives at their activities … The Catholic Church in particular has been more concerned with protecting the reputation of the institution and the clerical profession than in safeguarding real or potential child victims.

In other words, although individual perpetrators are indubitably responsible for their actions, we can still ask what institutional contexts enabled, even encouraged, the CSA of tens (if not hundreds) of thousands of children in the Catholic Church, several hundreds of children in ISKCON,[69] some scores in CoG, and possibly a couple of dozen in JF.[70]

Despite the important differences between the three religions, there were also significant similarities. Theological beliefs had inspired all three to live in socially isolated communities that drew sharp boundaries between themselves and the outside world. These boundaries were strengthened with negative terms for non-members – 'karmies' (ISKCON), 'systemites' (CoG) and 'worldlings' (JF) – and further reinforced by non-members pejoratively labelling the religions as 'cults'. Contact with non-members was mostly restricted to proselytising and fund raising; communication with previous friends and relatives who were not part of the movement was possible, but rare. Time not spent in work or sleep was commonly spent in religious rituals or some other kind of spiritual practice. Access to the media was either forbidden or restricted.

Educational arrangements tended to offer children little or nothing in the way of access to responsible outside contacts and frequently entailed separation from parents. CoG children were home-schooled, but this could be in homes other than those in which their families resided. ISKCON children were sent to *gurukulas*, usually miles, even continents, away from their parents. JF children attended local state schools but were not permitted to take part in extra-curricular activities or socialise with other children (including not having lunch at their school); different clothing and hair styles could lead to isolation or bullying. Once they reached their teens, they would often spend time in different community houses from their parents.[71]

Even when children were living under the same roof as their parents, biological families were considered subservient to the communities' beliefs and requirements. When James Chancellor asked a remorseful CoG mother whether she would have sent her 11-year-old daughter to another location, knowing that it would involve the daughter having sexual intercourse with an adult there, she replied, 'Yes. At that time, I would have sent her' (Chancellor 2000:142–3). Sometimes members could be shocked by what they observed, yet their movement's culture apparently left them impotent: 'I did not feel capable of changing things and felt it more important to pursue authentic bhakti [devotion to Krishna]'.[72]

Questioning those in positions higher than oneself was frowned upon. Beliefs and practices were 'givens'; to question was to show one's ignorance or disloyalty and was liable to be met with some form of punitive response. CoG and ISKCON children were regularly subjected to severe physical punishments (Kent and Hall 2000; Lutz 2010); JF children were subjected to 'rodding' in accord with the Biblical injunction 'He that spareth his rod hateth his son: but he that loveth him chasteneth him betimes' (Proverbs 13:24). Sometimes confused children would confess under pressure to sins they had not committed.

All three movements had what could be viewed as unconventional attitudes towards sex. Whilst CoG celebrated sex between consenting heterosexual adults, ISKCON and JF valued celibacy, although sexual relations between married couples were permitted for the purpose of procreation. CoG children were raised in a sexually liberal environment and taught that sex was natural and God-created with, during the 1980s, no obvious boundary being drawn between affection and sex. ISKCON and JF children were given little or no sex education; they too, albeit in an entirely different way, remained ignorant about what might be sexually acceptable and what not. When sexually abused, children were usually told not to tell; some thought it was their fault and/or feared (with reason) that they would be punished or not be believed (Lutz 2010:58).[73] Many, if not most, victims have suffered in silence well into adulthood (Radford et al. 2011:9).

Berg's interpretation of the 'Law of Love' was most obviously conducive to CSA. ISKCON's belief that the primary duty of devotees was to lead a life of devotion by chanting and promoting the movement through book distribution,[74] coupled with a requirement to respect and follow the wishes of one's guru and other figures of authority, could result in children being ignored, exploited and/or abused. JF children were placed in potential danger by the Fellowship's strong belief that it should demonstrate Christian compassion and love by extending dignity, shelter and employment to all, including addicts and former convicts, without question.

Although it may now be widely accepted that CSA is a reportable crime, religious bodies have found themselves facing what to them appeared to be some serious dilemmas: Should one risk sacrificing the group for an individual? Should the group publicly apologise or defend itself? Should confidential confessions be betrayed in order to warn others? Should those who repent their sins be forgiven and accepted back into the community? Does forgiveness encourage repetition? Should perpetrators and victims receive internal pastoral care or external judgement or counselling? To what extent should members be placed under surveillance or trusted with freedom?

Furthermore, as the Catholic and other traditional religions were discovering (Byrnes 2020; Jenkins 1996:125–34; Zambrana-Téar 2020), more material considerations could involve financial and other assets. Both ISKCON and JF had considerable wealth at risk. They also had to clarify their insurance status. CoG had practically no financial assets; their belief in an imminent Endtime had made considerations of taking heed for the morrow, let alone insurance, superfluous (Barker 2020:108–9).

None of the founders could be considered a 'good man' so far as preventing CSA was concerned. Berg promoted a culture that encouraged it and was himself involved in the practice. Stanton openly promoted celibacy but was accused of sexual and other abuses.[75] Prabhupada neither practised nor did he directly encourage abuse, but he was responsible for children being sent to the gurukulas and did little or nothing to prevent the triumph of that particular 'evil'.

It was up to 'good people' to remedy the situation. Initially, they could be ignorant of what was happening, but on hearing allegations of CSA, these could be met with disbelief that such things could happen in their community, perhaps finding it difficult to change their conception of someone they had known and respected for years. Those in leadership positions might dismiss accusations as rumours spread by disaffected former members and/or a salacious media – and/or quietly move the perpetrator to another location.

As rumours grew, and in the face of mounting proof, several good people left, disillusioned and feeling impotent; but others stayed to bring about change, even when they found themselves impeded in their reformatory efforts by a truculent and obstructive institution. Nonetheless, sufficient numbers persisted in their efforts to ensure that safeguarding eventually became firmly institutionalised as part of both the culture and structure of their respective movements (Anuttama 2017:147; CCPAS 2015).[76]

Despite all efforts, however, CSA continues. Exposés have continued to appear in the media, but most of these are now of historic abuse (see Borowik chapter in this volume),[77] and although reliable statistics for CSA within any religion are notoriously difficult to estimate (Jenkins 1996:83), there can be little doubt that the number of abused children in the religions discussed in this chapter has been radically reduced, and when current abuses do occur they are less likely to be in an ashram, gurukula or socially isolated religious community than within the context of nuclear family life, thereby mirroring the causes and patterns found within mainstream society, with the religions' structure and culture more likely to mitigate against rather than foster abuse (Rochford 1998a:62n.3; Wolf 2004:342).

To conclude, the religions described in this chapter have undergone radical changes since their inception (Barker 2020; Rochford 2007), a key factor having been their response to CSA. Many children suffered severely; some continue to suffer as a result of CSA they received in an environment in which good people did nothing – for some time. The eventual reduction in abuse was partly because of a growth in general social awareness of the evils of CSA, partly because of outside pressure and the protests of some abused children, but also partly as a result of radical changes in the movements' culture and structure brought about because there were 'good men and women' who did, eventually, 'do something'.

Notes

1 I would like to express my thanks to members and former members of the religions discussed in this chapter for sharing their experiences with me.
2 Attributed to, amongst others, Edmund Burke and John Stuart Mill.
3 https://www.cbsnews.com/news/vatican-reveals-how-many-priests-defrocked-for-sex-abuse-since-2004/; http://www.bishop-accountability.org/AtAGlance/USCCB_Yearly_Data_on_Accused_Priests.htm
4 See, for example, Finnigan and Hogendoorn (2019); Jenkins (1996); https://www.iicsa.org.uk/publications/investigation/ANGLICAN-chichester-peter-ball; https://www.METHODIST.org.uk/about-us/news/latest-news/all-news/church-issues-full-and-unreserved-apology-to-abuse-survivors/; https://JEWISHnews.timesofisrael.com/consensus-in-some-jewish-communities-not-to-tackle-child-sex-abuse/; https://apnews.com/ddd9660f63ae4433966684823f79d3e9/ISLAMIC-schools-in-Pakistan-plagued-by-sex-abuse-of-children; https://www.BUDDHISTdoor.net/news/alarm-bells-sounded-over-child-abuse-at-thailands-buddhist-temples; http://WWASPSURVIVORS.com/about-wwasp/wwasp-history/; https://time.com/longform/BOY-SCOUTS-sex-abuse/
5 https://www.who.int/news-room/fact-sheets/detail/child-maltreatment
6 https://www.iicsa.org.uk/

7 The patterns of roles and interactions between these roles, including authority and communication structures.

8 The shared beliefs, values and worldview of a social group.

9 Individual's independent psychological profiles, including genetic predispositions, personality and previous experiences.

10 https://www.iskcon.org/activities/food-relief-program.php; http://www.familyafrica.com/index.php/projects; http://www.jesusarmywatch.org.uk/scrapbook/cinema.htm

11 Women in both ISKCON and the Jesus Fellowship were commonly expected to be subservient to men, and had very little say in policy matters. However, Berg (1979) had named Maria as his successor and, even before his death, it was she who outlawed adult sex with children (Chancellor 2000:20–21); furthermore, many of the colonies were run by husband-and-wife teams and World Services was roughly balanced between female and male members (Shepherd and Shepherd 2010).

12 By 1991, ISKCON householders outnumbered renounced members and 70% had at least one child (Rochford 1998a:50).

13 https://surrealist.org/gurukula/timeline/standards.html

14 http://www.iskcon-truth.com/childabuse/childabu.htm

15 In 1997, Windle Turley had represented victims of sexual abuse by a priest who won a $120-million judgment in a sex abuse case against the Catholic Diocese of Dallas. The victims then agreed to a $30-million settlement. http://www.bishop-accountability.org/tx-dallas/resource-files/turley-documents.htmhttps://www.nytimes.com/1997/07/25/us/120-million-damage-award-for-sexual-abuse-by-priest.html

16 http://www.exfamily.org/pubs/ml/b4/ml0258.shtml; http://www.exfamily.org/pubs/ml/ml1999_main.shtmlhttps://www.xfamily.org/index.php/The_Devil_Hates_Sex; https://www.xfamily.org/index.php/The_Family%E2%80%99s_History,_Policies,_and_Beliefs_Regarding_Sex#The_Family.27s_History.2C_Policies.2C_and_Beliefs_Regarding_Sex_.E2.80.94Part_3

17 http://www.exfamily.org/pubs/ml/b4/ml0258.shtml

18 https://www.xfamily.org/images/0/06/Ff-report-docs.pdf

19 Thousands of MO letters, tracts written (mainly) by 'Moses' Berg, were distributed throughout the communities on a regular basis.

20 A compilation of the letters *The Story of Davidito* was published in 1982, but destroyed in 1989, then replaced by a sanitised version (Sarah 1997). Parts of the original are accessible at https://www.xfamily.org/index.php/Story_of_Davidito. In 2005, Ricky murdered Berg's former secretary and then committed suicide after making a video expressing his anger at his upbringing. https://www.youtube.com/watch?v=3p0-iLcx4es

21 Merry is referred to as MB in Ward's judgement.

22 E.g. https://www.xfamily.org/index.php/Main_Pagehttps://archive.xfamily.org/www.movingon.org/newcontent.asp.html

23 E.g. Edwards (2018); Jones et al. (2007).

24 Bugbrooke is a small village not far from Northampton in the English Midlands.

25 https://charismactivism.com/2014/06/05/the-mission-and-vision-of-the-jesus-army/

26 Stanton encouraged his followers to 'give their genitals to Jesus'. https://www.bbc.co.uk/news/av/uk-england-northamptonshire-53657504/jesus-army-founder-noel-stanton-preaching-about-sexual-sins. Those who chose celibacy included couples who already had children, and singles, some of whom might recognise themselves to be homosexual.

27 https://inews.co.uk/news/uk/jesus-army-no-voice-now-damaged-ex-members-must-heard-91830

28 http://www.jesusarmywatch.org.uk/scrapbook/online/022.htm; http://www.jesusarmywatch.org.uk/scrapbook/online/027.htm

29 https://www.northamptonchron.co.uk/news/jesus-army-sex-offender-who-was-based-northamptonshire-sentenced-string-indecent-acts-directed-children-1980s-860901; http://www.jesusarmywatch.org.uk/scrapbook/dwe/004.htm; http://www.jesusarmywatch.org.uk/scrapbook/ce/013.htm; http://www.jesusarmywatch.org.uk/scrapbook/ce/120.htm; https://inews.co.uk/news/uk/jesus-army-no-voice-now-damaged-ex-members-must-heard-91830

30 https://www.northamptonchron.co.uk/news/exclusive-sexual-and-financial-abuse-claims-made-against-founder-jesus-army-northampton-856646

31 https://gbc.iskcon.org/

32 https://www.latimes.com/archives/la-xpm-1999-jun-13-mn-46054-story.html

33 https://surrealist.org/gurukula/timeline/mothersletter.html

34 http://vaishnava-news-network.org/world/WD9903/WD14-3323.html

35 https://www.iskconchildprotection.org/-about

36 http://news.bbc.co.uk/1/hi/world/americas/788790.stm

37 See also http://www.people.vcu.edu/~dbromley/participantobservationresearchLink.html

38 https://www.nytimes.com/1998/10/09/us/hare-krishna-movement-details-past-abuse-at-its-boarding-schools.html

39 http://news.bbc.co.uk/1/hi/world/americas/788790.stm/; https://www.hinduismtoday.com/modules/smartsection/item.php?itemid=4177/

40 https://surrealist.org/jpgs/complaint_state.pdf, page 19.

41 https://surrealist.org/gurukula/timeline/lawsuitdocs.html

42 https://surrealist.org/gurukula/timeline/lawsuitdocs.html

43 http://www.safetemple.org/2012/01/04/guidelines/; https://11367181-1147-4490-b065-a691958b5ecd.filesusr.com/ugd/8a61c5_3cba6c1074e7427d893be8af35c40a79.pdf

44 There have been several subsequent editions of *The Love Charter*, the most recent being on TFI's website: https://portal.tfionline.com/en/pages/governing-documents/

45 https://www.myconclusion.com/apology-to-second-generation.html#more-1785

46 https://portal.tfionline.com/en/pages/charter-children/

47 https://www.xfamily.org/index.php/Main_Page

48 https://www.nytimes.com/1988/07/15/movies/tv-weekend-retrieving-youngsters-from-a-sex-exalting-cult.html; https://www.netflix.com/title/80106144; https://www.xfamily.org/images/6/6b/Mene_cover.jpg; https://www.nytimes.com/1988/07/15/movies/tv-weekend-retrieving-youngsters-from-a-sex-exalting-cult.html

49 See also http://news.bbc.co.uk/1/hi/world/americas/788790.stm

50 Now Thirtyone:Eight https://thirtyoneeight.org/

51 https://www.nytimes.com/1997/07/25/us/120-million-damage-award-for-sexual-abuse-by-priest.html; http://www.bishop-accountability.org/tx-dallas/resource-files/turley-documents.htm; https://www.nytimes.com/1997/07/25/us/120-million-damage-award-for-sexual-abuse-by-priest.html

52 Following his death in 2011, Savile was exposed as having sexually abused hundreds of children. https://www.dailymail.co.uk/news/article-3078225/Watchdog-says-Jimmy-Savile-caught-2008-Sussex-police-mishandled-victim-s-abuse-complaint.html; https://www.standard.co.uk/news/crime/blunders-meant-jimmy-savile-was-not-prosecuted-while-still-alive-8447827.html

53 https://www.whatdotheyknow.com/request/child_sexual_abuse_operations_32

54 https://www.cmpsolutions.com/

55 https://www.bbc.co.uk/news/uk-england-northamptonshire-53450901
56 https://jesusfellowshipsurvivors.org/
57 https://surrealist.org/gurukula/timeline/lawsuit.html; see section 'Where are they now?'
58 https://krishna.org/the-cost-of-silence-children-of-the-hare-krishnas/
59 https://satyavrata.wixsite.com/lokanathswami?fbclid=IwAR2lYQiWlyA4Lq1_ITFNlORrk
60 https://11367181-1147-4490-b065-a691958b5ecd.filesusr.com/ugd/8a61c5_3cba6c1074e7427d893be8af35c40a79.pdf
61 https://ochs.org.uk/
62 https://www.bbc.co.uk/programmes/articles/5bxBSyCZvhXMzJtsZg5lSsP/regular-contributors
63 See http://www.familyafrica.com/
64 https://jesusfellowshipsurvivors.org/bbc-report-on-the-jesus-army-jesus-fellowship/ @ 7:46. https://www.bbc.co.uk/news/uk-48447066
65 https://jesusfellowshipsurvivors.org/important-statements-from-the-jfsa-and-the-jfct-on-the-redress-scheme/
66 https://jesusfellowshipsurvivors.org/group-civil-claim-for-those-harmed-within-the-jesus-fellowship-jesus-army-under-the-age-of-21/
67 https://jesusfellowshipsurvivors.org/group-civil-claim-for-ex-community-members/
68 https://www.iicsa.org.uk/
69 http://news.bbc.co.uk/1/hi/world/americas/788790.stm
70 https://www.bbc.co.uk/news/uk-48447066
71 https://inews.co.uk/news/uk/jesus-army-no-voice-now-damaged-ex-members-must-heard-91830
72 https://surrealist.org/gurukula/timeline/jagadananda.html
73 https://inews.co.uk/news/uk/jesus-army-no-voice-now-damaged-ex-members-must-heard-91830
74 https://krishna.org/srila-prabhupada-book-distribution/
75 https://www.northamptonchron.co.uk/news/exclusive-sexual-and-financial-abuse-claims-made-against-founder-jesus-army-northampton-856646
76 https://www.thefamilyinternational.org/en/children-hope-future/
77 https://surrealist.org/gurukula/timeline/lawsuit.html; https://www.bbc.co.uk/news/uk-scotland-glasgow-west-53448774; https://www.northamptonchron.co.uk/news/special-report-alleged-victim-historic-abuse-reveals-traumatic-childhood-growing-jesus-army-840120

Bibliography

All URLs were accessed on 29 October 2020.

Amsterdam, Peter. 1995a. *World Services' Response to Mr Justice Ward.* September.

Amsterdam, Peter. 1995b. "The Ministry of Reconciliation: A Report." Appendix to *Response to Mr Justice Ward.* September.

Anderson, Barbara (Ed.). 2007. *Secrets of Pedophilia in an American Religion: Jehovah's Witnesses in Crisis. Court Documents: Charissa et al Coordinated Cases vs Jehovah's Witnesses.* CD Rom. McLean, VA: Watchtower Documents LLC.

Anuttama, Dasa. 2017. "The Changing Perception of ISKCON: Ancient Faith or Dangerous Cult?" pp. 134–151 in *'Cult Wars' in Historical Perspective: New and Minority Religions,* edited by Eugene Gallagher. Abingdon: Routledge.

Anuttama, Dasa. 2016. *A Statement on Child Protection within ISKCON*: ISKCON Communications Office. https://iskconnews.org/a-statement-on-child-protection-within-iskcon,5609/

Bainbridge, William Sims. 2002. *The Endtime Family: Children of God*. Albany, NY: SUNY.

Baldasty, Gerald J. 2005. *Vigilante Newspapers: A Tale of Sex, Religion, and Murder in the Northwest*. Seattle: University of Washington Press.

Barker, Eileen. 2020. "Denominationalization or Death? A Comparative Examination of Processes of Change within the Jesus Fellowship Church and the Children of God aka The Family International," pp. 99–117 in *The Demise of Religion: How Religions End, Die, or Dissipate*, edited by Michael Stausberg, Stuart A. Wright, and Carole M. Cusack. London: Bloomsbury.

Barker, Eileen. 2017. "The Changing Scene: What Might Happen and What Might Be Less Likely to Happen?" pp. 7–19 in *New and Minority Religions: Projecting the Future*, edited by Eugene V. Gallagher. Farnham: Routledge.

Barker, Eileen. 2016. "From The Children of God to the Family International: A Story of Radical Christianity and Deradicalising Transformation," in *The Handbook of Contemporary Christianity: Movements, Institutions & Allegiance*, edited by Stephen J. Hunt. Leiden: Brill.

Barker, Eileen. 2012. "Ageing in New Religions: The Varieties of Later Experiences." *Diskus: The Journal of the British Association for the Study of Religions* 12:1–23. http://jbasr.com/basr/diskus/diskus12/index.html

Barker, Eileen. 1984. *The Making of a Moonie: Brainwashing or Choice?* Oxford: Blackwell.

Berg, David. 1980. *The Devil Hates Sex! But God Loves It!* The Children of God. DFO999. https://www.xfamily.org/index.php/The_Devil_Hates_Sex

Berg, David. 1979. Berg, David. 1979. *THE SHEPHERDESS!* DO837. 25 September. http://www.exfamily.org/pubs/ml/b5/ml0837.shtml

Berg, David. 1977. *Child Brides!* The Children of God. DO 902. https://www.xfamily.org/index.php/Berg_on_Pedophilia#Child_Brides

Berg, David. 1976. *The Basic MO Letters*. Geneva: Children of God.

Berg, David. 1975. *Free Sex! Wildly Illustrated*. London: Children of God.

Bharata, Shrestha Das. 1998. "ISKCON's Response to Child Abuse: 1990–1998." *ISKCON Communications Journal* 6(1):71–79. https://content.iskcon.org/icj/6_2/62dhira.html

Borowik, Claire. 2013. "The Family International: Rebooting for the Future," pp. 15–30 in *Revisionism and Diversification in New Religious Movements*, edited by Eileen Barker. Farnham: Ashgate.

Bogdan, Henrik, and James Lewis (Eds.). 2014. *Sexuality and New Religious Movements*. New York: Palgrave Macmillan.

Borowik, Claire. 2018. "From Radical Communalism to Virtual Community: The Digital Transformation of The Family International." *Nova Religio* 22(1):59–86.

Bromley, David G., and James T. Richardson (Eds.). 1983. *The Brainwashing/Deprogramming Controversy: Sociological, Psychological, Legal and Historical Perspectives*. New York: Edwin Mellen.

Byrnes, Timothy A. 2020. "Catholic Bishops and Sexual Abuse: Power, Constraint, and Institutional Context." *Journal of Church and State* 62(1):5–25.

Chancellor, James D. 2000. *Life in The Family: An Oral History of the Children of God*. Syracuse, NY: Syracuse University Press.

CCPAS. 2015. *Safeguarding Review for Jesus Fellowship*. Swanley: CCPAS.

Collective of Women, A. 1997. "Sex, Lies, and Grand Schemes of Thought in Closed Groups." *Cultic Studies Journal* 14(1):58–84.

Cooper, Simon, and Mike Farrant. 1997. *Fire in Our Hearts: The Story of the Jesus Fellowship/Jesus Army* (1st edition: 1991). Nether Heyford, Northampton: Multiply Publications.

Davis, Deborah. 1984. *The Children of God: The Inside Story by the Daughter of the Founder, Moses David Berg*. Grand Rapids, MI: Zondervan.

Deadwyler, Gabriel (Yudhishthira das). 2004. "Fifteen Years Later: A Critique of Gurukula," pp. 346–356 in *The Hare Krishna Movement: The Postcharismatic Fate of a Religious Transplant*, edited by Edwin Bryant and Maria Ekstrand. New York: Columbia University Press.

Edwards, Flor. 2018. *Apocalypse Child: A Life in End Times*. Nashville: Turner Publishing.

Family, The. 1995. *The Love Charter*. Zurich: The Family.

Family, The. 1992, June. *Our Replies to Allegations of Child Abuse*. Zurich: World Services.

Finnigan, Mary, and Rob Hogendoorn. 2019. *Sex and Violence in Tibetan Buddhism: The Rise and Fall of Sogyal Rinpoche*. Portland, OR: Jorvik.

Gelberg, Steven J. 1988. "The Fading of Utopia: ISKCON in Transition," pp. 171–184 in *Sects and New Religious Movements*, edited by Anthony Dyson and Eileen Barker. Manchester, UK: Bulletin of the John Rylands University Library of Manchester.

Giambalvo, Carol, Michael Kropveld, and Michael Langone. 2013. "Changes in North American Cult Awareness Organizations," pp. 227–245 in *Revisionism and Diversification in New Religious Movements*, edited by Eileen Barker. Farnham: Ashgate.

Haines, Michael, et al. 2012. *Jesus Army Safeguarding Policy*. Palm Beach Gardens, FL: Jesus Fellowship Church.

Hubner, John, and Lindsey Gruson. 1988. *Monkey on a Stick: Murder, Madness, and the Hare Krishnas*. New York: Penguin.

Jagadish, Dasa. 1981. *Interview* ISKCON World Review 1(6).

Jahnavi, Dasi. 1999. "Children of Krishna." *Vaishnava News* 14 March. http://vaishnava-news-network.org/world/WD9903/WD14-3323.html

Jeffs, Rachel. 2017. *Breaking Free: How I Escaped Polygamy, The FLDS Cult, And My Father, Warren Jeffs*. New York: HarperCollins.

Jenkins, Antonia. 2008. "Third Statement of Antonia Jenkins." High Court of Justice. Exhibits 18; Fd0700454 Family Division.

Jenkins, Philip. 1996. *Pedophiles and Priests: Anatomy of a Contemporary Crisis*. Oxford: Oxford University Press.

Jones, Kristina, Celeste Jones, and Juliana Buhring. 2007. *Not Without My Sister*. London: HarperElement.

Kay, William K. 2007. *Apostolic Networks in Britain: New Ways of Being a Church*. Milton Keynes: Paternoster.

Kent, Stephen A. 2004. "Generational Revolt by the Adult Children of First-Generation Members of the Children of God/The Family." *Cultic Studies Review* 3(1):56–72.

Kent, Stephen A., and Deana Hall. 2000. "Brainwashing and Re-Indoctrination Camps in the Children of God." *Cultic Studies Journal* 17:56–78.

Kirkengen, Anna Luise. 2001. *Inscribed Bodies: Health Impact of Childhood Sexual Abuse*. Dordrecht: Kluwer.

Langone, Michael D. 2016. "Origins and Prevention of Abuse in Religious Groups." *ICSA Today* 7(3):11–13.

Lewis, James R., and J. Gordon Melton (Eds.). 1994. *Sex, Slander, and Salvation: Investigating The Family/Children of God*. Stanford, CA: Center for Academic Publications.

Lutz, Daniel. 2010. *My Karma My Fault*. Self-published.

McMillion, Andrew. 2002. "Growing Up and Leaving the Children of God." *FAIR News* 2:13–16.

Melton, J. Gordon. 2004. *The Children of God: 'The Family.'* Turin: Signature Books.

Muster, Nori J. 2001. *Betrayal of the Spirit: My Life Behind the Headlines of the Hare Krishna Movement*. Urbana: University of Illinois Press.

PADA (Prabhupada Anti-Defamation Association). 1993. *Child Molesters: Gurus?* http://harekrsna.org/child-molesters-gurus/

Patrick, Ted, and Tom Dulack. 1976. *Let Our Children Go*. New York: Ballantine.

Radford, Lorraine, et al. 2011. *Child Abuse and Neglect in the UK Today*. London: NSPCC. https://learning.nspcc.org.uk/media/1042/child-abuse-neglect-uk-today-research-report.pdf

Raine, Susan, and Stephen A. Kent. 2019. "The Grooming of Children for Sexual Abuse in Religious Settings: Unique Characteristics and Select Case Studies." *Aggression and Violent Behavior* 48(September–October):180–189.

Rasamandala, Das. 2020. *ISKCON and Hinduism. Exploring the Hare Krishna Movement and Its Broader Traditions*. Aldenham, Herts: ISKCON Educational Services.

Rochford, E. Burke. 2007. *Hare Krishna Transformed*. New York: New York University Press.

Rochford, E. Burke (with Jennifer Heinlein). 1998a. "Child Abuse in the Hare Krishna Movement: 1971–1986." *ISKCON Communications Journal* 6(1):43–69.

Rochford, E. Burke. 1998b. "Further Reflections on Child Abuse Within ISKCON." *ISKCON Communications Journal* 6(2):64–67.

Rochford, E. Burke. 1998c. "Reactions of Hare Krishna Devotees to Scandals of Leaders' Misconduct," pp. 101–117 in *Wolves Within the Fold*, edited by Anson Shupe. New Brunswick: Rutgers.

Rochford, E. Burke. 1985. *Hare Krishna in America*. New Brunswick: Rutgers University Press.

Sarah A. 1997 *Dito: His Early Years*. Zurich: World Services.

Saxby, Trevor. 1998. *The Call to a Christian Community Life Style*. Nether Heyford, Northampton: Multiply.

Shepherd, Gary, and Gordon Shepherd. 2013. "Reboot of The Family International." *Nova Religio* 17(2):74–98.

Shepherd, Gordon, and Gary Shepherd. 2010. *Talking with* the *Children of God: Prophecy and Transformation in a Radical Religious Group*. Urbana: University of Illinois Press.

Shinn, Larry D. 1987. *The Dark Lord: Cult Images and the Hare Krishnas in America*. Philadelphia: Westminster.

Stacey, James. n.d. *Kingdom Seekers*. Nether Heyford, Northampton: Multiply. https://www.yumpu.com/en/document/view/37285029/kingdom-seekers-new-creation-christian-community

Turley, Windle. 2000. *Submission to the Texas District Court I Dallas, by Law Offices of Windle Turley on Behalf of the Children of ISKCON*. http://iskcon-truth.com/documents/turley-complaint0606.pdf

Van Eck Duymaer van Twist, Amanda 2015. *Perfect Children: Growing Up on the Religious Fringe*. Oxford: Oxford University Press.

Van Zandt, David E. 1995. "The Children of God," in *America's Alternative Religions*, edited by Timothy Miller. Albany NY: State University of New York.

van Zandt, David E.1991. *Living in the Children of God*. Princeton NJ: Princeton University Press.

Ward, The Rt. Hon. Lord Justice Alan. 1995a (May). W42 in the High Court of Justice, Family Division: Principal Registry in the Matter of ST (a Minor) and in the Matter of the Supreme Court Act 1991. https://media2.xfamily.org/docs/legal/uk/ward-judgment/ward-judgment-scan-low.pdf

Ward, The Rt. Hon. Lord Justice Alan. 1995b (November). https://media.xfamily.org/docs/legal/uk/ward-judgment/ward-judgment-v2.pdf

Willey, Andrea, and Stephen A. Kent. 2017. "Prosecuting Child Sexual Abuse in Alternative Religions." *International Journal of Cultic Studies* 8:16–36.

Williams, Miriam. 1998. *Heaven's Harlots: My Fifteen Years as a Sacred Prostitute in the Children of God Cult*.New York: Eagle Brook.

Wolf, David. 2004. "Child Abuse and the Hare Krishnas: History and Response," pp. 321–344 in *The Hare Krishna Movement: The Postcharismatic Fate of a Religious Transplant*, edited by Edwin F. Bryant and Maria L. Ekstrand. New York: Columbia University Press.

Wright, Stuart and Susan, Palmer 2016. *Storming Zion: Government Raids on Religious Communities*. Oxford: Oxford University Press.

Yeomans, Peter. 2013. "'The Little Pebble': Cult Leader and Child Sex Offender." *Australian Police Journal* March:44–49.

Zambrana-Téar, Nicolás. 2020. "Reassessing the Immunity and Accountability of the Holy See in Clergy Sex Abuse Litigations." *Journal of Church and State* 62(1):28–58.

Zerby, Karen. 1993. "Getting Back on Track for Jesus! (Part 1)." Maria #205. DO 2890 September, http://www.exfamily.org/pubs/ml/b5/ml2890.shtml.

Zerby, Karen. 1989. "Child Abuse: A Final Warning." *June* DFO 2536. https://pubs.xfamily.org/text.php?t=2536

3 Children of Heimdall: Ásatrú ideas of ancestry

Karl E. H. Seigfried

This chapter examines the attitudes towards ancestry that have developed and changed over time in Ásatrú, a new religious movement that revives/reconstructs/reimagines pre-Christian Germanic religion with an emphasis on medieval Icelandic texts. From its founding by a small group of artist-activists in Reykjavík in 1972, Ásatrú has spread worldwide and is now part of a larger set of religious systems that adherents call 'Heathenry'. Emphasis on ancestry is a common theme among iterations of Ásatrú, yet definitions vary in various communities. In Iceland, ancestry and practice are integrally linked; members of the Ásatrúarfélagið (Ásatrú Fellowship) trace their ancestry via national database to figures in the medieval sagas that they also examine for evidence of pagan practice to (re)construct ritual. In America, race and religion are often paired; Ásatrú Folk Assembly founder Stephen McNallen advocates concepts of ancestry that have ranged from 'Viking' to 'European-American' as he promotes white identity politics focusing on DNA as determinant of religiosity. A third approach, exemplified by the international organization known as the Troth, responds to the overtly racialist approach by publicly forwarding conflicting arguments regarding the importance of ancestry for religious belonging. These three approaches are driven by different sociopolitical concepts and result in conflicting religio-cultural manifestations and revisions. A consideration of these related yet different groups and their attitudes towards ancestry provides a specific example of how new religious movements change over time and under different leadership.

Descendants of saga heroes: the Ásatrúarfélagið

The new religious movement known as Ásatrú dates to 20 April 1972 (Berg 2008: 269), when twelve individuals interested in reviving Iceland's pre-Christian religion gathered at Reykjavík's Hotel Borg to found the Ásatrúarfélagið (Hilmar Örn Hilmarsson 2016b). The Icelandic term *Ásatrú* has a contested origin, but its first appearance seems to be in the Danish form *Asatro*, used by N.F.S. Grundtvig in *Optrin af Norners og Asers Kamp* of 1811 (Grundtvig 1880: 333). In either language, the term means 'Æsir Faith' and

DOI: 10.4324/9781315226804-3

refers to belief in or loyalty to the main tribe of Norse gods; *Ásatrúarfélagið* means 'Æsir Faith Fellowship'. There is also a contested date for the first public *blót* (Ásatrú ritual) held in Iceland after the pagan rite's open performance was outlawed in 1000; it was on either summer solstice 1972 (Berg 2008: 269) or 5 August 1973 ("*Blótuðu Þór í Úrhellisrigningu*" 1973). By the summer of 1973, public curiosity about Ásatrú led to media members outnumbering Heathens at *blót* (Hilmar Örn Hilmarsson 2016c). Despite opposition from Iceland's Lutheran bishop, the Ásatrúarfélagið was recognised as a religious organization in May 1973 (Berg 2008: 270–1). Farmer, poet, and antiquarian Sveinbjörn Beinteinsson became the group's first *allsherjargoði* (roughly, 'high priest').

The impetus for the Ásatrú society's formation was the presence of Christian missionaries in Iceland during the winter of 1971–1972. Sveinbjörn later stated,

> At that time we were getting a lot of Jesus Children into Iceland, and I said to myself, 'Wait a minute, we have older beliefs in Iceland. Why should we not bring them back to life? How come we're bringing in all these other sects?' (Graichen 1986)

The first Ásatrú meetings were 'in direct opposition' to the foreign missionaries and sought to create a specifically Icelandic alternative: 'We wanted to give people a chance to belong to the old religion. The religion that was here on Iceland before there was Christianity, that was forbidden us in the same year that Iceland adopted Christianity' (Graichen 1986). Current *allsherjargoði* Hilmar Örn Hilmarsson clarifies details:

> We had these so-called Children of God that came to Iceland. This was a Christian sect founded by a man who called himself Moses David… He sent out young people to hand out leaflets and say, "Come back to Jesus" and stuff like that. Sveinbjörn was looking at this and saying, "Why do we have these young foreigners coming to tell us to go to Jesus? Why can't we just say to them, 'Go back to Thor and Odin'?" That was, in a way, an inspiration for him. (Seigfried 2011a: Part 2)

From its inception, Ásatrú was seen as specifically for Icelanders and rooted in the nation's pre-Christian past.

Sveinbjörn promoted the idea that pagan practice in Iceland never ceased after the conversion to Christianity, and that the creation of Ásatrú was therefore a return to public life rather than a recreation of a dead practice. During the millennium after conversion, according to Sveinbjörn, '[t]he country folk always believed in nature, in natural experience, and in beings that live in nature like elves, gnomes, and good, positive-natured beings which live near people and help them' (Graichen 1986). In this construction of Iceland's pagan history, the religion is passed down by personal contact in a nation that never fully committed to Christianity. 'The old people, the kind I knew as a kid, who were surely Christians,' says Sveinbjörn, 'but they didn't overdo it with the Christian thing. Normally, they had a mix of beliefs in Christianity but also in nature. They had a sense that there were elves and other beings around them' (Graichen 1986). Hilmar agrees, saying, 'I don't think we were as serious about Christianity as other people' (Seigfried 2011a: Part 1). This concept of superficial Christianity is often connected with stories presenting specific family members as pagan before the 1972 appearance of Ásatrú.

Jörmundur Ingi Hansen, Sveinbjörn's successor as *allsherjargoði*, connects his predecessor's idea of 'mild Christianity' (Seigfried 2011a: Part 1) with family continuity and a sense that pagan traditions are an intrinsic part of Icelandic identity:

> both my parents, my grandparents and my great-grandmother – they all looked at themselves as Christians. But the old traditions of the wights, the hidden people, the beings that live in every rock and everywhere in nature were so much part of my upbringing, like most Icelanders. (Dornoy 1999)

For Jörmundur Ingi, Ásatrú is an expression of Icelandicity:

> People realize that this is maybe the best way for the younger people to express that they are actually Icelandic. One reason that paganism is coming up could simply be because the church is losing ground. The strata that is underneath is only coming up when the patina of Christianity is starting to fade away. This is so much alive in Iceland that it is not considered strange to be a pagan. It is such a part of the national identity that it's very difficult to define Iceland without mentioning the ancient paganism. (Bocquet 2006)

The combination of (1) claiming that self-identified Christian family members held pagan beliefs and (2) asserting that Ásatrú expresses a primeval Icelandic identity is common among Ásatrúarfélagið members.

Jóhanna G. Harðaróttir, the organization's *staðgengill allsherjargoða* (deputy high priestess), also connects members of her family to pre-Ásatrú paganism under a Christian surface. Speaking of her father's beliefs during her childhood, she says,

> There was no Ásatrúarfélag at that time, but he was Ásatrúar, and he always was. He died two years ago, but he was a heathen. He was a pagan... He was teaching me about the old gods and telling me things about this religion, even if I didn't know that he was heathen. We never talked about *that*, really. I love nature, and I love the animals, and we had the same thing. (Seigfried 2011b: Part 1)

She states that her parents were registered in the National (Lutheran) Church of Iceland but stresses that registration was automatic. 'For Icelanders, church is for getting married and for giving your children names and for going when somebody dies, but church is not a big thing with Icelanders', she says. 'We are really very heathen people' (Seigfried 2011b: Part 1). Like Jörmundur Ingi, she connects paganism with Icelandicity in a way that overrides Christian identity:

> There's such a lot of people that are registered in the National Church that are heathen. It's in our hearts, being heathen. We love this country, and we love this lifestyle of being connected to the country – the land itself. That is, of course, part of being a heathen. It's very strong in our genes. (Seigfried 2011b: Part 1)

The claim of genetic connection to paganism refers to literal and verifiable descent from heroes and poets of early Iceland. Speaking of the 13th-century author of the *Edda*, the most coherent surviving record of Norse mythology, Jóhanna says,

> I'm very thankful for Snorri Sturluson – who was my twenty-seventh grandfather – for writing this down, because now we have *something*. But even if he didn't, I'm still myself, and I would still believe in the same things. (Seigfried 2011b, Part 3)

After this declaration of family connection to the myths and assertion of individual religious experience, she says, 'I guess maybe eighty percent of the nation is related. That's the funny thing about Iceland. You can dig up your forefathers all the way to Norway' (Seigfried 2011b, Part 3).

Tracing family trees in Iceland requires neither rummaging through dusty church archives nor delving into the work of amateur genealogists online. 'It's very easy in Iceland', says Jóhanna. 'We even have it on the web. It's called *Íslendingabók*. You just type your name in there, and it pops up. You click "find my forefathers," and there will come all the names' (Seigfried 2011b, Part 3). The *Íslendingabók* database 'contains genealogical information about the inhabitants of Iceland, dating more than 1,200 years back' (Íslendigabók 2016: 'English Summary'). Its goal is 'to trace all known family connections between Icelanders from the time of the settlement of Iceland to present times' (Íslendigabók 2016). Jóhanna claims an ancestry that includes the greatest pagan heroes of Icelandic literature, its best-known pagan poets, and the writer who preserved pagan mythology. She is not unique in this regard.

Although its membership has grown by over 35,000 per cent since its founding, and even though the organization welcomes any legal resident of Iceland from any national origin or ethno-racial background, over 99% of its membership consists of native Icelanders (Hilmar Örn Hilmarsson 2016a).

Nearly every member can therefore trace her ancestry to the subjects and authors of the texts the group mines for evidence of worldview and ritual. This deep connection to literature and history helps explain assertions of family connection and inherently Icelandic nature of Ásatrú. When virtually all members of a religion are related to their nation's oldest recorded practitioners, ancestry is taken for granted. The few non-native members are welcomed into what can be seen as an extended family, yet the sense of Ásatrú as the inheritance of those whose roots go back to settlement times remains at the Icelandic religious movement's core.

In 2016, the Ásatrúarfélagið was noticeably absent from the list of '180 organizations in over 20 different nations' that approved 'Declaration 127', a condemnation of 'discrimination on the basis of ethnicity, sexuality, and gender identity' by the U.S.-based Ásatrú Folk Assembly (Declaration 127 2019). Many of these groups were among the 'more than 1,300 signatories' of a statement of support for the Ásatrúarfélagið in response to the Icelanders 'receiving hate mail from reactionary and socially conservative foreign pagans' (Iceland Magazine 2015). Although willing to accept positive attention from non-Icelandic Heathens, Ásatrúarfélagið leaders are increasingly unwilling to engage with other Ásatrú organizations or publicly support foreign practitioners. As the first Ásatrúarfélagið generation passes on and members not yet born when the organization was founded step into leadership roles, it is unclear how the turn to disengagement will develop and whether the emphasis on deep Icelandic ancestry will be revised in light of the country's increasing diversity (Heleniak and Sigurjonsdottir 2018).

Race as religion: the Ásatrú Folk Assembly

Four years after the Ásatrúarfélagið's formation, an American version of Ásatrú appeared that went against Jörmundur Ingi's ideas of nourishing 'your local tradition', leading him to condemn the Americans for building a religion 'mostly from books' (Dornoy 1999). In 1976, former Army infantryman Stephen A. McNallen found the term *Ásatrú* in the book *Hammer of the North* (McNallen 2004: 208). Its Icelandic author uses the term anachronistically, stating that Norse religion in the Viking Age 'was called Ásatrú' (Magnusson 1976: 55). The find inspired McNallen to change the name of his Viking Brotherhood – 'a miniscule organization' focused 'on the assertion of individual will and freedom that the warrior epitomizes' (McNallen 2004: 206) – to the Ásatrú Free Assembly (AFA). The organization 'crumpled in 1986' when he asked members for 'financial compensation' and was refused (McNallen 2004: 208–9).

McNallen insists that the Ásatrú Free Assembly 'held to a middle ground on racial issues' but also that his version of Ásatrú is centred on the 'folk' and on 'folkish' ideology which forwards 'an innate connection between ancestry and religion' (McNallen 2004: 208, 203). Despite his denials that *folk* and *folkish* relate to German concepts of *Volk* and *völkisch* ideology from the 19th century through the reign of the Nazi Party, folkish and *völkisch* rhetoric agree in their main points. According to Goodrick-Clarke,

> During the nineteenth century, this term [*Volk*] signified much more than its straightforward translation 'people' to contemporary Germans; it denoted rather the national collectivity inspired by a common creative energy, feelings and sense of individuality. These metaphysical qualities were supposed to define the unique cultural essence of the German people. An ideological preoccupation with the *Volk* arose for two reasons: firstly, this cultural orientation was the result of the delayed political unification of Germany; secondly, it was closely related to a widespread romantic reaction to modernity. (Goodrick-Clarke 1985: 3)

This passage from Goodrick-Clarke's well-known work is echoed in McNallen's recent book:

> The late nineteenth and early twentieth centuries witnessed a revival of all things Germanic. The awakening was largely spurred by the creation of a unified German nation in 1871. Many Germans were disappointed with the resulting state; they had expected something more spiritually enriching than the prosaic politics of the day. Idealists, mystics, and romantics of all sorts reacted against this limited vision. (McNallen 2015: 170–1)

McNallen gives a positive spin, celebrating 'revival' and 'awakening' focused on the 'spiritually enriching'. His broadened scope posits a transnational racial group to which his audience owes 'a high degree of concern and loyalty' and that partakes of a 'spiritual connection and repository of past action which encloses and unifies all people of a given ancestral heritage' (McNallen 2015: 82, 201).

McNallen writes in the 'New Traditionalist' journal *Tyr* that his 1994 forming of a new AFA (Ásatrú Folk Assembly) was driven by feelings that 'the politically correct faction was making inroads into territory long denominated by the folkish' (McNallen 2004: 210–1). In his book, he alters the passage to say, 'a corrupt faction was making inroads into the Germanic religious movement in the United States' and insist that '[t]his error could not be allowed to become dominant' (McNallen 2015: 65–66). He also states the second AFA was founded in reaction to 'liberals, affirmative-action Asatrúers, black goðar, and New Agers' in American Ásatrú (Gardell 2003: 261). The organisation continues to define itself in opposition to these categories.

In his 2015 book, McNallen interchangeably uses terms such as 'Eurofolk', 'European-descended kin', 'Folk', 'Germanic peoples', 'indigenous Europeans', 'native European', 'people of Germanic heritage', 'peoples of the North', and

'Scandinavian/Germanic'. Although some of these overlap, they are not synonymous. Conflating European identities and excluding non-Germanic Europeans, he forwards a primeval racial core:

> We may refer to ourselves as Americans or English, Germans or Canadians, but behind these labels lurks an older, more essential identity. Our forefathers were Angles and Saxons, Lombards and Heruli, Goths and Vikings – and, as sons and daughters of these peoples, we are united by ties of blood and culture undimmed by the centuries. (McNallen 2015: 1)

Like the Icelanders, McNallen asserts direct pagan descent, but his line is mythological rather than genealogical; no website lets Americans trace family trees back two thousand years to the Common Era's first centuries. This concept of ancestry resembles *völkisch* theories positing the existence of a 'Nordic or Aryan race' and claiming its most exalted examples are those McNallen highlights: Scandinavians, Germans, and English (Evans 2010: 117–8).

Of his folkish concepts, McNallen writes, 'If this seems ethnocentric – well, so it is' (McNallen 2015: 82). He repeatedly references the '14 words', 'the most popular white supremacist slogan in the world' (Anti-Defamation League 2016). Coined by David Lane of 'the white supremacist terrorist group known as The Order', it states 'We must secure the existence of our people and a future for white children' (Anti-Defamation League 2016). McNallen uses paraphrases such as 'we place the highest priority on values such as the survival of our people and traditional culture' (McNallen 2015: 191). Further, the AFA *Declaration of Purpose* injects religion, stating that 'the survival and welfare of the European peoples as a cultural and biological group is a religious imperative' and 'the building of a secure future for our religion and our people' is an AFA goal (McNallen 2015: 192). McNallen connects the '14 words' with 88, white supremacist code for 'Heil Hitler' (since *H* is the alphabet's eighth letter): 'Some like the number 88... Some like 14, as in '14 words.' I like it shorter... eight words: 'The existence of my people is not negotiable' (Gardell 2003: 283).

McNallen's (1980) 'Metagenetics' essay is the keystone of his concept of the relationship between ancestry and religion. Its opening lines set out his core belief and address accusations of racism:

> One of the most controversial tenets of Asatru is our insistence that ancestry matters – that there are spiritual and metaphysical implications to heredity, and that we are thus a religion not for all of humanity, but rather one that calls only its own. This belief of ours has led to much misunderstanding, and as a result some have attempted to label us as "racist", or have accused us of fronting for totalitarian political forms. (McNallen 1980)

McNallen discusses extra-sensory perception (ESP) of twins and re-incarnation memory. He insists that archetypes theorised by Jung 'were in fact inherited – that is to say, genetic' and uses infant studies as evidence for religion's genetic predetermination (McNallen 1980). He concludes that 'Asatru is an expression of the soul of our race' and has promoted the idea ever since (McNallen 1980). In 2015, he called for 'the spiritual awakening of the European-descended peoples [in which] we as a group must reclaim our native spirituality', hoping that 'every thinking person of European heritage would at least be aware that we have a deep culture and religion' with 'bodies and souls... forever shaped by those long millennia in the European environment' (McNallen 2015: 180). His message is consistent: participation in Ásatrú is tied to ancestry. To join, one must claim European ancestors defined according to folkish ideas of whiteness parallel to *völkisch* ideas of Nordicity.

In the last few years, the Ásatrú Folk Assembly has undergone major changes. In 2016, McNallen retired from formal leadership (Pagan Community Notes 2016a). He and new leaders cast aside a decades-long policy of avoiding plainspoken racism and public embrace of white na-tionalism. In 2017, McNallen joined the Charlottesville pro-Confederate rally that led to Heather Heyer's murder and the Berkeley 'alt-right' rally that resulted in violent clashes, telling followers to engage in 'red pilling'[1] in order to 'control the narrative about Charlottesville [after President] Trump made his much-contested remarks about there being "violence on both sides"... Trump gave us an opening and we must exploit it to the hilt' (McNallen 2017a). Shortly after, McNallen's successor Matt Flavel posted a statement on the AFA Facebook page:

> Today we are bombarded with confusion and messages contrary to the values of our ancestors and our folk. The AFA would like to make it clear that we believe gender is not a social construct, it is a beautiful gift from the holy powers and from our ancestors. The AFA celebrates our feminine ladies, our masculine gentlemen and, above all, our beautiful white children. The children of the folk are our shining future and the legacy of all those men and women of our people back to the beginning. (Pagan Community Notes 2016b)

Backlash to the post led to Facebook taking down the AFA page and the organization's denunciation in 'Declaration 127'. In addition to the gender comments, the trigger was clearly use of the word 'white'. McNallen's euphemisms had long allowed sympathetic Heathens to insist he and his organization were not white nationalists. The change in language makes such dissembling more difficult.

Quickly embraced by the alt-right, Flavel appeared on white nationalist broadcast *Radio 3Fourteen* to discuss white identity and his 'spiritual journey' from Jehovah's Witness to AFA leader (Radio 3Fourteen 2016). McNallen promoted his '8 words' by sharing memes of the slogan (often with images of young white women, sometimes visibly pregnant) and signing social media posts '"The existence of our people is not negotiable". Wotan Mit Uns!' (McNallen 2017b), the latter phrase referencing Jung's 1936 'Wotan' essay and *Gott mit uns* ('God is with us') inscriptions on Nazi Wehrmacht belt buckles. In 1998, 'race-political extremist' and former Ásatrú Free Assembly member Wyatt Kaldenberg ridiculed McNallen for avoiding racist terminology: 'He never used the word *Aryan* or *white*. He said *folkish* a little now and then, but when you said *race*, he'd turn pink' (Gardell 2003: 178, emphasis in original). Twenty years later, McNallen and the AFA have adopted the language of the milieu they long sought to both distance themselves from and tap for recruits. One result of this rhetorical revision is the AFA's classification as 'perhaps this country's largest neo-Völkisch hate group' in the Southern Poverty Law Center's 'Extremist Files' (Southern Poverty Law Center 2019).

Spiritual kin: the Troth

When the Ásatrú Free Assembly collapsed in 1986, two long-time members formed new organizations. Michael Murray had been a member of the American Nazi Party and the National Socialist White People's Party's Nazi Motorcycle Club before founding the Odinist Fellowship and joining McNallen's first AFA. Murray (using the Icelandic name 'Valgard') formed the Ásatrú Alliance in 1987 as an organization 'inhabit[ing] a border area linking the magical/neopagan community with the millenarian theorists of the white supremacist world' (Kaplan 1997: 20–1). Stephen Flowers (using the Icelandic pseudonym 'Edred Thorsson') founded the Ring of Troth as an organization publicly welcoming the 'liberals, affirmative-action Asatrúers, black goðar, and New Agers' that were anathema to McNallen. However, what seem to be fundamental differences have not always been clearly defined.

Now known as the Troth, the organization engages in ongoing re-visionism that involves ousting leaders and shifting alliances with racist groups. After revelations of Flowers' membership in the Church of Satan and Temple of Set, involvement with 'shamanic sex magic', and 'magical use of sadomasochistic practices' (Kaplan 1997: 26), the group's founder was pushed out of a leadership role in the early 1990s. By 1995, the organization was led by William Bainbridge of the supposedly opposed Ásatrú Alliance. The Troth's 2004 *A Book of Blots* credits a man using the Icelandic alias Stefn Thorsman as the organization's 'Steersman' (leader); the 2009 *AFA Book of Blotar and Ritual* credits him as 'AFA Clergy co-ordinator'. The Troth's highest officer had moved into AFA leadership. The 2006 edition of *Our Troth* – the Troth book on history, mythology, and ritual practice – asserts that 'the Teutonic ways... do not involve racism or fascism' on a page crediting McNallen as contributor to and resource for the text (Grundy 2006: 123). Steersman Steven T. Abell's public association with the Troth ended after widespread condemnation of his *Patheos* column defending his friendship with McNallen and facilitation of co-operation between the Troth and AFA while attacking Heathens United Against Racism's Ryan Smith for 'aping corny Marxist propaganda' in his own article on McNallen's increasingly public use of far-right talking points (Abell 2016). In 2016, the AFA's Runestone Press published a revised edition of Flowers' 1989 *A Book of Troth*, blueprint for the Troth itself. It was produced with editors Joshua Buckley and Michael Moynihan, driving forces behind the *Tyr* journal that published McNallen's revision of Ásatrú's post-1972 history next to articles by Evola, de Benoist, and others embraced by a new generation of white nationalists.

The Troth draws a line between itself and the AFA regarding who is publicly declared welcome to join. Troth bylaws assert that '[d]iscrimina-tion... shall not be practiced by The Troth, its programs, departments, officers, or any affiliated group, whether in membership decisions or the conduct of any of its activities' and define *discrimination* as 'making dis-tinctions, limitations, or exclusions within the organization based on cri-teria such as race, gender, ethnic origin, or sexual orientation' (Troth 2019, 'Troth Bylaws'). This is underscored in the Troth mission statement's as-sertion that '[w]e welcome all people, whatever their religious, cultural, or ancestral background, gender or sexual orientation' (Troth 2019, 'Mission Statement'). In 2016, the High Rede (steering committee) announced an amendment of 'the oath that is taken by all titled representatives (Rede members, Officers, committee Chairs, Stewards, etc.)' to include a new statement: 'With the Troth I stand against any use of Germanic religion and culture to advance causes of racism, sexism, homophobia, white su-premacy, ableism, or any other form of prejudice' (the Troth Blog 2016). The Troth publicly announced the revision only two months after the AFA's 'white children' post. As at many other points in its history, the Troth reacted to AFA statements by publicly distancing itself from its rival.

Diana Paxson, editor of the Troth journal *Idunna*, obliquely challenges McNallen's 'Metagenetics' essay when she writes in *Essential Ásatrú* that 'there has been a great deal of discussion of the relationship between genetics and religion. My observation is that language and culture have a far greater influence on people's religious affinities than does genealogy' (Paxson 2006: 155). Her discussion of ethnicity in Ásatrú ends with kinship: 'When I meet someone who reads the same books, does the same rites, and honors the gods I do, it is the meeting of minds that identifies her to me as spiritual kin' (Paxson 2006: 156). For Paxson, 'spiritual kin' includes racist practitioners. Her discussion of American Ásatrú's development outlines the Ásatrú Free Assembly's founding, its dissolution, and the appearance of the later orga-nizations, yet makes no mention of racial politics involved or connections to the American Nazi Party (Paxson 2006: 48–52). In a section recommending organizations for newcomers to the religion, she writes that the Ásatrú Alliance 'characterizes itself as essentially conservative and libertarian in at-titude, but nonpolitical' without providing further information on the group's by then well-documented extremist connections. When re-commending the Ásatrú Folk Assembly, she likens 'a religion that belongs to people of indigenous European stock' to 'the traditional tribal religions be-long[ing] specifically to Native Americans' (Paxson 2006: 176). Nearly a decade later, after attending a session featuring 'leaders from a number of North and South American tribes' at the Parliament of the World's Religions in Salt Lake City, she concluded that she was 'once more willing to affirm that in origin and basic concepts, Heathenry is an indigenous as well as an ethnic religion' (Paxson 2015: 28). By asserting Ásatrú's indigeneity and ethnicity, she repeats a claim central to McNallen's folkish theory from his earliest publications through his latest writings.

Stephan Grundy has held Troth leadership positions and led the compilation of *Our Troth*. Written under Icelandic pseudonym Kveldúlf Gundarsson, his essay 'Ancestry and Heritage in the Germanic Tradition' begins by asserting that the organization's 'official, and unshakeable policy is that we do not permit racism of any sort' (Grundy 2020). Still available on the website of Paxson's Hrafnar (Icelandic 'ravens') kindred, the essay both challenges racist Ásatrú and promotes its core tenets. Grundy refers to a range of ancient Germanic peoples as 'the folk' and 'our folk' – the same conflation of Scandinavian, German, and English identities into generic white ancestry as in *völkisch* and folkish theory – as he calls for a return to 'the culture of our forebears' and claims that Heathenry 'is an ethnic tradition, largely stemming today from the interest in recovering a forgotten heritage' (Grundy 2020). After covering topics such as 'the Germanic folks' of long ago 'interbreeding' with Irish and Finnish people (as different, he asserts, from 'our forebears' as 'Orientals, Africans, or Amerindians'), Grundy writes at length about the importance of ancestry, bloodlines, and reincarnation – key subjects in McNallen's 'Metagenetics' essay. When he states that 'those folk whose clans do not include any Germanic ancestors, however distant, should be en-couraged at least to learn about and appreciate the beauty of their own per-sonal heritage before seeking out a stranger's faith' (Grundy 2020), he uses a folkish trope regularly appearing in AFA materials. Jeff Wolf's 2015 essay in AFA publication *The Voice* asks 'Can a non-Germanic person be Asatru?' and answers 'Sure they can, but we would have to ask them why they would want to do so and not follow their own ancestral path' (Wolf 2015). When Grundy asserts the importance of 'a unification of the individual's soul with the current of holy might which is the life-blood of the Germanic heritage' (Grundy 2020), he taps into the *völkisch* spiritualism that leads McNallen to write of 'Germanic magic and mysticism, an integral part of our religious heritage' as means of reaching 'a higher level of spiritual evolution' and rising 'to the levels of the Gods themselves' (McNallen 2015: 166, 172, 176). An essay that opens with assertion of 'official, and unshakeable policy' against 'racism of any sort' closes with rhetoric indistinguishable from that of racist Ásatrú.

In February 2017, Troth founder Stephen Flowers made a series of Facebook posts in response to an *Idunna* article on 'Heathenry's Racist

Heritage'. Flowers denounced the Troth as overtaken by 'radical universalists' and 'intellectual morons' while insisting that 'radical folkish ideology' with whiteness as a prerequisite 'has never existed' (Flowers 2017). Former Steersmen Thorsman and Abell joined the attack on the organization, its current members, and the new officer oath as intolerant of folkish beliefs. In fact, Troth bylaws state that '[g]eneral membership in other organizations is acceptable as long as it creates no conflict of interest' (Troth 2019: 'Troth Bylaws'), a policy that allows dual membership in the Troth and AFA. The reality that the Troth welcomes AFA members to join without renouncing membership in the folkish organization casts a shadow over the many public statements Troth leadership has made against the AFA.

In October 2017, the Troth's International Relations and Exchange Program produced 'Frith Forge', '[a]n international conference among inclusive Asatru/Heathen organizations and individuals' (Troth 2019: 'Frith Forge'). Held outside Potsdam, Germany, the event was hosted by Haimo Grebenstein of the *Verein für Germanisches Heidentum* (Association for Germanic Heathenry). The *Verein* was formed as German partner of the Odinic Rite, an organization with founders who 'had links to neo-Nazis' (Paxson 2017: 166) and which Caiani and Parenti include in their list of 'extreme right groups' (Caiani et al., 2012: 172). This partnership of two inclusive organizations with founders who began and/or ended up allied with folkish groups set the tone for a conference featuring clashing views on inclusivity itself. Many participants denounced the AFA, yet several echoed former Troth leaders by arguing that *inclusivity* means including folkish voices and that racist Heathens should be welcomed, with the goal of showing them 'a better way'. Throughout the three-day event, affirmations of inclusion were at odds with attendees' uniform whiteness, and there was a distinction made between *inclusivity* and *diversity*. The conference's dissonances are emblematic of the Troth's determination to promote an inclusive position not fully implemented at ground level or in the currently all-white High Rede. Given the Troth's democratic structure and regular leadership changes, it is unclear how these conflicts will develop and whether the organization will continue to revise itself in reaction to developments within the AFA.

'All the tribes': continuing revision

Arguably the single most important statement on Norse cosmogony and cosmology, the poem *Völuspá* ('The Prophecy of the Seeress') from the 13th-century *Codex Regius* begins by addressing its audience:

> Hearing I ask from all the tribes,
>
> greater and lesser, the offspring of Heimdall;

Father of the Slain, you wished me well to declare

living beings' ancient stories, those I remember from furthest back. (Larrington 2014: 4)

Heimdall is the god who guards the Rainbow Bridge against forces that threaten civilization, and his children form the classes of human society. The Father of the Slain is Odin, who wanders widely to seek information that will delay or mitigate the coming destruction of the worlds at *Ragnarök* (doom of the powers); the slain are those who die in the battles of this world. Since its founding in the early 1970s, Ásatrú has developed multiple conceptions of who makes up 'all the tribes'.

Icelanders in the Ásatrúarfélagið celebrate verifiable ancestral connections to saga characters in a modern society undergoing demographic change. McNallen and his Ásatrú Folk Assembly deny place in the religion to any who do not fit their racialist definition of European ancestry. The Troth publicly declares that all who wish to participate in the religion are welcome while maintaining a complicated relationship with their folkish counterparts. With McNallen's retirement from the leadership position he had held since the first appearance of American Ásatrú (excepting the break between the AFA's two versions), it remains to be seen whether the folkish version of Ásatrú will grow under new leadership or wither like its *völkisch* predecessor. The Ásatrúarfélagið's inward turn and the Troth's problematic relationship with inclusion make it difficult to predict future development of the two organizations.

As Ásatrú nears the 50th anniversary of its founding, practitioners of its various iterations continue to revise the religion that began in a Reykjavík hotel in 1972. As Ásatrú moved from Iceland to the United States, it became embroiled in American debates on racial identity. As it travelled from a functionally mono-racial society sharing a common ancestry to a fundamentally multicultural and diverse nation, Ásatrú was revised in two opposing yet intersecting ways – one embracing the United States' racial divisions, the other struggling with them. Revisions continue, including such offshoots as reconstructionism and tribalism; both offer critiques of earlier versions while reproducing many of the same fault lines. Mirroring today's political world, a harder turn to the right is opposed by more aggressive calls for diversity, especially by younger practitioners. As this process of argument and innovation progresses, Ásatrú offers a living model of revisionism in new religious movements.

Note

1 A reference to the 1999 film *The Matrix*, this is used by members of the 'alt-right' to mean 'enlightening' others and converting them to a far-right political worldview. See, for example, Dignam and Rohlinger (2019): 591.

Bibliography

Abell, Stephen T. 2016. "Letters from Midgard: Yes, Enough" in *Patheos* (30 January). Available at https://www.patheos.com/blogs/agora/2016/01/guest-post-yes-enough [accessed 5 July 2020].

Anti-Defamation League. 2016. "14 Words." Available at https://www.adl.org/education/references/hate-symbols/14-words [accessed 5 July 2020].

Berg, Jónína K. 2008. "Sveinbjörn Beinteinsson: A Personal Reminiscence" in *Tyr: Myth–Culture–Tradition*, Vol. 3: 263–272.

"Blótuðu Þór í Úrhellisrigningu". 1973. *Vísir* (7 August).

Bocquet, Greg. 2006. "Nordic Gods Alive in Reykjavík" in *The Reykjavík Grapevine* (1 December). Available at http://www.grapevine.is/mag/interview/2006/12/01/nordic-gods-alive-in-reykjavik/ [accessed 5 July 2020].

Caiani, Manuela, Donatella della Porta, and Claudius Wagemann. 2012. *Mobilizing on the Extreme Right: Germany, Italy, and the United States*. Oxford: Oxford University Press.

Declaration 127. 2019. Available at http://www.heathenhof.com/declaration127/ [accessed 5 July 2020].

Dignam, Pierce Alexander and Deana A. Rohlinger. 2019. "Misogynistic Men Online: How the Red Pill Helped Elect Trump" in *Signs: Journal of Women in Culture and Society*, Vol. 44, No. 3: 589–612.

Dornoy, Denis. 1999. "Interview with Jormundur Ingi" in *ECER: European Congress of Ethnic Religions* (7 March). Available at http://ecer-org.eu/interview-with-jormundur-ingi-by-denis-dornoy-march-7-1999-antwerpen-belgium/ [accessed 5 July 2020].

Evans, Andrew D. 2010. *Anthropology at War: World War I and the Science of Race in Germany*. Chicago: University of Chicago Press.

Flowers, Stephen 2017. Facebook post (10 February). Available at https://www.facebook.com/permalink.php?story_fbid=412799595729611&id=100009987222358 [accessed 5 July 2020].

Gardell, Mattias. 2003. *Gods of the Blood: The Pagan Revival and White Separatism*. Durham: Duke University Press.

Goodrick-Clarke, Nicholas. 1985. *The Occult Roots of Nazism: Secret Aryan Cults and Their Influence on Nazi Ideology*. Washington Square: New York University Press.

Graichen, Gisele. 1986. "Interview with Sveinbjörn Beinteinsson" in *Die neuen Hexen: Gespräche mit Hexen*. Hamburg: Hoffmann und Campe. Translated by "the Seiðman." Available at http://www.angelfire.com/nm/seidhman/beinweb.html# [accessed 5 July 2020].

Grundtvig, N. F. S. 1880. *Poetiske Skrifter*. Edited by Svend Grundtvig. Kjøbenhavn: Karl Schønbergs Forlag.

Grundy, Stephan (as Kveldúlf Hagan Gundarsson). (ed.). 2006. *Our Troth Volume One: History and Lore*. North Charleston: BookSurge Publishing.

Grundy, Stephan (as Kveldúlf Hagan Gundarsson). (ed.). 2020. "Ancestry and Heritage in the Germanic Tradition." Hrafnar website. Available at http://hrafnar.org/articles/kveldulf/ancestors/ [accessed 5 July 2020].

Heleniak, Timothy and Hjördis Rut Sigurjonsdottir. 2018. "Once Homogenous, Tiny Iceland Opens Its Doors to Immigrants" in *Migration Information Source*

(18 April). Available at https://www.migrationpolicy.org/article/once-homogenous-tiny-iceland-opens-its-doors-immigrants [accessed 5 July 2020].

Hilmar Örn Hilmarsson. 2016a. Email communication (9 July 2016).

Hilmar Örn Hilmarsson. 2016b. Email communication (10 July 2016).

Hilmar Örn Hilmarsson. 2016c. Email communication (11 July 2016).

Iceland Magazine. 2015. "Icelandic Pagan Association high priest moved by the outpouring of international support" in *Iceland Magazine* (16 July). Available at http://icelandmag.visir.is/article/icelandic-pagan-association-high-priest-moved-outpouring-international-support [accessed 5 July 2020].

Íslendingabók. 2016. Website. Available at https://www.islendingabok.is/english [accessed 5 July 2020].

Kaplan, Jeffrey. 1997. *Radical Religion in America: Millenarian Movements from the Far Right to the Children of Noah*. Syracuse: Syracuse University Press.

Larrington, Carolyne. 2014. *The Poetic Edda*. Oxford: Oxford University Press.

Magnusson, Magnus. 1976. *Hammer of the North: Myths and Heroes of the Viking Age*. New York: G.P. Putnam's Sons.

McNallen, Stephen A. 2017a. Facebook post (17 August). Available at https://www.facebook.com/stephen.mcnallen/posts/10210919767884276 [accessed 4 February 2018].

McNallen, Stephen A. 2017b. Facebook post (19 November). Available at https://www.facebook.com/stephen.mcnallen/posts/10211526675056576 [accessed 4 February 2018].

McNallen, Stephen A. 2015. *Asatru: A Native European Spirituality*. Nevada City, CA: Runestone Press.

McNallen, Stephen A. 2004. "Three Decades of the Ásatrú Revival in America." *Tyr: Myth–Culture–Tradition* 2: 203–219.

McNallen, Stephen A. 1980. "Metagenetics." Ásatrú Folk Assembly website. Available at https://web.archive.org/web/20161204190926/http://asatrufolkassembly.org/articles-essays/ [accessed 5 July 2020].

Pagan Community Notes. 2016a. "Michael Wiggins, Asatru Folk Assembly, Canadian Wildfires, and more!" in *The Wild Hunt* (9 May). Available at http://wildhunt.org/2016/05/pagan-community-notes-michael-wiggins-asatru-folk-assembly-canadian-wildfires-and-more.html [accessed 5 July 2020].

Pagan Community Notes. 2016b. "Pagan Community Notes: Denton CUUPS, Convocation, Asatru Folk Assembly, and more", in *The Wild Hunt* (22 August). Available at http://wildhunt.org/2016/08/pagan-community-notes-denton-cuups-convocation-asatru-folk-assembly-and-more.html [accessed 5 July 2020].

Paxson, Diana L. 2017. *Odin: Ecstasy, Runes & Norse Magic*. Newburyport, MA: Weiser Books.

Paxson, Diana L. 2015. With Robert Schreiwer and Lorrie Wood. "Heathens in the Hall: A Report on Troth Participation at the Parliament of World Religions" in *Idunna* 106 (Winter): 22–28.

Paxson, Diana L. 2006. *Essential Ásatrú: Walking the Path of Norse Paganism*. New York: Citadel Press Books.

Radio 3Fourteen. 2016. "Asatru: Native Spirituality of European Folk" (31 August). Available at https://redice.tv/radio-3fourteen/asatru-native-spirituality-of-european-folk [accessed 4 February 2018].

Seigfried, Karl E. H. 2011a. "Interview with Jóhanna G. Harðardóttir of the Ásatrú-arfélagið" in *The Norse Mythology Blog* (17 January). Available at http://www.norsemyth.org/2011/01/interview-with-johanna-g-harardottir-of.html [accessed 5 July 2020].

Seigfried, Karl E. H. 2011b. "Interview with Hilmar Örn Hilmarsson of the Ásatrúarfélagið" in *The Norse Mythology Blog* (23 June). Available at http://www.norsemyth.org/2011/06/interview-with-hilmar-orn-hilmarsson-of.html [accessed 5 July 2020].

Southern Poverty Law Center. 2019. "Neo-Volkisch." Available at https://www.splcenter.org/fighting-hate/extremist-files/ideology/neo-volkisch [accessed 5 July 2020].

Troth. 2019. Website, Including Pages on "Troth Bylaws", "Mission Statement", and "Frith Forge." Available at http://www.thetroth.org/ [accessed 5 July 2020].

The Troth Blog. 2016. "Updated Rede, Officer, Representative Oath of Office" (16 October). Available at http://thetroth.blogspot.com/2016/10/updated-rede-officer-representative.html [accessed 5 July 2020].

Wolf, Jeff 2015. "Asatru" in *The Voice* (July). Available at http://runestone.org/wp-content/uploads/2019/02/The-Voice-July-2015.pdf [accessed 12 December 2019].

4 Varieties of enlightenment: revisions in the Enlighten Next movement around Andrew Cohen

André van der Braak

Groups associated with various Asian traditions of philosophy, devotion, and meditation form an important subset of new religious movements in contemporary western societies (Dawson 2006, 3). An important aspect of many such new religious movements is the fascination with Indian gurus. This 'guru phenomenon' started with 19th-century teachers such as Swami Vivekananda (1863–1902), and went through a second wave in the 1960s, when various Indian-based gurus – such as Adi Da (1939–2008), Maharishi Mahesh Yogi (1918–2008), Bhagwan Shree Rajneesh or Osho (1931–1990), Ramana Maharshi (1879–1950), and Sathya Sai Baba (1926–2011) – offered their teachings in the West through various forms of religious and cultural interaction, translation, and transplantation (see Forsthoefel and Humes 2005). Arguably, since the 1980s, a third wave has occurred, consisting of western students and successors of Indian-based gurus who have created new religious movements. However, as Gleig and Williamson argue, the innovative styles of such western-born gurus reflect a distinctively western cultural and religious ethos and could be viewed as home grown (Gleig and Williamson 2013, 2).

This chapter will study the revisions to the beliefs and practices associated with the community of one such home-grown guru, the American spiritual teacher Andrew Cohen (b. 1955). It will investigate the various revisions and diverse understandings that took place during the rise and fall of the organisation around him that was consecutively called Moksha Foundation, Impersonal Enlightenment Fellowship, and EnlightenNext (a European organisation was called FACE [Friends of Andrew Cohen Everywhere]). This organisation served to facilitate the dissemination of his teachings, which originated in Advaita Vedanta, the Indian non-dualistic school of Hinduism, of which Ramana Maharshi is the best-known representative in the West.

I myself became a student of Cohen in 1987 and remained in his community until 1998, when I departed in a sphere of conflict and disillusionment. My experiences have been documented in my book *Enlightenment Blues*, which I will quote from extensively (Van der Braak 2003). I will also draw from various other insider accounts (Tarlo 2009; Yenner 2009; Sand

DOI: 10.4324/9781315226804-4

2015; the blog '*WHAT Enlightenment??!*' 2020), as well as academic publications within the field of NRM studies (Oakes 1997, 2010; Gleig 2013).

In this chapter, the rapid rise and gradual decline of the community – 'a slow devolution of Andrew Cohen's "mission" first to spin, then to lies, and then to bigger and more elaborate lies' (Yenner 2009, 8) will be investigated. The rise of various forms of verbally and physically violent behaviour will be connected to different revisions of the notion of 'enlightenment'.

Enlightenment

Cohen's teachings centred around the Indian religious notion of 'enlightenment': a spiritual insight or awakening to the true nature of reality. The English term 'enlightenment' is a translation of the term *bodhi* (awakening), which was popularised in the western world through the 19th century translations of Max Müller. The term is also being used to translate several other Buddhist and Hindu terms and concepts used to denote insight and knowledge, such as *kensho, satori, moksha,* and *nirvana.* In the West, the concept of enlightenment has taken on a romantic meaning, with connotations such as self-realisation, illumination, and ultimate nondual knowledge (see Van der Braak 2008). The vagueness of the term makes it very susceptible to creative appropriation, as is the case in many Asian-oriented new religious movements. Cohen's movement was no exception to this.

In a 2013 article, Ann Gleig traced Andrew Cohen's reinvention from a Neo-Advaita teacher to a leading proponent of 'evolutionary enlightenment' by distinguishing three stages in the evolution of Cohen's teachings of enlightenment. In the first stage, the focus was on 'personal enlightenment', in line with neo-Advaita Vedanta teachings. During the second stage, a split between Cohen and his Indian teacher led to a new teaching of 'impersonal enlightenment', which was accompanied by a war against the ego. The community claimed that a third stage of 'evolutionary enlightenment' had begun on 30 July, 2001, when a group of male students experienced what was referred to as collective or intersubjective enlightenment (Gleig 2013, 203). I will follow Gleig in her description of these three stages, and I will argue that each new stage was an attempt at explaining and justifying Cohen's increasingly harsh and violent teaching methods, often in response to heavy external criticism of those teaching methods. In 2013, a new round of criticism, this time internal, led to Cohen's departure and the demise of EnlightenNext.

After describing Cohen's three understandings of 'enlightenment', this chapter will argue that his various revisions of the notion of enlightenment also served to facilitate the legitimisation of the increasing occurrence of several forms of verbal and physical violent behaviour within the community. This chapter will focus on the interplay between internal reasons (changes in philosophical and spiritual understanding) and external reasons that led to these various revisions.

Andrew Cohen

During the 1960s and 1970s, many new religious movements based on the Eastern notion of enlightenment exploded onto the scene in Europe and the US. Westerners enrobed as Buddhist monks visited ashrams to study yoga and became followers of westernised Eastern teachers such as Bhagwan Rajneesh, Chögyam Trungpa Rinpoche, Suzuki Roshi, or Swami Muktananda. Enlightenment seemed at hand (Van der Braak 2003, 7).

It was in this cultural climate that the American spiritual seeker Andrew Cohen appeared. Born in New York City in 1955, he had a spontaneous spiritual experience at 16. Over time, he became a restless spiritual seeker, practicing martial arts, kundalini, and vipassana, but he could not find what he was after. Then he travelled in March 1986 to Lucknow, India, to meet a then little known Advaita Vedanta teacher Harilal Poonja (1913–1997), who had apparently been a disciple of Ramana Maharshi. On the third day of their meeting, Cohen claimed to have a powerful experience of awakening. Within three weeks of their initial meeting, Poonja told Cohen that 'their work was over', or so the story went. Poonja sent Cohen out to the West to go and teach enlightenment.

With a small group of students including his future Indian wife, Cohen moved to Devon, England, in September 1986 and would spend the next two years giving *satsang* – a neo-Advaita type of gathering with long periods of communal silence punctuated with question and answer exchanges – in various locations across Europe and in Israel. These satsangs can be qualified as what Stark and Bainbridge (1985, 27) call 'audience cults': loosely structured events at which an individual lectures on esoteric topics. A consistent following may arise, but the audience remains mere consumers of cultic goods.

> Initially, Cohen met with great success. In some mysterious way, he appeared to have spontaneously morphed from an insecure thirty year old into a charismatic spiritual teacher with a silver tongue, exuding great clarity and a mystical presence. Suddenly, Cohen was irresistible, and wherever he went people wanted to be around him and hang onto his every word. He seemed to possess an uncanny ability to transmit a deep glimpse of enlightenment, inspiring people to leave everything behind and become his disciples. Thousands of people still full of hope and longing flocked to see him. (Van der Braak 2003, 7)

Stage one: personal enlightenment

The first stage in Cohen's community was from 1986 to 1989. Cohen taught fairly traditional Advaita Vedanta teachings on enlightenment, defined by him as follows:

'Enlightenment', Andrew says with a smile, 'is relief. It is cessation. It is the end of becoming. It's the end of the struggle to become anyone or anything. It's coming finally to rest, here and now, in this life. [...] Enlightenment goes beyond definition, goes beyond thought. You can only experience it directly, if you dare to let go of your thinking mind for a moment'. (van der Braak 2003, 10)

Cohen's neo-Advaita teachings on enlightenment are most clearly expressed in *Enlightenment Is a Secret*, a book that he initially asked me to edit in 1989, based on the transcriptions of his talks. Enlightenment requires no effort because one is and always has been liberated:

In the end there's absolutely nothing to do, nothing to change and no one to become. When you are no longer interested in the past and you are no longer interested in the future, when you know you're completely helpless, these ideas of effortlessness versus effort won't have any meaning. (Cohen 1991, 86)

Time, the world, and the individual self are an illusion. Only the unchanging, eternal, and pure consciousness Self is real. Enlightenment can be attained instantly; a gradual approach only reinforces the illusory concept of time: 'Enlightenment is *not* far away. It does *not* need to take time. As long as you insist that it must take time, then you are still interested in protecting yourself' (Cohen 1991, 6).

No methods are necessary because practice and effort assume a dualistic framework: a separate self, attempting to achieve a future goal of enlightenment. To realise the Self all that is necessary is to surrender to the Self and one's passion for 'Liberation', which can be achieved in the presence of the teacher who is identical to the Self:

Where is your passion for Liberation? Without passion for Liberation there is no hope for Liberation. Passion for Liberation is your Liberation, and if you surrender to that passion and become a slave of that passion, your fate will be sealed. (Cohen 1991, 14)

Cohen's message was simple: nothing has to change, as everything is perfect as it is. He emphasised that clarity of intention was most important:

Do you really want to be free more than anything else? Are you willing to give up anything for it? If that's really true for you, you won't have any trouble reaching enlightenment. (Cohen, quoted in van der Braak 2003, 14)

Sangha as a joyous community of finders

During this first period (1986–1989), Cohen was very accessible to his students, living and travelling with them. An international community of devotees began to spontaneously form around him and in 1988, when the community relocated to Amherst, Massachusetts, it had grown to around 150 students (van der Braak 2003, 30). The lifestyle of the community at that time was firmly centred around the nightly satsang meetings with Cohen:

> To stay in touch with Andrew, we write notes to him to tell him about our experiences, about how satsang has struck us. Often Andrew reads our notes aloud in satsang. If it happens to be our own letter we're ecstatic. We're a close-knit group. We see each other every night in satsang, and the rest of the time we do everything together: eating, talking, discussing Andrew's teachings, blissing out, watching videos, listening to music. There's an indescribable sense of intimacy between us. We're family. (van der Braak 2003, 19)

The community at this time functioned at the level of what Stark and Bainbridge (1985, 28) would call a 'client cult' (a moderate-commitment social network where people exchange goods and services). Although the regular satsang meetings mobilised participants more fully than at the earlier stage of audience cult (a low-commitment social network), the mobilisation was still partial. The predominantly European followers of Cohen visited the U.S. for several months to be with him (often during summer vacations) and then returned to their lives and jobs in Europe.

Stage two: from personal to impersonal enlightenment

However, from 1989 on, Cohen's message began to change. Rather than the direct personal experience of enlightenment, Cohen began to stress the ethical imperative to fully live up to the implications of that experience. He still spoke about clarity of intention as the way to enlightenment, but he also started to speak about the need to make clear choices in one's day-to-day life, choices that would keep one's enlightened state free from obstacles, such as attachments and conditioned patterns. He started to emphasise the need to change, which meant letting go of old conditioned tendencies and no longer acting out of them (van der Braak 2003, 23). Further, he claimed that:

> Enlightenment [...] is an eternal reality beyond time and space that we can dip into at any time. You only need to have the guts to see your neuroses for what they are and take a leap beyond them into the unknown. Otherwise, what good would enlightenment be? If it doesn't

lead to a beautiful human being, what's the point? You can't say 'that's just the way that I am'. You have to change. It's a moral obligation to life, to the cosmos itself. You have to align yourself with the standard of enlightenment. (Cohen quoted in van der Braak 2003, 24)

As a result of this emphasis on the need to change, the intimate family-like atmosphere was increasingly punctuated with uncomfortable incidents. Cohen's emphasis on aligning oneself with the standard of enlightenment proved no simple matter. The standard of enlightenment, as defined by Cohen, proved difficult to meet:

> One by one, Andrew's housemates have to leave his house because they don't meet the standard. Kathy, an English girl who knew Andrew personally before his enlightenment, has to leave because she can be opinionated and have a bad temper. Alan, a fragile, former hippie from New Zealand, has to leave because he is too fearful and insecure. (van der Braak 2003, 24)

To keep the standard of enlightenment, regular house meetings were organised in which housemates gave each other feedback regarding the degree to which they were 'living the teachings'. Some verbal violence was not uncommon during those meetings (for an example, see van der Braak 2003, 25–7).

Now, the community around Cohen rapidly moved from a client cult to a cult movement: a full-fledged religious organisation that attempts to satisfy all the religious needs of its members (Stark and Bainbridge 1985, 29). In 1989, a formal community was established, a *sangha* (a Buddhist term for the community of monks and nuns). Cohen expressed the rationale for this as follows:

> A sangha is a community of finders, of people who've had a profound awakening experience. A sangha is a group of people who have come together only because they want to give themselves utterly to being free. In that complete giving they are committed to overcome anything that could ever interfere with the perfect expression of perfect enlightenment and perfect liberation. That's the meaning of sangha. (Cohen quoted in van der Braak 2003, 31)

Cohen's more dedicated students became part of his sangha. Other people, such as visitors from Europe, or those who did not make a formal commitment to Cohen' teachings, were called 'lay students'. The men and women of the sangha were to meet twice a week in separate meetings, to discuss Cohen's teachings and to increase the standard to which they were living them. These meetings soon took over the function of the house meetings.

Sangha as proving ground and showcase of enlightened living

The attempt to keep students to the standard of enlightenment led Cohen to stronger measures. An Italian student whom Cohen considered to be overly flirtatious and infatuated with her appearance was told to shave her head and take a vow of celibacy (van der Braak 2003, 32). Her example was soon followed by others. Eventually, about one-fifth of the community became shaven celibates. An American student, whom Cohen considered overly attached to his $20,000 Saab, was instructed to crush the car at the local junk yard (van der Braak 2003, 33). The men's and women's meetings turned into verbally violent confrontations that sometimes extended deep into the night. Students were harangued and confronted with their infractions of the standard of enlightenment. Cohen himself was not present at these meetings, but his close students carried out his wishes and instructions. Cohen justified such harsh measures with a reference to his teachings:

> Many people say they want to be enlightened, but very few people actually want to change, because change can be difficult and painful, and can require big sacrifices. A spiritual community should be a place where people who aren't serious about their own evolution wouldn't be able to survive. It should be far more challenging than living in the normal world where there is no standard, and where compromise is very acceptable. A true Sangha is a proving ground, a constant testing, where everyone finds out how serious they are. (van der Braak 2003, 35)

Such a notion of sangha was a different image of sangha from that of a joyous community of finders. It seemed more like a spiritual boot camp.

Due to the changes in his teaching, and his shifting emphasis from only 'clarity of intention' to the necessity of having to change in order to keep to the standard of enlightenment, Cohen increasingly began to question his teacher Poonja's perspective on the nature of enlightenment. He observed that despite many powerful enlightenment experiences, his students had not been fundamentally transformed:

> My Teacher always said someone was 'Enlightened', after this initial glimpse into their true nature. I soon realized this wasn't true. If a person was 'Enlightened', to me that meant they had to be able to manifest and express that Enlightenment consistently in their behavior. I had observed so many people who had experienced profound awakenings and yet still would be unable to manifest and express that realization in their outer lives. It seemed that in spite of 'Enlightenment', much neurotic and conditioned behavior usually remained. (Cohen 1991, 56–7)

This period saw the further development of the second major stage of Cohen's message: his teaching of impersonal enlightenment and the war against the ego:

> Pointing to the number of guru scandals, Cohen declared that the search for personal enlightenment was all too often motivated and corrupted by the fundamental self-concern of the individual ego. His community, however, had begun to manifest something beyond individual enlightenment – what he called impersonal enlightenment – in which enlightenment was realized for its own sake and not for the sake of the individual. (Gleig 2013, 195)

In 1991, Cohen asked me to serve as the first editor of an in-house journal, *What is Enlightenment?* (*WIE?*), to investigate the nature of enlightenment. Although my own editorship proved short lived, *WIE?* soon grew into an international magazine with a wide readership. Tackling topics such as the nature of the ego and the relationship between spirituality and sex, it featured many well-known Asian and western spiritual teachers and established Cohen as a major contemporary spiritual figure. To reflect the shift from personal to impersonal enlightenment, and to make Cohen's teachings accessible to a larger audience, the name of Cohen's organisation was changed from Moksha Foundation to Impersonal Enlightenment Fellowship.

Cohen's relationship with his teacher, Poonja, completely broke down. Gleig describes the main point of contention between them as the relationship between enlightenment and ethics:

> According to Cohen, Poonja insisted that the realization of the Self had nothing to do with worldly behavior and he did not believe that it was possible to fully transcend the ego. Poonja's perspective was that although karmic tendencies remained after enlightenment, the enlightened person was no longer identified with them and, therefore, did not accrue any further karmic consequences (Cohen 1991, 106–8). Moreover, ethical standards, being based in a dualistic understanding of reality and assuming an individual agent, could never be used to measure nondual enlightenment. For Poonja, the goal was the realization of the Self; the illusory realm of relative reality was ultimately irrelevant. Cohen, on the other hand, was adamant that the experience of enlightenment must manifest in flawless behavior. He insisted that it was possible to be fully liberated from karmic conditioning in order to perfectly express nondual realization in the world. (Gleig 2013, 194)

Cohen began to implement many traditional ascetic practices such as intensive meditation practice, prostrations, celibacy, and head shaving. He also became much more removed from his students and took an increasingly authoritative role in their lives, declaring whom they could have relationships with and where they should live. The early days of blissful satsang and effortless enlightenment were over, as I recalled in 2003:

> In the sangha there's a war going on: the war against the ego. Because of Andrew's new emphasis on impersonal enlightenment, the process of purification takes on a new and heightened significance. It is not only for our personal benefit, but for the evolutionary development of the whole human race. (van der Braak 2003, 54)

Cohen began to practice daily formal meditation with his students. From 1991 on, community life became immersed in spiritual practice, usually about two to three hours a day. Students daily performed 500 prostrations in the morning and the evening. Cohen started to give derogatory names to students who proved very resistant in his view. A man with a temper was called 'Raging Bull'; an immature student was called 'Q the Clown'; a woman who tended to space out was called 'Dizzy'. Later on, this was followed by such names as 'Unreal', 'Sincere', 'His Greatness', and others. The names were meant to bring about humility by continuously reminding the student of the vicious ego patterns that they were unwilling to let go of (van der Braak 2003, 54). In Cohen's new ideal of sangha, it was not a community of finders but a place to create heaven on earth, as I noted in 2003:

> Andrew speaks about creating heaven on earth. The Sangha should be a beacon of light in a dark and ignorant world – a laboratory and showcase of enlightened living, living without personal agenda. As long as at least some people will live justly and with integrity, there's still hope for the world. (van der Braak 2003, 69)

Starting around 1995, to implement such a 'heaven on earth', centres around the world were established. Cohen stressed that the time for sitting in satsang in a self-absorbed blissful bubble had passed. It was time to go out into the world, organise talks, video showings, meditation evenings, translate Cohen's books, spread Cohen's message, while throughout being a shining example of his teachings.

In 1996, Cohen devised a new methodology called 'the five fundamental tenets of enlightenment' that stressed complete dedication, total renunciation, taking full responsibility for one's actions and not personalising any experience (van der Braak 2003, 75). These were:

1. *Clarity of Intention*: The first tenet is the foundation of the spiritual life. To succeed liberating yourself from ignorance and self-deception, you have to have no doubt whatsoever that you want to be free more than anything.

2. *Volitionality*: It is within our power to change. 'Most of us like to see ourselves as unconscious victims. But in fact, we all know exactly what we are doing'.
3. *Face Everything and Avoid Nothing*: The third tenet is the ultimate form of spiritual practice. It asks: how awake are you to what is motivating you to make the choices that you make? Because only if you are paying close attention are you going to be able to bring the light of awareness into the darkest corners of your own psyche.
4. *Impersonality*: The fourth tenet states that every aspect of the human experience is a completely impersonal affair. It tells us that the illusion of uniqueness, the narcissistic self-sense that is ego, is created moment by moment through the compulsive and mechanical personalisation of almost every thought, feeling, and experience we have.
5. *For the Sake of the Whole*: The pursuit of enlightenment is for the transformation of the whole world, the enlightenment of the whole universe. It's ultimately for the evolution of consciousness itself (Cohen 2000).

The five tenets were to be discussed nonstop in the men's and women's meetings and were expounded by Cohen in his public teachings and in meetings with his students. During intensive practice periods, students were no longer allowed to have any personal conversations, only conversations about the five tenets (see Sand 2015). The target of these tenets was the ego, defined by Cohen as, 'the compulsive need to remain separate at all times'. (Cohen 2000) Such egoistic individuality prevented the perfect expression of the impersonal absolute on the relative level and he insisted that the 'compulsion with the personal' must be completely severed. As I recalled in 2003:

> Slowly but surely the community moves in a more 'impersonal' direction. Speaking about personal problems, personal interests, or ourselves is not considered helpful. Attention to 'our personal drama' is discouraged. Independent thinking outside the perimeters of Andrew's teaching becomes suspect. Why would you want to inquire into anything outside the five fundamentals when the five fundamentals are all that you need to focus on in order to realize freedom? (van der Braak 2003, 75)

In 1996, the community moved to an estate called Foxhollow in Lenox, Massachusetts. After this move, the extreme measures to the students increased, and the regimes of spiritual practice became ever more demanding. The male students were told to hold a 'pushup marathon' each Sunday, performing as many pushups without stopping as possible. The German translation of *Enlightenment Blues* is *Liegestütz zur Erleuchtung*, 'Pushup to Enlightenment' (van der Braak 2004), and my recollection of them is as follows:

> Pretty soon we are standing on our hands for three to five hours, doing push-ups in series of ten. Some of us manage to do thousands of push-ups; the record is ten thousand. This becomes too time-consuming, therefore the rules are changed: do as many push-ups as you can in an hour's time. You are supposed to break your record every week. (van der Braak 2003, 78–9)

The verbal abuse started to give way to physical abuse. In 1997, I spoke to an English student who told me he was physically roughed up by a few male students, to "force him to get in touch with his fighting spirit" (van der Braak 2003, 80). This was part of a systematic regime of:

> disciplinary face slapping – usually in response to a student's performance of some task failing to measure up to his expectations – in which it was difficult to discern any particular 'lesson' other than 'Shape up!' [...] In some cases, Andrew would direct one student to slap another; in others, he administered the slaps himself. (Yenner 2009, 31)

Such practices were symptoms of "the unprecedented degree of control that eventually came to pervade the atmosphere of the Foxhollow community, and 'groupthink' was certainly a consequence of this atmosphere of control" (Yenner 2009, 32). Several occasions of violence occurred at Foxhollow. One of these involved a student for whom Cohen:

> ordered that the walls, floor and ceiling of her office (which had been located to an unfurnished basement room) be painted red to signify the spilled blood of her guru. She was ordered to spend hours there contemplating the implications of her transgressions, with the additional aid of a large cartoon on the wall depicting her as a vampire and the word 'traitor' written in large letters next to it. (Yenner 2009, 32–3)

The transition from stage one to stage two in Cohen's community had been marked by his acrimonious conflict with his teacher, Poonja. Now, as stage two was progressing, Cohen came under increasing criticism from former students. In 1997, his own mother and student, Luna Tarlo, published *Mother of God*, a harsh indictment of her son and his teaching methods (Tarlo 2009). In 2003 I published my own *Enlightenment Blues* (van der Braak 2003). In 2004, a critical website was founded by former *WIE?* editor Hal Blacker (*WHAT Enlightenment??!*). Such external criticism led to vehement discussions of Cohen and his teaching style; Cohen himself claimed to have already moved on to a next stage, that of evolutionary enlightenment.

Stage three: evolutionary enlightenment

The third stage of 'evolutionary enlightenment' was claimed by the community to have been born on 30 July 2001, when a group of male students experienced what was referred to as collective or intersubjective enlightenment (Gleig 2013, 203). In his third phase, Cohen shifted his focus from the impersonality of enlightenment to the relationship between enlightenment and evolution. This had always been a theme in his teaching, but now 'evolutionary enlightenment' became an important revision in the community's teaching. Cohen framed evolutionary enlightenment as a combination of enlightenment (the nondual realisation revealed by Indian enlightenment traditions) and evolution (the deep time developmental perspective discovered by western science. See Gleig 2013, 201). Enlightenment was now seen as emerging through a collective.

In November 2005, a new significant emergence of collective enlightenment was claimed to have occurred in Cohen's community. According to Cohen, a shared experience of enlightenment had occurred across his entire student body and was sustained for a period of over a month. The point of realising enlightenment, according to Cohen, was no longer to escape the world of suffering (as in the traditional Indian notion of samsara), but to fully participate in the evolutionary process of life – to work in the service of evolution. Enlightenment was not only to be expressed in perfect ethical behaviour but became itself an ethical imperative to further evolution. With this change, 'Cohen reconfigures enlightenment from a world-negating and utterly transcendent state to a unique form of consciousness that both embraces and extends the universe' (Gleig 2013, 201). The emphasis in Cohen's message was now on being fully engaged and involved with the world. This evolutionary and world-affirming discourse led to a future-oriented remodelling of Cohen's community. The magazine *What is Enlightenment?* was relaunched as *EnlightenNext*; which also became the new name of the organisation, replacing Impersonal Enlightenment Fellowship. At the same time, Cohen's students were also renamed as 'evolutionaries'.

Cohen's teaching took place using multimedia methods such as a sophisticated interactive website, regular podcasts and virtual discussions, weekly webcasts and telephone conference calls, and monthly virtual workshops and seminars (Gleig 2013, 202). Cohen also set up an educational and training programme in which 60 qualified EnlightenNext instructors offered a variety of live and virtual events. As Gleig notes, this collective model of teaching marks a notable shift from the traditional guru-model that characterised Cohen's earlier community (Gleig 2013, 203). The emphasis in Cohen's community shifted to creating a global movement and a worldwide learning community. The community was deeply involved with alliances with the Integral community of thinkers such as Ken Wilber, Duane Elgin and Don Beck.

Conclusion

This chapter has described various changes with regard to Cohen's teaching of enlightenment: from his initial experience-based emphasis on personal enlightenment, Cohen went to an ethics-based emphasis on living one's life based on impersonal enlightenment, and ended up envisioning the future of mankind through evolutionary enlightenment. These three teachings of enlightenment came with three models of community. First, within the context of experiential enlightenment, spiritual community consisted in the voluntary association of enlightened individuals resulting in an ecstatic shared celebration of life ('a community of finders'). Second, within the context of ethical impersonal enlightenment, spiritual community became both an individual proving ground and a collective showcase for enlightened living ('creating heaven on earth'). Third, and finally, within the context of evolutionary enlightenment, Cohen's community was re-envisioned as an evolutionary collective aimed at bringing about evolution in the world.

Such heady rhetoric with regard to enlightenment and community served to explain and legitimise Cohen's harsh and inflexible teaching methods which facilitated various processes that encouraged increasingly violent behaviour within the EnlightenNext community, from verbal abuse and pestering to physical abuse bordering on torture. In the move from personal to impersonal enlightenment, the individual's experience was de-emphasised, and the greater collective good ('heaven on earth') became most important. In the epic war against the ego, individual suffering was part of the bargain. Collateral damage was unavoidable. In the move from impersonal to evolutionary enlightenment, all the individual suffering was reinterpreted as necessary in order to bring about the monumental evolutionary shift that had supposedly taken place in Cohen's community. As Gleig notes, Cohen himself claimed that this shift was only able to emerge as a result of his 'momentous efforts' to push his students beyond their egoistic selves (Gleig 2013, 204).

In order to explain the increasingly grandiose revisions of enlightenment and community in charismatic religious leaders such as Cohen, psychologists of religion often point to pathological narcissism. Australian psychologist Len Oakes, for example, argues that such cult leaders have a narcissistic personality, often characterised by isolation, autonomy, grandiosity and manipulativeness (Oakes 1997, 2010). And indeed, Cohen's inability to leave a good thing alone and stay with his community of finders may be connected to a narcissistic compulsion to prove his superiority to his own Advaita Vedanta teacher Poonja, as well as to other spiritual teachers who 'compromised' in his eyes.

However, such revisions could also be interpreted as a response to criticism from outside. Once Cohen was criticised by his own guru and by other teachers, he radicalised his message in order to prove his autonomy. The revision from personal to impersonal enlightenment shielded him from criticism with regard to his harsh teaching methods: those methods were necessary in order to win the war with the ego. As Gleig notes, Cohen and his supporters have utilised the Buddhist hermeneutic of crazy wisdom and skilful means (*upaya*) to legitimise his teaching methods as a form of transformative pedagogy (Gleig 2013, 199). Both Buddhist and Hindu traditions revere crazy wisdom teachers, enlightened gurus who use shocking methods including physical force and breaking religious ethics to awaken their students. Gleig also remarks on the irony of this argument, since the hermeneutic of skilful means assumes a skill and flexibility in teaching different individual students that has been notably lacking in Cohen (Gleig 2013, 200).

The revision from impersonal to evolutionary enlightenment allowed Cohen to remodel his community into a global movement and a worldwide learning community, thereby lessening the need to interact directly with his students. The focus shifted not only from individual to communal change, but even from communal change to cultural change. In this way, Cohen's controversial teaching methods were further shielded from public criticism.

Postscript

Gleig's article was published when Cohen was still going strong as a religious leader. However, in 2013, Cohen announced on his blog that he would step down from his role as guru and leader of EnlightenNext and take a sabbatical for an extended period of time (Cohen 2013). He also began apologising to some former and current students for misdeeds and abuses of the past. Core students in the leadership of EnlightenNext left the organisation and struck out on their own. Apparently, core members of EnlightenNext had been calling Cohen to task for some time, attempting to get him to change his autocratic and authoritarian style of leadership (Blacker 2013a, 2013b).

In May 2015, Cohen posted an extensive letter of apology to his former students on his website, *andrewcohen.org* (the letter was removed from the site afterwards), in which he expressed regret for the ways in which his unusual teaching methods, which often included forms of violence, had hurt and alienated many former students (Cohen 2015).

> I gradually lost sight of people's humanity, including my own [...] I have begun to see more and more clearly how over time my pride and my desire for fame and recognition slowly but surely began to blur and corrupt my vision. The worst part of it is that I was oblivious to the many different ways some of my students were being pushed too hard and at times too relentlessly to make breakthroughs and too often breaking down as a result [...] there were and have been too many moments where I simply have been wrong. Not only did my arrow miss

the target but it caused unnecessary pain and suffering to too many people. For this I am deeply and terribly sorry. (Cohen 2015)

To the horror of his former students, however, Cohen has recently begun teaching again through a new website platform (Cohen 2020).

Bibliography

All URLs were accessed on 17 June 2020.

Blacker, Hal. 2013a. "Andrew Cohen and the Fall of the Mythic Guru in an Age of PR Spin." Available at http://whatenlightenment.blogspot.nl/2013/06/andrew-cohen-and-fall-of-guru-in-age-of_21.html

Blacker, Hal 2013b. "The 'A' List: A Catalog of Trauma and Abuse." Available at http://whatenlightenment.blogspot.nl/2013/07/the-list-catalog-of-trauma-and-abuse.html

Cohen, Andrew. 2020. "Manifest Nirvana." Available at https://www.manifest.nirvana.com

Cohen, Andrew. 2015. "An Open Letter to All My Students upon Return from my Sabbatical." Available at http://www.opnlttr.com/letter/open-letter-all-my-former-students-upon-return-my-sabbatical-andrewcohenorg

Cohen, Andrew. 2013. "An Apology." Available at https://web.archive.org/web/20131213114227/http://andrewcohen.org/blog/apology

Cohen, Andrew. 2000. *Embracing Heaven and Earth: The Five Fundamental Tenets of Enlightenment*. Lenox, MA: Moksha Press.

Cohen, Andrew. 1991. *Enlightenment Is a Secret: Teachings of Liberation*. Larkspur: Moksha Foundation.

Dawson, Lorne L. 2006. *Comprehending Cults: The Sociology of New Religious Movements*. 2nd ed. Oxford, UK: Oxford University Press.

Forsthoeffel, Thomas A. and Humes, Cynthia Ann (eds). 2005. *Gurus in America*. Albany, NY: State University of New York Press.

Gleig, Ann. 2013. "From Being to Becoming, Transcending to Transforming: Andrew Cohen and the Evolution of Enlightenment." In *Homegrown Gurus: From Hinduism in America to American Hinduism*. Ann Gleig and Lola Williamson (eds.). Albany, NY: State University of New York Press, pp. 189–214.

Gleig, Ann and Williamson, Lola (eds). 2013. *Homegrown Gurus: From Hinduism in America to American Hinduism*. Albany, NY: State University of New York Press.

Oakes, Len. 2010. *The Charismatic Personality*. Bowen Hills, Australia: Australia University Press.

Oakes, Len. 1997. *Prophetic Charisma: The Psychology of Revolutionary Religious Personalities*. Syracuse, NY: Syracuse University Press.

Sand, Marlowe. 2015. *Paradise and Promises: Chronicles of My Life with a Self-Declared, Modern-Day Buddha*. Winchester, UK: O-Books.

Stark and Bainbridge. 1985. *The Future of Religion: Secularization, Revival and Cult Formation*. Berkeley, CA: University of California Press.

Tarlo, Luna. 2009. *The Mother of God*. Rhinebeck, NY: Epigraph.

van der Braak, André. 2008. "Enlightenment Revisited: Romantic, Historicist, Hermeneutic and Comparative Perspectives on Zen." *Acta Comparanda*, XIX: 87–97.

van der Braak, André. 2004. *Liegestütz zur Erleuchtung*. Winterthur: Spuren Verlag.

van der Braak, André. 2003. *Enlightenment Blues: My Years with an American Guru*. Rhinebeck, NY: Monkfish Publishing.

WHAT Enlightenment??! Blog. Available at http://whatenlightenment.blogspot.com (accessed 06 October 2020).

Yenner, William et al. 2009. *American Guru: A Story of Love, Betrayal and Healing – Former Students of Andrew Cohen Speak Out*. Rhinebeck, NY: Epigraph Books.

5 "Not all Druids wear robes": countercultural experiences of youth and the revision of ritual in British Druidry

Jonathan Woolley

When one thinks of a Druid, perhaps the first and clearest image that comes to mind is of a wise old man, with a white beard and white robes, sporting a staff or a golden sickle, standing in a forest grove, amidst a circle of standing stones (Rees and Rees 1989). This imaginary has little basis in the actual archaeological or historical record of the Iron Age, having been first invented by the 15th century humanist, Conrad Celtis (Hutton 2009: 50–1; 2013: 172–73). But the conjunction of age, gender, and hermetic power in this image has broad resonance with many other figures in Western cultures – not least the Jungian archetype of the 'senex' (Jung and Baynes 1976) – a resonance that gives the image great power. This stock character in popular fiction manifests in a wide variety of genres and media, from novels, to films, to television – so it is only natural that the Druid, who is implicated in many similar themes and tropes, should be conceptualised in much the same way. Indeed, the connection between the Celtic Druid and the English Wizard is very old – as the Anglo-Saxon word for magic of dry-craeft, literally 'druid-craft', indicates (Storm 1948). But behind this monolithic image, the exists the modern spiritual movement of Druidry – a community that includes some 4,189 people according to the 2011 census, of many different ages, genders, and backgrounds (ONS Digital 2015). The largest Druidic organization in Britain is the Order of Bards, Ovates, and Druids (OBOD), and it is with this organisation that this chapter is concerned. We shall see that at this significant point in the development of OBOD – the Order was re-founded in 1988, and so it is only now that it is becoming truly multigenerational – the rites of passage of young Druids and the broader history of their wider community intersect. Just as young Druids experience such rites as moments of great personal change; so the institution of these innovative ritual procedures represents a way in which Druids have adapted to the novel presence of multiple generational cohorts within their community.

My argument in this chapter takes its inspiration from Helen Berger and Douglas Ezzy's study of young people who participate in Witchcraft. Berger and Ezzy systematically interrogate the stereotypes attached to teenage Witches (Berger and Ezzy 2007), determining that – contrary to how they

DOI: 10.4324/9781315226804-5

are often depicted as spiritual dilletantes, even amongst older Witches – young Witches in fact showed a significant depth of understanding of their faith, and a high degree of investment in its practice. In this chapter, I examine the influence of the discourse that Berger and Ezzy critique – namely, that young people are shallow, and too superficial to engage constructively with spiritual matters – within the Druidic community, and how that discourse informs and is addressed by coming of age rituals. As OBOD's style of Druidry is heavily influenced by psychoanalytic thought – its former leader, Philip Carr-Gomm, is a trained Jungian psychotherapist – OBOD's mediations on age and intergenerational change are heavily influenced by archetypical thinking about elders and the young. In particular, I will suggest that the dialectic between the senex and the puer – the mean old man and the rebellious youth – characterizes both the Druidic commentary on intergenerational relations in Britain, but also the ways in which Druids themselves have sought to use novel ritual forms to heal the rift such a dynamic represents. Rather than resolving the dialectic, however, Druidic coming of age ceremonies represent a key site where old and young are brought together, and the tensions between different cohorts become overt, and prompt changes in British Druidry as a whole.

I conducted my fieldwork for this chapter by drawing primarily on my own experiences in the fashion of an 'auto-ethnographer' (Blain 2005: 182; Reed-Danahay 1997; Ellis and Bochner 2000) but also utilising participant observation to take careful note of the conversations, rituals, and daily activities that characterise camp life.[1] As a Druid myself and a member of the community before I began my research, I chose to embrace my role as an insider in the hope of producing a rich, detailed account of the practices I was involved in, but nonetheless approaching the culture of OBOD in a critically rigorous way.

Context: the Order of Bards, Ovates, and Druids and White Horse Camps

OBOD was founded in 1964 by Ross Nichols, a former member of the Ancient Druid Order (also known as the Universal Bond), a spiritual fellowship founded decades earlier by the Theosophist William McGregor-Reid that counted Gerald Gardener, the founder of one of the main schools of Wicca,[2] as one of its members (Carr-Gomm 2010; Nichols 1990). Throughout the latter half of the 20th century, interest in Celtic spirituality and pre-Christian religious practices increased throughout Britain and America, accompanied by a quickening of 'New Age' spiritualties and the consolidation of the ideas of the 1960s counter-culture. OBOD can be located squarely within this interlocking tradition of esoteric networks and cultural trends (Hutton 2009; Morris 2006). In 1988, Philip Carr-Gomm, Nichol's protégé, revived the Order after it had fallen into quiescence following Nichols' death in 1975. Together with Caitlin and John Matthews, two authors who had published a number of works on the myths recorded in Irish and Welsh manuscripts, Carr-Gomm compiled a series of distance learning courses that "offered a journey of spiritual and psychological exploration inspired by Druidry, and based upon the philosophy and the ideas that had become associated with it" (Carr-Gomm 2007). By the turn of the century, over 6,000 people were working with the material Carr-Gomm and the Matthews had compiled, and, according to the Order's most recent published figures, some 13,000 people internationally have taken the course.[3] Members of the Order meet in a series of 'groves' and 'seed-groups'[4] spread across Britain, Europe, North America, Australia, and New Zealand, and through the bi-annual 'gatherings', which take place in the UK in Glastonbury, Somerset.

White Horse Camps is a community of OBOD Druids, their friends, and families, scattered across England, Wales, Ireland, and Scotland. They come together four times a year to celebrate the major cross-quarter days of the Celtic Pagan Calendar – Samhain (1 November), Imbolc (2 February), Beltane (1 May), and Lughnasadh (1 August). Although interpersonal contact is maintained throughout the year on a smaller scale, particularly via social networking websites, the camps held at the four festivals have particular importance in that they allow members of the tribe to live, for a time, as a community. The camps themselves are therefore a temporary village, including two yurts for sleeping and for workshops; a mobile shower-and-sauna ('water-world'); a series of 'benders'[5] used for healing, welcoming new arrivals, ritual and storage; the central fire pit; a kitchen and compost toilets.[6] Many members bring their own tents, which are pitched on any spare flat land that is available. All of the equipment and structures ('tat') are transported from site to site in a large trailer and are erected by volunteers ('crew') in the weeks prior to and following each camp. Volunteering was, for much of the time I was at camps, an important way in which poorer members of the community could gain access – as it was possible to earn days at camp as payment in kind for working in the kitchen, or by setting up or taking down the communal structures. This system was deemed to be financially unsustainable and replaced by a smaller reduction in ticket price in 2015. The ticket price has changed over the years, but for most of the time I wasdoing fieldwork, the price was around £25 per person per day. The community does not yet own land, and so rents camping grounds from others – Imbolc camps are held at a retreat centre in the Midlands, while the Beltane, Lughnasadh and Samhain camps were until recently held on open farmland in the Vale of the White Horse, Oxfordshire. Since 2015, the Beltane and Samhain camps take place at the Midlands location, while Lughnasadh is held at a farm in Ceredigion, Wales.

It was usual for members of the Order to bring their families to camp, especially at Lughnasadh; a practice that was much less common at events organised centrally by the Order, which were usually members-only. This has meant that the children who have attended camps from early on have grown up with Druidry. The first camps – under the name of OBOD Camps – were held in 1994 and were organised directly by Carr-Gomm. In 2002, responsibility for the running of the camps was taken on by volunteers, and in 2012, OBOD Camps were renamed White Horse Camps and made financially and legally independent.

This relatively long history – 27 years – means that generational cohorts have been able to form at camps, building relationships over decades. Indeed, while I was at camp, three cohorts appeared to be in evidence. The 'adults' were those over 30 – predominantly OBOD members or their partners – who made up the majority of those attending the camp. The 'teenagers' were those between the ages of 15 and 30, including both the older children of the 'adults' and their friends amongst the membership who were of similar age. The 'children' were those under 15. Anyone under the age of 16 had to be accompanied by an adult sponsor and had to be registered separately at booking. If a large number of children were expected, the organisers would erect a dedicated 'Kids Space' – a yurt or bender filled with toys and children's books, set aside for playing. 'Teenagers' and 'adults' were not allotted dedicated spaces, and so would normally socialise outside each other's tents, or in communal areas like the kitchen bender. The reason for this lack of dedicated spaces for either 'teenagers' or 'adults' is provided by the current White Horse Camp's FAQ, which states that

> We welcome people of all ages & often have a dedicated kids' space & kids' activities though we do not usually provide a crèche where parents can leave their children. Some camps are more suitable for young children in terms of both accommodation & camp activities... Teenagers & young adults are welcome at camp but they are encouraged to join in with the camp rather than do their own thing. Again, some camps may be more or less suitable for young people.[7]

The statement that '[young adults] are encouraged to join with the camp rather than do their own thing' is, I suggest, particularly significant. It distils an important normative stance taken by many Druids; that the separation of young adults from their elders is 'anti-social'.

The senex and the puer: youth and age as dialectic

This norm distils two major lines of thinking about youth and adulthood in White Horse Camps – first, that the relationship between young people and adults in wider society was pathological, and second that the solution to this was greater integration at camps. Coming of age ceremonies form an integral part of this solution.

Within the community, there was a prevailing sense that the wider society did not respond to young people – or the life course in general – particularly well. White Horse Campers frequently articulated the view that the transitions between different life stages – from childhood to adulthood, from adulthood to elderhood, and from elderhood to death – were not recognized or celebrated sufficiently. This draws upon a broader view in OBOD, that

> One of the problems caused by the increasing secularisation of society is that these [life] events are often insufficiently acknowledged, even when part of us yearns to honour these special times in a meaningful and spiritual way. (Carr-Gomm 2014)

One Druid from White Horse Camps said to me that

> Druidry honours different stages of life – there is this respect there. So there's a very good relationship between the generations, there isn't so much of a gap... there's that relationship.

In Western society as a whole, however, that respect was not deemed to be there.

> But in general, there's a much bigger divide between generations. We don't respect our elders. And young people are portrayed in the media, as a bit of a nuisance, as a problem, so people don't trust them.

To this deficit, many members of the communities attributed a great many ills – from anti-social behaviour to intergenerational isolation – and their own personal anxieties about growing up, growing old, and dying. In contrast to this perceived lack of concord between the cohorts, the White Horse community was conceived of as a utopian project; an attempt to develop an alternative, more cohesive mode of social organization. Reflecting the influence of British folk (Boyes 1993), this organic, imagined village was one in which generations could live and work together, where the old and young could be reunited, for the benefit of all concerned. The reintroduction of age-related 'rites of passage' into the community, the thinking went, would help sustain this ideal state of harmony and cohesion, by assisting young people with their journey into adulthood. The introduction of these rites of passage took place over the course of the late 1990s and early 2000s, when an increasing number of the children of founding members of White Horse Camps began to reach mid-late adolescence. Reflecting the sentiment expressed in Carr-Gomm's quote above, the intention for these rituals was to honour the experience of growing up in this new cohort of young Druids – to solemnize this change in a way that would integrate them as adults, through a ceremonial event that was personally significant and imbued with spiritual meaning.

Sources of tension remained, however. One of the major areas of differentiation and discord between adults and teenagers was the fact that 'the teenagers' often sought to socialize separately – not taking part in the workshops and events arranged on the camp but spending their time with one another. Although this would occasionally be linked to active rule breaking – such as excessive drinking, or drug-taking, both of which were forbidden on camps – this was not always the case. One example that I witnessed first hand was when – during Beltane Camp 2013 – a group of us played a card game called *Magic: The Gathering* in one of the communal yurts. On a number of occasions while playing the game, older Druids entering the yurt to fetch their possessions or to enquire after other members of the community, would glare at us gathered together, mutter to themselves, or look visibly annoyed. Subsequently, complaints were made that we were being 'anti-social' and that the game 'was inappropriate'. One of the 'teenagers' involved confided that he found this response 'deeply hurtful'. As he explained;

> We decided to play *Magic: The Gathering* ... because the Beltane camp had been a washout. It rained constantly and, to keep ourselves entertained and also strengthen our bonds of friendship, we decided to play a card game.

He also referred to the fact that there was very little put on specifically for young adults to do and claimed that these led to drinking and drug taking as distractions. He contrasted this lack of facilities with a non-OBOD camp he had attended, where there was a dedicated space set aside for young adults – including a ping-pong table and other games. At this camp, he explained, there was less drinking, and no tension between young people and other members of the community. This desire for difference would become particularly visible during ceremony; while many of the 'adults' would have a set of robes that they reserved specifically for ceremonial uses, most of the 'teenagers' would wear simply their ordinary clothes. Over the period of my fieldwork, eschewing robes became increasingly salient for some younger members of the community, becoming a conscious choice that marked out the new generation as distinct from the older cohort.

My own position regarding these generational cohorts was complicated. As a member of OBOD who was not related to any of the older members, and who regularly attended workshops and talks, I was essentially conceived of as an 'adult', despite the fact that – at 22 years old – I was actually younger than some of the 'teenagers'. At one point, I was standing with two 'teenager' friends of mine, when we were approached by an elder, who wanted to organise a meeting with 'the young people on camp' about some of their behaviour the previous night. I asked when the meeting would be, and the elder looked at me a little confused, before replying 'Well, you can come if you want, Jonathan, but *you* don't need to be there...'. It was clear that 'young people' was implicitly a social category that was connected to discord, disruption, and 'un-Druidic' behaviour, rather than simply matter of age. In this respect, it appears that just as the role of the senex is the *sine qua non* of Druidic selfhood, the Jungian counterpart of the *puer* – the eternal, creative youth – provides the imprimatur for Druidic imaginaries around young people as a distinct group (Jensen 2009).

The primacy of elderhood in Druidic identity is reinforced by Druidry's interactions with wider society. Druids with a public profile – the most notable example perhaps being Arthur Pendragon – often consciously adopt the raiment most characteristic of the Druid-as-Senex, including white hair, a long beard, a white robe, eccentricity, and remote mystique, to court the attention of the media (Pendragon and Stone 2003; BBC 2011). Although Arthur is a controversial figure in the Druid community, many Druids adopt the white robes and long hair of the archetypical senex.

In fiction, the senex is often highly decontextualised relative to the protagonist of whom he is the counsellor, advisor, and teacher. While the hero-as-puer is almost always enmeshed in a dense network of social obligations and worldly events at the beginning and the end of such tales – with the departure from such relationships being one of the conditions of his personal transformation and the development of the ego (Neumann and Jung 2014) – the senex is in in many respects the opposite. He is often sought out by the hero in some wild, distant place. He is a hermit, seeking refuge from a fallen social order, who has abandoned ego (Graham 2013). Once the quest is over and the hero returns to society, the senex will normally return to his original, lonely state – letting go of social ties, in a way that is indicative of how the senex is associated intimately with loss (Hubback 1996). These features are identifiable in many characters that conform to the senex archetype in popular media, including Obi Wan Kenobi from the *Star Wars* franchise (Lucas 1977), Allanon in *The Shannara Chronicles* (2016), and Gandalf in *The Lord of the Rings* and *The Hobbit* (Jackson 2001, 2012). In all these cases, the senex is *a priori* separate to ordinary society, standing apart in grand isolation, only entering into social relations under exceptional circumstances, and then relinquishing them soon afterwards. This is perhaps exemplified by the figure of Merlin in T.H. White's *The Once and Future King* – a character who ages backwards. We see the same features in the Druidic image consciously embodied by Arthur Pendragon – an isolated figure, both ageless and aged, standing guard over the enspirited remains of a largely-forgotten world. By separating themselves from their elders – and failing to attend workshops, and engaging in 'inappropriate' activities – the young adults of OBOD are seen by their detractors in the elder cohort to fall short of this standard.

For rather than solely manifest in a positive guise – of a questing hero – as Louise von Franz has argued, the *puer* can symbolize 'youthful irresponsibility refusing to face up to the demands of adult life' (Walker 2014; von Franz 2000), a pathology that was clearly being alleged in the cases above. Following a line of thinking developed by James Hillman, it seems to me that the tension between 'adult' Druids and 'teenagers' deploys a polarization of the senex and puer archetypes – with the puer embodying rebellious adolescence, and the senex manifesting as the 'mean old man' (Walker 2014; Hillman 2005). This is the same polarization of young and old that Druids recognize and condemn in wider society, and so it is also being used to make sense of the – sometimes strained – relations between the cohorts. Despite the way in which Druids often position themselves in opposition to wider society, the popular media's use of Jungian themes and its characterisation of Druids serves to reinforce this dynamic; meaning that real-life Druidic communities are far from immune from the tension between youth and age.

An ethnographic case: coming of age rituals

We now turn our attention to the ritual structure of coming of age ceremonies in OBOD. Considering these rites in detail allows us to see how Druids attempt to respond constructively to demographic change by addressing the polarization of senex and the puer, while using a model of ritual practice that actually relies upon the power of the senex archetype. This results in these rituals' relative inability to address these tensions.

Druidic coming of age ceremonies are intensely personal events that often involve airing the intimate thoughts, feelings, and memories from the life of the passenger. Revealing the particular details of any one such event in the form of a detailed case study would not be appropriate here, as it would involve doing violence to the intimate, personal, and private nature of the experience. However, I will provide a brief description of the general features of coming of age rites involving young adults in OBOD and discuss their significance.

Coming of age rituals would normally be planned well in advance; organisers of individual camps required that people request any rites of passage they might wish to have with their booking. At the camp itself, the organisers – usually together with the parents of the individual being initiated – would then informally discuss the logistics of the ritual itself; where particular phases of the ceremony would take place on the site, and who from the community could perform specific roles in the ceremony. As the camps took place at a number of different locations, and different ceremonies would happen at each one, buildings and landscape features were generally not given fixed ceremonial purposes but repurposed as needed. A woodland glade might be the abode of a god one day, and a focal point for a Bardic initiation the next. Nonetheless, all such sites were considered to be the permanent home of particular spiritual beings – resident within trees, rocks, and water features – whose blessing and protection would be sought before any ceremonial activity. On the chosen day, the rite of passage would be announced with the other events of the day at the morning meeting, usually with public acknowledgement – rounds of applause and congratulations – of the individual undertaking it, if they were present. The entire community would then be invited to support the individual on their journey, by taking part in the ceremony, providing gifts or offering advice.

Coming of age rituals were gendered, with the women of the community initiating the girls, and the men of the community initiating the boys. The actual ceremony would normally take place during the afternoon or early evening. When the allotted time came, one person – usually an elder, occasionally accompanied by a parent – would meet the passenger at the central fire, where they would ask if they were ready to become an adult. There is no obligatory formal liturgy for coming of age ceremonies in OBOD, and so the precise wording would depend upon the taste of the elder performing the ceremony. Upon receiving an affirmative answer from the passenger, the elder would lead the passenger away from the campsite, to a quiet place where they might reflect upon their life's course. After a period of time – normally 50 minutes or so – had elapsed, the elder would bring the passenger out to a series of predetermined locations around the campsite, where the passenger would be met sequentially by one or more members of the community or spiritual beings.[8] These individuals would be responsible for testing the passenger's resolve. The precise nature of these tests would vary according to the passenger's own character, age, and wishes; they might involve a riddle or a feat of strength – I once saw a young man ford a stream in winter to retrieve a knife from the other side – a question of Druidic lore, or a more ceremonial challenge, involving the need to show courage in the face of a monstrous enemy, embodied by a member of the community in disguise. After these stages were completed, the passenger would be brought to a gathering of all the men or women of the community, according to the gender of the passenger, who would then each speak to the passenger directly, offering words of praise or welcome as an adult. The passenger would then themselves be invited to say a few words. Once this was done, the passenger would be brought back to the main campsite, accompanied by singing and drumming and celebration.

Within this ritual framework, we can see clear efforts to overcome the polarisation that Druids believe exists between younger and older generations – between the puer and the senex. The passenger is given the opportunity to reflect upon the course of their lives, confronted with the rigorous demands of personal responsibility, and then systematically encouraged by their elders – the rebelliousness of the puer is quashed, while their antipathy to the senex is diminished through demonstrations of overt support. Equally, we also see the positive qualities of the senex – as a source of wisdom and experience – being reinforced by this process. The actual structure of the ritual – a threefold process, involving an initial separation, followed by a challenge or challenges, concluded through a re-integration of the passenger into society – indicates the original source that inspired this ritual framework: the writings of Joseph Campbell (2008, 1972). Campbell is widely read amongst the OBOD community, and so his Jungian take on myth has been highly influential upon contemporary Druidic thought. Campbell's concept of the monomyth – a psychological structure that, Campbell argued, underpinned all the world's mythic tales – has been explored by Druids in the context of what Campbell felt was its original stimulus; rites of passage. As Campbell puts it, 'the standard path of the mythological adventure of the hero is a magnification of the formula represented in the rites of passage: separation – initiation – return' (Campbell 2008: 23). Campbell's placement of initiation as the central feature of rites of passage is a significant departure from the classic work on rites of passage by Arnold Van Gennep (2013; see also Ackerman 2012), where the threefold process is characterised rather differently. Whereas Van Gennep characterised preliminal, liminal, and postliminal rites as effecting the dissolution, suspension, and creation of social relationships (Praet 2014; Turner 1964), Campbell misinterpreted this as a psychological process: where the passenger leaves society to seek self-knowledge, and returns when this has been gained. As Lefkowitz points out, only a 20th century hero would undertake a journey purely for the purposes of self-discovery (Lefkowitz 1990: 432); Campbell's theories have more to do with the 're-ligion of self-development' (Lefkowitz 1990: 429) than they do with any sound cross-cultural comparison of rites of passage.

Gieser has argued this 'psychologizing tendency' permeates Druidry (Gieser 2008: 190). Indeed, it has guided the process by which Druids have designed all rites of passage, including coming of age ceremonies. As a mystery tradition, the OBOD community is initiatory in structure. There are three levels of initiation within the Order – the Bardic Grade, the Ovate Grade, and the Druid Grade – and movement between each one is solemnized through ceremonies the initiate completes on their own. White Horse Camps also offers initiation ceremonies that members can request after having done their own, solo initiations beforehand. The process by which a Grade initiation is booked and planned is identical to the procedure for a coming of age ceremony, and the content of the rite is basically the same, with a strong emphasis upon inner transformation, and a tripartite structure of separation/ initiation/return (Gieser 2008). One even sees crucial features of Campbell's process – from the call to adventure, to the presence of helpers, guides, and guardians – being referred to as such by Druids engaged in initiations.

In short, in seeking to cope with the appearance of a new cohort of younger Druids, the community has adapted an existing ritual structure with which they are familiar, to open up new forms of ceremonial life. Faced with the polarization of youth and old age in wider society, and a new cohort of young adults within their community, the elders of the Druid community have drawn upon a familiar Jungian paradigm, to revise their existing initiatory practices to into a new kind of rite of passage. Reflecting the 'psychologizing tendency' of Druidry as a whole, coming of age is dealt with as primarily a personal obstacle, to be resolved with greater self-knowledge.

However, the impact of these ceremonies has been complex. One young person spoke of her vivid memories of her coming of age ceremony, articulating a clear sense of being reassured of the support and wisdom of her fellow women. She also felt that there had been a positive change in her status after the ceremony – she was given greater responsibility by others (being asked to babysit and to lead kitchen shifts) and felt a sense of being trusted. But she admitted that this nonetheless 'was not a huge change' in terms of how other people had treated her already. Other experiences were far more negative. Another person stated his feelings very plainly:

> I desired the rite of passage to show to the group that I was not the child they viewed me as. I was a man, living in the world, doing things that deserved respect. Ultimately, however, this didn't happen... The coming-of-age ceremony itself made me hopeful for change. People said wonderful things to me as I walked around... [But] the day after, it was business as usual.

Despite their differing in terms of how positively they viewed the experience, both identify two key things – the ceremony was psychologically very profound, but it did not command much of an effect on their interpersonal relationships.

As we have seen, the senex is fundamentally a remote figure – separate from ordinary society, and from the hero to whom he provides teaching. Campbell's writing compounds this effect, as does Druidry's psychologizing tendencies. The fact that coming of age ceremonies are personally meaningful, but less socially transformative, serves to underscore the extent to which, despite employing a revisionist strategy to innovate and create new ritual forms, Druids nonetheless continue to work within these familiar frameworks of belief. Rather than providing an effective solution to the wider tensions between cohorts in Western society, these innovations simply serve to reinforce the deeper cultural themes that engender those tensions in the first place.

The senex and the fool: changes in Druidry and the problem of youth

The hermetic status of the senex makes for an elegant parallel with the tensions raised by coming-of-age in British Druidry. By increasingly focusing upon the personal development of the young, and neglecting their social relationships, especially with older adults, the ceremonialism of British Druid camps ultimately fails to satisfy the noble aspiration of bringing young and old together in community. The first cohort of members since the revival of the Order in 1988 did not face this problem – there was no older cohort with whom a destructive polarity could emerge. But as their children's generation has grown into adulthood, and the Order begins to become multi-generational, the inaccessibility of the senex – leading to its polarization from the puer – becomes at times a disruptive force within the Druid community. Attempts to create new ritual procedures that might negate this tension and bring the cohorts together are hindered by the fact that, ultimately, the image of what it properly means to be a Druid is connected so intimately with one extreme of that polarity. By deploying rituals that enhance individual personal development, rather than ones that transform social relations, Druids betray their allegiance to the isolated senex, in contrast to the socially embedded puer. Instead, these rituals can serve to simply make the tensions characterizing this shift in Druidry's social history more explicit, and the basic theological and cultural commitments that intersect with these tensions all the clearer.

Notes

1 At Imbolc I focused upon participant observation and interviews, while at Beltane I also took photographs and made recordings of camp life. My decision to avoid the use of photography at Imbolc was out of a desire to preserve the privacy of the landowners.
2 Wicca, one of the largest of the contemporary British Pagan spiritualties, is typically duotheistic, syncretic and involves a much greater focus upon ritual magic than Druidry.
3 Subscription to each course depends upon the desired format of the teaching materials, ranging from £195 (written *gwersi*) to £320 (written and audio *gwersi*). There is no additional membership fee other than the course cost, although subscription to *Touchstone* costs £20 annually.
4 'Groves' and 'seed-groups' are gatherings of members of the Order. The primary difference is size, but groves also tend to have more experienced members – a seed group requires two members of the Druid grade in order to become a grove.
5 Temporary constructions made of a bent hazel frame over which tarps are tied.
6 As Imbolc is held on a private smallholding, all the facilities are already provided, and so no shifts for tat-up and tat-down are required. Reflecting the cold climate that usually characterises February in Britain, indoor sleeping space is provided.
7 White Horse Camps (2016).
8 An important part of Druidic rituals involves 'drawing down' – a form of spirit possession, in which a god or other spiritual being is made manifest in the body of Druid celebrant (Adler 1986). This was not normally incorporated into rites of passage, but it would sometimes be deemed appropriate.

Bibliography

All urls were accessed on 2 July 2020.
Ackerman, Susan. 2012. *When Heroes Love: The Ambiguity of Eros in the Stories of Gilgamesh and David*. New York: Columbia University Press.

Adler, Margot. 1986. *Drawing Down the Moon: Witches, Druids, Goddess-Worshippers, and Other Pagans in America Today/Margot Adler*. Revised and expanded edition. Boston: Beacon Press.

BBC. 2011. "King Arthur Pendragon Loses Human Remains Legal Battle." *BBC News – Wiltshire*. http://www.bbc.co.uk/news/uk-england-wiltshire-14630468

Berger, Helen, and Ezzy, Douglas. 2007. *Teenage Witches: Magical Youth and the Search for the Self*. New Brunswick: Rutgers University Press.

Boyes, Georgina. 1993. *The Imagined Village: Culture, Ideology and the English Folk Revival*. Manchester: Manchester University Press.

Campbell, Joseph. 2008. *The Hero with a Thousand Faces*. Novato, CA: New World Library.

Campbell, Joseph. 1972. *Myths to Live By*. New York: Viking.

Carr-Gomm, Philip. 2014. "Rites of Passage." *Order of Bards and Druids*. http://www.druidry.org/druid-way/teaching-and-practice/rites-passage

Carr-Gomm, Philip. 2010. *Journeys of the Soul*. Lewes, Sussex: Oak Tree Press.

Carr-Gomm, Philip. 2007. "The History of Modern Druidism." *Order of Bards and Druids*. http://www.druidry.org/druid-way/what-druidry/brief-history-druidry/history-modern-druidism

Gieser, Thorsten. 2008. "Experiencing the Lifeworld of Druids: A Cultural Phenomenology of Perception." Unpublished Thesis, University of Aberdeen, Aberdeen. https://digitool.abdn.ac.uk/webclient/StreamGate?folder_id=0&dvs=1593717178554~437

Graham, Jack A. 2013. "Reimagining the Self: The Sage, the Wise Old One, and the Elder." *Jung Society of Atlanta*. http://www.jungatlanta.com/articles/summer13-the-sage.pdf

Hillman, James, ed. 2005. *Senex and Puer: Uniform Edition of the Writings of James Hillman*, Vol. 3, 1st edition. Putnam, CT: Spring Publications.

Hubback, Judith. 1996. "The Archetypal Senex: An Exploration of Old Age." *Journal of Analytical Psychology* 41(1): 3–18.

Hutton, Ronald. 2013. *Pagan Britain*. London and New Haven, CT: Yale University Press.

Hutton, Ronald 2009. *Blood and Mistletoe: The History of the Druids in Britain*. New Haven, CT, and London: Yale University Press.

Jackson, Peter. 2012. *The Hobbit: An Unexpected Journey*. Adventure, Fantasy.

Jackson, Peter 2001. *The Lord of the Rings: The Fellowship of the Ring*. Adventure, Drama, Fantasy.

Jensen, George H. 2009. "Introduction to the Puer/Puella Archetype." In *Perpetual Adolescence: Jungian Analyses of American Media, Literature and Pop Culture*, Sally Porterfield, Keith Polette, and Tita French Baumlin (eds.). Albany, NY: SUNY Press.

Jung, Carl G. 1976. *Psychological Types*. Edited by R. F. C. Hull. Translated by H. G. Baynes. Princeton, NJ: Princeton University Press.

Lefkowitz, Mary R. 1990. "MYTHOLOGY: The Myth of Joseph Campbell." *The American Scholar* 59(3): 429–434.

Lucas, George. 1977. *Star Wars: Episode IV – A New Hope*. Action, Adventure, Fantasy.

Morris, Brian. 2006. *Religion and Anthropology: A Critical Introduction*. Cambridge: Cambridge University Press.

Neumann, Erich, and Jung, Carl G. 2014. *The Origins and History of Consciousness*. Translated by R. F. C. Hull. With a Foreword by C. G. Jung. Princeton, NJ: Princeton University Press.

Nichols, Ross. 1990. *The Book of Druidry*. Edited by John Matthews and Philip Carr-Gomm. New York: Castle Books.

ONS Digital. 2015. "What Is Your Religion?" UK 2011 Census. London: Office of National Statistics. http://visual.ons.gov.uk/infographic-what-is-your-religion/

Pendragon, Arthur, and Stone, Christopher James. 2003. *The Trials of Arthur: The Life and Times of a Modern-Day King*. London, UK: Element.

Praet, I. 2014. *Animism and the Question of Life*. New York and Oxford: Routledge.

Rees, Alwyn D., and Rees, Brinley. 1989. *Celtic Heritage*. New edition. London: Thames & Hudson Ltd.

Storm, Godfrid. 1948. *Anglo-Saxon Magic*. Berlin: Springer.

The Shannara Chronicles. 2016. Adventure, Fantasy, Sci-Fi.

Turner, Victor W. 1964. "Betwixt and Between: The Liminal Period in Rites de Passage." In *The Proceedings of the American Ethnological Society, Symposium on New Approaches to the Study of Religion*, pp. 4–20.

Von Franz, Marie-Louise. 2000. *The Problem of the Puer Aeternus*. 3rd edition. Toronto, Canada: Inner City Books.

Van Gennep, Arnold. 2013. *The Rites of Passage*. London, UK: Routledge.

Walker, Steven. 2014. *Jung and the Jungians on Myth*. London, UK: Routledge.

White Horse Camps. 2016. *White Horse Camps – Frequently Asked Questions*. https://web.archive.org/web/20180325010539/http://whitehorsecamps.co.uk/?page_id=159

Part II

Technology and institutions as drivers of change

6   Santo Daime: work in progress

Andrew Dawson

The subtitle of this chapter, "Work in Progress", plays on the complementary interplay between exterior and interior dimensions of Santo Daime religiosity. It also plays on the transformative trajectory through which this Brazilian new religious movement has passed since its beginnings in the early-1930s and increasingly so since spreading beyond the Amazon region of its birth in the mid-1980s. In respect of its exterior dimension, the rituals of Santo Daime are frequently referred to as 'works' and treated as practical-symbolic events that demand application, discipline, focus, and exertion from beginning to end. Regarding the interior dimension of *daimista* ritual practice, human existence is understood as but a single stage within a much longer series of incarnations through which the higher-self undergoes a prolonged spiritual refinement by way of meeting and overcoming the myriad challenges associated with corporeality and embodiment. The individual self is, quite literally, a work in progress. Bringing these two dimensions together, daimistas believe that the self's cultivation of (interior) spiritual purification is most effectively (though not solely) achieved through participation in a rigorous (exterior) ritual regime, the psychophysical demands of which are both efficacious in their own right and analogous to the everyday 'trials' of embodied existence. Ritual space is, then, not only a source of spiritual strength (by way of the disciplines nurtured through meeting its exacting demands) but also a practical-symbolic microcosm of the psychophysical struggles associated with corporeality and its material deficiencies.

The complementarity of exterior ritual regime and interior self-betterment is informed by Santo Daime's particular amalgamation of various religio-cultural sources. As it emerged in the Amazon region of the early-1930s, Santo Daime was marked by the pragmatic supernaturalism of the popular Catholic, Amazonian-folk (*caboclo*) and Afro-Brazilian elements on which it drew. Over time, these foundational elements were complemented by, overlaid with, or marginalised relative to the ameliorative concerns of modern (here, post-1850s) esoteric, Spiritist and human potential movements. Owing to the ingression of urban-professional adepts and its subsequent spread beyond Amazonia, the daimista religious repertoire of the late-twentieth century was further augmented by the autopoietic preoccupations of New Age and

DOI: 10.4324/9781315226804-6

alternative spiritualities. Today, Santo Daime continues on an inter-nationalising trajectory begun as early as the 1990s and, as a consequence, undergoes further hybridisation as ritual practices and symbolic tropes are appropriated from an increasingly variegated range of religio-cultural (e.g. Aboriginal; Buddhist; Druidic; Heathen; Hindu; and Native American) worldviews. As with the individuals for whom it caters, Santo Daime is a work in progress (Dawson 2013b).

Irrespective of the socio-cultural context in which it occurs or the particular amalgam of beliefs and practices at play, Santo Daime's articulation of exterior regime and interior self-betterment is centred upon the ritualised consumption of ayahuasca. Ayahuasca translates from the Quechua language of the north Andes as 'soul vine' or 'vine of the dead' and has traditionally been consumed by indigenous communities (e.g. Aruák; Chocó; Jívaro; Pano; and Tukano) across the upper reaches of the Amazon River system in Bolivia, Brazil, Colombia, Ecuador, and Peru. Here, ayahuasca is most commonly consumed in liquid form as part of shamanic rituals designed to communicate with celestial supernatural forces or the spirits of the forest. Known by various names within its respective indigenous contexts, ayahuasca is a generic term commonly as-sociated with preparations of the mildly psychoactive vine *Banisteriopsis caapi* (the psychotropic effects of which are caused by three beta-carboline alkaloids: harmine, harmoline and tetrahydroharmine). Owing to their ability to intensify and prolong the psychotropic effect, other natural substances such as tree barks and coca or tobacco leaves may also be combined with the vine. Ayahuasca use passed from indigenous to non-indigenous contexts in the latter part of the nineteenth century through the combined forces of inter-marriage and contact with non-indigenes working in the region (Luna 1986).

Beyond indigenous communities, ayahuasca consumption most frequently occurs in two kinds of ritual contexts. First, ayahuasca is ritually consumed within the Brazilian 'ayahuasca religions' of Barquinha, Santo Daime and the União do Vegetal. These communities have many of the formal attributes (e.g. prayers, songs and ritual disciplines) customarily associated with mainstream traditional religions like Christianity, Islam and Judaism (Dawson 2017). Second, ayahuasca is consumed within a variety of more or less formal contexts such as new religious movements, enlightenment retreats, neo-shamanic workshops, self-discovery weekends, and eco-lodges specialising in spiritual-tourism (see Gearin 2015; Homan 2016). The most common form of non-indigenous ayahuasca consumption comprises the combination of the vine *Banisteriopsis caapi* with the leaves of the shrub *Psychotria viridis*. The foliage of *P. viridis* contains the psychoactive agent N,N-Dimethyltryptamine (DMT) which intensifies and prolongs the psychotropic effects of ayahuasca con-sumption. The consumption of ayahuasca beyond its indigenous contexts is legal in Brazil when undertaken as part of a religious ritual and regulated ac-cording to a number of stipulated principles (Labate 2011). However, as other parts of the world treat DMT as a Class A/Category 1 narcotic (alongside cocaine and heroin, for example), the ritual consumption of ayahuasca outside of Brazil engenders a range of issues impacting individuals, organisations and host nations alike. These issues are addressed in more detail below.

By way of contextualising the transformative trajectory of Santo Daime, the next section delineates the most relevant branches of the daimista movement and says something more about the understanding of ritual participation as 'work in progress'. The subsequent section forms the heart of this chapter and explicates the most radical changes experienced by Santo Daime since its beginnings in 1930s' Brazil. The radical changes treated are: reportorial diversity, organisational differentiation, and ritual reconfiguration. Exploration of each is intended to furnish appreciation of the transformational impact of Santo Daime's increasingly transnational character and urban-professional profile. The chapter concludes by reflecting upon the implications of these radical changes for the Santo Daime movement and its members.

The Santo Daime 'Family'

Santo Daime as a religion comprises a number of different branches or movements, all of which claim some kind of allegiance to or immediate descent from the central 'trunk' established in the early-1930s by Raimundo Irineu Serra (1892–1971) in what is today the Brazilian state of Acre. Known by daimistas as 'Master Irineu', Raimundo Serra is believed to be the reincarnation of Jesus Christ. Master Irineu and his close band of followers founded the community of Alto Santo (literally, Holy Height) which is today located in the outer suburbs of the Acrean capital, Rio Branco. Subsequent to the succession struggles and doctrinal dissensions that ensued subsequent to Master Irineu's death, the daimista community commenced on a gradual trajectory of organisational schism and progressive ritual and theological diversification. This is not to say that Santo Daime had existed as a homogeneous and static phenomenon from the period of its emergence to the death of its founder. Throughout the approximately forty years of its existence under Irineu Serra, Santo Daime underwent a series of evolutionary developments. Most notable among these developments were the increasing moralisation of ritual and organisational formats (e.g. in respect of alcohol, tobacco and gendered distinctions), formalisation of liturgical practices (e.g. through calendars, hymnals and uniforms) and rationalisation of doctrinal content (e.g. rejection of spirit possession in favour of introspective self-scrutiny). In common with other new religious movements, however, the death of Santo Daime's founder initiated a series of events and subsequent processes that went beyond the relatively smooth transitions experienced by the movement during his life-time (Dawson 2013b).

In contrast to what went before, the term Alto Santo today designates a number of disparate units that are more or less directly descended from the foundational community led by Master Irineu. The schisms that fractured the original Alto Santo community subsequent to Irineu Serra's death principally revolved around competing leadership claims (with kinship bonds playing an important part), doctrinal disputes (not least regarding spirit possession) and organisational relations (worldly-orientation) with society at large (Oliveira 2011). Restricted to the Amazon region, the Alto Santo network is only a small part of what is now a fully blown transnational movement. Whereas independent start-ups and breakaway groups exist in Brazil and beyond, the overwhelming majority of daimista communities outside of the Amazon region and throughout the world are members of or associated with the largest branch of Santo Daime founded in the early-1970s by Sebastião Mota de Melo (1920–90). Known as 'Padrinho ('Godfather') Sebastião' by his followers, Mota de Melo is believed by many daimistas to be the reincarnation of John the Baptist. Originally converted to Santo Daime through a healing performed by Irineu Serra in 1965, Mota de Melo was leading a semi-autonomous community by the time of Irineu Serra's death in 1971, but subsequently severed all ties with Alto Santo after a failed bid to succeed Master Irineu in 1973. It should be noted, however, that the details of this period and the events relating to succession and rupture are hotly contested by the different factions involved.

The independent movement subsequently founded by Padrinho Sebastião is now the largest and most widespread of Santo Daime's various branches. Legally established in the mid-1970s as the 'Raimundo Irineu Serra Eclectic Centre of the Universal Flowing Light' (Cefluris), the movement founded by Mota de Melo is now officially titled the 'Church of the Eclectic Cult of the Universal Flowing Light' (Iceflu). Catalysed by the growing involvement of urban-professional adepts from the mid-1970s onwards, Cefluris spread from the Amazon region to conurbations such as Brasília, Rio de Janeiro and São Paulo before further expanding to various parts of the world. Headquartered at Céu do Mapiá in the state of Amazonas, Cefluris (now Iceflu) is today led by Mota de Melo's son, Alfredo Gregório de Melo ('Padrinho Alfredo') and draws the majority of its membership from urban-professionals outwith the Amazon region (Lowell and Adams 2016). Certainly, the Brazilian diaspora of the late-twentieth century played an integral part in Santo Daime's relatively rapid transnationalisation (Groisman 2013). At the same time, Santo Daime's globalisation has been facilitated through its appropriation by non-Brazilian practitioners attracted to various aspects of its inclusive religious worldview and hybridising ritual repertoire (Labate and Assis 2016). Driven by the complementary processes of transnational diaspora and transcultural appropriation, Santo Daime was first practised outside of Brazil by the late-1980s (e.g. 1987 in Argentina and the United States and 1989 in Belgium and Spain) and has subsequently spread across the American continent (North and South), throughout Europe, and in parts of Africa, Australasia and the Middle East (Dawson 2013b). Unless otherwise explicit, all references to Santo Daime hereafter refer to Cefluris/Iceflu.[1]

Daimista Ritual

The ritual repertoire of Santo Daime is highly variegated and of a transformative kind. It is, in effect, a living and evolving palimpsest whose original components are overlaid but never wholly erased by subsequent additions and ongoing developments. Although a miscellany of established and *ad hoc* ceremonies are practised in various ways by contemporary daimistas, Santo Daime's mainstay religious repertoire comprises five distinct kinds of ritual. These are: the 'Dance', 'Mass', 'Concentration', *feitio*, and rituals of spirit possession. Celebrated at other points of the year (e.g. anniversaries), the Dance rituals at which Santo Daime sings its most important hymnals are mostly scheduled relative to the traditional Catholic calendar. Although very much a modified version thereof, the daimista ritual of the Mass likewise exhibits explicit derivation from its popular Catholic counterpart. Such derivation, however, is embellished by narrative and practical components borrowed from esoteric and Spiritist repertoires. Unlike the Dance and Mass, the ritual of Concentration owes little to the popular Catholic heritage of its creators and rather reflects the introspective preoccupations of the esoteric paradigm. Literally translating as 'making' or 'manufacture', the *feitio* ritual produces ayahuasca (known as 'daime' by practitioners) by way of combining the vine *Banisteriopsis caapi* with the leaves of *Psychotria viridis*. An increasingly important aspect of the daimista repertoire, spirit possession is practised in a growing number of contexts (e.g. the rituals of Saint Michael and White Table). Along with detailed descriptions of the Concentration, Dance and Mass, the progressive significance of spirit mediumship is treated in Dawson 2013b; while a much fuller description of the *feitio* is provided by Dawson 2013a.

Although each of these rituals has its own particular rationale, they share a common concern to generate a positive spiritual current that binds participants vertically to the cosmic plane and horizontally with each other. Once generated, the spiritual current is then harnessed for the benefit of both ritual participants (physical and spiritual) and those at a distance for whom this astral energy is mobilised and projected. Nuanced relative to the ritual in question, the generation of the spiritual current at all times requires the correlation of collective effort and individual application. The collective generation of the spiritual current thereby relies upon the sustained and focused contribution of individual ritual actors, while the individual participant is woven within a web of corporate obligation that delimits autonomous action relative to the wider dynamics of communal ceremonial practice. Employed by older generations of daimistas, the designation of rituals as 'trials' reflects their often arduous and demanding nature; while the now commoner term 'work' holds similar connotations. The psychoactive effects and physiological impact of daime (i.e. ayahuasca) engender a range of challenges for the individual involving vigilance and, at times, careful management. In combination with these factors, the physical demands of often prolonged ritual participation coupled with sustained collective co-ordination makes for a doubly demanding experience. Complementing the notions of trial and work, ritual practice is discursively framed by the virtues of discipline and steadfastness that enable participants to 'remain in your place'. In so doing, ritual actors meet the collective responsibilities of ceremonial participation while reaping the subjective rewards of individual focus and application.

Diversity, Differentiation and Reconfiguration in Santo Daime

The remainder of this chapter concerns itself with delineating three complementary dynamics which respectively exemplify the increasing variegation of Santo Daime's theological worldview, organisational structures, and ritual practices. In so doing, the following discussion treats the increasing repertorial diversity, organisational differentiation, and ritual reconfiguration associated with Santo Daime's progressively transnational profile. It also explains why Santo Daime is neither theologically averse nor institutionally resistant to the practical-symbolic transformations underway.

Repertorial Diversity

The daimista movement founded by Sebastião Mota de Melo and today led by his son, Alfredo, is theologically eclectic by nature. Indeed, the inclusion of the word 'eclectic' within the names of Cefluris and Iceflu intentionally signals an organisational willingness not just to acknowledge the validity of a broad range of beliefs and practices but also to be actively disposed, where fitting, to their incorporation within Santo Daime. Labate and Assis engage the theological hybridism of Santo Daime by appropriating Gilberto Freyre's notion of 'miscibility' (*miscibilidade*). In his classic study *The Masters and the Slaves* (1986), Freyre employs the concept of miscibility (i.e. the capacity to be mixed) to explicate the openness of Brazil's Portuguese settlers to the hybridising processes of socio-cultural miscegenation associated with the colonial enterprise. Locating the same openness within the cultural context from which Santo Daime emerged, Labate and Assis (2016: 61) identify within the movement "a similar aptitude for creative confluence, exchange, and mixing with multiple religions, incorporating elements of their cosmology and ritual practice". Santo Daime's theological eclecticism is also informed by the supernatural pragmatism of its popular religious roots, in which ritual utility and material necessity trump the niceties of doctrinal particularism. Such openness to appropriating whatever beliefs and practices will do the job at hand is further catalysed by a metaphysical holism inherited from traditional esoteric, Spiritist, and New Age paradigms. Informed by this metaphysical holism, daimistas regard particular beliefs and practices as contingent historical expressions of an all-embracing universal reality. Relativised through reference to this underlying, universal Whole, the beliefs and practices of different religions and worldviews are made readily transposable from one religious repertoire to another (Dawson 2013b).

The hybridising implications of Santo Daime's eclecticism impact not only the movement as a whole but also the individual communities of which it is comprised. In effect, and for the reasons stated below, individual communities commonly embody a relatively distinct, and sometimes starkly contrasting, means of expressing the Santo Daime religion. Paralleling its hybrid and evolving worldview, the concrete manifestation of daimista religiosity within particular communities is both highly diverse and transformative. A key factor enabling the practical-symbolic diversity at play across the movement is what I have elsewhere termed Santo Daime's 'minimal orthodoxy' (Dawson 2007: 93). Here, minimal orthodoxy contrasts with the maximal orthodoxy of, for example, conservative NRMs like Scientology which demands conformity in all matters of official belief and practice across the entire institution. The minimal orthodoxy operative within Santo Daime, however, requires the conformity of its communities only in respect of particular components of its ritual repertoire (e.g. calendrical schedules, specific ritual content and certain ceremonial form). As long as affiliated groups meet designated requirements relating to these components, they are, within reason, free not only to modify existing rites but to celebrate beliefs and practices totally unconnected with received traditions.

The 'charismatic' mode of authority in operation across the movement is another contributory factor to Santo Daime's reportorial diversity. In contrast to other forms of authority (e.g. 'rational-legal' and 'traditional'), charismatic authority is intimately connected with the personality and status of an individual regarded by his or her followers as being of an extraordinary quality and exceptional nature (Weber 1991). The prevalence of charismatic modes of authority within Santo Daime facilitates an autonomous style of leadership in which local leaders enjoy a considerably broad scope of self-determination. The directive latitude enjoyed by the local leadership thereby allows the development of relatively diverse community identities as each individual leader impresses a range of discourse and practice which, at points, reflects idiosyncratic preferences as much as, if not more than, broader organisational expectations. At the same time, the relative newness of communities often entails an absence of those able to distinguish between daimista discourse and practice rooted in received traditions and recent repertorial modifications or additions instigated by charismatic leaders at a local level.

Combined with its minimal orthodoxy (along with the organisational and demographic factors discussed below), the charismatic ethos of Santo Daime engenders increasing diversity in respect of the particular beliefs and practices instantiated by individual communities. For example, in a local community influenced by Afro-Brazilian traditions (e.g. Candomblé and Umbanda), ritual behaviour and subjective experience are framed and impacted by Afro-Brazilian symbols and practices that fuse with or sit alongside established daimista beliefs and behaviours. In the same vein, communities of a traditional esoteric (e.g. Theosophy) or New Age bent likewise refract the established motifs and inherited rituals of Santo Daime in ways which engender variations in both objective corporate practice and subjective religious experience. The same dynamics apply to communities shaped by aboriginal, Druidic, indigenous, and native beliefs and practices encountered in the increasing number of contexts to which Santo Daime is spreading (e.g. Dawson 2013b; Groisman 2013; López-Pavillard and de las Casas 2011; Menozzi

2011; Rhode and Sander, 2011; Sheiner 2016). Furthermore, and as well as introducing and merging local discourse and rituals with received beliefs and practices, communities outside of Brazil frequently downplay or eradicate explicitly Christian elements inherited from Santo Daime's popular Catholic foundations (e.g. Labate, Cavnar and Assis 2016; Watt 2018).

Organisational Differentiation

Responding to the diversifying dynamics of its progressive transnationalisation, Iceflu has developed the kind of bureaucratic organs (e.g. Administrative, Doctrinal, and Financial Councils) and representative mechanisms (e.g. Regional, National, and International Assemblies) found in many traditional and mainstream religions. Exemplified by the 'Higher Doctrinal Council', for example, these institutional structures are helping to manage the operational and religious issues implicated in the movement's continuing geographical expansion (www.santodaime.org). Despite these mechanisms, and in common with other institutions undergoing rapid and relatively large-scale growth, daimista organisational structures are subject to a typically centrifugal dynamic whereby executive power and authority are incrementally dispersed outwards from a traditional centre of operations. Certainly, the family and close associates of Padrinho Alfredo and the broader Amazonian matrix continue to exert considerable influence across the daimista network. In addition to the supply of ayahuasca and formal institutional support given to those subject to state attentions (see below), the veneration of 'authentic' Amazonian spirituality personified by the leadership of Santo Daime plays a significant part in continuing to uphold their status and authority throughout the now global daimista movement. At the same time, however, the development of local community structures and regional networks in various parts of the world increasingly gives rise to organisational arrangements which, of necessity, have their own executive powers and alternate authorities. The power and authority traditionally concentrated in the administrative and spiritual heartland of the Amazon is thereby progressively dispersed and weakened in effect. Developments concerning the legalisation of daimista communities in Oregon, USA, offer a pertinent working example.

The broader processes involved, and judicial procedures undertaken in respect of the legalisation of Santo Daime in Oregon, are detailed elsewhere (Haber 2011). Of more immediate interest here, though, are the organisational dynamics associated with the Oregon communities' push for legalisation that encountered both hostility from other daimista groups across the USA and outright opposition from the Iceflu leadership based in Céu do Mapiá, Brazil. Resistance to the kind of proactive move for legalisation as that undertaken in Oregon was and continues to be informed by four factors, the latter two of which are the more substantive. The least impactful, though still influential, factor informing internal resistance to legalisation relates to an entrenched countercultural ethos among certain members of Santo Daime in various parts of the world. This countercultural ethos sits uncomfortably with the mainstreaming implications of Santo Daime's legalisation and the movement's ensuing socio-cultural normalisation. It also revels in the default clandestinity and below-the-radar tactics that, of necessity, accompany the ritual consumption of what many jurisdictions define as a Class A/Category 1 narcotic. Although in the minority, such countercultural preoccupations go some way to reinforcing other more impactful factors that inform a quasi-default resistance to proactively pursuing legalisation.

The second factor informing resistance to legalisation campaigns is the desire of certain communities to avoid what they regard as the attendant adminis-trative headaches, unduly burdensome bureaucracy and additional financial costs that would accompany the legalisation of ritual ayahuasca consumption. As legalisation would comprise an exemption from, rather than removal of, established legal restrictions in respect of DMT, the ritual use of daime would continue to be framed by and subject to a broad range of rules and require-ments. For example, the conditions under which daime is imported, stored, distributed, and financed would be stipulated in complex fashion, onerous to comply with and accompanied by numerous costs to be borne by a relatively small group of practitioners. Add to these matters the vexing issues of locally cultivating the non-indigenous (and potentially invasive) flora of vine and bush and manufacturing daime through their combination, then it is little wonder that many communities, in union with the other factors delineated, decide to eschew legalisation and thereby avoid its attendant administrative burdens.

A third more determinative factor in respect of engendering resistance to the proactive pursuit of legalisation is the very pragmatic question of: 'If the answer is "no", then what?' The sacramental character of daime (i.e. aya-huasca) makes it a *sine qua non* of ritual practice, without which Santo Daime ceases to be what it is. Certainly, the holistic worldview of daimistas allows them to regard other religions as valid means to spiritual fulfilment and the sacrament of daime as a non-exclusive aid or 'short cut' to achieving the same end (Polari de Alverga, 1999). Nevertheless, Santo Daime ritual without the sacrament of daime is, for adepts, tantamount to Christianity without Christ or Buddhism without the Buddha. Consequently, and in view of existing political wariness, established juridical frameworks and prevailing public opinion, many daimistas regard the attendant risks of declaring their hand and relying upon the sympathies of others as too great to take. Believing the odds to be stacked against success, Santo Daime has thereby eschewed the proactive pursuit of legalisation in favour of a publicity-avoidance policy embodying a 'don't ask, don't tell' approach.

The fourth, and perhaps most influential, factor informing reluctance to pursue legalisation is the significance of other naturally occurring psychoactive agents to the daimista (here, Iceflu) worldview. As with the sacrament of daime, psychotropic 'sacred plants' such as cannabis sativa, the fly agaric mushroom, the iboga shrub, and the San Pedro cactus are regarded as 'en-theogens' (Ruck *et al* 1979) by and through which the spiritual realm, or

particular aspects thereof, can be efficaciously accessed. Most commonly referred to as 'Santa Maria' (Holy Mary), cannabis is by far the most widely used
of these other psychoactives and, for a good number of daimistas, enjoys the
same kind of sacramental status as ayahuasca. The origins, ritual use and attendant sacralising discourse in respect of Santa Maria are detailed elsewhere
(e.g. Dawson 2013b; MacRae 1998). Of particular note here, though, is the
entrenched position of Santa Maria as a staple of daimista practice such that a
significant portion of the movement would rather eschew legalisation than give
up its ritual (*viz.* communal) consumption. This, however, is precisely what the
daimista communities of Oregon elected to do upon deciding to pursue the
legal right to ritually consume ayahuasca.

The pursuit of legalisation in the State of Oregon was a long, arduous and
often fraught campaign (Haber 2011). Whereas legal battles fought by daimistas have elsewhere occurred as reactions to the arrest and prosecution of
members or confiscation of daime, the Oregon group was proactive in its initial approach to the state court in the mid-2000s. Encouraged by legal developments initiated by another ayahuasca religion (the União do Vegetal), the
Oregon communities began debating moves to legalisation and, as part of this
process, consulted with the leadership at Céu do Mapiá. The leadership was,
however, strongly opposed to any proactive moves to legalisation and, up until
the very eve of the first court hearing, exerted as much pressure as possible to
get the Oregon group to withdraw from the judicial processes initiated by it. In
view of aforementioned institutional dynamics, however, the Santo Daime
leadership was ultimately powerless to stop the Oregon communities from
pursuing an organisational strategy to which it fiercely objected. Moving ahead
in defiance of the Brazil-based leadership, the Oregon group showed Iceflu to
be more an umbrella organisation of affiliated but self-determining members
than a tightly controlled, centre-led institution.

Ritual Reconfiguration

The progressive expansion of Santo Daime beyond its original Amazonian
context has coincided with the increasing dominance and practical-symbolic
impact of an urban-professional constituency. Geographical growth and demographic shift are two sides of the same coin that are reconfiguring not only
Santo Daime in particular but also the worldwide ayahuasca diaspora as a
whole (see Dawson 2016). As I've argued elsewhere (Dawson 2013b), the now
preponderant urban-professional membership's progressive remodelling of
Santo Daime's received beliefs and practices is shaped by a number of
practical-symbolic dynamics. These dynamics comprise: the *subjectivised* va-
lorisation of the individual as the ultimate arbiter of religious authority and the
primary agent of spiritual self-transformation; an *instrumental* (i.e. strategic
and reflexive) religiosity oriented to the goal of absolute self-realisation; a
holistic worldview which both grounds the individual self in an overarching
cosmic whole and relativises religious belief systems as contingent expressions

of otherwise universal truths; an *aestheticised* demeanour characterised by strong experiential preoccupations manifest through inward self-exploration and outer self-expression; a *meritocratic-egalitarianism* which is both expectant of rewards for efforts expended and qualifies traditional hierarchical structures; a *this-worldly* ethos which looks for the benefits of spiritual transformation as much in the 'here and now' of this life as in the 'there and then' of any future incarnation; and, an enhanced *religious mobility* characterised by the consecutive or concurrent participation in any number of groups and movements. In combination, these typically self-oriented dynamics qualify collective modes of belonging through their subordination to subjectivised preoccupations of an experiential, exploratory and expressive kind.

The experiential, exploratory and expressive preoccupations of Santo Daime's urban-professional membership impacts its traditional ritual repertoire in respect of, for example, divisions of ritual labour, use of ritual space and respect for ritual conventions. Customarily, Santo Daime has managed the distribution of ritual roles relative to the spiritual status and social standing of the individuals concerned. As a result, high profile ritual roles such as mediumship, the playing of musical instruments or composition of hymns were restricted in their allocation and reinforced through typically communal hierarchies and collective authority structures. The same corporate determination has also traditionally applied to the use of ritual space, with participants being assigned a particular place relative to sex, age and status and expected to remain in their allotted place until told otherwise. In the same vein, established conventions demand that ritual practitioners avoid disturbing or unduly interacting with those immediately around them and, unless appropriate, refrain from publicly disclosing the contents of visions received under the influence of daime. By way of ongoing challenges or constant transgressions, however, inherited modes of regulating ritual labour, managing ritual space and reinforcing ritual conventions are being progressively eroded and ultimately modified along typically subjectivised lines. For example, and no doubt motivated by the enhanced experiential, exploratory and expressive possibilities on offer, increasing numbers of adepts are infringing traditional restrictions upon where, when, how, and by whom spirit mediumship may be practised. Such is complemented by the expansion of those both looking to play musical instruments and claiming to receive hymns worthy of official adoption. The increasingly popular practice of publicly disclosing recently experienced visions is another indication of the ongoing transformation of inherited modes of collective determination, as is the progressive transgression of established spatial boundaries by individuals leaving their allotted place (in order to lie down or 'do my own thing') or moving to parts of ritual space traditionally out of bounds to them. The idiosyncratic customising of official ceremonial uniforms[2] is a further case in point, as is the increase in individuals interacting with or unduly disturbing their ritual co-participants (e.g. through overly flamboyant dance steps or melodramatic mediumistic practices).

As with other religious repertoires, the combined forces of globalising modernity impact Santo Daime by way of recalibrating individual–communal dynamics such that traditional forms of collective authority and corporate determination are relativized while typically subjectivised modes of self-orientation are progressively prioritised. At the same time, and albeit chiefly unintended, the subjectivised preoccupations of urban-professional daimistas refract individual engagement with received authorities and collective demands in a manner which further qualifies the established foundations of the Santo Daime repertoire and modifies its contemporary format along increasingly self-validating lines. Intimately associated with its now dominant urban-professional membership, the progressive change in the Santo Daime movement reflects a range of processes and dynamics which owe far more to the contemporary landscape of globalising modernity than they do to the Amazonian context in which the daimista repertoire was first forged. Certainly, within the overwhelming majority of Santo Daime communities, the beliefs and rituals inherited from the Amazonian context furnish a much-revered template by which individual discourse and practice are orchestrated. Nevertheless, while some communities pride themselves on their connectedness with or level of adherence to an ideal template, others do not, preferring instead to view the alterations and additions they make as legitimate variations on the daimista theme. While urban-professional members continue to articulate a deep-seated respect for the structures, beliefs and practices inherited from the Amazonian context, they view and occupy the world in ways which are markedly different from daimistas of earlier generations. Imbued with values, concerns and aspirations not straightforwardly compatible with established traditions, the now dominant urban-professional constituency is incrementally transforming Santo Daime in a manner which renders it increasingly conducive to meeting the needs and expectations associated with a typically modern and increasingly globalised existence.

Conclusion

In the earliest years of the Cefluris/Iceflu movement, close ties with Padrinho Sebastião and the Amazonian context, the mutual dependence of fledgling communities and the relative youthfulness and modest size of the Santo Daime network combined to limit the forces of repertorial diversity, organisational differentiation and subjectivising ritual reconfiguration. Traditional constraints upon the forces of diversity, differentiation and reconfiguration are, however, being incrementally diminished as each of these historical factors is eroded or cedes precedence to other influences. Nevertheless, and implicated in its ongoing transnationalisation, three dynamics continue to act as limit-factors constraining the theological, organisational and ritual impact of the combined forces of diversity, differentiation, and reconfiguration. First, practical and symbolic preoccupations with an authentic daimista experience underwrite frequent visits to and from Brazil through which personal bonds are forged and organisational ties strengthened. For example, visits to Brazilian communities (especially, Céu do Mapiá) are frequently made by leaders who are intent on reinforcing their credentials and accruing symbolic capital through association with the movement's hierarchy – not least, those descended from or having worked with foundational figures such as Padrinho Sebastião. In the same vein, staging a visit by a Brazilian dignitary or working party (e.g. teaching hymn-singing or spirit mediumship) is a popular means of strengthening ties and underwriting both individual and communal status.

Second, the overwhelming majority of Santo Daime communities around the world continue to rely on supplies of daime furnished by *feitios* undertaken in Brazil. On the one hand, hostile environmental conditions serve to limit the number of places in which vine (*B. caapi*) and leaf (*P. viridis*) can be successfully cultivated outside of South America.[3] Despite their clandestine cultivation, however, the relative scarcity and immaturity of these plants continues to limit their ability to provision domestic ayahuasca production. On the other hand, the precarious legal status of ayahuasca consumption outside of Brazil places severe restrictions on the ability to cultivate and process its constituent parts. Even in those jurisdictions where the ritual consumption of ayahuasca is protected by law, such juridical protections do not extend to the actual manufacture and distribution of ayahuasca (Labate and Feeney 2012; Tupper 2008). Managed through strategic alliances and accompanied by organisational dependencies, reliance upon Brazil to supply the sacrament of daime thereby continues to underwrite both horizontal inter-communal relations and vertical institutional hierarchies.

Third, formal organisational association with the *bona fide* religious tradition that is 'Santo Daime' goes some way to ameliorating the precarious legal position in which non-Brazilian communities commonly find themselves. While I and other academics may submit expert witness statements arguing that daimista communities subject to police action possess a sufficient number of characteristics to be legitimately defined as a 'religion' (and therefore, by implication, enjoy the rights pursuant to this definition), such arguments are both abstract and, quite literally, academic. However, when those arrested and/or prosecuted by the state can mobilise formal documentation of institutional belonging to a legal (at least elsewhere) religious entity such as Iceflu, backed up with official supporting statements by a constituted organisational leadership, the case for defence, if only in part, is mitigated in a manner better suited to the judicial arena (e.g. Haber 2011; Plas 2011; Walsh 2016). If only on pragmatic grounds as a kind of insurance policy, institutional membership of Santo Daime nevertheless entangles non-Brazilian communities within a transnational web of organisational obligations and commitments. Combined with the dynamics of authenticity and sacramental supply, the pragmatics of institutional association go some way to impacting, if not delimiting, the aforementioned processes of change (i.e. diversity, differentiation and reconfiguration) implicated in Santo Daime's ongoing transnationalisation.

Notes

1 The address of the official website of Cefluris/Iceflu is: www.santodaime.org (accessed on 5 June 2020).
2 Although differing in style and ceremonial use, ritual uniforms are employed by all three ayahuasca religions (Dawson, 2013a). Dawson elsewhere (2013b: 67–8) discusses the origins, use and modification of ritual uniforms in Santo Daime.
3 To my knowledge, and despite numerous attempts, vine and leaf have only been successfully transplanted to two other regions of the globe (Dawson, 2013a).

Bibliography

All urls accessed on 5 June 2020.

Dawson, Andrew. 2017. "Brazil's ayahuasca religions: Comparisons and Contrasts" in *Brill Handbook on Contemporary Religions in Brazil*. Steven Engler and Bettina Schmidt (eds). Leiden: Brill. pp. 233–252.

Dawson, Andrew 2016. "If Tradition Did Not Exist, It Would Have to be Invented: Retraditionalization and The World Ayahuasca Diaspora", in Beatriz C. Labate, Clancy Cavnar and Alex Gearin (eds) *The World Ayahuasca Diaspora: Reinventions and Controversies*. London: Routledge. pp. 19–37.

Dawson, Andrew 2013a. "Making Matter Matter: The Santo Daime Ritual of Feitio", *Making Spirits: Materiality and Transcendence in Contemporary Religion*. Nico Tassi and Diana Espirito Santo (eds) London: I. B. Tauris, 229–252.

Dawson, Andrew 2013b. *Santo Daime: A New World Religion*. London: Bloomsbury.

Dawson, Andrew 2007. *New Era – New Religions: Religious Transformation in Contemporary Brazil*. Aldershot: Ashgate.

Freyre, Gilberto. 1986. *The Masters and the Slaves: A Study in the Development of Brazilian Civilization*. Berkeley: University of California Press.

Gearin, Alex. K. 2015. ""Whatever you want to believe": Kaleidoscopic individualism and ayahuasca healing in Australia." *The Australian Journal of Anthropology*, 26(3): 442–455.

Groisman, Alberto. 2013. "Transcultural Keys: Humor, Creativity and Other Relational Artifacts in the Transposition of a Brazilian Ayahuasca Religion to the Netherlands" in *The Diaspora of Brazilian Religions*. Cristina Rocha and Manuel Vásquez (eds). Leiden: Brill. pp. 363–385.

Haber, Roy. 2011. "The Santo Daime Road to Seeking Religious Freedom in the USA" in *The Internationalization of Ayahuasca*. Beatriz C. Labate and Henrik. Jungaberle (eds). Berlin: LIT Verlag. pp. 301–318.

Homan, Joshua. 2016. "Disentangling the Ayahuasca Boom: Local Impacts in Western Peruvian Amazonia", in *The World Ayahuasca Diaspora: Reinventions and Controversies*. Beatriz C. Labate, Clancy Cavnar and Alex K. Gearin (eds). Abingdon: Routledge. pp. 165–181.

Labate, Beatriz. C. 2011. "Comments on Brazil's 2010 resolution regulating ayahuasca use" in *Curare*, 34(4): 298–304.

Labate, Beatriz C. and Assis, Glauber L. de. 2016. "The Religion of the Forest: Reflections on the International Expansion of a Brazilian Ayahuasca Religion" in *The World Ayahuasca Diaspora: Reinventions and Controversies*. Beatriz. C. Labate, Clancy Cavnar and Alex K. Gearin (eds). Abingdon: Routledge. pp. 57–76.

Labate, Beatriz C., Cavnar, Clancy and Assis, Glauber L. de. 2016. "Religious Battle: Musical Dimensions of the Santo Daime Diaspora." *The World*

Ayahuasca Diaspora: Reinventions and Controversies. Beatriz C. Labate, Clancy Cavnar and Alex K. Gearin (eds). Abingdon: Routledge. pp. 99–121.

Labate, Beatriz C. and Feeney, Kevin. 2012. "Ayahuasca and the process of regulation in Brazil and internationally: implications and challenges" in *The International Journal of Drug Policy*, 23: 154–161.

López-Pavillard, Santiago and de las Casa, Diego. 2011. "Santo Daime in Spain: a Religion with a Psychoactive Sacrament" in *The Internationalization of Ayahuasca*. Beatriz C. Labate and Henrik Jungaberle (eds). Berlin: LIT Verlag. pp. 365–374.

Lowell, Jonathan T. and Adams, Paul C. 2016. "The routes of a plant: ayahuasca and the global networks of Santo Daime" in *Social & Cultural Geography*. Published online: http://www.tandfonline.com/doi/full/10.1080/14649365.2016.1161818.

Luna, L. Eduardo. 1986. *Vegetalismo: Shamanism Among the Mestizo Population of the Peruvian Amazon*. Stockholm: Almqvist and Wiksell International.

MacRae, Edward. 1998. "Santo Daime and Santa Maria – The Licit Ritual Use of Ayahuasca and the Illicit Use of Cannabis in a Brazilian Amazonian Religion" in *The International Journal of Drug Policy*, 9: 325–338.

Menozzi, Walter. 2011. "The Santo Daime Legal Case in Italy" in *The Internationalization of Ayahuasca*. Beatriz C. Labate and Henrik Jungaberle (eds). Berlin: LIT Verlag. pp. 379–388.

Oliveira, Isabela 2011. "Um desafio ao respeito e à tolerância: reflexões sobre c campo religioso daimista na atualidade" in *Religião e Sociedade*, 31(2): 154–178.

Plas, Adele V.D. 2011. "Ayahuasca under International Law: The Santo Daime Churches in the Netherlands" in *The Internationalization of Ayahuasca*. Beatriz C. Labate and Henrik Jungaberle (eds). Berlin: LIT Verlag. pp. 327–338.

Polari de Alverga, Alex. 1999. *Forest of Visions: Ayahuasca, Amazonian Spirituality and the Santo Daime Tradition*. Rochester: Park Street Press.

Rhode, Silvio A. and Sander, Hajo. 2011. "The Development of the Legal Situation of Santo Daime in Germany" in *The Internationalization of Ayahuasca*. Beatriz C. Labate and Henrik Jungaberle (eds). Berlin: LIT Verlag. pp. 339–352.

Ruck, Carl A. P., Bigwood, Jeremy, Staples, Danny, Ott, Jonathan and Wasson, R. Gordon. 1979. "Entheogens" in *Journal of Psychoactive Drugs*, 11(1/2): 145–146.

Sheiner, Eli O. 2016. "Culling the Spirits: An Exploration of Santo Daime's Adaptation in Canada" in *The World Ayahuasca Diaspora: Reinventions and Controversies*. Beatriz C. Labate, Clancy Cavnar and Alex K. Gearin (eds). Abingdon: Routledge. pp. 79–97.

Tupper, Kenneth. W. 2008. "The globalization of ayahuasca: harm reduction or benefit maximization?" in *The International Journal of Drug Policy*, 19: 297–303.

Walsh, Charlotte. 2016. "Ayahuasca in the English Courts: Legal Entanglements with the Jungle Vine" in *The World Ayahuasca Diaspora: Reinventions and Controversies*. Beatriz C. Labate, Clancy Cavnar and Alex. Gearin (eds). London: Routledge. pp. 243–260.

Watt, Gillian. 2018. "Santo Daime in a 'post-Catholic' Ireland" in *The Expanding World Ayahuasca Diaspora: Appropriation, Integration and Legislation*. Beatriz C. Labate and Clancy Cavnar (eds). London: Routledge. pp. 61–75.

Weber, Max. 1991. "The Sociology of Charismatic Authority" in *From Max Weber: Essays in Sociology*. Hans H. Gerth and Charles W. Mills (eds). New Edition. London: Routledge. pp. 245–252.

7   A Song of Wood and Water: the ecofeminist turn in 1970s–1980s British Paganism

Shai Feraro

This chapter will highlight the turn towards ecofeminist ideology and praxis among adherents of Contemporary Paganism(s) in the Western world and will centre on its emergence during the 1970s and 1980s. Focusing the analysis on Britain, the Pagan magazine scene of the period will be examined, with *Wood and Water* – a feminist-inclined Pagan publication – and the milieu associated with it serving as a case study. Following an introduction to Contemporary Paganism and Goddess Feminism, I will broadly examine the rise and development of feminist and ecological discourses within the Pagan milieu and then proceed to focus on *Wood and Water* magazine, the ecofeminist community that revolved around it, and its embeddedness in the British Pagan scene during the late 1970s and throughout the 1980s.

Contemporary Paganism and Goddess Feminism

The contemporary revival of Paganism in the Western world owes much of its existence to Gerald Gardner (1884–1964), a retired British civil servant, who embarked upon a quest to revive what he had described as the ancient religion of pagan witchcraft (or Wicca, as it came to be known) during the late 1940s and early 1950s. In the years following Gardner's death, Wicca evolved into the most widely known and influential of the denominations that comprise Contemporary Paganism today (Hutton 1999). All Wiccans characterise themselves, by definition, as Witches as well as Pagans. However, not all of the individuals who subscribe to the broader definition of 'Witch' would also characterise themselves as Wiccan. Indeed, some – especially in the UK – would be at pains to point out that they are 'not Wiccan'.[1] A further complication is caused by the inclination of many individuals in the United States – especially of the 'Teen Witch' variety (Berger and Ezzy 2007; Johnston and Aloi 2007; Lewis 2012) – to identify as Wiccans, although they have not undergone initiation into a coven which subscribes to one of the branches of the religion. In Britain, and more generally in Europe, these individuals are recognised as 'Pagan,' but not as 'Wiccan.' The label 'Pagan,' in turn, includes both initiated Wiccans and non-initiates who are influenced by a Wiccan-derived Paganism, but also those who follow Druidry or Heathenry. Up until

DOI: 10.4324/9781315226804-7

the late 1980s and early 1990s, however, the Pagan community in Britain was dominated almost exclusively by Wiccans and by Wicca-inspired Pagans and Witches (Hutton 1999: 374).

There exists a clear and direct correlation between Contemporary Paganism and Goddess Feminism, as both movements call for restoring the connections between human beings, the natural world, and the Sacred Feminine (Eller 1993; Rountree 2004; King 1989; Griffin 2005). That is not to say that all spiritual feminists would also subscribe to a 'Pagan' label. Indeed, spiritual feminists can be divided into three overlapping and interacting groups (Raphael 1999). The first is a large core of women who define themselves as feminist Witches/Wiccans who act either in a coven or as solitaries (Rountree 2004; Salomonsen 2002). The second group contains women who practise in ritual and study groups that do not regard themselves as Wiccan or necessarily as Pagan. Here, I shall describe them as 'Goddess Feminists' (Eller 1993; Griffin 2005). Most of them understand 'the Goddess' as a liberating metaphor, or as a symbol of their own personal and political energies, while some do see her as a real and independent force. The third group – who will not be dealt with in this chapter – consists of spiritual feminists who keep their Jewish/Christian identity and try to bring about feminist changes within the Judeo-Christian traditions.

Feminism, ecology, and the new animism in Contemporary Paganism(s)

By the time of Gardner's death in 1964, Wiccan ideology and ritual praxis had already included important 'naturist' elements such as the celebration of nudity and rurality, no doubt due to its main propagator's interest in nudism and due to the influence of Romanticism on British occultism in general. By 1964, Wicca had 'emigrated' to America due to the work of Raymond Buckland (b. 1934), an initiate of Gardner, who brought knowledge of the new 'Old' religion with him back to America (Clifton 2006: 15, 24). It was during the 1960s–70s – as America was evolving into the new centre for Pagan thought and activity – that the religion of Wicca came under the influence of 'second-wave' radical and cultural feminism(s) and the ecology movement. Radical feminist thought developed in the United States during the late 1960s out of the dissatisfaction of some women who were working within the 'male-dominated' political left, and as a reaction to the so-called 'second-wave' liberal feminism. Early radical feminists claimed that women, oppressed by the universal patriarchy, must break away from male institutions, culture, and language and form a new women's movement. Some researchers claim that by the mid-1970s, a new tendency had developed within radical feminism, called cultural feminism.[2]

While early radical feminists focused simply on the elimination of what they understood as a gender-based class system, cultural feminists emphasised biological differences between males and females in their quest to recreate what they understood to be female values and nature, long defaced by the rule of patriarchy. These brands of feminism were to become a dominant transforming force within the American Pagan movement (Berger 1999: 13, 46; Raphael 1999: 31, 119; Greenwood 2005: 185–6; Griffin 1995: 40), and as the 1970s drew to a close, that influence was already evident in the US through the writings of Miriam 'Starhawk' Simos (b. 1951) and Zsuzsanna Emese Mokcsay (b. 1940), who developed feminist and Dianic Witchcraft, respectively, becoming by far the most popular spokespersons for the American Pagan community (Melton and Poggi 1992: 209; Starhawk 1989 [1979]; Budapest 1999 [1980]). As I show elsewhere, Goddess Spirituality and feminist interpretations of Wicca soon found their way across the Atlantic, and the contacts and cross-fertilisations between British Wiccans, Goddess women, and feminist Witches that existed during this period contributed to the shaping of contemporary British Paganism (Feraro 2013).

The feminist turn that swept through large significant sections of the Pagan milieu in both the United States and Britain was also accompanied by the adoption of an ecological discourse. This was mainly due to the popularity of James Lovelock's 'Gaia Hypothesis', which maintained that the earth's ecosystem behaved as a single, live, organism (Hutton 1999: 352–5). At the turn of the 1980s, ecological concerns coalesced with feminist discourse and ecofeminist campaigning groups with a significant Pagan presence began to emerge. The Women and Life on Earth group was formed in the United States during March 1980 and by November 1980 had carried out the Women's Pentagon Action. Starhawk, for instance, joined with 300 other women in San Francisco in organising a ritual demonstration in support of the thousands of women who marched on the Pentagon and was arrested together with 1900 other protestors during the Abalone Alliance's ten-day blockade of the Diablo Canyon Nuclear Power Plant in 1981, which was also the site of similar rituals (Starhawk 1982).

Meanwhile, in Britain, a Women and Life on Earth network was founded in September 1980, with Stephanie Leland, an American expatriate, serving as its national coordinator. Later renamed as Women for Life on Earth, on September 1981 the organisation sponsored a group of 39 women and children (and a few men) who arrived at the entrance to the Greenham Common military airbase after a nine-day walk from Cardiff in order to protest the plan to place 96 American nuclear Cruise missiles within it as deterrent against the Soviet Union. Upon arrival, the marchers established a peace camp near the main entrance to the base. The peace camp – which quickly became a 'women-only' space – was the scene of large-scale radical feminist protest activities which included a significant presence by Goddess women and feminist/Dianic Witches throughout the 1980s (Feraro 2016).

During the latter part of the decade, the Paganlink Network, which served as a campaigning organisation and information service for newcomers to Paganism in Britain, became increasingly associated with 'political' ecologically minded rituals. One of Paganlink's key activists was Rich Westwood (d. 1989), who co-edited the Pagan magazine *Moonshine* with his wife Kate. In 1989, Westwood co-published a booklet titled *Awakening the Dragon: Practical Paganism, Political Ritual and Active Ecology*, which drew directly from Starhawk's *Dreaming the Dark* and encouraged 'Pagans to mix ritual and magical practices with political action ...' (Letcher 2004: 183–4).

By the 1990s, the main site of struggle for ecopagans shifted to the road protests movement, which challenged the government's plans for building a new bypass and highway expansions with non-violent resistance, protest camps, and political rituals. These rituals were led by the Dragon Environmental Group that was founded in 1990 with an initial membership of about 30 London-based Pagans and occultists, and which peaked in 1996 with 300 members, organised across the country in 13 local groups (Letcher 2004: 186–7).

The 2000s ushered in a development in both academic and practitioner-based discourses on animism, which is being transformed from its earlier Victorian definition as the belief in spirits residing in trees, rivers, stones etc. to an understanding of human existence in terms of a relationship with the larger-than-human world, a world inhabited by myriad other-than-human beings. These discourses on 'new animism' and 'Dark Green Religion', propagated within academia by figures such as Graham Harvey and Bron Taylor, are simultaneously informed by developments among Pagan practitioners while being debated by Pagans themselves (Harvey 2005, 2014; Taylor 2009).

Wood and Water magazine

The remainder of this chapter will illustrate the ecofeminist turn in British Paganism during the late 1970s and throughout the 1980s by focusing on *Wood and Water* magazine – the first specifically feminist-inclined Pagan publication to appear on the British scene – and the community that revolved around it during said period as a case study.

The magazine was the brainchild of Hilary Llewellyn Williams and Tony Patfield, who both shared a passion for the preservation and veneration of sacred wells. Llewellyn-Williams had 'long been attracted to Wicca without ever having been involved in a coven' (H.L.W. 1981: 24). In the autumn of 1978, the two published a short leaflet on the subject and the interest it attracted eventually led to the publication of the first issue of *Wood and Water* in 1979. During its first couple of years, the scope of the magazine broadened into a wider ecopaganism, with an emphasis on 'the restoration of female values and the primacy of the Goddess' (Llewelyn Williams and Padfield 1981aLlewelyn Williams Llewelyn Williams 1981; Hilary and Tony 1980, 9–11). *Wood and Water*'s emphasis on Goddess Feminism was called into question early on by some of the early subscribers, who were interested primarily in wells and were not necessarily Pagan.

This prompted Llewellyn-Williams to clarify the importance, in her mind, of Goddess primacy and matriarchal societies' presumed peacefulness vis-à-vis patriarchal 'aggressive and competitive values', as well as their 'cyclical [...] life-centreed' time perception compared to 'continuous', 'industrial', and 'death-centreed' patriarchal time (Llewelyn Williams 1979). Her sources were Penelope Shuttle (b. 1947) and Peter Redgrove's (1932–2003) *The Wise Wound*, an article by Goddess Feminist Monica Sjöö on menstruation – which appeared in her Pamphlet *Women are the Real Left* – as well a piece titled 'Towards a Matriarchal Manifesto', which appeared in the London Matriarchy Study Group's *The Politics of Matriarchy* pamphlet (Llewelyn Williams 1979).[3] Sjöö made similar claims in an editorial published in the magazine's fifth issue and added that it aimed at challenging '[t]he oppression of [...] mechanistic society' – signalling her influence by Carolyn Merchant's (b. 1936) prominent book, *The Death of Nature* ('Editorial' 1980).

During April 1980, *Wood and Water* organised a spring gathering in a Quaker Meeting House at Pickering, Yorkshire (on the edge of the North York Moors National Park), which was also publicised in advance by *The Cauldron*, an important British magazine representing practitioners of Wicca and Witchcraft ("The Wood & Water Gathering 4–7 April, 1980. 1979/1980"; "Ecopagan Gathering" 1980). Matriarchy and matrifocality were among the subjects debated in the gathering's discussion groups.[4] In its wake, plans for a nationwide, loose network of active and autonomous spiritual/ecology 'Gaia' groups – which would keep contact with other ecological and feminist organisations – were announced in the summer of 1980 in both *Wood and Water* and *The Cauldron* (H & T., 1980: 6; "Eco News" 1980).

In 1981, Llewellyn-Williams and Padfield announced an initiative to establish the 'Spiral Centre [...] a Free School, Education and Resource Centre based on a mixed Matrifocal Pagan Community':

> The key feature of Spiral Centre will be the primacy of women, round which the whole Spiral will revolve. The community will be organized around the rhythms and needs of women and young children; women and men will work side by side as loving and respected equals, but in all important decisions affecting the life of the community and its work women will determine the final outcome – and in spiritual matters will be the initiators and creators. This 'positive discrimination' is for good reason. Our very existence will be a challenge to patriarchy and an alternative to patriarchal values. [...] We believe that the ancient matriarchies were peaceful, filled with positive energy [...] and we will be working to re-awaken the spirit of the Goddess-centreed communities of old, adapted to our needs in the present times. (Llewelyn Williams and Padfield 1981b)

A second weekend 'Wood and Water Spring Gathering' was held at Cwmdulais Farm (set in rural southern Wales) in May 1981 to celebrate Beltane. One visitor and performer from overseas who stayed for the duration of the gathering was Batya Podos – an American feminist who had been initiated into a British Hereditary Witchcraft tradition in the States.[5] Advertisements for both *Wood and Water* and the gathering were inserted in the March 1981 issue of *Spare Rib*.[6] Monica Sjöö (1938–2005) and Rufus Brock Maychild (who co-founded Pagans Against Nukes and co-edited its organ, *The Pipes of PAN*) participated in the gathering as well.[7] Recently, Maychild recalled that the participants at this gathering "were a motley bunch of [... the magazine's] subscribers", and at least one of them – Ken Rees – was a Wiccan initiate.[8]

Changes in the magazine's editorial makeup

Wood and Water's pioneering ecofeminist vision in the British Pagan scene was not met with the enthusiasm hoped for by its editors, though, and by late February to early March of 1981, Llewellyn-Williams felt that the their original aim, of initiating

> a *network of people* [sic] to care for and reclaim sacred springs, i.e., who would go out [sic] and look for wells that needed attention[...], [...] meet together from time to time, and keep in touch through Wood & Water[...] hasn't happened,

and that '[i]deas like "Gaian groups" evoked little response' as well.[9] By August 1981, Llewellyn-Williams and Padfield had 'lost the energy, will, time and finances to continue producing' the magazine (Hilary and Tony 1981: 1–2). Subsequently, *Wood and Water* was edited by a London-based collective, and following the relocation of two of its members, the task of editing was subsequently carried out by Daniel Cohen (b. 1934) and Jan Henning.[10] Some readers, such as Nicola Miles, felt uneasy with what they described as a turn towards a matriarchal 'hardcore' feminist discourse and wrote that

> it seems that the magazine is in some danger of moving away from gentle, Goddess-oriented Earth Magic and into the realm of feminism/politics, which I feel would be a great shame. I noticed a tendency to promote matriarchy as preferable to patriarchy, which it may well be, but the promoters of this idea seem to have forgotten that the natural order of things does consist of both male and female elements and that in order to achieve a balanced and harmonious universe both sexes must co-operate with each other [...] (Editorial Collective 1981: 2–3)[11]

This 'unbalanced' approach, as Miles described it, was already visible in the magazine's first incarnation, in an article titled "Mother Earth, Father Sky… Beware of the Patriarchal Lie!" by Goddess Feminist Janet McCrickard (b. 1952), who argued against the relegation of the Goddess to the position of Earth Mother, fertilised by a male Sky Father. This, claimed McCrickard, was an act of dismemberment perpetrated by patriarchy:

> in confining the Goddess to the earth, patriarchy buries Her, entombs Her… establishing that polarity where activity, will, fire and the spirit are part of exalted or 'higher' being, i.e. maleness. Father Sky is high and dry, while down beneath him lies Mother Earth, waiting – for what? to be got pregnant by his thunderbolts, for she has no fruitfulness of her own – will, conception, […] creativity are all inevitably contained in the image of Father Sky. The essence and purpose of the Earth Mother/Sky Father theme is the justification of male power; […] Each time the lie is reiterated, the Goddess is raped, dismembered, buried. (McCrickard 1981: 14)

Influenced by Mary Daly (1928–2010), McCrickard added that this reflected another example of patriarchy's 'devious reversals'[12] and called on women to 'reclaim the true images [of the goddess] … [in] a process of exorcism. It is', continued McCrickard, 'as Mary Daly says, "RE-MEMBERING" [sic] the dismembered Goddess' (McCrickard 1981: 14).[13] In effect, McCrickard was urging women active in the British Pagan scene to enact a revision of Wiccan-based dualistic male-female polarity in terms of its cosmology, theology, and daily ritual praxis, in much the same way as was previously done by American Dianic Witches. In the aftermath of McCrickard's article, the magazine's editors reported receiving two negative comments from male readers which (in their eyes) 'managed to combine triviality, manipulative-ness, aggression and self-pity in various proportions'.[14]

The fluctuations *Wood and Water* underwent during the turbulent early 1980s can be observed by monitoring the changes in the way its editors chose to describe the magazine in advertisements placed in another Pagan publication – *The Cauldron*. Around August 1981, as Llewellyn-Williams and Padfield co-edited their last *Wood and Water* issue, it was described as an 'Ecopagan/Gaian magazine featuring holy wells & sacred springs' (The Cauldron 1981a: 8). Under the new editorial board, the pre-existing feminist element was highlighted and the magazine was described during late 1981 as a 'radical ecopagan, anarch-feminist magazine dedicated to the sacred places and the ways of the Goddess and the God' (The Cauldron 1981b: 8). By early 1982 – perhaps in reaction to the concerns raised above by subscribers such as Nicola Miles, this radical element was dialed down somewhat and the magazine was being described as an 'ecopagan magazine dedicated to the sacred places and the God and Goddess' (The Cauldron 1982a: 8). In May of that year, it has become a 'feminist influenced, ecologically minded, Goddess centreed magazine' (The Cauldron 1982b: 8), and the following August its description finally became secured as a 'feminist, ecological Goddess centreed magazine' (The Cauldron 1982c: 8).

Ken Rees, who was involved in the magazine's earlier incarnation, resigned from the new editorial collective in protest at 'the censorship applied to balanced criticism of extreme feminist views and object[ed] to the development of WW in the direction of one-sided matriarchal feminism to the exclusion of more moderate views' (Editorial Collective 1981: 2–3). He obviously included Starhawk as a representative of the latter view, since his book review – published in the same issue – hailed *The Spiral Dance* as 'a sophisticated text where virtually every line conveys meaning and vitality'. He particularly recommended chapter two, on the Worldview of Witchcraft, and chapter six, on the Horned God, and concluded that '[i]t is perhaps an open question as to how many groups in this country provide for their members the level of intellectual awareness or degree of systematic training found in Starhawk's covens' (Rees 1981: 23).

Wood and Water's embeddedness in the Pagan and Goddess Spirituality milieus

Since its inception, *Wood and Water* was connected with the Goddess Spirituality scenes in both the United States and Britain. Hilary Llewellyn-Williams contributed a poem to a 1982 issue of *Womanspirit* magazine,[15] and *Wood and Water* published details on the 1982 Goddess Rising conference, which was organised in Sacramento by Ann Forfreedom and included speeches by many American Pagan luminaries such as Starhawk, Margot Adler (1946–2014), Selena Fox, and Carol Christ (Llewelyn Williams 1982: 13; *Wood and Water* 1981: 16). Furthermore, in a piece written several years later for the British-based *Matriarchy Research and Reclaim Network Newsletter* (*MRRN*), Monica Sjöö noted that the *Wood and Water* was probably known to many *MRRN* readers (Sjöö 1990). The Greenham Common cause received full backing as well. In late 1980, *Wood and Water* published an extract from *The Pipes of PAN*'s first issue simultaneously with the latter's debut (Wood and Water 1980c). It also included the initial call by Women for Life on Earth regarding the march from Cardiff to Greenham, which culminated in the founding of the Women's Peace Camp (Anon 1981: 17). Hilary Llewellyn-Williams likewise took part in the 'Embrace the Base' demonstration at Greenham in December 1982 and wrote a report on the proceedings for the magazine.[16]

Under the new co-editor, Daniel Cohen – who produced the magazine between 1981 and 2003 – *Wood and Water* continued with its commitment and connection to Goddess Feminism and feminist Witchcraft. Cohen hails from a Jewish background and was raised by atheist parents. His interest in spirituality developed during the mid-1970s around the age of forty after reading Merlin Stone's (1931–2011) *The Paradise Papers* and via Colin

Murray's (1942–1986) Golden Section Order[17] – whose rituals he attended with Asphodel Long (1921–2005) and other women who were active in the London Matriarchy Study Group. Growing up during the war, Cohen was accustomed as a child to women performing what had previously considered 'male' jobs, such as law and medicine, and consequently developed a liberal feminist political view as he matured.[18] During the latter half of the 1970s, he was a member of Alternative Socialism, together with Asphodel Long and other members of the London Matriarchy Study Group.[19] Cohen had no close acquaintances who were part of a Wiccan coven as late as May 1980 and had met only a few 'men who described themselves as pagan' during the preceding months.[20] On the eve of May Day 1980, through his contact with Asphodel Long of the London Matriarchy Study Group, Cohen took part in a full moon walk up the maze of the Glastonbury Tor which was set up by Kathy Jones (b. 1947)[21] and Geoffrey Ashe[22] (a proponent of Arthurian legends) and included Monica Sjöö as well.

Cohen read *The Spiral Dance* during April 1980 and immediately wrote to Starhawk, noting that he was 'very taken by it' (Letter from Danny Cohen to Starhawk). He applauded her for developing a tradition of feminist spirituality which 'gives the God, and so men, a place which is highly important without, as too often happens, his usurping the place of the Goddess' (Letter from Danny Cohen to Starhawk). Cohen visited the 1982 Goddess Rising conference, which was organised by the feminist Witch Ann Forfreedom in California and included Starhawk (and many others) among its speakers. He joined Starhawk's 1982 tour of Ireland and made connections with some of its American participants (Personal Interview with Daniel Cohen). Cohen was on good terms with her (she later stayed in his London flat during her 1985 visit to the UK), and in May 1982, he announced to the readers of *Wood and Water* that he could get some copies of *Dreaming the Dark* – which was to be published during the late summer – directly from Starhawk (*Wood and Water* 1982: 13; Starhawk 1987: 252). He reviewed the book in a later issue of *Wood and Water* in an overall positive manner but took issue with Starhawk for failing to refer to the potential problems which could arise in mixed ritual and political groups (due to deeply set patriarchal conditioning) (Cohen 1983: 12). His close relationship with Asphodel Long, who co-authored a paper titled 'Is it Worthwhile Working in a Mixed Group?', no doubt affected this.[23] Vicky Noble's *Motherpeace – A Way to the Goddess Through Myth, Art and Tarot* (1983), and its accompanying tarot pack, were also reviewed in *Wood and Water* during the spring of 1984 (Henning 1984: 16; Catriona 1984). Cohen himself read many radical and cultural feminist texts, and as late as 1987, Cohen referred to Susan Griffin (b. 1943) – author of *Woman and Nature: The Roaring Inside Her* (1978) – as 'one of the most profound and moving feminist writers' (Personal Interview with Daniel Cohen; Cohen 1987: 5-6).[24]

Another noted contributor and supporter of *Wood and Water* was archaeologist, Wiccan initiate, and a rotating Magister of the Cornish-based

Cuilna Sidhe coven – Jo O'Cleirigh.[25] O'Cleirigh was first introduced to feminist ideas by a lesbian friend during the mid-1970s and began to feel that Goddess Spirituality 'balanced the somewhat conservative Wicca... [he] was studying' at the time.[26] O'Cleirigh was involved in *Wood and Water* almost from its inception and began writing for the magazine in late 1979 (O'Cleirigh 1979/1980). His vision for *Wood and Water*'s 'Gaia Groups' derived 'some important insights' from Starhawk's *The Spiral Dance*.[27] Several months later he also quoted from the book in a review essay on 'Native Peoples, Womanspirit and Neopaganism', terming it 'a classic in Neopagan literature' (O'Cleirigh 1981: 13). The essay was dedicated mainly to Margot Adler's *Drawing Down the Moon* (1979), which made O'Cleirigh 'realise far more than I have... which people and groups in the American scene most harmonise with my own views, and with ... the ... ethos of wood & water' (O'Cleirigh 1981: 13). He also called for *Wood and Water* subscribers to give more support to local Goddess Feminists such as Monica Sjöö and the women of the Matriarchy Study Group (13). O'Cleirigh eventually met Starhawk in 1984, and the two 'spent a lot of time together in Cornwall and Glastonbury'.[28]

Another writer closely associated with *Wood and Water* – and who, incidentally, also met Starhawk during the latter's 1985 visit to the UK (Sjöö 1989a: 5) – was Goddess Feminist Monica Sjöö, who wrote several pieces for the magazine,[29] and attended its 1981 Beltane Gathering.[30] In a two-part article titled 'No Real Changes: Continuing Sexist Assumptions in the "New Age"', published in *Wood and Water*'s Samhain 1981 and Beltane 1982 issues, Sjöö voiced her continuing discontent with the Wiccan insistence of acknowledging a male aspect of the divine. While the editors of *Wood and Water* described it at the time as a 'feminist influenced, ecologically minded, Goddess centreed magazine' (See ad in *The Cauldron* 1982b: 8), it certainly had a wider readership and Sjöö's piece attracted so many critical and supporting response letters that after two issues the magazine editors decided to conclude the subject by printing just one more response. This letter's writer was Michael Howard (1948–2015) of *The Cauldron*, which was one of the two most important British Pagan magazines at that time and was not feminist-influenced. Howard expressed agreement with much of Sjöö's view regarding women's oppression and validated her individual choice of acknowledging only the female aspect of the divine.[31] A year earlier, he reviewed Sjöö and Mor's *The Ancient Religion of the Great Cosmic Mother* in *The Cauldron* and heralded it as an 'academic tour-de-force... which should be on every Pagan's book shelf as a standard reference work' (Howard 1981: 8). As I argue elsewhere (Feraro 2015), this was clearly a change from British Wiccans' negative attitudes towards Goddess Feminists and Dianic Witches during the mid-1970s, exemplified by John Score's treatment of lesbian separatist Dianics as an abomination over the pages of *The Wiccan* – organ of the Pagan Front (John Score, alias 'M.' 1976: 1).

Conclusions

This chapter has focused on the ecofeminist turn among adherents of Contemporary Paganism(s) in the Western world, with an emphasis on its emergence during the 1970s and 1980s. The period's British Pagan magazine scene has been analysed – with an emphasis on *Wood and Water* and the milieu associated with it – in order to show the turn, in comparison with 1950s–1960s Gardnerian and Alexandrian Wicca. It should be noted, of course, that *Wood and Water* was by no means the only British Pagan magazine to have centred on a combination of ecological and feminist activism during the 1970s and 1980s. *The Pipes of PAN*, the mouthpiece of Pagans Against Nukes, was another prime example, and magazines associated with Paganlink, such as Rich and Kate Westwood's *Moonshine* or Phil Hine's *Pagan News*, had somewhat similar leanings. *Greenleaf* centred on ecopaganism, and more 'mainstream' Pagan publications such as *The Cauldron* and *The Wiccan* frequently contained debates on these issues. During the 1970s and 1980s, encounters with ecologically minded feminist Witches and Goddess Feminists forced British Wiccans and Wiccan-derived Pagans to react – as well as occasionally to change and adapt – to the ecofeminist challenge. This cross-fertilisation between British Wiccans and feminist Witches and Goddess Feminists greatly contributed to the shaping of contemporary British Paganism, and its fruits became visible during the 1990s road protest movement and the 'new animism' discourse of the early 21st century.

Notes

1 These would include, for instance, feminist Witches influenced by Starhawk (b. 1951), whose Reclaiming tradition fuses Wicca with radical and cultural feminist ideologies. Another example would be the adherents of 'British Traditional Witchcraft', who claim to follow a path which pre-dates Gardner's Wicca teachings. To further complicate matters, in the United States, the term 'British Traditional Witchcraft' or BTW is often used to refer to initiatory-based Wicca.

2 The term 'cultural feminism' was coined by a radical feminist called Brooke Williams, who defined it as '[a] belief that women will be freed through an alternative female culture'. Researcher Alice Echols used and expanded this term significantly. See (Echols 1983; 1991 [1989]).

3 For a study of the Matriarchal Study Groups that operated in Britain during the latter half of the 1970s and throughout the 1980s see (Komatsu 1986).

4 See the letter from John Billingsley in the letters section in *Wood and Water* (1980a: 21).

5 From a brochure for the gathering, found clipped to the second issue of *Wood and Water*, housed in the Museum of Witchcraft's library.

6 Letter from Hilary Llewellyn-Williams and Tony Padfield to 'Phillip', [n.d.], found clipped to the second issue of *Wood and Water*, housed in the Museum of Witchcraft's library.

7 Personal correspondence with Rufus Brock Maychild, March 2014. For more information on Pagans Against Nukes, which was another important group that combined feminism with ecological discourse during the 1980s, see Feraro (2019).

8 Personal correspondence with Rufus Brock Maychild, March 2014.
9 Letter from Hilary Llewellyn-Williams and Tony Padfield to 'Phillip'.
10 Also, personal email correspondence with Daniel Cohen, 22 October 2014.
11 See her comment in 'Letters' (1982: 22).
12 Daly claimed that patriarchy operates by way of 'reversals', or debasements of female values and ideas. This happens because 'the female self is the Otherworld to the patriarchs, their intent is to close... [women] off from... [their] own selves, deceiving' them by turning positive female qualities and myths as weapons against them (Daly 1978: 46–7).
13 Her references section sported the 1980 edition of Daly's *Gyn/Ecology*, published in the UK by The Women's press (McCrickard 1981: 14).
14 Letter from Hilary Llewellyn-Williams and Tony Padfield to Phillip. It is worth noting that a quick browse through the issues of *Wood and Water* would show McCrickard seems to have been part of its inner circle of contributors. Furthermore, copies of the letter– which included a plea for help in continuing to run the magazine – were sent to a small group of individuals who included McCrickard as well as Monica Sjöö, Daniel Cohen, Jo O'Cleirigh and Ken Rees.
15 *Womanspirit* operated between 1974 and 1984 and 'helped [to] shape the nascent Goddess Movement in the U.S. and elsewhere'. At its height, the magazine had a print run of 3,000 per issue, though its editor estimated that each copy was probably read by a dozen women, thus increasing its exposure manifold (Griffin 2014: 14, 19).
16 See her letter in *Wood and Water* (1983: 14).
17 The Order was based at Murray's London home and was founded around 1976 in order to encourage 'the preservation of Celtic lore, monuments and antiquities' (New Celtic Review 1980: 1). Its meetings brought together speakers and participants in many aspects of Celtic study and lore, and a magazine titled *The New Celtic Review* was set up in order to further discussion of these matters. Based on his own interpretation of Celtic religion, Murray also organised ritual gatherings corresponding with the eight seasonal festivals. These were open to spiritual seekers regardless of their denomination, and each festival was held in a location deemed appropriate to it: Beltane, for instance, was held at the 'Druid Oaks' in Glastonbury, which became the main home of the Order outside London (Long 1986; Hutton 2003: 251).
18 Personal Interview with Daniel Cohen.
19 See Daniel Cohen's website at: http://www.decohen.com/articles/chauvinism.htm. Interview with Daniel Cohen; Email Correspondence with Daniel Cohen, 22 October 2011. He was active in the pro-feminist men's movement in Great Britain from its early beginnings in the early 1970s and has also participated in conferences of the related American movement. See his website at http://www.decohen.com. Alternative Socialism operated in Britain during the 1970s with close links to *Peace News* magazine, but eventually collapsed due to the tensions which arose out of its nature as a mixed organisation based on cooperation between male and female feminist activists (Rowan 1987: 26–7). See also (Long and Coghill 1977).
20 Letter from Danny Cohen to Starhawk, May Day 1980. In Starhawk Collection/GTU 2002-4-01/Box 5/24.
21 Jones – who is known today as the key proponent of Goddess Spirituality in Glastonbury and in the whole of the UK – was also a member of the Glastonbury Women's Group, with ties to the Matriarchal Study Groups network, and visited Greenham on several occasions during the 1980s (Jones 1996: 12, 14).
22 Letter from Danny Cohen to Starhawk.

23 According to Cohen, Asphodel 'was my dearest friend and partner for over 25 years. We led very independent lives, and I usually visited her about one day a week. Our discussions, theological, spiritual, political, literary, enlivened my life and deepened my thinking'. See Daniel Cohen's website at: http://www.decohen.com/articles/asphodel.htm.
24 Personal Interview with Daniel Cohen, as well as Cohen (1987: 5-6).
25 For background information on O'Cleirigh see Howard (2012: 36–43).
26 See Howard (2012: 42) as well as Letter from Jo O'Cleirigh to the Author, 24 May 2012; Letter from Jo O'Cleirigh to the Author, 3 August 2012.
27 See his concluding remarks in *Wood and Water* (1980b, 15).
28 See Jo O'Cleirigh's recollections in White (2017: 136–138). I have stated in previous publications prior to 2020 that Starhawk's first visit to the UK was conducted during May 1985, and am now happy to amend that statement.
29 (Sjöö 1981: 4–7; 1983: 4–10; 1984a: 6–11; 1984b: 6–8; 1989b: 2–6). Sjöö's books (co-written with Barbara Mor), *The Ancient Religion of the Great Cosmic Mother* (1981) and *The Great Cosmic Mother: Rediscovering the Religion of the Earth* (1987), were warmly reviewed in *Wood and Water* during the 1980s (Llewelyn Williams 1981: 23–24; 'Book Reviews' 1987: 5–6).
30 Personal correspondence with Rufus Brock Maychild, March 2014.
31 (Anon, 1982: 22). It might also be relevant to add that Howard avidly supported Pagan groups who linked their spirituality with ecological awareness,and included an 'Econews' section in *The Cauldron* since 1980. See for instance "Eco News" (1980: 5; 1981: 3; 1983: 5); and "Ecopagan Gathering" (1980: 5).

Bibliography

All URLs were accessed on 22 June 2020.
Anon. 1981. "Women's Action for Disarmament: Women for Life on Earth 1981" in *Wood and Water*, 1(10), 17.
Anon. 1982. "No Real Changes! Editorial Note" *Wood and Water*, 2(4): 22.
Berger, Helen A. 1999. *A Community of Witches: Contemporary Neo-Paganism and Witchcraft in the United States*. Columbia: University of South Carolina Press.
Berger, Helen A. and Douglas Ezzy. 2007. *Teenage Witches: Magical Youth and the Search for the Self*. New Brunswick: Rutgers University Press.
"Book Reviews". 1987. *Wood and Water*, 2(22), 5–6.
Budapest, Zsuzsanna. 1999 [1980]. *The Holy Book of Women's Mysteries*. Oakland: Wingbow Press.
Catriona. 1984. "Books". *Wood and Water*, 2(14).
The Cauldron. 1982a. 27, p8.
The Cauldron. 1982b. 26, p8
The Cauldron. 1982c. 25, p8.
The Cauldron. 1981a. 24, p8.
The Cauldron. 1981b. 23, p8.
Clifton, Chas S. 2006. *Her Hidden Children: The Rise of Wicca and Paganism in America*. Lanham, MD: AltaMira.
Cohen, Daniel. 1987."John Rowan. The Horned God" *Wood and Water*, 2(22): 5–6.
Cohen, Daniel. 1983. "Starhawk: Dreaming the Dark: Magic, Sex and Politics" *Wood and Water*, 2(7), 12.

Daly, Mary. 1978. *Gyn/ecology: The Metaethics of Radical Feminism*. Boston, MA: Beacon Press.

Echols, Alice. 1991 [1989]. *Daring to Be Bad: Radical Feminism in America, 1967–1975*. Minneapolis: University of Minnesota Press.

Echols, Alice. 1983. "The New Feminism of Yin and Yang" in *Powers of Desire: The Politics of Sexuality*, Ann Snitow, Christine Stansell and Sharon Thompson (eds). New York: Monthly Review Press, pp. 439–459.

"Eco News". 1983. *The Cauldron*, 29: 5.

"Eco News". 1981. *The Cauldron*, 21: 3.

"Eco News". 1980. *The Cauldron*, 19: 5.

"Ecopagan Gathering". 1980. *The Cauldron*, 17: 5.

"Editorial". 1980. *Wood and Water*, 1(5): 3.

Editorial Collective. 1981. "Editorial" *Wood and Water*, 2(1): 2–3.

Eller, Cynthia. 1993. *Living in the Lap of the Goddess: The Feminist Spirituality Movement in America*. Boston: Beacon Press.

Feraro, Shai. 2019. "Playing the Pipes of PAN: Pagans Against Nukes and the Linking of Wiccan-Derived Paganism with Ecofeminism in Britain, 1980–1990" *Magic and Witchery in the Modern West*, Shai Feraro and Ethan Doyle White (eds). New York: Palgrave Macmillan, pp. 45–64.

Feraro, Shai. 2016. "Invoking Hecate at the Women's Peace Camp: The Presence of Goddess Spirituality and Dianic Witchcraft at Greenham Common During the 1980s" *Magic, Ritual and Witchcraft*, 11(2): 226–248.

Feraro, Shai. 2015. "Connecting British Wicca with Radical Feminism and Goddess Spirituality During the 1970s–1980s: The Case Study of Monica Sjöö" *Journal of Contemporary Religion*, 30(2): 307–321.

Feraro, Shai. 2013. "'God Giving Birth' – Connecting British Wicca with Radical Feminism and Goddess Spirituality During the 1970s–1980s: A Case Study of Monica Sjöö" *Pomegranate: The International Journal of Pagan Studies*, 15(1–2): 31–60.

Greenwood, Susan. 2005. *The Nature of Magic: An Anthropology of Consciousness*. Oxford: Berg.

Griffin, Wendy. 2014. "The Land Within" in *Sacred Lands and Spiritual Landscapes*, Wendy Griffin (ed). Tucson: ADF Publishing, pp. 9–24.

Griffin, Wendy 2005. "Webs of Women: Feminist Spiritualities" in *Witchcraft and Magic: Contemporary North America*, Helen A. Berger (ed). Philadelphia: University of Pennsylvania Press, pp. 55–83.

Griffin, Wendy. 1995. "The Embodied Goddess: Feminist Witchcraft and Female Divinity" *Sociology of Religion*, 56(1): 35–48.

H & T. 1980. "Towards a Network of 'Gaian' Groups?" *Wood and Water*, 1(5): 6.

Harvey, Graham. (ed). 2014. *The Handbook of Contemporary Animism*. London: Routledge.

Harvey, Graham. 2005. *Animism: Respecting the Living World*. New York: Columbia University Press.

Henning, Jan. 1984. "The Motherpeace Tarot Pack" *Wood and Water*, 2(14): 16.

Hilary and Tony. 1981. "Editorial". *Wood and Water*, 1(10): 1–2.

Hilary and Tony. 1980. "Wood and Water – Past and Future" *Wood and Water*, 1(4): 9–11.

H.L.W. 1981. "Review" *Wood and Water*, 1(10): 24–25.

Howard, Michael. 1981. "The Ancient Religion of the Cosmic Mother of All" *The Cauldron*, 23, 8.

Howard, Mike. 2012. "Interview with Jo O'Cleirigh: Archeologist & Veteran Pagan" *The Cauldron*, 143: 36–43.

Hutton, Ronald. 2003. *Witches, Druids and King Arthur*. London: Hambledon and London.

Hutton, Ronald. 1999. *The Triumph of the Moon: A History of Modern Pagan Witchcraft*. Oxford: Oxford University Press.

Johnston, Hannah E. and Peg Aloi. (eds). 2007. *The New Generation Witches: Teenage Witchcraft in Contemporary Culture*. Aldershot: Ashgate.

Jones, Kathy. 1996. *On Finding Treasure: Mystery Plays of the Goddess*. Glastonbury: Ariadne Publications.

King, Ursula. 1989. *Women and Spirituality: Voices of Protest and Promise*. Houndmills: Macmillan.

Komatsu, Kayoko. 1986. *An Empirical Study of Matriarchy Groups in Contemporary Britain and their Relationship to New Religious Movements*, MA thesis, University of Leeds.

Letcher, Andy. 2004. "Raising the Dragon: Folklore and the Development of Contemporary British Eco-Paganism" *The Pomegranate*, 6(2): 175–198.

"Letters". 1982. *Wood and Water*, 2(2): 22.

Lewis, James R. 2012. "The Pagan Explosion Revisited: A Statistical Postmortem on the Teen Witch Fad" in *The Pomegranate*, 14(1): 128–139.

Llewelyn Williams, Hilary. 1979. "The Goddess and the Well". *Wood and Water*, 1(2), 7–10.

Llewelyn Williams, Hilary. 1981. "Review". *Wood and Water*, 1(10): 23–24.

Llewelyn Williams, Hilary. 1982. "Poem". *Womanspirit*, 34: 13.

Llewelyn Williams, Hilary and Tony Padfield. 1981a. "Introduction" in *Out of the Fountainhead: Selected from Wood & Water 1979-81*, Hilary Llewelyn Williams and Tony Padfield, (eds). Swindon: Wood & Water.

Llewelyn Williams, Hilary and Tony Padfield. 1981b. "A note on Spiral Centre: March 1981" in *Out of the Fountainhead: Selected from Wood & Water 1979-81* in Hilary Llewelyn Williams and Tony Padfield (eds). Swindon: Wood & Water.

Long, Asphodel P. 1986. "Collin Murray – In Memoriam" in *Wood and Water*, 2: 20.

Long, Pauline and Mary Coghill. 1977. *Is It Worthwhile Working in a Mixed Group?* London: Beyond Patriarchy Publication.

'M.' 1976. "Homo'-Les'" *The Wiccan*, 51: 1.

McCrickard, Janet. 1981. "Mother Earth, Father Sky... Beware the Patriarchal Lie!" *Wood and Water*, 1(8): 14.

Melton, J. Gordon and Isotta Poggi. 1992. *Magic, Witchcraft, and Paganism in America: A Bibliography*. New York: Garland Publishing.

New Celtic Review. 1980. January Issue: 1.

O'Cleirigh, Jo. 1981. "Native Peoples, Womanspirit and Neopagans" in *Wood and Water*, 1(9): 11–13.

O'Cleirigh, Jo. 1979/1980. "Nemeton and the Sacred Play of the Year" *Wood and Water*, 1: 3.

Raphael, Melissa. 1999. *Introducing Thealogy: Discourse on the Goddess*. Sheffield, UK: Sheffield Academic Press.

Rees, K.I. 1981. "The Spiral Dance" in *Wood and Water*, 2(1): 23.

Rountree, Kathryn. 2004. *Embracing the Witch and the Goddess: Feminist Ritual-Makers in New Zealand*. London, UK: Routledge.

Rowan, John. 1987. *The Horned God: Feminism and Men as Wounding and Healing*. London, UK: Routledge & Kegan Paul.

Salomonsen, Jone. 2002. *Enchanted Feminism: The Reclaiming Witches of San Francisco*. London: Routledge.

Sjöö, Monica. 1990. "Challenging New Age Patriarchy" in *Matriarchy Research and Reclaim Network*, 63.

Sjöö, Monica. 1989a. "Some Thoughts About the New Age Movement" in *Wood and Water*, 2(28): 2–6.

Sjöö, Monica. 1989b. "Pilgrimage to the USA (Part 1)" in *Wood and Water*, 2(29): 2–7.

Sjöö, Monica. 1984a. "The Bleeding Yeh Mother and Pentre Ifan Cromlech" in *Wood and Water*, 2(12): 6–8.

Sjöö, Monica. 1984b. "Discovering Sacred Places and Holy Wells" in *Wood and Water*, 2(10): 6–11.

Sjöö, Monica. 1983. "Danish Wells and the Goddess" in *Wood and Water*, 2(9): 4–10.

Sjöö, Monica. 1981. "No Real Changes: Continuing Sexist Assumptions in the 'New Age'" in *Wood and Water*, 2(1): 4–7.

Starhawk. 1989 [1979]. *The Spiral Dance*. San Francisco, CA: Harper&Row.

Starhawk. 1987. *Truth or Dare: Encounters with Power, Authority and Mystery*. San Francisco, CA: HarperCollins Publishers.

Starhawk. 1982. *Dreaming the Dark: Magic, Sex & Politics*. Boston, MA: Beacon Press.

Taylor, Bron. 2009. *Dark Green Religion: Nature Spirituality and the Planetary Future*. Berkeley: University of California Press.

"The Wood & Water Gathering 4–7 April, 1980. 1979/1980" in *Wood and Water*, 1(3), 16–17.

White, Rupert. 2017. *The Re-enchanted Landscape: Earth Mysteries, Paganism & Art in Cornwall 1950–2000*. Antenna Publications.

Wood and Water. 1983. 2(6): 14.

Wood and Water. 1982. 2(3): 13

Wood and Water. 1981. 1(10): 16.

Wood and Water. 1980a. 1(7).

Wood and Water. 1980b. 1(6): 15.

Wood and Water. 1980c. 1(5): 21.

8 When galaxies collide: the question of Jediism's revisionism in the face of corporate buyouts and mythos 'retconning'

Beth Singler

This chapter is a preliminary investigation into the response of a new religious movement to sudden changes in what could be seen as the primary 'text' of their faith. Specifically, I will be discussing real-world Jediism, which draws upon the Star Wars films originally created by George Lucas. This is a loosely affiliated and primarily online group that has raised questions about the definitions and boundaries of what we call 'religion', and which has been variably described by scholars as an 'invented religion' (Cusack 2010), or as a 'hyper-real religion' (Possamai 2005), and as a religious category promoted online during the lead up to the 2001 and 2011 UK Censuses (Singler 2014). In this chapter, I propose that a consideration of the real-world Jedi's response to real-world changes such as corporate buyouts and structure changes, as well as the 'ret-conning'[1] of their initial source narrative, clearly demonstrates subsequent changes in the world framing of the real-world Jedi. In particular, radical changes in both their relationship with the creator of 'canon' and in their understanding of the importance of that 'canon'. Canon is in this account the 'official storyline': in this case, the initial and original material that was created by George Lucas, the creator, to tell his story of Star Wars. Canon is a word used in fandom[2] culture that obviously has religious origins and resonances, which are also worth bearing in mind in this chapter.

This chapter's consideration of the real-world Jedi assumes that the reader is at least partially familiar with the existing films of the Star Wars series. They may also be aware that there are further films currently planned for production. These will include further spin-off films and prequels that fill in details of the overall story, introducing events that occurred between the existing films. I hope that I can make this assumption because of just how thoroughly Star Wars has permeated into the public consciousness, and perhaps even into its subconscious. Evidence can be easily found for this cultural permeation: in 2005, the expression 'May the Force be with you' was judged the eighth most recognisable film quote of the past 100 years by the American Film Institute (AMC Filmsite 2016), and the franchise has only grown in popularity since then.[3]

DOI: 10.4324/9781315226804-8

Furthermore even those who have not seen the films or even go to the cinema regularly will recognise how Star War's quotes and ideas have become a part of our contemporary vocabulary. Popular culture scholar Will Brooker, in his 2002 book on the Star Wars fandom, *Using the Force*, says that:

> For many people... it is the single most important cultural text of our lives, it has meshed with memories of our childhoods, with our homemade tributes – from the amateurish childhood comics to the professional product of an adult fan – with our choices of career or education, with our everyday experiences. (Brooker 2002: xii)

Further, he states:

> Star Wars references are so deeply embedded in our popular consciousness that we encounter them every day without trying. (Brooker 2002: 2)

Images and iconography from the universe of Star Wars have also been employed in other contexts. For example, a Volkswagen car advertisement shown during the 2011 American Football Superbowl shows a small boy dressed as legendary fallen Jedi and Sith Lord Darth Vader attempting to use his telekinetic powers around his house with little success. Finally, his parents make use of their car's locking system to make its lights flash and doors whir from a distance just as he gestures towards them, surprising and delighting the small Vader. In an image, the elusive graffiti artist Banksy illustrates and remixes Vader's famous line, '... I am your father' by having one large military vehicle from the Star Wars Universe saying it to a smaller vehicle type. A cat meme, anecdotally described as one of the primary products of the Internet, shows a cat with balled up green socks on its head, as Princess Leia Organa's famous bun hairstyle, desperately saying her famous line, 'Help me Obi Wan'. The 2011 hit song 'Somebody that I used to know' by Kotye, featuring Kimbra, had its iconic music video remixed with Darth Vader as Gotye and George Lucas as Kimbra, playing out the account of an emotional break up and the feeling of distance that time brings. Vader sings instead, 'What happened to the Star Wars that I used to know?', describing how he feels betrayed by Lucas for having his past revealed ineptly in the prequel films and for Lucas's retrospective changes to canon (ret-conning). The latter changes will be shown to be integral to this chapter's consideration of the development of the real-world Jedi.

How might we understand these later developments and remixes of the images and tropes of Star Wars? Scott Lash and Celia Lury explain in their 2007 book, *Global Culture Industry: The Mediation of Things*:

> our cultural objects are self-organizing systems, sometimes operationally closed at other points emergent, singularities forming connective syntheses, at many points actualizing themselves into events. (Lash and Lury 2007: 15)

I propose that the emergence of the new religious movement based on the fictional Jedi of the Star Wars universe, Jediism, is just one such an 'actualised event'. However, as Brooker also reminds us, Star Wars is also very much a corporate as well as a cultural entity:

> Star Wars is not a dead franchise, kept alive in the cultural memory by the fan minority, but an industry, delivering products to a worldwide audience. (Brooker 2002: xvi)

The influence of Star Wars goes beyond more qualitative cultural influences, it is also apparent in the success of the companies behind and related to the film series. In 2012, Lucasfilm, George's Lucas' production company, was named the no. 2 global producer of entertainment products by Forbes Magazine (Forbes 2012) and 17th most powerful global brand by License magazine, in May 2011 (License Magazine 2011). Since being bought by Disney, it has merged with that influential powerhouse too, and we will discuss the influence of this purchase in this chapter.

Therefore, this chapter explores the interaction of this event – the emergence of the real-world Jedi – with the cultural and commercial objects that catalysed its actualisation. Specifically, what happens when those original cultural objects, the multi-element containing cultural worlds of the Star Wars mythos, are involved in a process of financially driven change and retrospective correction, or 'retconning'. First, we must consider the question, who are the Jedi?

The Jedi

In the films/source materials, the information to answer this question has oscillated between intentional vagueness to fully-fleshed back stories and pseudo-scientific explanations, and back again. In the Massively Multiplayer Online role-playing games (MMORPGs), produced by LucasArts (the video game creation arm of Lucasfilm) and Sony, a certain mystique was initially generated by making the Jedi extremely rare. As Michael Clarke explains, in his chapter, 'Branded Worlds and Contracting Galaxies: The Case of Star Wars Galaxies':

> exactly who they are, what they do, and the nature of the intentionally vague Force was left mostly blank, only filled in gradually with each additional text, but never completely resolved – there is always more about the Jedi that we do not know. (Clarke 2014: 216)

This is in contrast to the attempts at back story and explanation seen in the Star Wars prequel films of 1999, 2002, and 2005: the new material that inspired the Gotye parody music video with Vader and Lucas. These films introduced more lightsabers, more races that appeared as Jedi, and the much debated (in the fan community) microscopic 'midichlorians': a testable, scientific, indicator of Jedi ability. The sequels of 2015, 2017, and 2019 varied in their portrayal of the Jedi, but on the whole they were still a much diminished group, even long after the events of the prequels, and little new canon material was introduced.[4]

The games and film makers, and perhaps ultimately Lucas himself as the initial generator and authenticator of canon, responded to what they had perceived as the frustration of fans by making the Jedi much more commonplace in the games and prequels. For example, in 2003, LucasArts began a game series set in an earlier period of the history of the Star Wars universe when Jedi were numerous, opening up the possibility for all gamers to play as Jedi: *Knights of the Old Republic*. I argue that a parallel can be drawn with the real world, where over time people have come to see that they too can be Jedi, or that the Jedi can be 'restored' to our world (as in the 2015–2019 sequels). They can be Jedi, not only as fans and gamers, or even as role-players, but as real Jedi in the real world. A key role in the emergence of the real-world Jedi was played by censuses, and I will now briefly outline how the response, an on and offline 'event', took place, which I have also written about elsewhere (see Singler 2014).

In 2001, population censuses held in Australia, New Zealand, Canada, and the United Kingdom asked about religious affiliation and received hundreds of thousands of responses with Jedi written into a blank box. Prior to these censuses an email that quickly went 'viral' (an epidemiological metaphor used to mean that it was shared rapidly and widely, generally meaning online) claimed that if enough people claimed to be Jedi on their census forms then the governments requesting the answer would be forced, through sheer force of numbers, to recognise Jediism as a legitimate religion. The e-mail stated, with no evidence or precedent to back up its claim, that:

> It usually takes about 10,000 people to nominate the same religion [to get a state to recognise a new religion]. It is for this reason that it has been suggested that anyone who does not have a dominant religion to put Jedi as their religion.

Responses to this plan varied between enthusiasm and cynicism. However, the UK media covered this particular census finding with a touch of mischievous humour. For example, a BBC News article on the result included a picture of Jedi Master Yoda with a quote from him underneath, saying in his usual reversed syntax that, 'Presbyterian my real religion is' (BBC News 2001). However, we should note that the intentions behind the e-mail campaign were not entirely religious and might also have been a bit more mischievous in nature:

> If this has been your dream since you were six years old… do it because you love Star Wars. If not … then just do it to annoy people. [Ellipses in original][5]

Even if annoyance was the aim for these 'trolls'[6] who encouraged others to annoy people, an unexpected outcome was that even ten years later many were still writing in 'Jedi' to their 2011 UK censuses, perhaps for more benign reasons as Internet trolling rarely has that kind of stamina. The 2011 UK census produced a result of 176,632 Jedi in England and Wales and 11,746 in Scotland. This was certainly a decline since 2001, when it had been around 390,127 in England and Wales and 14,052 in Scotland.[7] This decline was parodied in the media: it was described as the result of the fictional Sith's massacre of the Jedi, as originally described in the first three films and finally dramatised in the 2005 prequel *The Revenge of the Sith*. However, even with this large decline in numbers this response, ten years after the original email campaign, is significant.

For some, writing Jedi in the box was a rebellion, either aimed at the Census creators for even asking a question about religion or aimed at religion itself. However, for others, only a minority of the overall number perhaps, writing in 'Jedi' was an act of publicly declared self-definition. It was seen as a chance to express a genuine religious affiliation. Online research quickly finds numerous real-world Jedi groups that have formed, using forums and other social media, to share their desire to instantiate the religion IRL (in the real world). This actualisation of a cultural object like Star Wars and the Jedi shows that, 'intentional or unintentional references in popular culture can have the effect of solidifying beliefs', as Debra McCormick explains in her article, 'From Jesus Christ to Jedi Knight: Changing Paradigms in the Study of Religious Affiliation'. I have also described this process as a 'snowballing legitimation' as conversations online make the religion a 'fact' (Singler 2014). Images are easy to find online of official Jedi events. For example, a 'knighting' which took place in 2015 shows an officiant wearing dark robes. There are also individuals presenting themselves as spokespeople and providing training manuals for the Jedi. I have been in contact with some of these in researching this chapter, including Master Thompson of the Ashla Knights who has developed Sabre Flow, a Jedi inspired martial art. Material from my conversations with Master Thompson and others will be presented in 'The Jedi Response' section, but first we need to consider further the relationship between the original fiction and more recent corporate changes in the real-world.

Fiction and corporate changes

The move of the MMORPG Star Wars games further back into the history of the Star Wars Universe to allow more people to play as Jedi did not actually change that fictional history, nor did it have an effect on the later offline instantiation of the religion. However, a more recent corporate action has changed how the real-world Jedi understand themselves. In 2012, George Lucas sold Lucasfilm, and all the rights to the Star Wars Universe to the Walt Disney Company for $4.04bn (approx. £2.5bn in 2012). Clarke explains that:

> Speaking directly to the media, George Lucas framed his October 2012 sale of Lucasfilm and its affiliated intellectual properties to Disney as an effort to ensure the longevity of the brand. (Clarke 2014: 213)

This sale also guaranteed the production of the new sequels and stand-alone films, as well as spin offs in other media, including new television shows such as *The Mandalorian* (2019–), and animated series. However, another result of this purchase was the shrinking of the Star Wars 'Expanded Universe', as the Star Wars canon of official material and stories was streamlined for potential new audiences who would not be familiar with all its intricacies. The Star Wars Universe's collective history was changed to align with this shrink in the scope of the story, and the method known as 'retconning' was employed – new information was seeded backwards into the history of the universe with the presumption that audiences would accept that these story elements had always been present. I would describe this change in the Star Wars universe as a 'Big Crunch', in contrast with the usual 'Big Bang' of universe expansion. These two terms, 'canon' and the 'Expanded Universe' need explaining further to understand why this crunch was a potentially dramatic change, first for the fandom and secondly for the real-world Jedi.

'Canon' is a debated term among Star Wars fans. Often it is applied solely to those characters, events, and objects created by George Lucas himself. Sometimes the concept of canon is widened out to include the projects created by others that Lucas as the first creator has given initial sanction to and signed off on. Or canon can be applied to those projects developed externally by approved licensees of the original parent company, Lucasfilm. The 'Expanded Universe' contains material from all three of these realms of canon, and in the 1990s, this canon, and its associated universe, expanded rapidly. As Clarke explains, 'with no SW [Star Wars] sequels forthcoming, attitudes at Lucasfilm underwent a sea change with regard to its relationships with licensees, resulting in the creation of the so-called Expanded Universe' (Clarke 2014: 209). The parent company made deals with external companies such as Bantam Books and Dark Horse Comics, as well as developing the in-house LucasArts game production company to produce games such as the MMORPGs already mentioned earlier. This expansion inevitably led to the emergence of editor-archivists who had the job of maintaining the continuity of this Expanded Universe of canon through the 'Holocron', a massive database of everything that ever existed in the fictional Star Wars Universe. In July 2012 the Holocron contained at least 55,000 discrete entries on such objects as characters, planets, races, and events (Chee 2012).

The fandom relationship to canon has long been problematic. Fan interest directly powers the economy of cultural objects but often also plays with them in new, creative, and occasionally problematic ways. Brands, of which Star Wars has become a pivotal example as I have shown, benefit from the creative passions of fans. Brands can, however, also have a negative reaction to fan uses of their intellectual properties for new stories that might not match or suit their existing understanding of the material. Sometimes they will 'aggressively attack instances of emergence when they constitute use deemed unofficial' (Clarke 2014: 207). Such attacks by Lucasfilm have happened over the decades since the original films first inspired fans. In the 1980s, Lucasfilm cracked down on fan magazines, or 'zines', after previously having supported, archived and critiqued them on behalf of fans. In the 1990s, it was believed that Lucasfilm would tolerate fanfiction in the Star Wars universe if it was family friendly, i.e. not erotic straight or Slash fiction,[8] but still the parent company regularly shut down fan websites through initiating legal action against the companies providing hosting for their pages. In 2000, Lucasfilm offered official Star Wars web spaces to fans, but their legal Terms of Service meant that Lucasfilm would own the rights to any material posted there by fans (Brooker 2002: 169). Following this history of litigation, Brooker concludes that, 'Lucasfilm has been one of the most aggressive corporate groups in trying to halt fan cultural production [...] The deep irony is that Lucas's core concepts of SW itself borrow heavily from pre-existing material' (Brooker 2002: 176, 218). Brooker specifically addresses the influence of Jack Kirby's *Fourth World* science fiction stories on Lucas' world building in Star Wars.

Disney, which bought the Star Wars universe in 2012, is also well known for the adoption and adaption of mythological, literary, and speculative resources: 'Disney and firms like it are acting a mass cultural assemblers, combining, collecting and remixing popular culture' (Clarke 2014: 214). Therefore, it is not just the fans who are engaged in creative play with fiction's canons – but there are hierarchies of power at play between the fandom and the corporation as communities. Ultimately, Lucasfilm, and now Disney, had the narrative power to contract that same canon, just as they had the legal power to crush those fan constructions. The former is exactly what happened after the corporate buyout for $4.05bn (£2.5bn) in 2012.

The Jedi response

To understand the real-world Jedi's response to Disney's 'Big Crunch' of the Star Wars Universe, I spoke to members of the Temple of the Jedi Order and the Ashla Knights through their forum boards and via e-mail in 2016–2017. Below are some indicative responses, which actually demonstrate a surprising lack of interest in the corporate buyout and its effect on the fiction of Star Wars. This disinterest will be explored further below, but, for example, 'Ryujin'[9] told me that:

> the fiction has almost no influence from my perspective... non, zippo, el zilcho, nada... while I may on occasion quote something from the fiction it is merely out of convenience.

'Darren' and 'Goken' took a more universalist approach, a stance which I had noted previously among the Jedi I have spoken to in earlier research:

Darren: Personally, I really like some of the fictional Jedi philosophy, but I think it's more important for us to look at the sources that inspired those philosophies, which I think we do pretty well round these parts ☺ [smiley emoticon]

Goken: I am still very much a Star Wars fan, but it has less to do with my Jedi path. I like some of the symbols and phrases but I incorporate symbols and phrases from many places, some from other fictional sources and some from other religions

Ryujin also emphasised the importance of the individual's path over, and separate to, the narrative or the corporation's actions:

Ryujin: The fiction opened the door and stepped aside... I did the rest.

'Lone Star' suggested that Lucas might have been inspired by the Force *itself*, thus arguing for the fictional concept's objective reality, and they also recognised the original movies as a significant source comparable to the religious texts of another religion:

Lone Star: To my mind if one is to genuinely accept the Force one would need to accept the real possibility that it (the Force) was using Lucas and the movies as a means to instigate the creation of the Jedi Religion, or something similar, in the real-world. This being said, Jedi distancing themselves from the movies themselves would be a bit like a Hindu distancing themselves from the Mahabhrata [sic], but then again these are the words of someone who is less than a neophyte in Jediism

Other Jedi were more pragmatic, such as 'Edan', seeing the films as an important source, but one that could be moved beyond by the Jedi; even if the new films created more public interest in them and their beliefs as real-world Jedi. Concerns about the litigious tendencies of Lucasfilm, described in relation to fandom and fanfic above, were also recognised by 'Akkarin':

Edan: The use of the word Jedi is very much an homage. In the IP (initiate programme) we study the inspiration for the films, without studying the films themselves. We use the name as a way of saying that we see where that inspiration led.

Akkarin: The biggest impact the films are likely to have at the Temple will be an increase in membership simply from people being more conscious of the existence of Star Wars [...] What might be an issue of contention is whether they decide to aggressively enforce their IP (Intellectual Property). In the past Lucas has never done this (stopped people using the word Jedi for instance) and by this point, seeing as TOTJO is in its ninth year, they may not even have the legal ability to do so – but that doesn't mean that they couldn't try. That might bring some headaches, but we'll have to wait and see.

Akkarin recognised Lucas's (and subsequently, Disney's) general control of the original intellectual property, but emphasised that the temple's material was different and separate from that canon because of its years of independence. This rhetoric of indifference and difference was also apparent in the response of Master Thompson of the Ashla Knights to my questions:

Jediism, though based on teachings and understandings of "The Jedi Way", has labored long and hard to distinguish its practices and path from what is presented in the movies or in the new Star Wars universe. [If it fails to resonate usefully with] the philosophy then the chasm that already exists between scion and progeny will widen even more... However, when the new movie is released and the new expanded universe timeline begins to take shape, I foresee a great many things that will require deep discussion.

However, after considering these responses from my informants, I started to question whether the expressions of indifference and/or differences between Jediism and the Star Wars Canon were a result of the most recent changes or a more inherent characteristic of the real world Jedi and the fan-culture to which they are ultimately linked. As I have already explained, Star Wars canon has *always* shifted, both through the influence of the fandom, and through Lucasfilm's interventions. For example, in the 1990s, when the Special Editions of the original film trilogy were released Lucasfilm made, based on Lucas' decisions, 'official' changes to canon. Lucas described the 1990s Special Edition versions of the first trilogy as being *necessary* for the technological maintenance and preservation of the original films. However, Lucas also added scenes that he claimed had been impossible to create due to their expense and time constraints when the films had first gone into production and post-production. Fans have made it their personal mission to track these changes, frame by frame (see DoubleOFive 2010).

In the 20 years between the original three Star Wars films and the Special Edition versions, the effect of the Expanded Universe of graphic novels, novels etc. on the films themselves was apparent. The Special Edition included specific images and characters from this new Expanded Universe, including the intergalactic capital planet, Coruscant, which was first introduced in an Expanded Universe novel.[10] Other changes were, however, more problematic than the introduction of a new location. In the original versions of the films, one of the main characters, Han Solo, appears to shoot a bounty hunter called Greedo before he has a chance to shoot him. In the Special Edition the scene was re-edited to make it clear that the previously more morally ambiguous Han actually shot Greedo *after* the alien had first aggressively drawn his blaster on him. George Lucas made this change and therefore it should have been canon, even if *ret-conned* canon. However, 'this authorial intention holds little weight with other fans who, over the past 20 years in some cases, have built up their own firm ideas about what characters would and wouldn't do' (Brooker 2002: 77). Likewise, the real-world Jedi, and much of the fandom, had their own firm ideas about the nature of the Jedi. And when these ideas are under pressure due to ret-conning or creator elaboration, the real-world Jedi find their own path.

Conclusions

The changes made to the first Star Wars films for the first Special Edition emphasised the dominance of Lucasfilm over canon. They also mark the point where the real-world Jedi started to move away from Lucas as an authority, and these changes came much earlier than the 2012 Disney purchase. These ret-conned films were of course also released *prior* to the 2001 census and the emergence of the Jedi into public consciousness, but many real-world Jedi that I have spoken to have emphasised that they believed *prior* to the 2001 UK Census and the trolling e-mail campaign that was covered by the media. In summary, canon based on fiction will always be contentious and subject to the will of its creator. When a new religious movement emerges based on a fictional canon this change could be momentous; almost as though a new 'revelation'. However, we have seen that in the case of the the real-world Jedi their reaction to this 'createdness' and the changing canon is a rhetoric of indifference. Both to Lucas and Disney, and to the obvious fictional canon for their faith. I also argue that if there had been earlier moments of conflict between the creator and those 'inspired' by his works, either culturally or spiritually, this attitude and associated rhetoric may have arisen earlier.

However, I also saw that this rhetoric goes further. It is also employed in boundary work among the Jedi as they assert their spiritual place in relation to the larger 'secular' Star Wars fandom. For example, on the Temple of the Jedi Order home page, the first introduction one has to their form of Jediism is:

> Jedi here are not Star Wars role-players, but a church of the Jediism religion and/or Jedi way of life. Jedi at this site are not the same as those portrayed within the Star Wars franchise. Star Wars Jedi are fictional characters that exist within a literary and cinematic universe.

While the members of the Temple of the Jedi Order are at pains to make it clear that they are not role players, I argue that there is an element of 'serious play' at work here as in Tanya Luhrmann's discussion of modern pagan witchcraft in *Persuasions of the Witches Craft* (1989). In the wider socio-logical study of Religion, the few attempts that there have been to categorise Jediism have relied primarily on capitalist/entrepreneurial explanations of contemporary religious invention. Or, as an online phenomenon, Jediism has also been described as a 'growing shift from collective – expressive church membership in the past to individual-expressive religious involvement' (McCormick 2006: 5, citing Phillip Hammond, in Warner 1993: 1075).

I argue that Jediism *is* a collective endeavour. Capitalistic interpretations of religious innovation are out of date and ill-fitting in an 'attention economy' (Bergquist and Ljungberg 2001) that does not rely heavily on financial interactions but still engages a community through creations, shared story-telling and collective serious and non-serious play. Likewise, the Jedi rhetoric of difference and indifference that distances the real-world Jedi from the corporate manoeuvres of Lucas and Lucasfilm contradicts the assumption that Star Wars was attractive as a canon for creative religious play because it presented a neatly pre-packaged religion, as McCormick has claimed:

> the archetypal characters and the values they espouse provide universal appeal to a generation looking for answers not necessarily found in traditional religion but offered in a ready-to-wear package from the mind of Hollywood. (McCormick 2006: 9)

This assumption, based on perceiving Jediism as an appealing religious brand, is problematic. First, it is not a ready-to-wear package. There is very little cosmology or theology provided with the canon, even if the greater number of Jedi in prequels and some video games has made them seem more commonplace. Second, the original sources, the first trilogy of films, are now so familiar that it is hard to see how unusual and 'un-Hollywood-like' they were when they first started inspiring people to think about actually being Jedi. Third, the characters might seem archetypal, and Lucas' reliance on Joseph Campbell's 1949 work of comparative mythology, *The Hero with a Thousand Faces,* is well known, but the philosophies the fictional Jedi do espouse are more like anti-logical koans than a clear path. Jediism in the films is extremely vague and incomplete, and perhaps purposefully so!

Further, in terms of successful branding and creative play, Clarke argues that 'Consumers must be able to immediately recognise brands as a surface effect at the same time that brands must allow for deep engagement through history, memory and fantasy' (Clarke 2014: 208). However, Lucasfilm, and more recently, Disney, have limited this 'deep engagement' by retconning beloved history, deleting favourite memories, and preventing fan fantasy from using their intellectual properties. Therefore, while the canon Jedi allowed for only a shallow engagement, the corporate model forced the real-world Jedi to distance themselves and to revise their relationship with canon as believers as far back as the 1990s. This of course predates the 2001 census, and scholars considering the real-world Jedi need to bear in mind that while the census was an event that brought Jediism to public awareness, Jediism was being considered online long before that.

Therefore, I am sorry to disappoint in that this chapter, unlike the Star Wars stories themselves, is not presenting the story of an epic battle between religious rebels and the corporate Empire. A more subtle distancing and revisionism actually started back in the 1990s, even as Jediism was taking form online, and, further, it was a natural result of having taken cues from an active and corporately controlled fiction franchise. What of the future of Jediism? Will these corporate changes and influences have any bearing on that? When I spoke to Master Thompson of the Ashla Knights for this research he told me that the largest problem facing the Jedi was not Disney or Lucas, but their own lack of consensus as a movement:

> The future is in motion…it's always changing as a wise Jedi Master has said; but if I had to speculate based on what I know from experience from having been around the many interpretations and practices of the Jedi Way, I'd say Darkness is one likely and not too distant future for Jediism. In practice there is no unity and no standard of understanding, there is no consensus. Because of this, observers of the philosophy are constantly embroiled in fighting over asinine perspectives and outlandish teachings.

This is an insider's account, and therefore we could approach it with a hermeneutics of suspicion; being aware of the informant's intentions in furthering a rhetoric of difference. The various claims of religious perennialism or universalism made by the Jedi also need careful criticism, and might be better understood as a part of further boundary work opposing the larger non-believing Star Wars fandom. However, I tend to agree with Master Thompson's analysis. The corporate shifts and changes will have little impact on a movement that is already in the process of separating itself from the source of its canon. Public changes to canon, especially when including additional films, will only inspire interest and garner new members, but they will not be key to the real-world Jedi's conception of their own extended universe of spirituality.

Notes

1 'Retroactive continuity' (Cook 2013: 269).
2 'The community that surrounds a TV show/movie/book etc. Fanfiction writers, artists, poets, and cosplayers are all members of that fandom' (Urban Dictionay 2017).
3 'A ballot was distributed in 2004 with 400 Nominated Quotes from Films to a jury of 1,500 leaders from the film community, including filmmakers, actors, historians, scholars, journalists and industry types. Voters could submit up to five write-in choices not included among the 400 nominees.' From AMC Filmsite, http://www.filmsite.org/afi100quotes.html (accessed 2 June 2020).
4 2017's *Star Wars: The Last Jedi* was roundly criticised for a pessimistic portrayal of an older and more cynical Luke Skywalker. However, 2019's *Star Wars: The Rise of Skywalker* returned to the writer/director of 2015's *Star Wars: The Force Awakens*, and much of this pessimism was undone by a storyline that emphasised the powers of the main Jedi characters and a more hopeful ending with Rey, a Jedi in training but now with no master, declaring herself a 'Skywalker' and continuing the legacy of Luke.
5 Jedi Campaign e-mail quoted on BBC News website: http://news.bbc.co.uk/1/hi/technology/1271380.stm (accessed 8 August 2013).
6 'To troll', 'to be a troll': to post incendiary comments with the intent of provoking others into conflict, as described by Hardaker (2010: 224).
7 Numbers for Northern Ireland are impossible to compare, as Jedi in the 2001 Census were included in the 'no religion' response with no breakdown of specific responses. In 2011 they were still placed in the 'no religion' category, but a breakdown was recorded, including the figure of 1,462 for Jedi or Jedi Knight.
8 Slash: 'a productive fan fiction strand in which same-sex television or film characters are subversively made into queer subjects' (Dhaenens et al. 2008: 1).
9 I have maintained the Jedi's online pseudonyms rather than double anonymising them as these were comments given with informed consent as a part of this research, and also I do not believe the content of these comments to hold potential for harm for my informants.
10 Coruscant did remain a part of canon, appearing significantly in the events of the 1990s prequel films, but it did not have a role to play in the sequels of 2015–2019.

Bibliography

All URLs were accessed on 2 June 2020.

AMC Filmsite. 2016. "America's Greatest Quotes in the Movies, 100 YEARS...100 MOVIE QUOTES, 100 Greatest Movie Quotes by American Film Institute (AFI)". Available at http://www.filmsite.org/afi100quotes.html

BBC News. 2001. "Jedi Makes the Census List". Available at http://news.bbc.co.uk/1/hi/uk/1589133.stm

Bergquist, Magnus and Ljungberg, Jan. 2001. "The Power of Gifts: Organizing Social Relationships in Open Source Communities" in *Journal of Information Systems*, 11: 305–320.

Brooker, Will. 2002. *Using the Force: Creativity, Community and "Star Wars" Fans*. London, UK: Bloomsbury.

Campbell, Joseph. 1949. *The Hero with a Thousand Faces*. New York: Pantheon Books.

Chee, Leland Y. 2012. "What Is the Holocron?" Blog post, July. Available at http://www.starwars.com/news/what-is-the-holocron

Clarke, Michael. 2014. "Branded Worlds and Contracting Galaxies: The Case of Star Wars Galaxies" in *Games and Culture*, 9 May: 203–224.

Cook, Roy T. 2013. "Canonicity and Normativity in Massive, Serialized, Collaborative Fiction" in *The Journal of Aesthetics and Art Criticism*, 71(3): 271–276.

Cusack, Carole. 2010. *Invented Religions: Imagination, Fiction and Faith*. Aldershot, UK: Ashgate.

Dhaenens, Frederick, Bauwel, Sofie Van and Biltereyst, Daniel. 2008. "Slashing the Fiction of Queer Theory Slash Fiction, Queer Reading, and Transgressing the Boundaries of Screen Studies, Representations, and Audiences" in *Journal of Communication Inquiry*, 18 July, 32(4): 335–347.

DoubleOFive. 2010. "Star Wars Special Edition Visual Comparisons". Available at https://doubleofive.wordpress.com/swsevc/

Forbes. 2012. "Disney Princess Tops List of the 20 Best-Selling Entertainment Products". *Forbes Magazine*, Jenna Goudreau, 17 September. Available at http://www.forbes.com/sites/jennagoudreau/2012/09/17/disney-princess-tops-list-of-the-20-best-selling-entertainment-products/#2d83c89e252d

Hardaker, Claire. 2010. "Trolling in Asynchronous Computer-Mediated Communication: From User Discussions to Theoretical Concepts" in *Journal of Politeness Research*, 6(2): 215–242.

Lash, Scott and Lury, Celia. 2007. *Global Culture Industry: The Mediation of Things*. Malden, MA: Polity.

License Magazine. 2011. "Top 125". Available on the Wayback Machine at https://web.archive.org/web/20170504213308/http://www.licensemag.com/license-global/top-125 (accessed 9 December 2016).

Luhrmann, Tanya. 1989. *Persuasions of the Witches Craft*. Cambridge, MA: Harvard University Press.

McCormick, Debra. 2006. "From Jesus Christ To Jedi Knight – Validity and Viability Of New Religious Movements in Late Modernity" in *Proceedings Social Change in the 21st Century Conference 2006*, Queensland University of Technology. Available at http://eprints.qut.edu.au/6636/1/6636.pdf

Possamai, Adam. 2005 *Religion and Popular Culture: A Hyper-Real Testament*. Brussels, Belgium: Peter Lang.

Singler, Beth. 2014. "'SEE MOM IT IS REAL': The UK Census, Jediism and Social Media" in *Journal of Religion in Europe*, 7(2): 150–168.

Urban Dictionay. 2017. "Fandom". Available at http://www.urbandictionary.com/define.php?term=fandom&defid=786878

Warner, R. Stephen. 1993. "Work in Progress Toward a New Paradigm for the Sociological Study of Religion in the United States" in *The American Journal of Sociology*, 98: 1044–1093.

Part III

Change as a part of a process of legitimation

9 Regulating religious diversification: a legal perspective

Frank Cranmer and Russell Sandberg

In 1967, Michael Segerdal, a minister of the Church of Scientology and acting chaplain of the Church's chapel at Saint Hill Manor in Sussex, applied unsuccessfully to the Registrar General of Births, Deaths and Marriages for it to be registered for the solemnisation of marriage under the Places of Worship Registration Act 1855. The Court of Appeal subsequently approved the Registrar General's refusal, with Lord Denning MR declaring that the chapel was not a 'place of religious worship' because 'worship' required 'reverence or veneration of God or of a Supreme Being' and the creed of the Church of Scientology was 'more a philosophy of the existence of man or of life, rather than a religion'.[1]

In 2011, the Registrar General refused to register the Church's London chapel under the 1855 Act and Louisa Hodkin, a member and volunteer at the chapel who wished to get married there, sought judicial review of that decision.[2] She was unsuccessful in the lower courts, which felt bound to follow the earlier decision in *Segerdal*, but the Supreme Court held that the chapel could be a 'place of meeting for religious worship' under the 1855 Act. Lord Toulson declared that the 1855 Act had to be interpreted 'in accordance with contemporary understanding of religion and not by reference to the culture of 1855' and that 'the understanding of religion in today's society is broad'.[3] For Lord Toulson, religion could now be described in summary as:

> a spiritual or non-secular belief system, held by a group of adherents, which claims to explain mankind's place in the universe and relationship with the infinite, and to teach its adherents how they are to live their lives in conformity with the spiritual understanding associated with the belief system.[4]

This *volte-face* reflected not only a changing sociological climate concerning religion or belief that had developed over the course of forty years but also a transformed legal framework. The late 20th and early 21st centuries saw a number of legal developments that protect religious rights. Discrimination on grounds of religion or belief became expressly forbidden, the Racial and

DOI: 10.4324/9781315226804-9

Religious Hatred Act 2006 outlawed stirring up religious hatred and the Human Rights Act 1998 articulated an explicit recognition of individual and collective religious freedom at common law by giving domestic effect to the protection in Article 9 of the European Convention on Human Rights of the right to manifest religion or belief as both an individual and a collective right.

Given both the increased protection of religious rights and the increased recognition of religious pluralism, the broadening of the definition of 'religion' and the recognition in *Hodkin* of the Church of Scientology as a place where religious marriages can be conducted in England and Wales[5] may be thought to have been inevitable. But that would be to paint too simplistic a picture of the trajectory of English and Scots law; that would be to confuse happenstance with evolution and to equate pragmatic and often ill-thought-out changes in the letter of the law with idealised notions of progress. The picture is more complicated than that.

Indeed, despite the avalanche of new laws, many religious believers feel that legal protection has decreased rather than increased.[6] New legal provisions have led to a landslide of cases, many of which have not only set confused precedents, and the way in which simplified versions of the disputes have made headline news has underlined how divisive and ill understood religion is in the public sphere. This has become an age in which religious and other differences have become stigmatised, loyalty to a source of authority other than the nation state is treated with suspicion and terrorist atrocities supposedly in the name of religion have cast a long shadow. A 2012 inquiry by Christians in Parliament (an official All-Party Parliamentary Group) concluded that 'Christians in the UK face problems in living out their faith and these problems have been mostly caused and exacerbated by social, cultural and legal changes over the past decade'.[7]

A legal analysis, therefore, can be particularly helpful to explore the intended and unintended consequences of the transformed legal framework around religion or belief. Interdisciplinary insights are valuable. not least in contextualising legal accounts; however, there is also a place for doctrinal legal studies exploring the contours of legal rights and the legal ramifications explicit and implicit within judicial decisions. This chapter, therefore, seeks to rely solely on primary legal materials to bring a legal perspective to the theme of this collection and to explore how English and Scots law deal with diversification within religious groups, looking not only at how the law deals with schisms within new religious movements and more traditional religions but also at the extent to which the law recognises new forms of religiosity or doctrinal developments. As the chapter will demonstrate, although the law in both jurisdictions is supposed to protect a right to manifest religion or belief in any form, in reality the courts readily assume a direct link between credal belief and behaviour and often fail to protect those who profess membership of a religion but adhere to a personalised interpretation of that religion and so feel themselves bound to manifestations that are not common or mandated within their religion as a whole.

The chapter will examine how the courts have dealt with new forms of religiosity through two case studies: the first will explore how the courts have dealt with mainstream religious groups that have splintered and the second will look at the extent to which the courts have dealt with individual claims concerning manifestations of religion that differ or deviate from the mainstream of the religion in question.

Dealing with collective religious freedom: splintering religious groups and schisms

Any consideration of the fissiparous tendencies of faith communities should begin with a statement of an obvious truth that is frequently overlooked: that almost every religious body that has come into existence in Great Britain since the English and Scots Reformations has at some point been a 'new religious movement'. And not only that: it is likely to have been a new religious movement cruelly persecuted for its temerity in departing from what the authorities regarded as 'true religion'.

A mere handful of post-Reformation examples will suffice. In England in the 1660s the so-called Clarendon Code[8] imposed considerable disabilities on Puritans and Dissenters, while in Scotland attendance and preaching at the Covenanters' dissident open-air conventicles were banned[9] and many Covenanters were killed resisting Government troops sent to suppress their worship. Then, after the enactment of the Claim of Right 1689, Scottish Episcopalians who would not 'qualify' by accepting the legitimacy of the House of Hanover suffered periods of disability, not least because they were suspected of Jacobite sympathies; and they were not fully tolerated until the enactment of the Scottish Episcopalians Relief Act 1792.

Even where the 'new religion' is tolerated – that is to say, not considered unlawful – there are likely to be a number of legal ramifications. This is especially true where the group holds property. Although England has seen many religious groups split off from the Established Church of England – most obviously the Methodists, who in their turn gave rise to the Salvation Army – it is perhaps in Scotland that the phenomenon is most obvious and it was a Scots case – *General Assembly of the Free Church of Scotland v Lord Overtoun*[10]– that, perhaps, had the greatest influence on the development of the legal response to schisms in both jurisdictions.

The Scots Reformation is generally held to have begun with the passing of the Confession of Faith Ratification Act 1560; but the Presbyterian polity of the Church of Scotland was not finally settled until the accession of William and Mary and the Confession of Faith Ratification Act 1690. However, Church government was not the only divisive issue; patronage – the right of the heritors of the parish to call a minister to a vacant charge – caused a major rift between Evangelicals who felt that it usurped 'The

Crown Rights of the Redeemer' and Moderates who regarded it as a mere property right. After the Church Patronage (Scotland) Act 1711 restored patronage, so bitter was the dispute that riots were not uncommon when a Moderate was presented to a parish where the congregation was unsympathetic to patronage.

The General Assembly attempted to abolish patronage with the Veto Act 1834,[11] but the Court of Session ruled that the Assembly did not have the power to do so.[12] That judgment triggered the events that led ultimately to the Disruption of 1834, when two-fifths of the ministers present demitted their charges, withdrew from the General Assembly and founded 'The Church of Scotland Free', installing Thomas Chalmers as the first Moderator. But they nevertheless maintained that it was the duty of the State to support the Church: as Chalmers explained at the first Free Church General Assembly:

> Though we quit a vitiated Establishment, we go out on the Establishment principle; we quit a vitiated Establishment, but would rejoice in returning to a pure one. To express it otherwise, we are the advocates for a national recognition and national support of religion – *and we are not Voluntaries.*[13]

There had been a much smaller First Secession in 1733, as a result of an Act of Assembly in 1732[14] that had restricted to heritors and elders the right to call a minister to a vacancy where the patron had failed to nominate within six months, and a Second Secession in 1761. In 1847, the two Secession Churches came together as the United Presbyterian Church, and there was then a gradual *rapprochement* between the Free Church and the United Presbyterians that led, ultimately, to their union in 1900 as the United Free Church. But the United Presbyterians opposed Establishment; and Free Church dissidents who held to 'the Establishment principle' refused to enter the union, claiming that the majority had jettisoned a basic tenet of the Free Church. They sued the General Assembly, essentially for breach of trust–*and won*. In the House of Lords, Halsbury LC said this:

> I do not suppose that anybody will dispute the right of any man, or any collection of men, to change their religious beliefs according to their own consciences; but when men subscribe money for a particular object and leave it behind them for the promotion of that object, their successors have no right to change the object endowed... [T]here is nothing in calling an associated body a Church that exempts it from the legal obligations of insisting that money given for one purpose shall not be devoted to another.[15]

As to what might this mean for new religious movements arising from older ones, the first and most obvious lesson is, *'be careful'*. The *dictum* that funds entrusted for one purpose may not necessarily be used for another (or, at any rate, not for a purpose inimical to the intentions of the settlor or truster) is still good law;[16] and one of the reasons why recent Church unions have been effected by private Act of Parliament is presumably that statutory authority overrides any possible conflicts in the trust deeds of the uniting bodies.[17] The second is possibly this: it is not necessary to be radically different from the body from which one is separating in order to run into legal conflict. In 2000, dissidents in the Free Church of Scotland left to establish the Free Church of Scotland (Continuing), largely as a result of what they saw as growing liberalism in the Free Kirk's theology. To an outsider – even to a sympathetic outsider – their theological differences do not seem great; but those differences have already given rise to two lots of litigation.[18] English and Scots law continue to lack any simple, non-contentious mechanism for dealing with splintering religious groups that differentiates between them and recognises that religious freedom includes the right to schism and diversity.[19]

In passing, it should be noted that the Charity Commission for England and Wales has taken a more liberal but seemingly inconsistent approach where new religious movements have sought registration as trusts for the advancement of religion. When the Church of Scientology applied for registration as a charity in the 1990s, the Commission refused to register it,[20] concluding that it was not charitable as an organisation established for the advancement of religion because it was not a 'religion' for the purposes of English charity law. Even if Scientology *were* otherwise established for the advancement of religion, public benefit could not be presumed, given its relative newness and the public and judicial concern expressed about it. Further, its central practices – 'auditing' and training – were of their nature private rather than public activities. That, together with the practice of requesting advance donations for services, led the Commission to conclude that any benefit flowing from Scientology was of a private rather than a public nature and that the public benefit test was not met. Nor has the Supreme Court's decision in *Hodkin* changed that situation – yet.

Subsequently, the Commission has considered applications for registration from new religious movements case by case, and no discernible general principle seems to have emerged. In the case of the Gnostic Centre, the Commission concluded that it had not sufficiently demonstrated "that there is an identifiable positive, beneficial, moral, or ethical framework promoted by the belief system, that this is being promoted to the public and is capable of impacting upon the public in a beneficial way"[21] – and that in spite of the fact that Gnosticism is a belief system (or, from an orthodox Trinitarian Christian perspective, a heresy) that goes back to the second century CE. Similarly, the Commission refused an application from The Way of the Livingness, the Religion of the Soul Trust, whose objects, *inter alia*, are for the benefit of the public to advance The Way of the Livingness as a religion by encouraging and facilitating Soul-full religious practice by existing followers and adherents by means of: (a) living in full the principles of the Way of the Livingness (b) the provision and maintenance of buildings used for religious practice and for religious instruction (c) the conducting of religious ceremonies (d) to provide buildings open to the public for people to enter and benefit from personal soulful contemplation.

Again, the rejection was on the grounds of failure to satisfy the public benefit test.[22]

Subsequently, the teachings of The Way of the Livingness (otherwise known as Universal Medicine) were scrutinised by the Court of Appeal in *Re S (Parental Alienation: Cult).*[23] An estranged father sought variation of a child arrangements order to provide for his 9-year-old daughter, 'Lara', to live with him rather than with her mother, who was an adherent. Relying in part on the judgment of the Supreme Court of New South Wales[24] in an unsuccessful libel suit brought by The Way's founder, Serge Benhayon, which found it to be a socially-harmful cult, the Court decided to postpone a final decision to allow the mother 'one last chance to take her own steps to leave Universal Medicine, start intensive therapy, and reverse the process of alienation of Lara from her father', adding that 'we warn that we foresee that without a wholesale transformation in the mother's position the court at the further hearing is likely to find it necessary to transfer Lara's care to her father'.[25] When the case returned to the Family Division, Williams J found that the mother had failed to comply with the Court of Appeal's directions to disassociate herself from Universal Medicine, gave the father exclusive custody of the child and refused an application for permission to appeal.[26]

On the other hand, when the Druid Network applied for registration in 2010, the Commission concluded that the Druids constituted a religion in charity law and provided public benefit – and stated that its decision was significant because it 'had to consider the definition of a religion both in charity law and human rights law'.[27] Nevertheless, it noted that

> the charity law definition of a religion … differs from the definition of a religion or belief system protected by Articles 9 and 14, not least that charity law requires that advancing a religion or belief system must be for public benefit.[28]

Later, in *Temple of the Jedi Order,*[29] the Commission refused the application of the Order to be constituted as a Charitable Incorporated Organisation ('CIO') and entered on the register of charities. The purposes of the proposed CIO were to advance the religion of Jediism for the public benefit worldwide in accordance with the Jedi Doctrine and to advance such charitable purposes as the Trustees saw fit from time to time.[30] The Commission was not satisfied that the reverence of the Jedi for 'the Force' was characterised by the belief in one or more gods or spiritual or non-secular principles or things necessary to constitute a 'religion' in charity law: 'Despite being open to spiritual awareness, there is scope for Jediism and the Jedi Doctrine to be advanced and followed as a secular belief system. Jediism therefore lacks the necessary spiritual or non-secular element'.[31] The Commission also noted that in *Hodkin* Lord Toulson had excluded secular belief systems from his description of religion.[32]

Nor was the Commission satisfied that Jediism as promoted by the Order demonstrated sufficient coherence and a sufficiently distinct set of beliefs, principles, and practices as to demonstrate the promotion of ethics or morals that could be shown by evidence to be for the benefit of the public. It was not sufficient to advance spirituality or spiritual beliefs on their own, nor was there a presumption that individuals would behave in a way that impacted beneficially on society.[33] There was also a lack of clarity as to what beliefs, principles, and practices were promoted,[34] and insufficient evidence that moral improvement was central to the Order's beliefs and practices – particularly as the Jedi Doctrine could be accepted, rejected and interpreted by individuals as they saw fit.[35] Nor was there sufficient evidence of Jediism directly promoting moral improvement within society generally.[36]

The Commission concluded that there was insufficient evidence to demonstrate either that the purpose of the Order was the promotion of moral or ethical improvement for the benefit of the public[37] or that it had beneficial effects.[38] In short, it was not satisfied that Jediism and its doctrines were sufficiently structured so as to have a beneficial impact[39] or that the public benefit requirement had been met, either for the advancement of religion or for the promotion of moral or ethical improvement.[40]

Whether or not the decision on the Druid Network represents the beginning of a closer engagement by the Commission with Article 9 remains to be seen, though the subsequent decision on the Jedi would appear to suggest that it does not; in any event, however, given the public benefit requirement in section 3 of the Charities Act 2006[41] and the fact that what is of benefit to the public is to some extent in the eye of the beholder, we suspect that recognition of the activities of new religious movements as charitable will be a very gradual, *ad hoc* process.

Dealing with individual religious freedom: new forms of religiosity and doctrinal developments

English and Scots law have long protected novel and individual religious beliefs and manifestations provided that such recognition was not contrary to public policy. For instance, in *Thornton v Howe*[42] a trust for printing, publishing and propagating the sacred writings of Joanna Southcott (which were alleged to declare, maintain or reveal that the Holy Spirit had impregnated her and a second Messiah was to be born) was held to be a valid charitable trust for the advancement of religion. However, it was held that the trust would only have been declared void if it had been the case that 'the tenets of a particular sect inculcate doctrines averse to the very foundations of all religion, and that are subversive of all religions'.[43]

Such permissiveness is a legacy of a process of toleration whereby legal disabilities that prevented the practice of forms of religiosity other than those of the established Church of England were removed, including limitations on holding certain public offices. Rather than any general recognition of religious rights, specific disabilities were removed piecemeal over a long period of time[44] with the result that, unlike in many Continental jurisdictions, English and Scots law neither developed a mandatory system of registration for religious groups nor articulated positive rights on grounds of religion. However, an unfortunate side effect was to define religion by analogy and, therefore, to take a conservative approach that discriminated against new forms of religiosity.[45] Rather than a rights-based approach to religious manifestation, the position at common law was that, absent any legal prohibition, people were permitted to do as they wished. As Donaldson MR noted in 1990, 'the starting point of our domestic law is that every citizen has a right to do what he likes, unless restrained by the common law ... or by statute'.[46] Legal mechanisms, therefore, generally favoured individual freedom of action.

The protection and articulation of religious rights in recent years, chiefly through human rights and anti-discrimination laws, have altered this historic common law stance. There are now many more rights conceded on grounds of religion or belief, and it would be expected that the earlier conservative attitude had been overtaken by the increasingly liberal approach culminating in the decision in *Hodkin*. However, detailed analysis of the case law shows that this has not happened. Rather, conservatism (or to put it more provocatively, the implicit disadvantaging of novel forms of religiosity) has continued to be evident in the interpretation of new religious rights. Courts and tribunals, though reluctant to determine what constitutes a religion or belief, have shown no inhibitions about determining what is a manifestation of a religion or belief, or what constitutes a disadvantage to a person's religion or belief; and in those contexts they have deemed themselves competent to answer theological questions.

A classic example is the decision in *Playfoot*,[47] in which Supperstone QC, sitting as a High Court judge, held that the wearing of a 'purity ring' by a schoolgirl as a sign of her sexual restraint was not a manifestation of her religion or belief since she 'was under no obligation, by reason of her belief, to wear the ring; nor does she suggest that she was so obliged'.[48] This suggested that manifestations of religion would only be protected if they were not only shared by coreligionists but also deemed to be obligatory;[49] nor, it might be noted in passing, did His Lordship consider whether or not wearing a 'purity ring' might have been a manifestation of Ms Playfoot's *philosophical or conscientious* belief in sexual abstinence before marriage that merited the protection of Article 9 – which protects freedom of thought and conscience as well as freedom of religion.

This requirement that religious manifestations need to be mandatory, or at least shared with others of the same faith, has meant that, in discrimination law, beliefs held by a few individuals that are not doctrinally obligatory (including beliefs held by a minority of believers within a larger religious group) have been denied protection. This is evident from the cases of *Eweida v British Airways* and *Chaplin v Royal Devon & Exeter NHS Foundation Trust*, which were the subject of domestic litigation before being heard by the European Court of Human Rights at Strasbourg.[50]

Both cases involved alleged indirect discrimination on grounds of religion or belief under the Equality Act 2010. To establish indirect discrimination, the claimant must prove that there has been a 'particular disadvantage' and that the disadvantage was not justified. There is a 'particular disadvantage' where the respondent has applied a provision, criterion or practice (PCP) equally to persons who do not share the claimant's religion or belief but, at the same time, that PCP puts persons who share the claimant's religion or belief at a particular disadvantage compared with others and actually disadvantages the claimant. In the domestic courts, the two claims failed for lack of evidence that the PCP placed persons who shared the claimants' religion at a particular disadvantage. In both cases, the fact that the PCP did not seemingly disadvantage coreligionists because they did not share the claimants' interpretation of their religion or belief was fatal to the claim.

Nadia Eweida, a part-time member of the check-in staff at British Airways (BA), sought to wear a silver cross in breach of BA's then uniform policy which prohibited visible religious symbols unless wearing them was mandatory. She was sent home by BA and remained there unpaid for five months before returning to work once the policy had been changed. The Employment Appeal Tribunal held that there had been no indirect discrimination because, though the uniform policy was a PCP, it did not put Christians at a particular disadvantage. Elias J held that 'the whole purpose of indirect discrimination is to deal with the problem of group discrimination' and, in this case, the lower tribunal was plainly entitled to conclude that there was no evidence of group disadvantage.[51] The Court of Appeal agreed, holding that there was no evidence either that practising Christians considered the visible display of the cross to be a requirement of the Christian faith or that the provision created a barrier to Christians employed at BA.[52] Sedley LJ held that it was 'entirely right' that equality laws required the court to determine 'whether an identifiable group is adversely affected, whether actually or potentially' and rejected the argument that the reference to 'persons' could include an entirely hypothetical peer-group, holding that there was no indication that solitary disadvantage should be sufficient.[53]

Shirley Chaplin, a nurse, had always worn a crucifix on a chain around her neck at work but a change to a V-neck uniform made the crucifix visible. She was asked by her Senior Matron to remove it at work on grounds of health and safety, the concern being of risk of injury when handling patients. When she refused, she was redeployed to a non-clinical role in which the hospital had no objections to her wearing the crucifix. The Employment Tribunal dismissed her claim of indirect discrimination, again on the basis that the uniform policy did not 'place "persons" at a particular disadvantage'.[54] Despite evidence that another nurse, Mrs Babcock, had been asked to remove her cross and chain,[55] the Employment Tribunal held that Mrs Babcock had not been put at a particular disadvantage since the word 'particular' meant that the disadvantage suffered needed to be 'noteworthy, peculiar or singular' and those criteria had not been met, because Mrs Babcock's religious views were not so strong as to lead her to refuse to comply with the policy. The Tribunal held that this was 'sufficient to dispose of the case', because the test for indirect discrimination referred 'to "persons" in the plural rather than the singular and here we have evidence that only one person, the claimant, was placed at a particular disadvantage'.[56]

Taken together, the domestic decisions in *Eweida* and *Chaplin* suggest that an objective approach is being taken whereby the test for indirect discrimination has been interpreted to require proof that a claimant's particular belief is not only shared by his or her coreligionists[57] but is deemed compulsory. There will only be indirect discrimination where coreligionists agree that it is obligatory (and, according to *Chaplin*, where at least one coreligionist is aggravated to the same extent as the claimant). The problem of this approach is that the courts assumed that all members of a particular religion share identical beliefs; and because manifestations of beliefs that were not regarded as obligatory according to a claimant's coreligionists were denied protection, it did not matter what the individual claimant believed – an extraordinarily conservative approach that disadvantaged new interpretations of religion and/or belief.

It was therefore unsurprising that the European Court of Human Rights rejected this interpretation.[58] The claim in *Eweida* focused on whether or not the decisions of the domestic courts and tribunals had violated the claimants' Article 9 rights and was the first case in which Strasbourg institutions found the United Kingdom to be in breach of Article 9. The Court rejected the UK Government's submission that the claimants'

> desire to wear a visible cross, while it may have been inspired or motivated by a sincere religious commitment, was not a recognised religious practice or requirement of Christianity, and did not therefore fall within the scope of Article 9.[59]

The Court stressed that Article 9 protects 'views that attain a certain level of cogency, seriousness, cohesion and importance' and, provided that threshold was satisfied, 'the State's duty of neutrality and impartiality is incompatible with any power on the State's part to assess the legitimacy of religious beliefs or the ways in which those beliefs are expressed'.[60] Although accepting that not 'every act which is in some way inspired, motivated or influenced by it constitutes a "manifestation" of the belief', the Court clarified that this only meant that 'acts or omissions which do not directly express the belief concerned or which are only remotely connected to a precept of faith fall outside the protection of Article 9'.[61] Moreover, though 'an act of worship or devotion which forms part of the practice of a religion or belief in a generally recognised form' would clearly be a manifestation, 'the manifestation of religion or belief is not limited to such acts'; rather, 'the existence of a sufficiently close and direct nexus between the act and the underlying belief must be determined on the facts of each case'. The Court was clear that 'there is no requirement on the applicant to establish that he or she acted in fulfilment of a duty mandated by the religion in question'.[62]

It is therefore clear that statements in the domestic case law that, in order to be 'manifestations', actions had to be mandated by the religion in question were incorrect interpretations of Article 9. In respect of *Eweida*, the Court held – unlike the domestic decisions – that Ms Eweida's wish to wear a crucifix 'was a manifestation of her religious belief, in the form of worship, practice and observance, and as such attracted the protection of Article 9'[63] and that the interference with that right had been disproportionate:[64] the domestic courts had afforded too much weight to her employer's wish to project a certain corporate image and not enough to her desire to manifest her religious belief.[65] In *Chaplin*, however, though the Court again accepted that Mrs Chaplin wore her crucifix at work as a manifestation of her religious belief,[66] there had been no violation of Article 9 because the interference had been justified to protect health and safety on a hospital ward and 'was inherently of a greater magnitude than that which applied in respect of Ms Eweida'.[67] Although the brevity of the Court's analysis of this point is problematic, in that it runs the risk of writing a blank cheque wherever health and safety concerns are invoked, the Court's overall message in these two claims was clear: the domestic courts had erred in holding that there was no interference with Ms Eweida or Mrs Chaplin's Article 9 rights merely on the basis that Christians do not generally regard wearing a cross or crucifix as obligatory.

The Strasbourg judgment raises the question of whether or not the test for indirect religious discrimination – requiring proof that the claimant's particular belief is shared by his or her coreligionists – breaches Article 9.[68] The logic of the Court's elucidation of general principles is that an individual's belief will still be protected under Article 9 *even if it is shared by no-one else*. This would suggest that a rule under indirect discrimination law that requires evidence that the belief is shared would breach Article 9. To date, however, this matter remains unresolved in domestic law.[69]

Conclusions

The letter of English and Scots law concerning religious freedom has changed dramatically over the last twenty years. Freedom of religion is now articulated as a human right and includes both individual and collective religious freedom. However, in practice, there has been much less change in relation to how the two jurisdictions protect religion. The decision in *Hodkin* does not represent a sea-change but, rather, the kind of *ad hoc*, progressive development that has long characterised the common law in both jurisdictions. Neither has developed any mechanism for dealing with splintering religious groups beyond the law of trusts and the use of private Acts of Parliament; and the fact that such groups are religious has no discernible effect upon the way in which the courts arrive at their decisions. It remains the law that there is 'nothing in calling an associated body a Church that exempts it from the legal obligations of insisting that money given for one purpose shall not be devoted to another';[70] and it is questionable whether this stance is compatible with the letter or the spirit of Article 9, given that religious belief is not a static phenomenon.

Even when bodies such as the Charity Commission have attempted to consider the definition of religion in human rights law, the end result has been pragmatic rather than principled. To begin from the Commission's premise that 'the charity law definition of a religion ... differs from the definition of a religion or belief system protected by Articles 9 and 14' is not only problematic inasmuch as it assumes that the Article 9 definition is somehow negotiable, it is likely to prove fatal to the vast majority of applications for registration from new religious movements – as the failure of the application by the Jedi demonstrated.

When it rejected Jediism, the Charity Commission cast doubt on the observance of the Force as the 'belief in one or more gods or spiritual or non-secular principles or things' necessary to be recognised as a religion in charity law and noted that Jediism could be 'advanced and followed as a secular belief system', concluding that Jediism therefore lacked the necessary spiritual or non-secular element to merit recognition. We would suggest that, in reaching that conclusion, the Commission went too far, appearing to adopt a distinction between the secular and the non-secular that is difficult to defend and operating from the assumption that 'religion' is something that can be described objectively, rather than a manifestation of the personal convictions of believers: in short, it took too little account of the *forum internum* under Article 9(1) ECHR.

It remains questionable, therefore, whether the Human Rights Act 1998 has had any great effect upon *collective* religious freedom. It has had an obvious effect in terms of *individual* religious freedom, as shown by an increase in the number of high-profile cases and a prevailing discussion of religious rights, but the actual legal effect has again been limited. The domestic judicial interpretation of Article 9 has been inherently conservative and was subject to much correction by the European Court of Human Rights in its *Eweida* judgment. Notwithstanding that decision, however, it remains unresolved whether or not solitary disadvantage can be sufficient for the purpose of indirect religious discrimination law. Ironically, despite the enactment of a number of religious rights provisions that regard religious freedom as an *individual* right, the law provides a lesser degree of protection for those who profess membership of a religion but adhere to a personalised interpretation of that religion.

The problem, as we see it, is that neither jurisdiction has yet fully embraced the letter and spirit of Article 9. Legal actors are not yet appreciating that religious freedom is both an individual and a collective right. The novelty of the human rights framework has led to a timid response that has largely failed to take into account the role of religion and belief in the formation of personal identities. English and Scots law need fully to embrace the notion that religion is a matter of private judgment and that a right to manifest religion or belief should mean exactly what it says: that people should have the right to manifest *any* religion or belief, provided only that to do so does not involve something otherwise illegal. And even Christianity was once a 'new religious movement': the principal concern of the Council of Jerusalem in Acts 15 was precisely whether it would be a development within Judaism or a new religion in its own right.

Notes

1 *R v Registrar General, ex parte Segerdal* [1970] 2 QB 679, 707.
2 *R (Hodkin & Ors) v Registrar General of Births, Deaths and Marriages* [2012] EWHC 3635 (Admin); see also *R (Church of Scientology) v Registrar General of Births* [2012] EWHC 3751 (Admin) granting a certificate under s.12 of the Administration of Justice Act 1969 to allow an application directly to the Supreme Court for permission to appeal.
3 *R (Hodkin & Anor) v Registrar-General of Births, Deaths and Marriages* [2013] UKSC 77, [34], [56].
4 [57]. It might also be noted in passing that Lord Toulson's description teeters on the brink of including humanism within its scope – though not atheism. Atheism is, however, protected under other areas of law such as the Equality Act 2010, under which laws prohibiting discrimination on grounds of religion or belief include lack of religion or belief.
5 There was no such bar in Scotland, which licenses *celebrants* rather than *buildings*.
6 A national opinion poll carried out by the *Sunday Telegraph* in May 2009 found that three quarters of Christians polled felt there was less religious freedom than twenty years ago: http://www.telegraph.co.uk/news/religion/5413311/Christians-risk-rejection-and-discrimination-for-their-faith-a-study-claims.html, accessed 1 June 2020.
7 See the 'Clearing the Ground Inquiry', published by the Evangelical Alliance on behalf of Christians in Parliament: https://www.eauk.org/current-affairs/publications/clearing-the-ground.cfm, accessed 1 June 2020. Though the inquiry's conclusion is by no means uncontested, it clearly accords with the *perceptions* of many Christians, whether or not it accords with the reality.
8 Corporations Act 1661, Act of Uniformity 1662, Conventicles Act 1664, Nonconformists Act 1666 (commonly known as the Five Mile Act), Test Act 1673.

9 Act against Conventicles 1670.

10 [1904] AC 515.

11 Act XII of 1834, anent Overtures and Interim Acts on the Calling of Ministers.

12 *Kinnoull (Earl of) v Presbytery of Auchterarder* (1838) 16 S 661.

13 *Proceedings of the General Assembly of the Free Church* (1843) 12 [emphasis added].

14 Act VIII of 1732, anent the Method of Planting Vacant Churches.

15 *General Assembly of the Free Church of Scotland v Lord Overtoun*, 626–7.

16 See, for example, *Shergill & Ors v Khaira & Ors* [2014] UKSC 33 [48]: "The jurisdiction of the courts is not excluded because the cause of the disciplinary procedure is a dispute about theology or ecclesiology. The civil court does not resolve the religious dispute. Nor does it decide the merits of disciplinary action if that action is within the contractual powers of the relevant organ of the association … Its role is more modest: it keeps the parties to their contract".

17 See, for example, the United Reformed Church Acts 1972–2000.

18 *Free Church of Scotland (Continuing) v General Assembly of the Free Church of Scotland* [2005] CSOH 46, *Smith & Ors v Morrison & Ors* [2011] CSIH 52.

19 Even when the dispute is about ecclesiastical jurisdiction rather than doctrine. For example, *Dean v Burne & Ors* [2009] EWHC 1250 (Ch): a dispute about jurisdiction in the Orthodox Church.

20 Decisions of the Charity Commissioners for England & Wales: *Church of Scientology* (17 November 1999).

21 Decisions of the Charity Commissioners for England & Wales: *Gnostic Centre* (16 December 2009). para 63.

22 Decisions of the Charity Commissioners for England & Wales: *The Way of the Livingness, The Religion of the Soul Trust* (24 August 2011).

23 [2020] EWCA Civ 568.

24 *Benhayon v Rockett (No 8)* 2019 NSWSC 169.

25 *Re S (Parental Alienation: Cult)* [104].

26 *Re S (Parental Alienation: Cult: Transfer of Primary Care)* [2020] EWHC 1940 (Fam).

27 Decisions of the Charity Commissioners for England & Wales: *Druid Network* (21 September 2010).

28 *Druid Network*, para 13.

29 Decisions of the Charity Commissioners for England & Wales: *The Temple of The Jedi Order: Application for Registration* (16 December 2016).

30 *Temple of The Jedi Order*, 4.

31 *Temple of The Jedi Order*, 18.

32 *Temple of The Jedi Order*, 18.

33 *Temple of The Jedi Order*, 40, 42.

34 *Temple of The Jedi Order*, 43.

35 *Temple of The Jedi Order*, 44.

36 *Temple of The Jedi Order*, 45.

37 *Temple of The Jedi Order*, 48.

38 *Temple of The Jedi Order*, 54.

39 *Temple of The Jedi Order*, 46.

40 *Temple of The Jedi Order*, 60.

41 Subsumed into the Charities Act 2011 as s.4.

42 (1862) 31 Beavan 14.

43 This was approved in *Re Watson* [1973] 1 WLR 1472 at 1483–84.

44 Possibly the last vestige was the removal by the Universities Tests Act 1871 of the religious test for graduation from Oxford, Cambridge and Durham.

45 There were some exceptions where this did occur such as in relation to the interpretation of the Places of Worship Registration Act 1855 discussed above.

46 *AG v Guardian Newspapers Ltd (No 2)* [1990] 1 AC 109.

47 *R (Playfoot (A Child)) v Millais School Governing Body* [2007] EWHC Admin 1698.

48 [23].

49 This a stance that was incompatible with the previous House of Lords judgment in *R v Secretary of State for Education and Employment and others ex parte Williamson*[2005] UKHL 15, [33] and which was later critiqued by a High Court decision which held that: 'There is nothing within Article 9 that requires there to be a perceived, much less an objectively demonstrable, obligation for the manifestation of religious belief to be protectable': *R (Bashir) v The Independent Adjudicator* [2011] EWHC Admin 1108, [21].

50 The Strasbourg decision is reported as *Eweida and Others v United Kingdom* (2013) 57 EHRR 8.

51 *Eweida v British Airways* [2008] UKEAT/0123/08LA (20.11.08).

52 *Eweida v British Airways* [2010] EWCA Civ 80, [8].

53 [8] and [15].

54 *Chaplin v Royal Devon & Exeter NHS Foundation Trust* [2010] ET/ 1728886/2009.

55 [15].

56 [28].

57 In *R (Eunice Johns and Owen Johns) v Derby City Council* [2011] EWHC Admin 375, the High Court subsequently confirmed that in indirect discrimination claims concerning Christians it is now 'necessary to show 'particular disadvantage' or 'group' disadvantage to Christians or the particular denomination of Christianity' [101].

58 (2013) 57 EHRR 8.

59 [58].

60 [81].

61 [82]. The first limb of this test is easier to interpret than the second. It is difficult to find a clear example of an action that would fail the 'remote connection' test, especially where the 'direct expression' test had been met (note that the word 'or' is used in the judgment).The judgment suggests that courts will now have to assess 'remoteness'.

62 Ibid. The same point was expressed clearly in the partly dissenting opinion of judges Bratza and Björgvinsson, [2].

63 [89].

64 [94].

65 [94].

66 [97].

67 [99]. The NHS Trust also offered her a 'reasonable accommodation': to wear her crucifix as a brooch [98].

68 This point is noted but not dealt with in paragraph 9 of the partly dissenting opinion of judges Bratza and Björgvinsson.

69 See, most notably, the Court of Appeal decision in *Mba v London Borough of Merton* [2013] EWCA Civ 1562 where the 'core component' test had been applied by an Employment Tribunal. Although the Court of Appeal dismissed the appeal because the Employment Tribunal's ultimate conclusion that the disadvantage had been proportionate was plainly and unarguably right, it did note that there had been errors of law in the Employment Tribunal's decision.

70 *General Assembly of the Free Church of Scotland v Lord Overtoun*, 626–7.

Bibliography

All URLs were accessed on 1 June 2020.

Statutes

Act Against Conventicles 1670.
Act of Uniformity 1662.
Charities Act 2006.
Charities Act 2011.
Church Patronage (Scotland) Act 1711.
Claim of Right 1689.
Confession of Faith Ratification Act 1560.
Confession of Faith Ratification Act 1690.
Conventicles Act 1664.
Corporations Act 1661.
Equality Act 2010.
Human Rights Act 1998.
Nonconformists Act 1666.
Places of Worship Registration Act 1855.
Racial and Religious Hatred Act 2006.
Scottish Episcopalians Relief Act 1792.
Test Act 1673.
United Reformed Church Acts 1972–2000.
Universities Tests Act 1871.

Cases

AG v Guardian Newspapers Ltd (No 2) [1990] 1 AC 109.
Benhayon v Rockett (No 8) 2019 NSWSC 169.
Chaplin v Royal Devon & Exeter NHS Foundation Trust [2010] ET/1728886/2009.
Dean v Burne & Ors [2009] EWHC 1250 (Ch).
Eweida v British Airways [2008] UKEAT/0123/08LA.
Eweida v British Airways [2010] EWCA Civ 80.
Eweida and Others v United Kingdom (2013) 57 EHRR 8.
Free Church of Scotland (Continuing) v General Assembly of the Free Church of Scotland [2005] CSOH 46.
General Assembly of the Free Church of Scotland v Lord Overtoun [1904] AC 515.
Kinnoull (Earl of) v Presbytery of Auchterarder (1838) 16 S 661.
Mba v London Borough of Merton [2013] EWCA Civ 1562.
R v Registrar General, ex parte Segerdal [1970] 2 QB 679.
R v Secretary of State for Education and Employment & Ors ex parte Williamson [2005] UKHL 15.
R (Bashir) v The Independent Adjudicator [2011] EWHC Admin 1108, [21].
R (Church of Scientology) v Registrar General of Births [2012] EWHC 3751 (Admin).
R (Eunice Johns and Owen Johns) v Derby City Council [2011] EWHC Admin 375.

R (Hodkin & Ors) v Registrar General of Births, Deaths and Marriages [2012] EWHC 3635 (Admin).
R (Hodkin & Anor) v Registrar-General of Births, Deaths and Marriages [2013] UKSC 77.
R (Playfoot (A Child)) v Millais School Governing Body [2007] EWHC Admin 1698.
Re S (Parental Alienation: Cult) [2020] EWCA Civ 568.
Re S (Parental Alienation: Cult: Transfer of Primary Care) [2020] EWHC 1940 (Fam).
Re Watson [1973] 1 WLR 1472.
Shergill & Ors v Khaira & Ors [2014] UKSC 33.
Smith & Ors v Morrison & Ors [2011] CSIH 52.
Thornton v Howe (1862) 31 Beavan 14.

Decisions of the Charity Commissioners for England and Wales

Church of Scientology (17 November 1999).
Druid Network (21 September 2010).
Gnostic Centre (16 December 2009).
The Temple of The Jedi Order: Application for Registration (16 December 2016).
The Way of the Livingness, The Religion of the Soul Trust (24 August 2011).

Others

Act VIII of 1732 anent the Method of Planting Vacant Churches [*Church of Scotland*].
Act XII of 1834 anent Overtures and Interim Acts on the Calling of Ministers [*Church of Scotland*].
Christians in Parliament. 2012. Clearing the Ground. London: Evangelical Alliance. Available at http://www.eauk.org/current-affairs/publications/clearing-the-ground.cfm
Proceedings of the General Assembly of the Free Church (1843).

10 Revision or re-branding? The Plymouth Brethren Christian Church in Australia under Bruce D. Hales 2002–2016

Bernard Doherty and Laura Dyason

In November 2013, the Australian tabloid television program *Today Tonight* aired a report entitled 'Religious Rebrand' in which they looked at the recent adoption of the name Plymouth Brethren Christian Church (PBCC) by the group popularly known as the 'Exclusive Brethren'. The report claimed this was 'an attempt to reinvent its tattered image' and showed public relations material produced by the group, which was described by the reporter as being 'complete with new warm and fuzzy image'. The report painted a highly stylised negative portrait of the Brethren that the presenter claimed was 'at odds with the Brethren's new wholesome public profile' (Uechtritz 2013). No stranger to sensationalist reporting on minority religious groups, *Today Tonight*'s report was hardly unique, with its timeslot rival *A Current Affair* producing a similar negative program on the Brethren a few months later (Williams 2014). These reports and others like them demonstrate the mixed ways in which recent changes within the PBCC (henceforth referred to as the Brethren),[1] a numerically small evangelical Protestant sect that has been a subject of intermittent controversy, have been received.

Since at least the 1950s, the Brethren have been a subject of episodic negative attention from the news media, politicians and regulatory bodies in a number of countries. The Brethren's strict communal boundaries and highly regulated community norms have sporadically occasioned disputes between the religious group and its surrounding environment. While the Brethren's *raison d'être* centres around a historical commitment to the beliefs and practices which underpin the 'Recovery of the Truth'[2] begun under their ostensible founder John Nelson Darby in the late 1820s, the way in which the Brethren have expressed and lived their beliefs has undergone a number of changes over their history – often as the result of changing social conditions, both internal and external to the Brethren community. Some of these occurred most dramatically during the 1950s and 1960s when the then leader James Taylor Jr. reinforced the group's commitment to the principle of 'Separation from Evil'[3] by implementing various rules governing the Brethren's social interactions within and outside their community in an effort to 'reinforce existing principles in changing

DOI: 10.4324/9781315226804-10

social circumstances' (Wilson 1983: 83). This exercise in boundary maintenance led to widespread negative press coverage at the time and a large exodus of members.[4] More recently, changes within the Brethren have again become particularly visible and highly publicized since Bruce D. Hales replaced his late father, John S. Hales, as worldwide leader of the group in early 2002. It is this recent period of revision which we focus on in this chapter.

In Australia, the Brethren constitute a sizable religious minority of around 15,000 members, whose public profile has increased exponentially in recent years owing to significant media attention since the mid-2000s.[5] The Brethren's higher public profile has ensured that scrutiny of their activities has also increased, as has the number of their critics from various sectors of Australian society, including journalists; state and federal politicians; trade unions representatives; members of the judiciary;[6] cult-watching groups; and former members. Negative external reactions to change within the Brethren have been numerous and highlight a series of areas in which this group's complex 'mode of insertion' (Beckford 1978: 77) into Australian society has provided multiple sites for conflict with sectors of the wider community. Moreover, these mixed responses to change highlight the multiple ways in which developments within the Brethren have been understood, both within the movement itself, but, of equal importance, by outside observers (Figure 10.1).[7]

Since Bruce Hales became 'Minister of the Lord in the Recovery'[8] several changes have been seen. The Brethren have sought to reconcile with estranged former members who Brethren acknowledged had been unjustly treated. Brethren senior members have been linked to political campaigning. Brethren businesses, schools, and households have cautiously adopted various forms of technology previously forbidden or restricted. Brethren communities have developed a network of government subsidized schools teaching the predominantly secular national curriculum. Brethren have permitted a small number of younger members to pursue university level higher education. And Brethren members have engaged in highly-publicized charity work directed to those outside the Brethren community. In this chapter, we analyse a selection of these developments,[9] noting where recent internal and external factors may have influenced change within the Brethren community in an Australian context.[10]

In analysing this example of religious revisionism, we focus both on the changes involved in Brethren approaches to the Review, politics, education, technology, and charity, and how these changes have been interpreted. To this end, we describe how different observers have accounted for recent changes in the Brethren, by looking at how the meaning attached to these changes is largely in the eye of the beholder and might be understood as either revisionism or re-branding (or neither as suggested by a current member of the Brethren), depending on an interpreter's perspective. We also provide some wider background to these changes and identify some of the major societal factors that have influenced them.

Figure 10.1 PBCC Meeting Room Canberra (Photograph by Eileen Barker)

'The Review'

In 2002, not long after Bruce Hales assumed leadership of the Brethren, reports began to emerge in the media and on Internet forums of overtures being made to former members by the Brethren seeking reconciliation and encouraging them to return to the fold. Some contact between long-estranged former members and Brethren family members was permitted and even encouraged, and some assembly leaders wrote to former members, apologising for the ways in which they may have maltreated them during past disciplinary procedures. This situation, generally referred to by observers as 'The Review' sought on the Brethren's part to acknowledge that past disciplinary decisions by individual assemblies may have been unjust and that some former members who had been 'withdrawn from'[11] may have been unfairly treated.

The motives for this gesture, however, have been variously interpreted and serve to demonstrate the contested narratives surrounding recent change in the Brethren. Within the Brethren fold the position taken has been that Hales' decision to seek rapprochement with former members was a gesture not only of good will, but also a recognition that at times disciplinary procedures in individual assemblies may have been unduly harsh and unjust. According to printed Ministry,[12] Hales told Brethren in Sydney at the time:

> See, we look back and in some sense it's been widespread, failure in administration, lack of discernment, lack of priestly skill, lack of wisdom, and that's caused suffering for the brethren. Some assemblies, long periods of suffering because of a failure in administration. (Hales, Bruce 2002: 6)

Some outside the Brethren viewed things with more scepticism. Several former members, including some who have penned lengthy auto-biographical accounts about their time within the movement, were clearly affronted by this. They suggested that such actions were a ploy to gain financial advantage by drawing successful former members back into the fold, or were an attempt to strengthen the population in a group which does not actively recruit and relies almost solely on current members having large families to ensure the continuation and growth of the group.[13] Other former Brethren suggested that Hales' motives related to a steady stream of young members who had left during the 1990s. As David Tchappat, who had left in 1992, wrote:

> It appeared Mr Bruce had realised the sad state of affairs regarding large groups of teenagers leaving the Brethren. He had to do something to stem the flow. He began relaxing the rules a little, starting with families having more contact with their children who had left. Instead of treating them as outcasts and lepers, he urged parents to re-build their relationships with their children, but at the same time eating or having regular contact was not allowed. (Tchappat 2009: 197)

Tchappat's subsequent account of a meeting with his family demonstrates how many former members viewed these overtures, 'as with any approach by the Brethren, it was a double-edged sword. It was always a nice exchange with pretty words but underneath was inevitably, a hidden agenda' (Tchappat 2009: 199).

Those former members we interviewed who witnessed the Review from the inside recall confusion and uncertainty, with familiar rules they were raised to follow being changed, and widespread leadership changes as leading brothers, blamed for unjust dealings with former members, were themselves withdrawn from or demoted. Colin, a former member who left after the Review recalls:

It was a time of upheaval within the church as people questioned everything they'd been raised to believe was right. For instance, my grandmother spent decades believing her husband was a wicked person, only to be told around 2002 that the church had made a mistake and he should never have been thrown out in the first place. Of course by then it was too late. There was …a lot of anger and resentment.

Other former members and critics suggest that not only did the instigation of the Review gain Hales 'enormous popularity', particularly with members who had lost family members to excommunication; it also provided him with 'a good chance to purge the Brethren leadership of anyone who was not loyal to [him] and the new direction he was taking'. Former members describe being told that the Review was needed to remedy past disciplinary decisions made by local leaders who had not acted in accordance with the instructions of the leader at the time, or worse, had deceived him about the true facts of administrative matters resulting in harsher than necessary judgments. As part of the Review, the local leaders were required to admit to their responsibility for these mistakes, on occasion resulting in their own discipline. According to former member Mike:

Part of the process was to place the blame on local leaders, thereby absolving the universal leadership of any responsibility. Another side-effect (possibly intended) was that a great many local leaders were demoted or fell from favour, so all Hales' potential rivals for the leadership were effectively neutralised.

Whatever the case may have been, if the Review was intended to bring former members back (which the Brethren note was not their purpose), it was unsuccessful. By May 2003, Hales was already expressing concern regarding a growing laxity since his father's death. Former members who did not wish to return, but had been given reason to hope that they would be able to rebuild relationships with estranged family members found contact again restricted. Kelvin, a young man who was at the time a member, and had enjoyed briefly being able to communicate with older siblings who had already left the Brethren recalls it as a confusing and painful time:

The review of the Review was the hardest part to stomach. When it became apparent that many of those approached had no mind to return to the fold, that the Brethren had not substantially changed… and that standards had been compromised too much… family members were told to cease contact once more with the ex-members. The *Letter of May '03*[14] was the epitome of the about face. It left many young ones confused, angered and even determined not to accept any more reversals and inconsistencies. However, the "review" appeared to have achieved significant power consolidation for Hales, which I now believe was the initial motive.

Despite the cynical motives attributed to Hales by critics, his printed Ministry and his followers clearly maintain that the purpose of this process was to rectify administrative injustices. If the intention was to remedy past wrongs, as the Brethren maintain, it still appears to have been largely unsuccessful, and in terms of outcomes in many instances simply re-traumatised former members and provoked some to more active opposition against the Brethren.[15]

Politics

While tragic stories of family estrangement have become a mainstay of media coverage of the Brethren, the major reason they first came to such media prominence in Australia relates to what former member Colin called their 'naïve attempt to influence the political process in their favour'.[16] During the mid-2000s, a number of individual Brethren across the globe were linked by investigative journalists to a series of conservative political pamphlets. While this was a clearly identifiable international trend, it attracted little attention in countries other than Australia and New Zealand, where the Brethren population was larger and where particularly polarised political contexts facilitated wider media scrutiny.

In Australia, these pamphlets first appeared around the time of the 2004 federal election. During this election campaign, the future funding of non-government schools – a matter of importance to the Brethren's growing number of schools – was a major topic of debate. Furthermore, this election saw conservative incumbent Prime Minister John Howard, whose policies on marriage, the economy, and national security were popular amongst Brethren, pitted against the firebrand Mark Latham whose policies, Brethren believed, threatened the funding of their schools, and were less in line with their values and interests.

On the one hand pamphlets provided support for the incumbent Coalition government, whilst, on the other hand, expressing disapproval at what the Brethren considered the permissive and morally damaging policies of the progressive Australian Greens. While these pamphlets later became a major talking point in subsequent parliamentary debates and media reports, at the time of their first appearance very few people recognised the provenance of these materials. When the source of the materials was identified in 2005, the Brethren's critics utilised them to attack the Howard government for associating with the controversial group and to question the desirability of Brethren (and, indeed, wider religious) involvement in political processes.

The perceived inconsistency between the Brethren's longstanding refusal to vote on conscientious grounds and their political involvement surprised not only the public, but also current and former members. Mike, who had left many years earlier, recalls that when he was with the Brethren, they did not vote or campaign. However, according to former member Chris, 'under Bruce Hales this all changed and Brethren all over the world were pressured into all sorts of political activities in order to get right wing governments elected'.

In spite of the reported existence of a letter signed by Hales and seven other leading Brethren brothers encouraging members around the world into political action,[17] the Brethren leadership has consistently maintained that no political activity was organised by the group itself, claiming instead that various individual members felt conscience-bound to act of their own accord. Records show that the Brethren as a group did not make monetary contributions to political parties or campaigns. Third-party advertising material was, as claimed, funded by individual Brethren businessmen. However, Chris recalls being asked to make his workplace available for young Brethren members to conduct a phone campaign in a marginal electorate, a request which he allowed in spite of having little personal interest himself in influencing the outcome of the campaign. Colin, who left the group a few years later, recalls:

> Political involvement in New Zealand began in earnest with the 2005 general election. There was active lobbying on behalf of the National Party, and the Brethren mobilised a large force of volunteers across the country to cold-call and deliver pamphlets on behalf of National candidates. Publicly the church denied involvement, and insisted that all volunteering was the decision of individuals. This simply was not true, and I remember discussing with other young people in the church our discomfort at the way church elders appeared to be lying – or at least being extremely economical with the truth – when questioned publicly about Brethren involvement.

While in some countries, such as New Zealand, the political campaigning was more widely known about among the Brethren members, several of the former members questioned during this research said that most of the congregation had little knowledge of what was going on:

> Rank and file members of the church were unaware of the extent to which senior Brethren leaders were involved with the political process in various countries… we were unaware of what exactly they were doing, and on occasion, revelations in the media were the first we heard.

This media reporting, both in New Zealand and Australia, was unrelenting and often savage and Colin recalls this being a challenging time for members as 'the public scrutiny was difficult for many members of the church, who struggled with seeing the Brethren berated in the press'.

While it is true that Brethren have traditionally abstained from voting, the Brethren have always maintained what they call 'witness to government', usually in the form of approaching local members on issues of moral concern to the Brethren community. What does appear to have been new here was the degree of visibility and the degree of widespread organised activism by a minority of Brethren members.

Technology

To the outside world the Brethren's historical reluctance to either utilise certain forms of technology such as computers, radio, mobile phones, and television, or heavily restrict the use of other forms of technology, such as fax machines, is perhaps one of their most distinctive feature.[18] As new forms of Information and Communications Technology (ICT) have become ubiquitous in the business and education sectors, the Brethren have been forced to embrace forms of ICT that they had hitherto been treated as defiling and dangerous. Changes have been cautiously introduced over the period of Bruce Hales' leadership, much to the surprise of some current members, and the disbelief of former members, including some who had been 'withdrawn from' for using forms of technology before they were sanctioned by the leadership.

As far back as the ministry of Darby and F.E. Raven, Brethren have viewed major developments in the technological and scientific spheres warily, seeing them as a potential distraction capable of leading believers away from a godly life. From the outset Brethren were ambivalent about technology, for example, in 1902 Raven had puzzled why people were so 'amazed in the present day at wireless telegraphy' (1902: 107) and remarked on how Scripture recorded that Christ wrought miraculous healings from a distance centuries before (like that of the centurion's servant in Matt. 8: 5–13). Popular Brethren writer C.A. Coates frequently noted the moral risk posed by having a wireless within the home, believing Brethren would be 'open to the influences that are broadcast in this present evil world' ([1926]: 115), and perhaps even tempted by 'the siren voices of the world' (n.d.: 116). James Taylor Sr. was more pronounced here, noting that listening to a radio in the home was 'letting the filth of the world into the house' and 'destructive to spiritual growth' (1965: 154). Taylor Jr. continued this line of thinking, frequently referring back to his father's ministry and extending the restrictions to include the new medium of television.

Ministry about the dangers of technology continued under Symington who expanded Brethren concerns to encompass more recent developments such as computers and fax machines. Indeed, in 1982, Symington connected technological and scientific developments to eschatological concerns and a scientific 'build-up' which would 'reach tremendous proportions before the rapture' and the arrival of the Man of Sin (1982: 52). Symington's ministry here set the standard for the approach to technology maintained under John Hales and in the ministry of Bruce Hales.

In his ministry, Bruce Hales adheres to this traditional Brethren interpretation of technology, even initially holding seminars to teach the Brethren how to prosper in business without over using technology. In 2003, for example, Hales recounted to Brethren in Sydney a conversation he'd had with a non-member, in which he noted:

> I was telling him why we didn't have all this electronic gear that people think is essential, mobiles and all that rubbish. I pointed out to him that I thought it was the greatest tool of disorganisation that business had ever got in possession of…that there was no future in the thing… See we don't have computers here, we don't have television in our homes, we don't have radios. (Hales, Bruce 2003a: 145)

Aside from believing technology was unnecessary for business, Hales also echoed the concerns of his predecessors regarding the morally detrimental effects of certain forms of ICT referring to it as recently as 2009 as an 'electronic labyrinth of evil and corruption' (Hales, Bruce 2009: 218). Hales seems to have had in mind the Internet, which he referred to in 2011 as a 'labyrinth of wickedness' (Hales, Bruce 2011: 129), and concerns about unfiltered access to objectionable material appears to have been paramount in the gradual manner in which the Brethren have slowly adopted filtered computers, whilst holding firm on television and radio.

Despite ongoing concerns about Brethren being ensnared by the trappings of the world, as early as 2002 there were signs that Hales was willing to accommodate the usage of such technology in business and education, subject to careful oversight. For example, in 2002, he granted that television screens, running on a closed circuit, might be used within Brethren schools for educational purposes, whilst still maintaining in 2004 that broadcast television was 'an instrument of hell' (Hales, Bruce 2004a: 70). By 2004, the Brethren were beginning to permit the limited usage of mobile phones, with tight restrictions on what numbers could be called or sent text messages, whilst still echoing the words of Taylor Sr. on radios, 'that's what mobile phones are, and computers, they're a pipeline of filth' (Hales, Bruce 2004b: 228). Colin who was in fellowship at this time described this transition:

> Brethren beliefs on technology changed rapidly during my time in the church. When I was a child…basic technologies such as fax machines and mobile phones were forbidden. We weren't even supposed to use cordless landlines. When I began working in [a Brethren business in the mid-2000s] we used to have our faxes sent to the non-Brethren business next door to work around the ban. After Bruce Hales assumed the leadership, use of fax machines was centralised under a trust administered by church

leaders. Mobile phones remained forbidden until around 2008, as were computers. These things were also introduced under the guise of a central trust, and remained tightly controlled by the church. Members were unable to access websites…that had not been preapproved.

The first computers, Wordex[19] machines, began to emerge around the late 2000s distributed by the Brethren-run Universal Business Team.[20] Since this time, as filtering software has advanced significantly, the Brethren have been able to utilise more technology, whilst maintaining their moral boundaries and community standards. The FAQ on their official website explains:

> The prime concern has been how to use these technologies without any harm to the user. As the ability to do this has developed, tools have been embraced to enable Plymouth Brethren members to operate this technology safely and effectively. (PBCC 2015)

With the speed of technological change, the Brethren have been forced to come to terms with contingencies which they had not previously encountered. While these changes offer a fascinating insight into how tight-knit sectarian groups negotiate their use of technology, it remains an open question how far Brethren will be able to permit further change, especially when to outsiders this appears to directly contradict earlier teachings.

Tertiary education

The Brethren have always been suspicious of aspects of higher education and since the late 1960s they have shunned university education completely, considering it to be unnecessary and potentially morally corrupting. Brethren leaders have cited a number of reasons for this, including that university education might involve young Brethren moving from the family home to dormitory-style accommodation, as Taylor Jr. noted in 1960:

> You want to keep your children at home, and not let them leave your home to go to college to learn. That is the whole trouble. We do not regard the household properly and then our children go out, and they get out of our control. If our children could go to college and not leave home, they would be that far safe [sic]. (Taylor Jr., 1960a: 146, 1960b)

While Taylor Jr. and his predecessors emphasized 'there is nothing wrong with education itself', the knowledge of God taught within the Brethren assembly and in printed ministry was considered superior to secular learning and should take precedence.[21] As Taylor Jr. noted in speaking of God giving the tablets of the Law to Moses on Mount Sinai (Exod. 31: 18):

> He [God] was the Legislator, in other words, He was the head of the
> university, He will give you the diploma. You will be glad of that one
> and you will cancel all the others you have, you will throw them in a
> basket; you will do the same with any degrees you have. (Taylor Jr.,
> James 1963: 275)

Symington took a harder line on tertiary education throughout his ministering years. For example, in 1982, Symington claimed that, 'a degree is
worse than worthless because of the damage that goes with it, or is likely to
go with it' (127). John Hales continued this position, quite frequently
questioning the value of worldly degrees (he himself had obtained one) and
those who boasted of secular learning, reminding followers, 'Christianity is
so practical. You don't have to go through a whole degree, a six-year
course, to get to the end...you can practice as a Christian right away...you
can do it immediately' (Hales, John S. 2009: 323).

Unsurprisingly, such attitudes have caused consternation amongst former
members, who considered that the ban on university education limited
opportunities for young people should they eventually choose to leave the
Brethren community. As former member Luke told us, 'I was one of the last
Brethren members [in our town] to obtain a tertiary qualification. This was
a life-saver for me, as I was able to obtain a job independent of the
Brethren'. Similar attitudes have been expressed by critics, most notably
former Australian Greens Senators Bob Brown and Christine Milne, who
both raised this matter in parliament on several occasions.

While to outsiders these restrictions are disconcerting, and the general
feeling amongst the former members questioned was that being denied the
opportunity for further education was a significant downside of a Brethren
upbringing: degrees are not requirement for employment in Brethren
businesses nor are they esteemed in the Brethren community to the extent to
which they are in wider society. Indeed, within the Brethren community the
possession of a university degree has often been disparaged in no uncertain
terms in Brethren Ministry as a sign of worldly pride.

Regardless, the tone of the more recent ministry of Bruce Hales has been
more pragmatic and indeed, in some aspects, conciliatory. While the simple
knowledge of God and the 'recovery of the Truth' still features heavily in
the Ministry, Hales has displayed some leniency toward practical university
degrees of potential benefit to the Brethren community. Despite this,
Brethren continue to consider university campuses corrupting environments
and young Brethren are encouraged to obtain any degrees through correspondence. While this shows a softening of the earlier Brethren misgivings
about tertiary education, it is also suggestive of a demographic issue within
the Brethren community; that is, the small number of tertiary educated
professionals within the community who obtained their degrees during the
1950s and 1960s are now an ageing cohort. As former member Stephen
noted:

> When I left ...the Brethren were making moves toward higher education. This usually took the form of accounting, law, or medicine. It has been around 50 years since university was banned by the church, and there was a need to permit members to become trained in some higher skills so that they could replace older accountants and doctors within the church.

Of the students who graduated from the largest Brethren school in 2013, nearly all have gone on to fulltime or part-time employment and 65 per cent were enrolled in some aspect of tertiary-level study (MET School 2013). This move towards what Brethren call 'postgraduate study' is a significant and quite recent shift. Little information is publicly available regarding the number of Brethren undertaking correspondence courses through tertiary providers, though anecdotal evidence suggests the numbers enrolled in university degrees remains small, and Vocational Education and Training (VET) sector training remains far more common. Nonetheless, this is still a significant, if incremental, shift in Brethren practice.

Charity

The Brethren's recent more public embrace of charitable activities – mainly though not exclusively in the form of the Rapid Relief Teams (RRT) Inc. – has attracted commentary in the media and from former members. Among former members questioned few recalled organised charity playing any substantial part in the Brethren way of life when they were members. As one former member, Naomi, remembers, Brethren were not encouraged to be involved with 'any community or charitable work whatsoever. We were strictly told that we were "in the world but not of it" this directive applying to the widest range of activities that it is possible to imagine'.

This sentiment was echoed by others questioned, with the consensus amongst former members being that the activities of the RRT and other charitable activities by the Brethren (e.g. fundraising for secular charities or substantial donations) have at best been, to quote Colin, a case of 'doing the right thing for the wrong reasons'. While most former members concede that it would be, as one remarked, 'churlish' to criticise charitable works, and indeed some have suggested that involving young Brethren in such activities may have a positive impact in the long-term, as a rule they remain highly sceptical, and at times even cynical, about the Brethren's motives. As Kelvin related, 'this rapid change, and the fact that most of the charitable efforts are accompanied by extensive PR, makes me highly sceptical that the Brethren's intentions are truly charitable'. Some also noted that the timing of this change was anything but coincidental. The reason for what these former members' claim has been a timely about-face are certainly quite easy to identify, as we will discuss in due course.

For the Brethren, their primary obligation has always been to members of their community. Taylor Jr. clearly illustrated this attitude ministering to Brethren in Barbados in 1967 when he noted:

> We take care of the poor...You do not have to give to all these charities – I do not, anyway, I give any money I have to the assembly, for that is where it belongs. Do not give to all these other things, because if these [other] churches looked after their poor we would not hear anything about this poverty in the world. (1967: 133)

For Brethren, Taylor's ministry assumed the status of a rule whereby Brethren were expected to direct their charitable giving to the upkeep of the Brethren concerns. In practice, this has meant that for poorer members of the Brethren community a safety net exists, and provision is made for them. This attitude seems to have continued largely unabated under Symington and John Hales, however, the latter did note in reply to a question about giving to institutions helping the homeless and destitute:

> I have no difficulty. I wouldn't want to be connected up with anything in a religious connection, but I have no difficulty. If it is a properly constituted organisation and it was operating on right lines, I would have no difficulty. That would be for persons who could spare it. (1991: 275)

In this sense then, any Brethren reservations about charity relate not to charitable giving in itself but with the Brethren practice of not aligning themselves – being 'unequally yoked'[22] – with other churches or worldly organisations. Certainly, individual Brethren give to secular charities, but until recently as a community they had no over-arching program for charity directed towards outsiders, equivalent to those found in other church groups. Their unostentatious and predominantly inwardly directed focus has on occasion presented difficulties, especially when recent changes in legislation regarding charity in the United Kingdom and Australia threatened to bring into question the registration of Brethren meeting hall trusts as charities.[23]

The major reason for these difficulties was the removal – in the United Kingdom Charities Act 2011 – of the presumption of benefit, that is, the presumption that any recognised religious group was automatically given the status of a charity because religion was in essence for the public benefit. This led to changes in how charitable status is accessed in the United Kingdom and lengthy debate surrounding the Brethren's Preston Down Trust between 2012 and 2014. This trust had been refused registration in 2012 when the Charities Commission for England and Wales raised questions about how far the Brethren's activities were a public benefit outside the Brethren community. After due consideration, and submissions by parties for and against (including former members), the Brethren's trust was eventually registered with a Deed of Variation in January 2014.[24]

While there has been a major overhaul of how charities are regulated in Australia in recent years, and some murmuring from politicians,[25] the Brethren have encountered no difficulty registering their religious activities under the Charities Act 2013 heading of 'advancing religion'. Not long after the establishment of the Australian Charities and Not-for-profits Commission (ACNC) in 2012, the Brethren were also able to register the Rapid Relief Team (RRT) as a charity under the subtype of a 'public benevolent institution' for 'the relief of such poverty, sickness, suffering, distress, misfortune, disability, destitution or helplessness as arouses pity or compassion in the community' (RRT 2013: 8). Soon after this occurred news reports began to emerge about the charitable activities of the RRT in serving complimentary food and drinks to emergency services personnel during times of crisis, catering free-of-charge at a wide range of public events, and providing free meals for the disadvantaged in areas where the Brethren reside.[26]

The list of those organisations assisted by the RRT since its inception is extensive,[27] however, how many of these organisations are aware that the RRT is run by the same Brethren who continue to be accused in the media of less than charitable behaviour toward former members is unclear, and media reports suggest that in many instances the link has not been made.[28] As former member Matthew astutely observed:

> I am convinced that many members of the public are unaware that the EB, with its negative baggage from earlier media analysis, is exactly the same organisation as the PBCC, with its family-friendly image, new website and smiling, helpful young RRT members doing all this wonderful charitable work in nursing homes, at fun runs and at natural disasters.

The motives for its establishment aside, the RRT certainly represents a significant shift in the Brethren's approach to charity and engagement with the wider community.

Conclusion

While the image of the Brethren illustrated by the television report with which we began this chapter was one of inflexibility and intransigence to change, what this chapter has demonstrated is a recent and cautious willingness by the Brethren under Hales' leadership to modify long-held community practices. Rather than maintain their historical reluctance pertaining to new forms of technology, the Brethren have instead worked to implement changes in ways which minimise the compromise of long-held community norms. In relaxing strictures on tertiary education, the Brethren are making some provision for the future welfare of their community through permitting some further study in areas of practical concern for the maintenance of the group.

Brethren members' brief foray into politics did not meet with the same success, nor, arguably, did the Review, both of which were perhaps naive and led to unwanted media scrutiny as well as making political enemies. Perhaps their greatest success – at least in the short term – has been in terms of their charitable work. In a short period, the RRT has demonstrated a willingness on the part of the Brethren to engage with the wider community and assist the less fortunate. However, this success may be due to marketing it under the RRT and PBCC brand names and the significant amount of positive media attention paid to the RRT has led some to speculate the motives for this were driven more by public relations than a spirit of community mindedness.

Regardless, the decision to adopt the less controversial name of Plymouth Brethren Christian Church has been explained by the Brethren as 'a decision to revert to its historic name'.[29] While we leave it to the reader to draw their own conclusions about whether this is a positive case of revisionism or a cynical exercise in rebranding, this account shows that the Brethren in recent years have changed much more than just their name.[30]

Notes

1 For an overview of the PBCC's history and beliefs see Doherty (2014b). This group has been known by various names over its history. The most common in English are Exclusive Brethren, Plymouth Brethren IV, and Raven-Taylor-Symington-Hales Brethren. On their relation to other Brethren groups see Doherty (2016); Introvigne & Maselli (2008); and Piepkorn (1970).

2 For Brethren this phrase refers to the theological and spiritual insights into the pristine understanding of Scripture and God's relationship with His people recovered under John Nelson Darby (1800–1882) and continuing through a set of subsequent leaders including F.E. Raven (1937–1903); James Taylor Snr. (1870–1963); James Taylor Junior (1899–1970); James H. Symington (1913–1987); John S. Hales (1922–2002); and Bruce D. Hales (1953). For a history from the group's perspective see Gardiner (1951).

3 Brethren adhere to a literal reading of 2 Tim. 2: 19–22, holding that they must separate themselves from worldly evil, "And, let everyone that nameth the name of Christ depart from iniquity" (v. 19). This is spelled out in detail in J.N. Darby's 1834 pamphlet *Separation from Evil God's Principle of Unity* and has been developed at length in later Brethren Ministry.

4 The Taylor period has been discussed at length elsewhere, see e.g. Scotland (1997) and Wilson (1967, 1983).

5 For the circumstances occasioning this see Doherty (2012, 2013).

6 See e.g. Thornthwaite (2011).

7 To this end the authors asked a small, snowball sample of former Brethren who had left the group between five and fifty years previously to respond to a short questionnaire covering five topics: The Review; technology; education; charity; and politics. Respondents' names have been changed to maintain their anonymity. Responses are reported throughout this chapter using single names.

8 The Brethren's succession of worldwide leaders, collectively referred to as these 'Great men', are referred to by a number of honorific titles drawn from Scripture, including 'Elect Vessel', 'Man of God', and 'Paul of Our Times'.

9 Due to space constraints, we will not cover the complex issues surrounding Brethren schools in Australia, for this see Doherty (2015).

10 This paper also, on occasion, makes some reference to wider international issues, where these issues help to illuminate the local situation.

11 This phrase, alluding to 2 Tim. 2:19, is used by Brethren to describe the situation of a member who has been excommunicated and is thus the subject of social avoidance by members in good standing. Because of their perceived sin/evil the Brethren had 'withdrawn' from fellowship with these former members.

12 Brethren communal life is punctuated by a weekly schedule of religious meetings known as Readings and Gospel Preachings (as well as other meetings relating to prayer and administration) and regular and more formal national and international community gatherings. While these occur in every local assembly of Brethren, those attended by the world leader are printed and distributed to members for their edification and study. In this chapter, we will use the upper-case Ministry when referring to these writings.

13 See the autobiographies of Nason (2015); Tchappat (2009); and Thomas (2005). For additional suspicious reactions also see Bachelard (2008).

14 A reprimanding letter from Bruce Hales to all Brethren in which he raised the increase of 'worldliness and substandard activities' since he had become leader. See Hales (2003a).

15 On provoking opposition see Dyason and Doherty (2015).

16 This section draws on Doherty (2012; 2013). For an alternative perspective see Bachelard (2008) and Mutch (2007).

17 See Bachelard (2008: 173). The authors have not seen a copy of this letter so cannot vouch for its authenticity.

18 It is worth noting here that other strands of the Brethren movement have also been wary of technology, see Grass (2006).

19 A type of heavily modified computers with restricted software which allowed Brethren to perform basic word processing and accounting functions for business and educational purposes.

20 See their website at http://www.universalbusinessteam.com/ (accessed 13 December 2016).

21 As Taylor Jr. told followers elsewhere: "The thing is to be spiritual, and then be a scholar...the great thing is education in the house of God first. We better not trust ourselves to this higher education, where the mind of man is coming in to defeat what God is at" (1960a: 235).

22 This phrase alludes to 2 Cor. 6:14–18 and the Brethren avoidance of links with the world.

23 Most notably in the late 1970s and early 1980s when the Charity Commission of England and Wales refused to register some of their meeting rooms as charities, see Wilson (1983).

24 The details of this case can be read in Charity Commission for England and Wales (2014) and in Charity Commission for England and Wales (2016). For a former member's perspective see McKay (2015). Similar legislative changes were also mooted in Australia in 2010 following concerns raised about the activities of the Church of Scientology see Doherty (2014a).

25 In the August 2014 *A Current Affair* report, Independent Federal Senator Nick Xenophon asked, "Why should we be subsiding an organization that is involved in this sort of appalling behavior?" (Williams 2014). Here Senator Xenophon

was merely reiterating his earlier position on the Church of Scientology. See Doherty (2014a, 2014b).

26 See the Newspaper Articles section listed in the References for this paper (Shuff 2005; Shuff 1997).

27 These have included well-known Australian charities like Uniting Care; SIDS-and-Kids; Relay-For-Life; Walk Against Poverty; Ronald McDonald House; White Ribbon Day; Walking Wounded; and annual events like Mental Health Week and NAIDOC Week. More information can be found on the group's website: http://www.rapidreliefteam.org/ (accessed 13 December 2016).

28 Note that all the newspaper articles either do not mention the link with the PBCC or use the Brethren's relatively recent incorporated name of PBCC or just Plymouth Brethren. No article refers to them as the Exclusive Brethren.

29 This is not an unwarranted claim. It was J.N. Darby who first remarked that: "Plymouth, I assure you, has altered the face of Christianity to me, from finding brethren, and they acting together" cited in Doherty (2014b). Moreover, other strands of the wider Brethren movement have also adopted name changes, albeit in an attempt to distance themselves from controversies surrounding the PBCC (see Doherty 2016).

30 The authors would like to thank Dr. Ian McKay for his invaluable assistance and feedback as we researched and wrote this chapter. All opinions expressed are those of the authors alone.

Bibliography

All URLs were accessed on 6 June 2020.

Anon. 2016. "Refuel for those living rough." *The NewsMail*, 2 February.

Anon. 2015a. "Rapid relief sizzle set-to stay." *Ballarat Courier*, 17 December.

Anon. 2015b. "TAFE celebrate the end of a successful term." *Lithgow Mercury*, 14 September.

Anon. 2015c. "Team offers relief." *Campbelltown Advertiser*, 9 September.

Anon. 2015d. "Brian proudly walking for the wounded." *Parkes Champion Post*, 28 July.

Anon. 2015e. "Taking youth program to the students." *Lithgow Mercury*, 22 June.

Anon. 2014a. "Relief team serves up fund-raising feast." *Parramatta Sun*, 27 November.

Anon. 2014b. "Community spirit alive." *The Ararat Advertiser*, 21 January.

Auerbach, Taylor. 2014. "Church in mourning for a hero." *The Daily Telegraph*, 25 November.

Bachelard, Michael. 2008. *Behind the Exclusive Brethren*. Melbourne, Australia: Scribe.

Beckford, James. 1978. *Cult Controversies: The Societal Response to New Religious Movements*. London: Tavistock.

Carylon, Peta. 2015. "Tasmanian firefighters receive 14 new tankers as tough season looms." *ABC News*, 19 October. Available at: http://www.abc.net.au/news/2015-10-19/new-fire-trucks-leave-tasmania-better-prepared-for-fire-season/6866342

Charity Commission for England and Wales. 2016. *Preston Down Trust: Case Report*. Available at: https://www.gov.uk/government/uploads/system/uploads/attachment_data/file/500364/preston_down_trust.pdf

Charity Commission for England and Wales. 2014. *Preston Down Trust: Decision of the Commission.* Available at: https://www.gov.uk/government/uploads/system/uploads/attachment_data/file/336110/preston_down_trust_summary_decision.pdf

Dann, Shannon. 2015. "Team offers relief." *Singleton Argus*, 18 June.

Doherty, Bernard. 2016. "The Brethren Movement: From Itinerant Evangelicals to Introverted Sectarians." *Handbook of Global Contemporary Christianity: Movements, Institutions, and Allegiance.* Stephen Hunt (ed.). Leiden: Brill, pp. 357–381.

Doherty, Bernard. 2015. "'The Nurture and Admonition of the Lord': Brethren Schooling and the Debate on Religious Schools in Australia." Paper presented at CESNUR, Tallinn, Estonia. Available at: http://www.cesnur.org/2015/doherty_brethren_tallinn_2015.pdf

Doherty, Bernard. 2014a. "Sensational Scientology! The Church of Scientology and Australian Tabloid Television" in *Nova Religio*, 17(3): 38–63.

Doherty, Bernard. 2014b. "The Plymouth Brethren Christian Church. World Religions and Spirituality Project." Available at: http://www.wrs.vcu.edu/profiles/PlymouthBrethrenChristianChurch.htm (accessed 13 December 2016).

Doherty, Bernard. 2013. "The 'Brethren Cult Controversy': Dissecting a Contemporary Australian 'Social Problem'" in *Alternative Spirituality and Religion Review*, 4(1): 25–48.

Doherty, Bernard. 2012. "Quirky Neighbors or the Cult Next-Door? An Analysis of Public Perceptions of the Exclusive Brethren in Australia" in *International Journal for the Study of New Religions*, 3(2): 163–211.

Dyason, Laura and Bernard Doherty. 2015. "The Modern Hydra: The Exclusive Brethren's Online Critics" in *St Mark's Review*, 233: 116–134.

Geddes, Jeff. 2015. "Can Assist bowled over by support." *Lithgow Mercury*, 16 September.

Grass, Tim. 2006. *Gathering to His Name: The Story of the Open Brethren in Britain and Ireland.* Exeter, UK: Paternoster.

Introvigne, Massimo and Domenico Maselli. 2008. *The Brethren: From Plymouth to Present.* Turin, Italy: CESNUR.

McKay, Ian. 2015. "Exclusive Brethren 'The End Times.'" *Joy & Sorrow*. Joy Nason (ed.). Sydney, Australia: Centennial, pp. 241–257.

MET School. 2013. *Annual Report.* Oatlands, Australia: MET School.

Millet, Carolyn. 2015. "Almost 700 people availed themselves of free food." *Northern Daily Leader*, 7 August.

Mutch, Stephen. 2007. "Cultish Religious Sects and Politics: The Brethren v. Green Contest and Other Controversies Involving Minor Religious Sects Down Under" in *Cultic Studies Review*, 6(3): 298–310.

Nason, Joy. 2015. *Joy & Sorrow: The Story of an Exclusive Brethren Survivor.* Sydney, Australia: Centennial.

Norris, Sam. 2015. "Bringing a smile to Maitland's homeless." *Maitland Mercury*, 9 August.

Piepkorn, Arthur C. 1970. "Plymouth Brethren (Christian Brethren)" in *Concordia Theological Monthly*, 41: 165–171.

Plymouth Brethren Christian Church (PBCC). 2015. "Has the Brethren Approach to Technology Changed Recently?" Available at: http://www.plymouthbrethrenchristianchurch.org/faq-category/technology-law-politics/

Scotland, Nigel. 1997. "Encountering the Exclusive Brethren: A Late Twentieth Century Cult" in *European Journal of Theology*, 6(2): 157–167.

Shuff, Roger. 2005. *Searching for the True Church: Brethren and Evangelicals in Mid-Twentieth-Century England*. Bletchley, Milton Keynes, UK: Paternoster.

Shuff, Roger. 1997. "Open to Closed: The Growth in Exclusivism Amongst Brethren in Britain 1848-1953" in *Brethren Archivists and Historians Network Review*, 1: 10–23.

Tchappat, David. 2009. *Breakout: How I Escaped from the Exclusive Brethren*. Sydney, Australia: New Holland Publishers.

Thomas, Ngaire. 2005. *Behind Closed Doors: A Startling Story of Exclusive Brethren Life*. Auckland, New Zealand: Random House NZ.

Thompson, Rod. 2014. "Hungry helpers." *Singleton Argus*, 23 October.

Thornthwaite, L. 2011. "Separatist religious sects, the Family Law Act and shared parenting: an examination of cases involving the Exclusive Brethren" in *Australian journal of family law*, 25(1): 54–72.

Uechtritz, Max (executive producer). 2013. *Today Tonight*. Religious Rebrand, first broadcast 22 November by Channel Seven.

Williams, Grant (executive producer). 2014. *A Current Affair*. The Exclusive Brethren Exposed, first broadcast 11 August by Channel Nine.

Wilson, Bryan R. 1992. *The Social Dimensions of Sectarianism: Sects and New Religious Movements in Contemporary Society*. Oxford: Clarendon Press.

Wilson, Bryan R. 1983. "A Sect at Law" in *Encounter*, 25: 81–87.

Wilson, Bryan R. 1967. "The Exclusive Brethren: A Case Study in the Evolution of Sectarian Ideology." *Patterns of Sectarianism: Organisation and Ideology in Religious and Social Movements*. Bryan Wilson (ed.). London, UK: Heinemann, pp. 287–342.

Brethren Ministry and Literature

Coates, C.A. n.d. *An Outline of the Song of Songs*. Hampton Wick, Kingston-on-Thames, UK: Stow Hill Bible and Tract Depot.

Coates, C.A. 1926. *An Outline of the Epistle to the Romans*. Hampton Wick, Kingston-on-Thame, UK: Stow Hill Bible and Tract Depot.

Gardiner, A.J. 1951. *The Recovery and Maintenance of the Truth*. Kingston-on-Thames, UK: Stow Hill Bible and Tract Depot.

Hales, Bruce D. 2011. *Instruction and Teaching from a Visitation*. Hounslow, Middlesex, UK: Bible and Gospel Trust.

Hales, Bruce D. 2009. *Conflict at the Ephesian Level*. Hounslow, Middlesex: Bible and Gospel Trust.

Hales, Bruce D. 2004a. *Christianity is a Heart Matter*. Hounslow, Middlesex, UK: Bible and Gospel Trust.

Hales, Bruce D. 2004b. *Preparedness for What's Entirely New*. Hounslow, Middlesex, UK: Bible and Gospel Trust.

Hales, Bruce D. 2003a. *A Man of Understanding*. Hounslow, Middlesex, UK: Bible and Gospel Trust.

Hales, Bruce D. 2003b. *RE: Attendance at Fellowship Meetings, 3 Day Meetings and Special Meetings*. Letter dated 5 May.

Hales, Bruce D. 2002. *Fatherhood*. Hounslow, Middlesex, UK: Bible and Gospel Trust.

Hales, John S. 2009. *Notes of Meetings Australia, Britain, Germany and New Zealand 1971-1972*. Chessington, Surrey, UK: Bible and Gospel Trust.

Hales, John S. 1991. *To Set Him Among Nobles*. Hounslow, Middlesex: Bible and Gospel Trust.

Symington, James H. 1982. *How to Counter the Man of Sin*. Vol. 107. Kingston, Surrey, UK: Bible & Gospel Trust.

Taylor Jr., James. 1967. *The Importance of Directives*. Hampton Wick, Kingston-on-Thames, UK: Stow Hill Bible and Tract Depot.

Taylor Jr., James. 1965. *Ministry*. Vol. 21. New Series. Hampton Wick, Kingston-on-Thames, UK: Stow Hill Bible and Tract Depot.

Taylor Jr., James. 1963. *The Service of Song*. Hampton Wick, Kingston-on-Thames, UK: Stow Hill Bible and Tract Depot.

Taylor Jr., James. 1960a. *The Foundations of the Gospel*. Hampton Wick, Kingston-on-Thames, UK: Stow Hill Bible and Tract Depot.

Taylor Jr., James. 1960b. *The Outpouring of the Holy Spirit*. Hampton Wick, Kingston-on-Thames, UK: Stow Hill Bible and Tract Depot.

11 Appendix to revision or re-branding? The Plymouth Brethren Christian Church 2002–2016

Remarks from the Brethren

In 2012, the Brethren (sometimes referred to as Brethren IV or Exclusive Brethren) decided to revert to its historic name, the Plymouth Brethren. They believe their historic name, 'Plymouth Brethren Christian Church' better reflects their true identity and relationship with the broader community. The name originates from over 180 years ago, when J. N. Darby, having begun the movement in Dublin during 1827, moved to Plymouth where a large gathering formed. The Brethren movement has endured, maintaining the doctrines set out by J. N. Darby, whilst responding to the challenges and changing conditions of the modern day.

To the observer, it may appear that the Brethren have undergone a 're-branding' or altered course to suit prevailing conditions. However, it is hoped the following remarks will show that they have in fact remained true to their core values in finding a path through this present age, whilst at the same time finding a way to do good towards all (Galatians 6:10).

The review

Although J.N. Darby set out principles for assembly administration, which included the need for grace and compassion, it is acknowledged these have not always been followed by individual Brethren assemblies. This was particularly so in the 1970s and 1980s when a small number of unqualified persons exercised a negative influence within the Brethren. The so called 'review' in the early 2000s was to humbly acknowledge this, both in the Church and to individuals who had been affected. Since then, the Brethren have renewed their committal to fairness and compassion and to follow carefully procedures that reflect Christian love and tenderness in situations where persons, especially younger ones, decide to leave the fellowship.

DOI: 10.4324/9781315226804-11

Representation to authorities

Brethren believe that governments should be respected as appointed by God (Romans 13:1) and meet regularly to pray for the strengthening of good government. They recognise the challenges that face the authorities in an increasingly unstable and dangerous world and are sympathetic. The Brethren Church takes no political ground, but individual members, however, may approach their governments, as is their right as citizens; not only about issues that concern them as Christians but also over matters that affect the interests of their countries and society.

Technology and the Internet

The Brethren have developed a pragmatic approach to the use of IT and the Internet as it rapidly evolves, affecting all areas of society. They remain concerned about indiscriminate use of the Internet and make no apology for taking measures to protect their young people from damaging material by using industry-standard filtering programs. Brethren make full use of technology for business and education, and as individuals without compromising their core beliefs and values.

Schooling

Brethren are committed to providing quality education, including tertiary courses, for their students. The Brethren's international 'OneSchool' education system uses innovative methods such as Self Directed Learning and Virtual Classroom Technology to educate students and equip them with the skills and values needed for their future careers. Non-Brethren teaching staff are recruited, and generally the national curriculum of a country is taught. Because many Brethren students wish to enter business, they prefer to enroll in vocational programs and courses that enable them to continue to study for diploma or graduate certificates whilst starting their careers.

Charitable activities

Charitable and humanitarian activities have been a feature of the Brethren from the earliest days, and their support in the Irish potato famine of 1847 and the Franco-Prussian war of 1870 are well documented examples. Much of this was carried out in private, but after the Charity Commission in England questioned the Brethren's public benefit in 2012, it became necessary for their charitable activities to be publicly structured and coordinated under the global Rapid Relief Team which was established in 2013 and is now a global charitable organisation, fully accredited and registered in several countries. The Brethren, from the outset, have stated that RRT is formed by volunteers from the Church and their official website has a clear link to the RRT website and vice versa. Many hundreds of Brethren members are voluntarily donating considerable amounts of their time and money to do what they can in their local communities.

Conclusion

The Brethren seek to remain true to their core beliefs and Christian values as maintained since J.N. Darby's time and their commitment to the weekly celebration of the Lord's Supper – the basis of their fellowship.

Although regarded as a very conservative Christian group, the Brethren are far more connected than some may think with the wider community, where there is daily interaction both at work, where many members run their own family businesses that collectively employ thousands of non-Brethren, and in the ordinary suburbs of towns and cities all over the world where Brethren live.

Often, when observers take account of the significant youth population amongst Brethren, the thriving education system, almost zero unemployment, negligible family breakdown and drug and crimes problems, they are led to remark "they must be doing something right". For their part, the Brethren simply see themselves as Christians holding to the truth and teaching of the Bible, awaiting the hope of His second coming, in a rapidly changing modern world.

For more information: www.plymouthbrethrenchristianchurch.org, www.rapidreliefteam.org, www.oneschoolglobal.com

12 Diversification in Samael Aun Weor's Gnostic Movement

David G. Robertson

Although little known in Europe, the Gnostic Movement and its related organisations have a significant presence in Latin America, US cities with a large Hispanic population (including San Francisco, Miami and particularly Los Angeles), as well as a smaller presence in Japan, Australia, Canada, Europe, and elsewhere. Although figures are hard to establish, at least in part because what constitutes 'membership' is not easy to define, affiliation is considerable, with estimates ranging upwards from tens of thousands (Introvigne 1993). The Gnostic Movement was founded by Samael Aun Weor (1917–77) in 1976, although he had been teaching his system (often referred to simply as 'the Gnosis') since the 1950s, and his students have gone on to form a number of sattelite groups in the years since his death.

Some of these have offices, vestments and liturgy adapted from Roman Catholicism – led by Bishops, performing Mass and describing themselves as a church (*igreja*). In all cases, however, these groups appeal to Gnosticism as the original (and by implication, most authentic) form of Christianity. In fact, Weor's teachings have little-to-no relationship to early Christian Gnostics (if such a thing can even be said to have existed), and instead derive from the Western Esoteric 'occult revival' of the 19th and early 20th centuries. In particular, sexual magic is central to Weor's teaching, which he in turn was taught by Arnoldo Krumm-Heller, a high-ranking member of the German Rosicrucian group, the Ordo Templi Orientis (OTO). Weor actually portrayed his sexual teachings as a re-storation of primitive Christian practice, although as this chapter will dis-cuss, in general this is not made explicit in modern versions of Weor's Gnosis.

In this chapter, I will show how much of the Gnostic Movement has sought to distance itself from its roots in Western Esotericism and instead promote itself as a mainstream Christian organisation. At the same time, and increasingly since Weor's death in 1977, other sections of the Gnostic Movement have sought to position the movement within the more diffuse New Age or 'self-spirituality' milieu. This has the considerable benefit of being more easily disseminated via the Internet, and to appeal to a broader spiritual milieu, particularly in post-Protestant countries where the

DOI: 10.4324/9781315226804-12

Christian elements may be considered off-putting. To achieve this, however, these groups have similarly played down the sex magic aspects of Weor's teachings. By diversifying along these two different lines, the Gnostic Movement has been able to appeal to a broad constituency, and to thrive when many groups with their roots in 19th century Western Esotericism have declined. At the same time, it presents a great case study of how academic categories can become mobilised by practitioners, even if they are historically inaccurate.

A brief history of Gnosticism

I want to briefly outline Gnosticism, as the subject has not been prominent in the study of New Religious Movements. I would like further to give you a simple definition, but unfortunately I cannot, as the term has been so widely and variously interpreted that to do so would mean my giving you what I wished Gnosticism to be. As Henry Green suggests:

> it appears, in our opinion, that we have only a variety of statements made with words by a variety of different writers with a variety of different intentions and as such, there is no history of an idea to be written, but only a history of various people who used the idea and of their varying social situations. (Green 1977: 133)

What I shall do, therefore, is to give a brief genealogy of the term which will show both why it is such an impossible category to delineate, and why it has been considered to be of such importance by such a wide variety of groups. The English word 'gnosis' is derived from the Greek γνώσεως, usually translated as 'knowledge', although gnosis is nowadays typically taken to indicate a particular type of knowledge which is experiential, rather than theoretical, often with a salvific aspect. '*Gnosticism*', however, only appeared in the late 18th century.

We first learned about Gnostics from Christian heresiologists in the second to fourth centuries of the Common Era, including Irenaeus, Tertullian, and Clement of Alexandria. For these men, embroiled in a battle to establish 'true' Christian orthodoxy, Gnostics were heretics, pure and simple. Their Otherness was constructed through a polemic that described their theology, which rejected the God of the Hebrew Bible and Jesus' suffering (docetism), and their practices, which were either described as radically ascetic or shockingly libertine (King 2003: 20–40).

Several early Christian works came to light in the 19th century: the Bruce Codex, containing the first and second books of Jeu and several untitled Coptic fragments, was published in 1892; the Askew Codex, containing a different version of Pistis Sophia from that later discovered at Nag Hammadi, was discovered in a London bookshop in 1773; in 1896, the Berlin Codex was found in Cairo, containing The Gospel of Mary, the Apocryphon of

John and two other texts (Pagels 1979: xxiv). These were universally re-garded as being Gnostic, despite the difficulty in reconciling them with the heresiological polemic. Nevertheless, this narrative found its way into later works on Gnosticism, such as those of the *religionswissenschaft* school, which sought an Iranian origin for Gnosticism. This narrative, which continued through into World War II, as an early (i.e. pre-Christian) Asian (and, therefore, Aryan) origin for Gnosticism, would have serious implications for the legitimacy of Christianity and the legitimacy of National Socialist paganism (Culianu 1992: 52–3; Junginger 2008: 7–18). At the same time, many Theosophists, including Blavatsky (1877 [1997]: 140) and G. R. S. Mead (1904 [1960]: 41), were appealing to Gnosticism as a perennial, underground spirituality, and the forerunners of the 'occult revival'.

This latter understanding is the one most prominent in the contemporary alternative religious milieu, fitting well with widespread notions of perennialism and individual experience over institutionalised forms of religion. Wouter Hanegraaff went so far as to posit Gnosis (which he constructs as a third 'pillar' of knowledge between scientific rationality and religious faith) as the essential phenomenon behind New Age and the entirety of Western Esotericism (2008). Other scholars, including Elaine Pagels (1979) and April DeConick (2016), continue to present Gnosticism as Christian heresy, albeit one that disagreed with aspects of contemporary church doctrine that the authors take issue with, for example, the centrality of women and the sacred feminine in the form of Sophia, and of (again) direct experience rather than faith mediated by priests and other functionaries.

Others, such as Carl Jung (1916 [1989]) and Hans Jonas (1934), interpreted the category idiosyncratically to bolster their own philosophical ends. At the 1966 International Association for the History of Religion Conference in Messina, Italy, in an attempt to reduce the confusion surrounding the category, a set of definitions of 'gnosis', 'Gnosticism', and 'Gnostics' were debated, agreed, and published. The definition of 'gnosis' was defined vaguely and broadly as 'knowledge of divine mysteries for an elite' (Markschies 2003: 13), whereas Gnosticism was defined as referring to 'a particular group of systems of the second century after Christ' which were typified by

> the idea of a divine spark in man, deriving from the divine realm, fallen into this world of fate, birth and death, and needing to be awakened by the divine counterpart of the self in order to be finally reintegrated. (Williams 1996: 27)

Unfortunately, this discussion of definitions was happening just as the contents of the Nag Hammadi corpus, a cache of circa fourth century papyri that had been discovered in a cave in the Egyptian desert in 1945, were beginning to be understood. These texts constitute by far the largest source on the so-called Gnostics, and the debates on their contents continue to the present. Scholars are still struggling to reconcile earlier conceptions of Gnosticism based on heresiologists with the contents of the texts. They are enormously diverse, with at least two traditions being identifiable (Valentinian and Sethian, although these in no way represent the totality of the material), and, importantly, no text which corresponds exactly to the narrative which had been presented as the essence of Gnostic theology (and continues to be so). Moreover, the presence of an oddly-translated copy of Plato's *Republic* and a good deal of Jewish and Platonic terminology showed that the Gnostics were certainly connected to the rest of the world, and no texts suggested the extreme asceticism or libertinism of the heresiologists' accusations.

In short, Nag Hammadi showed that Gnosticism did not really exist, at least not in the form that scholars and the public typically understand, a point made forcefully by Michael Williams (1996). What seems to be the case is that there was a more diverse range of positions existing within a milieu of religious innovation in the early centuries CE, in which aspects of Judaism and Hellenism mixed in different ways, but as a normative Christian theology and Rabbinic Judaism began to coalesce. Some of these competing groups were demonised as heretics, and this Othering was strengthened by the construction of a collective category, 'Gnostics'.

Yet, as has been the case with other polemical constructions (such as Shamanism, Hinduism and Witchcraft), Gnosticism has taken on a life of its own – or perhaps an afterlife, to extend the metaphor of 'zombie categories' (Beck and Beck-Gernsheim 2001). Despite Gnosticism's historical non-existence, there are now self-identifying Gnostics, with several competing traditions of Gnosticism operating in the contemporary religious milieu. Indeed, the 2009 Parliament of World Religions in Melbourne, Australia, included Gnostics for the first time. Samael Aun Weor's Gnostic Movement are well-established in Latin America, and, as we shall see, are continuing to increase their influence in Europe and beyond, making them the largest Gnostic religion today – and in all likelihood, ever.

Samael Aun Weor

Victor Manuel Gómez Rodríguez was born in Santa Fé de Bogotá, Colombia, on 6 March 1917. Some hagiographic descriptions of his youth describe him as able to teleport or take on animal forms (Dawson 2007: 54). Certainly though, as a young man, Rodríguez was very much a 'seeker', involved to a more or less degree with a range of alternative religious practices. He was involved with Freemasonry, the Theosophical Society, and a number of Spiritualist groups (Smith 1995: 211). Significantly, he also had an interest in the teachings of the Armenian-Greek 'guru' George Ivanovich Gurdjieff (1866–1949). Gurdjieff taught that humans generally spend their lives in a state of waking sleep, essentially operating as machines, passively receiving and reproducing impressions, and incapable of acting with conscious will.

Among Gurdjieff's complex, multifaceted, and often obscure and incomplete teachings (often referred to as the Fourth Way) was the idea that humans' role in the cosmos was part of a chain in which energies were raised from densest material to highest spiritual levels. This was achieved through a sort of 'inner alchemy' by 'work upon oneself' – that is, strenuously overcoming one's mechanical physical nature. Johanna Petsche (2014) has recently argued that Gurdjieff's teachings may be more concerned with sex than is generally considered to be the case. Not only did he consider the 'sex centre' to be uniquely able to 'receive the fine food of impressions', meaning it is particularly able to transmute matter to finer forms but also that sexual activity and/or abstinence can provide the 'shock' needed to propel matter into a higher 'octave' (2014: 134–5). This idea in fact appears in Gurdjieff's magnum opus, *Beelzebub's Tales to his Grandson*:

> The result of these serious ponderings of theirs was that the conviction first arose in them that this self-perfection could probably be actualized by itself, by abstaining from the ejection from oneself in the customary manner of these substances formed in them called sperm, and certain of them decided to unite and exit together in order to convince themselves in practice whether such abstinence could indeed give the supposed results. (1976 [1950]: 399)

As Zoccatelli outlines, Weor rarely cited Gurdjieff in his writings, and never attributed his ideas to him, yet he was undoubtedly drawing from them (2013). For example, Weor's description of the production of 'hydrogen SI-12' through *coitus reservatus* and its role in the production of an astral body (1991: 127) is almost identical to that of Gurdjieff, as recorded in Ouspensky's *Fragments of an Unknown Teaching* (1949 [1987]: 254–9). As Zoccatelli notes, 'we might say that in Weor's system Gurdjieff provided the theory and Krumm-Heller the practice' (2013: 145).

Rodríguez encountered Arnoldo Krumm-Heller (1876–1949) in the mid-1940s. Krumm-Heller was a native German who had settled in Columbia, where he founded a group called the Fraternidad de Rosacruz Antiqua and adopted the name Frater Huiracocha (Dawson 2007: 55). Krumm-Heller became Rodríguez' mentor and influenced Weor's later teachings in two significant ways. First, Krumm-Heller had been a member, possibly high-ranking, of the Ordo Templi Orientis (OTO) before leaving for Latin America in 1910 (König 1998: 23, note 31; c.f. 22). The OTO is an initiatory order founded in 1896 by Carl Kellner, a wealthy German Freemason who claimed to have been initiated by Arab and Hindu adepts (King 1973: 22). The OTO existed in name only until Kellner's death in 1905, whereupon leadership passed to Theodor Reuss (King 1973: 25). Reuss elaborated upon the Theosophical and Tantric influences using the teachings of Paschal Beverley Randolph (1825–75), a mixed-race Spiritualist and equal rights campaigner from New York, and pioneer of sex magic (Urban 2006: 96–7).[1]

The central idea of sex magic is that, at the moment of orgasm, individuals are at their greatest degree of openness and connection to the 'divine', and therefore at their most magically powerful (Pearson 2007: 78; c.f. Deveny 1997). In keeping with many other esotericists, Randolph saw the orgasm as a uniquely powerful event in which 'the souls of the partners are opened to the powers of the cosmos and anything truly willed is accomplished' (Urban 2006: 67). The OTO's teachings differed markedly from Randolph's rather conservative morality, however: the first seven degrees were based upon 'opening the chakras', apparently drawing from Tantric sources; eight and nine alone taught sex-magic techniques (apparently semen retention and possibly mutual 'adoration of the phalli'); and the tenth was entirely titular, being conferred upon the leader in each territory (König 1998: 12).[2]

Second, Krumm-Heller published several journals, including *Rosa-Cruz* and *Gnose*, which, alongside more standard esoteric material, reprinted material from the French 'Gnostic Revival' churches of the late 19th century. Principle among these was the Église Gnostique, founded in 1890. In fact, there was a considerable number of links between these churches and the OTO as, in 1908, Theodor Reuss had been consecrated as a Bishop of an offshoot, the Église Gnostique Universelle, which would eventually become the Ecclesia Gnostica Catholica in 1919 under Crowley's leadership (Pearson 2007: 46-7). This would seem to be where Weor would later take the Gnostic terminology that defines his later work.

Krumm-Heller died in 1949. Rodríguez was allegedly then contacted by the 'Venerable White Lodge' and underwent a series of mystical experiences that culminated in 1954 with his final initiation in an underground temple in Santa Marta, Columbia (Dawson 2005: 7). Here he was charged with a sacred, threefold mission: 'forming a new culture', 'forging a new civilisation' and 'creating the Gnostic Movement' (Dawson 2004: 345). He took the name Venerable Master of the Bodhisattva Samael Aun Weor and began promoting to esoteric and spiritualist groups a system he called 'The Gnostic Philosophy' or simply 'The Gnosis', described as 'the Synthesis of all Religions, Schools and Sects' (Smith 1995: 211). He was not successful initially, however, and was for a short time incarcerated in Columbia on charges of 'quackery' (Dawson 2007: 55).

His system was presented in *El Matrimonio Perfecto ('The Perfect Matrimony')* in 1950 (revised in 1963), which remained his most popular book, despite his publishing more than sixty other books. He proclaimed the commencement of the Age of Aquarius on 4 February 1962, and declared himself the avatar of the Christ spirit for the New Age (Dawson 2007: 56). He moved to Mexico and legally founded the Movimiento Gnóstica Christiano Universal (MGCU) in 1976, shortly before his death on 24 December 1977.

The teachings of Master Samael

The Gnosis is taught in free courses by all the different groups which make up the Gnostic Movement. It is presented in three levels; in the first, the 'exoteric' or 'First Chamber', students are taught meditation and relaxation, many clearly showing the influence of Gurdjieff, along with lectures on a range of standard esoteric material with a Theosophical heritage (Smith 1995: 212). The specifics of this varies depending on the particular concerns of the group giving the teaching, but the general structure is the same in each case. With the 'mesoteric second chamber', students move from theory to practice. In this level, initiated students are taught how to apply the 'Three Factors of the Revolution of the Consciousness' to their lives – that is, the loss of the ego, the birth of higher spiritual bodies and the passing on of The Gnosis (Zoccatelli 2013: 146). They are also introduced to specific rituals, such as the Gnostic Mass, taken from the French Gnostic Churches, probably through Krumm-Heller (Dawson 2007: 60).

However, the central secret of The Gnosis is only put into practice in the 'esoteric third chamber': 'He who wants to become a God, should not ejaculate the semen' (Weor 1963 [2001]: xviii). By retaining the semen, Weor claims that the energies it possesses are made available to drive the spiritual development of the (male) individual (1963 [2001]: 59), specifically by crystallising the Astral body.[3] This, he claims, is the essential truth transmitted by all initiatory groups and their symbolism, and was the original core teaching of Christianity (Weor 1963 [2001]: 63, 147). While Weor presented this as being drawn from Tantra (Dawson 2007: 59), this teaching is in fact drawn from Gurdjieff, though Aun Weor never acknowledges this.

While there is a long history of connecting the so-called Gnostics of the second to fourth centuries CE with sexual impropriety, these accusations come entirely through their detractors. There is no evidence of sexual rituals from the Nag Hammadi texts, and the descriptions of orgies of gluttony and fornication described by Epiphanius and others may be dismissed as a standard strategy for demonising heretics. Less hysterically, however, Hyppolytus, writing in the early third century CE, describes Naassenes as associating semen with the Logos and viewing it as numinous (Smith 1995: 215). Yet, Weor seems to have had little knowledge about these historical Gnostic groups – in fact, he actually includes Irenaeus and others who demonised these groups in a list of those whom he considers to have been members of his 'Primitive Catholic Christian Gnostic Church' (1961: 71–2). There is a clear tension between Weor's claims to be restoring the church, and what mainline Christians would see as unorthodox, or even heretical.

The Universal Christian Gnostic Movement

Even during his lifetime, the Gnostic Movement was riven with strife, and today, Weor's teachings are promulgated by a number of different interrelated organisations, often with confusingly similar names. At the highest organisational level is the organisation founded by Weor himself, the Movimiento Gnóstica Christiana Universal (MGCU). The ecclesiastical arm of the MGCU is the Iglesia Gnóstica Christiana Universal (IGCU). The MGCU also has a number of secular arms, including the Gnostic Association of Scientific, Cultural and Anthropological Studies (AGEACAC) and the Latin American Christian Workers' Party, and it is through these organisations that Weor's teachings are most widely disseminated (Dawson 2007: 56).

Following Weor's death in 1977, there was a long battle to determine his successor, and today dozens of different groups exist, differing significantly on points of doctrine (Zoccatelli 2013: 141). Weor's wife, Arnalda Garro Gómez (1920–1998; generally known as Maestra Litelantes) was elected to head the AGEACAC, although she left to found the Gnostic Institute of Anthropology Samael and Litelantes (IGASL) in 1989 following a dispute over the copyright on Weor's works (Introvigne and Zoccatelli 2002: 1228). IGASL currently has perhaps 18,000 members under the leadership of Weor's and Gómez' son, Osiris Gómez, and Roberto Tajeda.[4] The original AGEACAC still exists, under the leadership of Weor's and Gómez' daughter, Hypatia Gómez, and Victor Manuel Chavez (Introvigne and Zoccatelli 2002: 1229).

Eventually, Joaquin Amortegui Valbuena (1926–2000; generally called the Venerable Master Rabolú) assumed leadership of the MGCU (Gnostic Movement 2016). Rabolú also founded the Gnostic Christian Movement in the New Order in Columbia in 1960, a group which emphasised an apocalyptic element to Weor's teachings (Introvigne and Zoccatelli 2002: 1229). Most famously, Rabolú's book *Hercolubus or Red Planet* includes the claim that a giant planet called Hercolubus had previously caused the destruction of Atlantis, and was soon to approach Earth again, causing volcanic eruptions, the reversal of the Earth's magnetic poles and ultimately wiping out humanity (Rabolú 1999 [2001]). Only those who 'work on their spiritual regeneration' through 'elimination of psychological defects' and 'astral projection' would be 'taken to a safe place' (Alcione Association 2009). Rabolú's claimed authorisation for his adaptations from Weor himself, who talked of Hercolubus in several lectures (Weor 1975, 1976). Rabolú also claimed that Weor had told him in 1976 that only five of his books should be used, as the others all contained mistakes (Gnostic Movement 2016). In the Latin American popular millennial milieu, Herolubus has been conflated with Niburu and Planet X and incorporated into 2012 narratives, thus receiving renewed attention in recent years.

A British branch of the Rabolu line, the Gnostic Centre, founded in Leeds, came under some press attention when it applied for charitable status in 2010. The Charity Commission of England and Wales decided to reject the application. They argued that it did not have an educational agenda that was 'based on broad values that are uncontroversial and would generally be supported by objective and informed opinion' and that 'it was not demonstrated that the benefit was to the public or a sufficient section of the public' (Charity Commission 2009). Interestingly, while the board agreed that Gnosticism 'possessed some of the legal qualities of a religion, such as belief in a supreme being', it did not promote 'a positive, beneficial, moral or ethical framework' because it focused too narrowly on the spiritual welfare of individuals (Charity Commission 2009). At the time of writing, the Gnostic Centre appears to be inactive.

The Gnostic Christian Universal Church was founded in Uruguay by Teofilo Bustos (1936–2005; known as the Venerable Master Lakshmi).[5] Lakshmi also claims to be the designated successor of Weor and has written a number of books elaborating on practical and theoretical aspects of the Gnosis, including several volumes of *Jewels of the Yellow Dragon*. This group continues to exist today, offering introductory courses in the Gnosis through the Internet and at Gnostic centres throughout Latin America. In Spain, the Gnostic Association of Anthropological, Cultural and Scientific Studies[6] was founded in 1992 by Oscar Uzcátegui Quintero as a branch of the AGEACAC (Introvigne and Zoccatelli 2002: 1229). Quintero lived and worked with Weor during the last three years of his life and also claimed succession upon his death (CESNUR 2016).

The largest body teaching The Gnosis today is Brazil's Igreja Gnóstica do Brazil (IGB), which is an independent entity (Dawson 2007: 60). The official Curitiba office of the MGCU closed in 1977 due to a lack of interest, but a group of loyal Weorites founded the Gnostic Association of Philosophical, Scientific, and Cultural Studies in 1979. In 1983, they started a charitable foundation, Fundação Samael Aun Weor (FUNDASAW), which had become independent by 1987. FUNDASAW is considered the 'first chamber' of The Gnosis in Brazil, operating as an esoteric school open to all. FUNDASAW produces Portuguese translations of Weor's books and talks, original introductory works and offers an introductory course in the Gnosis ('Curso de Nova Gnose') and a number of more in-depth courses in subjects such as astral projection, meditation, and kabbalah (Dawson 2005: 8). These are offered at a purpose-built centre in Curitiba, although at present, the Internet is the primary point of distribution, reaching several thousand students a year (Dawson 2007: 60). FUNDASAW members then founded an ecclesiastical wing, the Igreja Gnóstica Cristê Universal do Brazil, which gained legal status as a religious organisation in April 1994, changing its name to the Gnostic Church of Brazil (IGB) in 2001 (Dawson 2007: 56.). The IGB is the 'Second Chamber', dedicated to the 'preservation and practice of the rituals of Samael Aun Weor', and operates with a liturgical calendar and functionaries inherited from Rosicrucian orders. A third wing, Associação Benificente Santa Clara, which focusses on social action, was granted charitable status in 1998.

Although these are legally and functionally distinct entities, they are run from the same location by the same individuals and towards the same ends and members frequently use IGB and FUNDASAW interchangeably (Dawson 2007: 56–7). As with Lakshmi and Rabolú, the IGB identify themselves as the legitimate heirs of the Gnosis and that they gained this authority upon Weor's death. They stress two differences with other would-be heirs: the amount of meditation and yoga practice required of students (two hours minimum as opposed to an average of thirty minutes); and the importance placed upon the daily practice of sexual magic, which the IGB refer to as 'Arcano A.Z.F.' (Dawson 2007: 58).

The largest English-language branch of the Gnostic Movement was founded in New South Wales, Australia, by Mark Pritchard, who also used the name Belsebuub. Pritchard was a former student of Rabolú, in the MGCU lineage. He was not recognised by other MGCU groups; however, Rabolú actually revoked Pritchard's permission to use his books. Belsebuub, however, argues that Rabolú's death in 2000 meant that he was his chosen successor, as he had allegedly 'said he would not die until he left a disciple on the path to carry on the work' (Gnostic Centre 2016). Pritchard's Gnostic Movement was active from 2000 to 2011 and claimed more than 90,000 participants during this time. It describes itself as 'a spiritual school that offered many opportunities to learn, participate in, and practice spirituality' (Gnostic Centre 2016). Again, while there were physical workshops offered, the GM's teaching mostly took place online through their website, mysticweb.org, offering free 9-week courses entitled 'Astral Travels and Dreams', 'Searching Within', 'Esoteric Wisdom', and 'Advanced Investigation', each of which was later published in book form. The latter two courses introduce 'the transformative practice which Samael Aun Weor called alchemy' – note the euphemistic language, apparently to avoid putting off potential clients (Gnostic Centre 2016).

The Internet and Diversification

The Internet allows for a greater degree of control over the public image of religious organisations and charismatic individuals, while ironically *appearing* to do quite the opposite (Baffelli 2011). As Dawson notes, this 'allows an enhanced degree of elasticity between what [a group] says it is and what it actually is' (2005: 20). The IGB and the IGCU, the ecclesiastical branches promoting Weor's teachings, do so in a language drawn from Roman Catholicism, describing themselves as 'churches' (*igreja*), practicing a formal liturgy derived from the Catholic model via the *fin de siècle* Gnostic Churches (including a 'Gnostic Mass'), carried out by 'priests' in buildings designed to resemble Catholic churches. This has allowed them to receive legal recognition as religious organisations, as noted above. Yet, this is in direct contradistinction to the majority of groups and individuals in the esoteric milieu in Brazil (and, for that matter, elsewhere), who are hostile to such traditional religious material (Dawson 2005: 20). However, the actual teachings of the Weor groups are firmly within that esoteric tradition, both in terms of theories and practices, as I have shown.

Moreover, all of the various online courses mentioned earlier entirely avoid any of either the Catholic language or the esoteric/Rosicrucian background, instead presenting themselves as part of the broader decentralised spirituality or New Age milieu. In these presentations, The Gnosis is presented as a 'spiritual-psychological' practical philosophy, rather than as of either the 'esoteric' or 'religious' tradition of practice (terms from Siqueira 1998). This is clearly more likely to find a responsive audience among the broader esoteric milieu, particularly in places where such esoteric discourse typically involves a distrust of or hostility to traditional forms of Christian practice. Moreover, the client has greater freedom to 'pick-and-choose' those elements of The Gnosis which appeal (Dawson 2007: 63). More problematically, these presentations downplay the presence of sex magic (at least, at first), despite its centrality to Weor's teaching.

In fact, the Internet has been the faultline along which the two fundamentally contradictory directions of the Gnostic Movement have separated since the death of Aun Weor. On the one hand, where they have been able to establish real-world institutions, the Gnostic Movement stress their Christian heritage, referring to themselves as churches, using biblical texts such as the Revelation of St. John, using liturgy and functionaries drawn from Roman Catholicism, and (paradoxically) identifying themselves as a restoration of pre-Roman Christianity. On the other, the mainly online sections of the movement downplay the Christian aspect and instead promote The Gnosis as an example of decentralised 'spiritual-psychological' practise in keeping with the New Age/spiritual marketplace of the 1980s and after. Both of these trajectories, however, downplay the Western Esoteric heritage and the centrality of sex magic to the Movement.

The Internet has been central to the rebranding of the movement, as well as disseminating it in territories where it has not traditionally had any firm footing, such as the UK and Australia. We can only assume that this trajectory will continue, yet the relative popularity of online outreach may mean that as the temple-based communities (such as the IGB) age and gradually fall away, the 'spiritual-psychological' aspects become the entirety of teaching of The Gnosis (Dawson 2007: 64). Thus, the success of the ideas of the Gnosis may ultimately come entirely at the expense of the practical aspects.

In terms of the broader theorisation of New Religious Movements, we must also bear in mind how different is the relationship outside of Europe between Christianity – and Catholicism in particular – with the broader religious milieu. Whereas in Europe, Catholicism seems to represent the 'old guard', tied up with issues of power and tradition (ironically, particularly in the Protestant areas), in Latin America this is not the case, and often it is seen as a liberating force. We can also note that in the US, Edgar Cayce's ostensibly Christian version of New Age was far more successful than Blavatsky's more atheist version had been. But religions old and new diversify and 'course correct'. The task of the sociologist of religion is to remain aware of this at the same time as we record the fascinating flowering of new forms. This volume is an important contribution towards that end.

Notes

1 Intriguingly, James Webb argues that Gurdjieff may have learned his sexual material from Randolph (1980: 532–3). Randolph, like Gurdjieff, claimed to have been trained by Middle Eastern adepts (Urban 2006: 66).
2 These were later considerably expanded upon by Aleister Crowley. However, Krumm-Heller rejected these innovations (König 1998: 207).
3 This gender imbalance is reinforced by Weor's frequent descriptions of male energies as active/producing and female as passive/receiving. Dawson's research suggests that such an imbalance was played out in the institutional roles within Weor groups, so his findings that the groups were predominantly male (68% to 32% female) is perhaps understandable (2005: 23).
4 http://www.gnosisusa.org (accessed 22 June 2020).
5 https://lumendelumine.org/ (accessed 22 June 2020).
6 http://www.ageac.org (accessed 22 June 2020).

Bibliography

All URLs were accessed on 22 June 2020.
Alcione Association. 2009. "Hercolubus: The Planet of the End of the World." Available at: http://www.dailymotion.com/video/x8abnj_hercolubus-the-planet-of-the-end-of_news
Baffelli, Erica. 2011. "Charismatic Blogger?: Authority and New Religions on the Web 2.0." in *Japanese Religions on the Internet: Innovation, Representation, and Authority*. Erica Baffelli, Ian Reader and Birgit Staemmler (eds). London and New York, NY: Routledge. pp. 118–135.
Beck, Ulrich and Elisabeth Beck-Gernsheim. 2001. *Individualization: Institutionalised Individualism and its Social and Political Consequences*. London, UK: Sage Publications.
Blavatsky, Helena P. 1877 [1997]. *Isis Unveiled: Secrets of the Ancient Wisdom Tradition*. Michael Gomes (ed and trans) Wheaton, IL: Quest Books.
CESNUR. 2016. "L'A.G.E.A.C." Available at: http://www.cesnur.com/chiese-e-movimenti-Gnostici/la-g-e-a-c/
Charity Commission for England and Wales. 2009, 16 December. Available at: https://www.gov.uk/government/uploads/system/uploads/attachment_data/file/324274/Gnosticdec.pdf
Culianu, Ioan P. 1992. *The Tree of Gnosis: Gnostic Mythology from Early Christianity to Modern Nihilism*. H.S. Wiesner and I. P. Culianu (trans). New York, NY: HarperCollins.
Dawson, Andrew. 2007. *New Era, New Religions: Religious Transformation in Contemporary Brazil*. Aldershot, UK: Ashgate.

Dawson, Andrew. 2005. "The Gnostic Church of Brazil: Contemporary Neo-esotericism in Late-Modern Perspective" in *Interdisciplinary Journal of Research on Religion*, 1(8): 1–28.

Dawson, Andrew. 2004. "The Universal Christian Gnostic Church." in *Encyclopedia of New Religions: New Religious Movements, Sects and Alternative Spiritualities*. Christopher Partridge (ed). Oxford, UK: Lion.

DeConick, April. 2016. *The Gnostic New Age: How a Countercultural Spirituality Revolutionized Religion from Antiquity to Today*. New York: Columbia University Press.

Deveny, John P. 1997. *Paschal Beverly Randolph: A Nineteenth-Century Black American Spiritualist, Rosicrucian, and Sex Magician*. Albany, NY: SUNY Press.

Gnostic Centre. 2016. "The Story of the Gnostic Centre." Available at: http://rememberingtheGnosticmovement.com/about/story/

Green, Henry. 1977. "Gnosis and Gnosticism: A Study in Methodology" in *Numen*, 24(2): 95–135.

Gurdjieff, George I. 1976 [1950]. *Beelzebub's Tales to His Grandson: An Objectively Impartial Criticism of the Life of Man*. London, UK: Routledge & Kegan Paul.

Hanegraaff, Wouter J. 2008. "Reason, Faith, and Gnosis: Potentials and Problematics of a Typological Construct." in *Clashes of Knowledge: Orthodoxies and Heterodoxies in Science and Religion*. Michael Welker Peter Meusbuger and Edgar Wunder (eds). Klaus Tschira Stiftung/Springer. pp. 133–144.

Introvigne, Massimo. 1993. *Il Ritorno dello Gnosticismo*. Carnago, Italy: SugarCo.

Introvigne, Massimo and PierLuigi Zoccatelli. 2002. "Gnostic Movement (Samael Aun Weor)." in *Religions of the World: A Comprehensive Encyclopedia of Beliefs and Practices*. J. Gordon Melton and Martin Baumann (eds). Santa Barbara, CA: ABC-CLIO. pp. 1228–1229.

Jonas, Hans. 1934. *Gnosis und spätantiker Geist. 1. Die mythologische Gnosis*. Göttingen, Germany: Vandenhoeck & Ruprecht.

Jung, Carl G. 1916 [1989]. "The Seven Sermons to the Dead written by Basilides in Alexandria, the City where the East toucheth the West." in *The Gnostic Jung and the Seven Sermons to the Dead*. Stephan A. Hoeller (ed, trans, commentary). Wheaton, IL: Quest Books.

Junginger, Horst. 2008. "Introduction." in *The Study of Religion Under the Impact of Fascism*. Horst Junginger (ed). Leiden: Brill.

King, Francis. 1973. *The Secret Rituals of the OTO*. London, UK: C. W. Daniel.

King, Karen L. 2003. *What Is Gnosticism?* Cambridge, MA, and London: The Belknap Press of Harvard University Press.

König, Peter R. 1998. *Ecclesia Gnostica Catholica*. Munich, Germany: Arbeitsgemeinschaft fur Religions-und Weltanschauungsfragen.

Markschies, Christoph. 2003. *Gnosis: An Introduction*. London and New York, NY: T & T Clarke.

Mead, George R. S. 1904 [1960]. *Fragments of a Faith Forgotten*. New York, NY: University Books.

Ouspensky, Petr D. 1949 [1987]. *In Search of the Miraculous: Fragments of an Unknown Teaching*. London, UK: Arkana.

Pagels, Elaine. 1979. *The Gnostic Gospels*. New York, NY: Random House.

Pearson, Joanne. 2007. *Wicca and the Christian Heritage: Ritual, Sex and Magic.* London, UK: Routledge.

Petsche, Johanna. 2014. "Gurdjieff on Sex: Subtle Bodies, Si I2, and the Sex Life of a Sage." in *Sexuality and New Religious Movements.* Henrik Bogdan and James R. Lewis (eds). New York, NY: Palgrave Macmillan. pp. 127–148.

Rabolù. 1999 [2001]. *Hercólobus, or Red Planet.* Varese: Còradi.

Siqueira, Deis. 1998. "A construção metodológica do sujeito-objeto de investigação." Paper delivered to VIII Jornadas sobre Alternativas Religiosoas na América Latina. São Paulo, 22–25 September 1998.

Smith, R 1995. "The Revival of Ancient Gnosis." *The Allure of Gnosticism: The Gnostic Experience in Jungian Psychology and Contemporary Culture.* Robert A. Segal, with June Singer and Murray Stein (eds). Chicago, IL: Open Court. pp. 204–223.

Urban, Hugh B. 2006. *Magia Sexualis: Sex, Magic, and Liberation in Modern Western Esotericism.* Berkeley, CA: University of California Press.

Webb, James. 1980. *The Harmonious Circle: The Lives and Work of G. I. Gurdjieff, P. D. Ouspensky, and Their Followers.* New York, NY: G. P. Putnam's Sons.

Weor, Samael Aun. 1991. *Carpa Solari: Messaggio di Natale 1967-68.* Florence: Instituto Gnostico di Antropologia.

Weor, Samael Aun. 1976. "End of the Kali Yuga." Available at http://Gnosticteachings.org/lectures-by-samael-aun-weor/621-the-end-of-the-kali-yuga.html

Weor, Samael Aun. 1975. "Closing Speech at the 1975 Gnostic Congress." Available at http://Gnosticteachings.org/lectures-by-samael-aun-weor/696-closing-speech-at-the-1975-Gnostic-congress.html

Weor, Samael Aun. 1963 [2001]. *The Perfect Matrimony: The Door to Enter into Initiation.* Brooklyn, NY: Thelema Press.

Williams, Michael A. 1996. *Rethinking "Gnosticism": An Argument for Dismantling a Dubious Category.* Princeton, NJ: Princeton University Press.

Zoccatelli, PierLuigi. 2013. "Sexual magic and Gnosis in Colombia: Tracing the Influence of G. I. Gurdjieff on Samael Aun Weor." *Occultism in Global Context.* PierLuigi Zoccatelli (ed). London: Acumen. pp. 135–150.

13 Using the New Religious Movements framework to consider LGBT Muslim groups

Shanon Shah

Public debates are still rife with notions that Islam 'inherently' condemns homosexuality and opposes the rights of lesbian, gay, bisexual, and transgender (LGBT) individuals. In the West, some commentators allege or insinuate that Muslims are therefore more anti-LGBT than other sectors of the general population (e.g. Perraudin 2016). Some politicians and media commentators even cast anti-LGBT attitudes among Muslims as a marker of their propensity for radicalism or extremism, despite the wide range of Muslim attitudes on sexuality (e.g. Moyer 2014; Trayner 2015). These perceptions are reinforced whenever certain people who claim Islamic authority make gruesome pronouncements that condemn LGBT individuals (e.g. Lubin 2016; Mosbergen 2015; Wyke 2015). However, an uncritical division of Muslims into the binary opposites of 'moderate'/'extremist' or 'liberal'/'fundamentalist' only serves to obscure the diversity *among* Muslims, which is constantly being shaped and re-shaped within particular social contexts.

In this chapter, I suggest that analysing the experiences of LGBT Muslims through a New Religious Movement (NRM) framework can help us move beyond simplistic dichotomies to explain Muslim attitudes towards gender and sexual diversity. I focus my discussion on Imaan, the British-based LGBT Muslim group. I argue that, on one level, an NRM framework allows us to look at how Imaan has innovated on Islamic teachings – including encouraging mixed-gender and woman-led congregational prayers and advocating that religious rulings do not forbid or condemn homosexuality – and its shifting modes of engagement with wider society. On another level, this framework also shows how this dynamic within Imaan reflects similar patterns of religious innovation and diversification among other Muslim groups in Britain.

The chapter begins with a brief review of the usefulness of the NRM framework to analyse movements associated with Islam as well as of various innovations introduced by NRMs in regard to gender and sexuality. Within the same section, I outline the conceptual criteria with which I will be investigating the experiences of Imaan, drawn mostly from work by Eileen Barker (2013) and David Bromley (2013). The chapter then

DOI: 10.4324/9781315226804-13

introduces Imaan and discusses the conditions in which the group was founded as well as key turning points in its organisational development. I devote the next section to discussing the specific theological innovations that Imaan has engaged in and continues to promote. I then appraise Imaan's inter-related organisational development and theological innovations through the approaches suggested by Barker and Bromley. The chapter ends by evaluating what this perspective of revisionism and diversification within Imaan can tell us about the wider landscape of Islam in Britain.

An NRM analysis of LGBT Muslim experiences

In politicised, ideologically driven debates on Islam, attitudes towards LGBT rights are increasingly a marker that is seen to separate so-called 'moderate' and 'extremist' Muslims. Whether 'moderates' or 'extremists' are viewed positively or negatively depends upon the political context. In several Muslim majority countries, the government and/or Islamic authorities often aggressively push for interpretations of Islam that are anti-liberal, anti-feminist, and anti-LGBT (e.g. see Kamal 2015; Hidayana 2015) – for them, 'good' Muslims are anti-LGBT, among other things. In Britain, some political actors, media outlets, and human rights activists portray anti-LGBT attitudes as an indication of so-called Islamic extremism, an affront to 'British values' or a 'failure' of multiculturalism (Tatchell 2007; Trayner 2015; UK Prime Minister's Office 2011). For these actors, 'good' British Muslims should be pro-LGBT, among other things.

This is not to deny that some Muslim individuals and groups do advocate extreme anti-LGBT attitudes based on their particular interpretations of Islam, as mentioned above. However, the division of Muslims using terms such as 'extremist' and 'fundamentalist' or 'moderate' and 'liberal' based on their attitudes towards LGBTs is flawed and simplistic. Furthermore, these divisions carry grave political consequences when they become part of debates suggesting that anti-LGBT attitudes are inextricably linked with the 'radicalisation' of Muslims (see Rory 2015).

From a sociological point of view, Marat Shterin and Ahmet Yarlykapov argue that analysing Muslim groups disproportionately from a radicalisation perspective prevents us from 'developing a better understanding of the real people engaged in a *variety of different groups* – people with specific interests, motivations, actual beliefs, practices (as opposed to official ideologies) and relationships with their social surroundings' (2011: 303). They add that such a narrow focus fails 'to present members of new Islamic groups as human agents who actually created these movements through their own choice and decision-making' and propose that some Muslim groups can be better analysed as new religious movements (NRMs) (Shterin and Yarlykapov 2011: 304–5). In addition to Shterin and Yarlykapov, scholars of religion have started looking at various Muslim groups as

NRMs including those advocating 'Jihadism' (Firestone 2012: 270) and 'neo-Sufism' (Sedgwick 2012: 198–9). As far back as the 1980s, Daniel Regan (1989: 124, 138–9) proposed approaching Muslim social movements – which many academics were then analysing under the framework of 'revivalism' – as NRMs. My suggestion is that an NRM framework can be useful to investigate debates on Islam and sexual diversity, inspired by this growing body of scholarship.

It must be noted that there is also growing academic research of the ways in which NRMs experiment with gender relations and expressions of sexuality, including analysing LGBT Christian movements as NRMs (Hunt 2010: xvi). These movements can be viewed as part of 'the religions of the gaps' that emerged in the West after the Second World War, seeking to fulfil 'individual needs in a way that traditional religion, by which was usually meant the Christian churches, could not' (Hunt 2010: xiv). This suggests that approaching LGBT Muslim groups as NRMs could be fruitful. That is, to investigate how they fulfil people's needs in ways that traditional Islamic institutions cannot. Yet, there is still a reluctance among many scholars of Islam to analyse new Muslim groups as NRMs (Shterin and Yarlykapov 2011: 305). Shterin and Yarlykapov (2011: 305) suggest that this reluctance 'reflects the widespread exceptionalist view of Islam as a religion that produces its own unique ideologies and movements'. This chapter is therefore an attempt to take up their approach and extend it by analysing an LGBT Muslim group – the British-based Imaan – by using an NRM framework. By doing this, I am not suggesting that Imaan or any other LGBT Muslim group should be considered NRMs or that an NRM framework is applicable to all of them. Rather, I am proposing that an NRM framework in this case can provide fresh insights into how Imaan has shaped and been shaped by the wider landscape of Islam in Britain.

To analyse Imaan in this way, I will refer to the sociological characteristics commonly associated with NRMs, namely having 'a predominantly first-generation membership' which is 'atypical of the rest of the population'; the presence of a 'charismatic' leader; experimentation with and promotion of 'an alternative set of beliefs and/or practices ... in tension with the rest of society'; and the propensity 'to undergo some fundamental changes within a relatively short time of their founding' (Barker 2013: 2; Bromley 2013: 247). To frame my analysis of the developments within Imaan from its founding to the present, I will draw upon Eileen Barker's (2013: 2, 5) notions of 'revisionism' and 'diversification' as well as David Bromley's (2013: 247, 251, 256) notions of the 'envisioning'/'concentration' phases in an NRM's founding period and its subsequent 'revisioning'/ 'diversification'.

My analysis of Imaan is based primarily upon ethnographic fieldwork and in-depth interviews carried out between October 2012 and September 2013 in Malaysia and Britain. In Britain, I interviewed ten Imaan members and two non-Imaan members who identified as gay Muslims – men and women – while in Malaysia, I interviewed 17 gay Muslim men and women, supplementing all of these with media analysis for context setting. In addition to providing an in-depth perspective into the everyday lives of gay Muslims, my qualitative research also enabled me to compare how their individual practices and beliefs did or did not produce a common group belief or movement ideology. Among other things, my encounters with gay Muslims in Britain within and beyond Imaan enabled me to observe how they interacted with others, namely non-LGBT Muslims and the wider non-Muslim LGBT movement. My analysis also draws upon my own insights and experiences as a gay Muslim man born and raised in Malaysia and now based in Britain.

Imaan's journey

In September 1998, the founder of the US-based LGBT Muslim group, Al-Fatiha Foundation,[1] placed an advertisement in the *Pink Paper* – a British publication on gay and lesbian issues which was circulated around gay venues in London including nightclubs, restaurants and cafes (Imaan 2020; Pink News 2009).[2] The paper was relatively accessible to LGBT Muslims who were part of the larger gay scene, specifically those who went to Asian-themed events or Bhangra clubs such as Club Khali and Shakti. The advertisment called for a meeting of LGBT Muslims in London and brought together the individuals who would become the founding members of the British chapter of Al-Fatiha.

By 2001, Al-Fatiha UK was poised to hold a national conference on the various issues confronting LGBT Muslims. The group's growing visibility prompted Al-Muhajiroun – the Hizbut Tahrir splinter group headed by Omar Bakri Mohammed, subsequently banned by the British government – to issue a fatwa denouncing Al-Fatiha members as apostates (Guardian 2001). The conference went ahead, albeit with a heavy police presence in light of continuing condemnations and threats by Al-Muhajiroun and other vocally anti-LGBT Muslim groups.

Eventually, Al-Fatiha UK changed its name to Imaan to reflect its autonomy as a British LGBT Muslim group and operated independently of Al-Fatiha Foundation.[3] Al-Fatiha and Imaan were founded when it was extremely risky and ground-breaking for LGBT Muslims to proclaim their religious and sexual identities openly, even in the context of the rapidly liberalising attitudes on sexuality in Western countries. Their early members faced hostility from extremist and violent groups such as Al-Muhajiroun, and at the same time encountered racism and Islamophobia within the gay scene. These external factors were the driving forces behind the founding generation of Imaan's activism to pioneer an organisation that defended both the sexual and religious identities of LGBT Muslims in Britain.

Apart from its inaugural conference as 'Al-Fatiha UK', Imaan also began organising support meetings for LGBT Muslims and set up a website which included a discussion forum for registered users. In practice, membership was open to anyone who identified as LGBT and Muslim, was a registered user of the online forum, and/or attended Imaan events regularly. Imaan also began participating in the London Pride march, albeit with many members seeking to protect their anonymity by wearing particular styles of clothing and/or not giving their names when approached by the press. In 2005, the group courted controversy amongst the wider LGBT community when its members marched in 'rainbow hijabs' and niqabs (full-face veils). Imaan defended this decision, describing it as a means of representing the diversity among Muslims and opposing Islamophobia within LGBT circles, but it was criticised by some secular LGBT activists for capitulating to misogynistic interpretations of Islam.[4]

By 2006, Imaan had attracted around 300 members (Carlile 2006). The same year, the group officially declined to participate in the Channel 4 television documentary *Gay Muslims* but co-founder and former leader Adnan Ali agreed to be featured in an individual capacity (Mirza 2007). In fact, Ali was the sole interviewee to use his real name and to consent to showing his face on camera. In 2009, the popular BBC soap opera *EastEnders* pioneered a storyline about a gay Muslim character, Syed Masood, who struggled with his sexuality and fell in love with an openly gay Englishman (Mahmood 2009). While the storyline was criticised by some Muslim organisations for allegedly feeding into wider Islamophobic stereotypes, it was lauded by Imaan for its candid portrayal of an LGBT Muslim character. In fact, shortly after the *EastEnders* storyline premiered, the number of registered users of Imaan's online forum doubled from around 1,500 to 3,000.[5] During the period of my research, I joined the confidential Imaan group on the social networking site Facebook, More recently, Imaan set up a Facebook page which has more than 3,200 'Likes' at the time of writing.

This first decade also saw numerous leadership struggles and the emergence of internal factions within Imaan.[6] In October 2001, for example, some tensions within the group led to the formation of a separate organisation, Safra Project, focusing specifically on LBT Muslim women (Decolonizing Sexualities Network 2020). The management and governance of Imaan was also heatedly debated as members tried to work out viable forms of leadership. The founders consciously structured Imaan as a charitable non-governmental organisation with its own constitution, policies and democratic elections to select a Chair and Board of Trustees.[7]

Elections sometimes highlighted unresolved tensions between various factions that had competing visions of Imaan's *raison d'être* and *modus operandi*, despite a general consensus that it needed to be inclusive and politically progressive. For example, some factions advocated a more confrontational style of activism, whether against anti-LGBT Muslim groups or anti-Muslim sentiments in the wider LGBT community, while others favoured more conciliatory approaches. Some members wanted more activism while others wanted the organisation to focus on internal community building and self-improvement. There were also arguments about the dominance of particular groups within Imaan, specifically ethnic British-born Pakistani males, and about the alleged marginalisation of women, bisexuals, transgender individuals, and other ethnic minorities. Crucially, there was also the question of the extent to which Imaan needed to integrate Islamic values and spirituality within its activities and policies. These competing visions sometimes resulted in acrimonious arguments at Annual General Meetings, especially for the years when elections were held.[8] These tensions were exacerbated by an ambiguous definition of membership and the existence of various online platforms – the forum, the Facebook group, and several groups on the social networking application WhatsApp – that allowed for various factions to organise their own internal campaigns behind the scenes.

While these factional dynamics continued in the background, Imaan's leadership post-2010 made several efforts to engage with other more mainstream British Muslim groups. At Imaan's 2012 national conference, for example, one of the panel discussions was an intra-Muslim dialogue between the LGBT Muslims who attended the conference and representatives of various Muslim charities including the Muslim Women's Network, the Islamic Society of Britain and the Association of British Muslims (Shah 2012). After this conference, Imaan continued to forge new partnerships and cooperation with these and other Muslim groups – for example, it participated in panel discussions organised by the City Circle. In 2014, Imaan also initiated and co-organised a two-day conference with the Muslim Institute on the topic of diversity in Islam (Muslim Institute, The, and Imaan 2014).

These developments not only signalled a departure in Imaan's own approach but also the changing landscape of British Muslim activism. As one Imaan founding member and former Trustee put it at the 2012 conference:

> When we started our first conference, only one Muslim group wanted to have anything to do with Imaan – that was Al-Muhajiroun and they wanted to shut us down. More than a decade later we have all these Muslim groups wanting to cooperate or at the very least have dialogue with us.

Some Muslim activists point out that this was partly a result of the shifts that occurred when Muslim activists and intellectuals began participating in statutory panels on diversity, equality, and inclusion alongside LGBT activists.[9] This opened up fresh opportunities for 'both sides' to get to know each other and cooperate, which became more salient after the passage of the first Equality Act in 2006. In other words, Imaan's proactive efforts to engage with other Muslim organisations were positively received by those Muslim activists who were already predisposed to forming pro-LGBT

Figure 13.1 Imaan London Pride, 2015 (Photograph by Shanon Shah).

attitudes. Additionally, Imaan also became more visible by participating more actively in events and activities organised by Jewish, Christian and non-religious LGBT collectives (Figure 13.1).[10] Amid these nascent collaborations, Imaan also finally managed to register officially as a fully-fledged charity in 2014 (Charity Commission 2020).

These developments gave rise to new internal rivalries, specifically from Imaan's founding generation who were uncomfortable with many of these changes. In 2016, these tensions came to a head and resulted in the departure of a few key members, some of whom went on to set up Hidayah, a separate Muslim LGBT organisation.[11]

The trajectory of Imaan's organisational development thus does not represent a black-and-white struggle between its LGBT Muslim members and monolithically anti-LGBT and/or anti-Muslim groups. Rather, it shows that succeeding generations of Imaan leaders and members constantly experimented with internal forms of organising alongside building diverse external alliances and networks of support. The turning points discussed here tell the story of Imaan's developing organisational structure and external networks. There is also the issue of the theological innovations adopted by Imaan's leadership and grassroots members which are discussed below.

Theological innovations among and beyond LGBT Muslims

Many Imaan events and activities are injected with religious content. For example, at its AGMs there is often time set aside for those who wish to conduct congregational *salah* (obligatory prayers) and its meetings usually open and close with a *du'a* (supplication). During Ramadan,[12] a Trustee will usually be put in charge of organising a collective *iftari* (fast-breaking dinner) on a convenient day of the week, usually Saturday, for members to get together and socialise. Such *iftaris* will also be punctuated with the congregational *salah* for *Maghrib* (the sunset prayer).

As a matter of policy, Imaan explicitly endorses mixed-gender and woman-led prayer which is also non-sectarian – Sunnis and Shi'as of various sub-schools pray together. Prayers are also inclusive and non-coercive – non-Muslims are often invited to join in while both Muslims and non-Muslims who do not wish to participate are free to just watch or mingle elsewhere. In this, Imaan is inspired by wider trends among progressive Muslim activists and intellectuals who challenge the existing norms upheld by conventional Islamic authorities around the world. An example would be the historic Friday prayers and *khutbah* (sermon) conducted by amina wadud, an African-American Islamic feminist theologian and activist, in New York in 2005, which was condemned by numerous Islamic authorities (BBC 2005). Conventional authorities maintain that only a male can become the *imam* (prayer leader) for congregational *salah*, during which men and women must be segregated. For Imaan, inclusive, mixed gender and non-coercive congregational *salah* thus becomes a powerful symbol of the struggle for LGBT equality in the wider *ummah* (community of Muslims). It also becomes a significant basis for building an LGBT Muslim community and collective identity.

Apart from incorporating inclusive worship into its events, Imaan also attempts to reinterpret conventional Islamic teachings affecting people with sexual and gender identities that do not conform to the norm. Historically, the group has engaged directly with openly gay Muslim academics and imams (religious leaders), such as Scott Siraj Al-Haqq Kugle, and Daayiee Abdullah, to articulate pro-LGBT interpretations of Islam. When I became acquainted with the group in 2010, I offered to conduct full-day workshops voluntarily on the social and historical constructions of Islamic rulings on gender and sexual diversity. My offer was met enthusiastically by several Trustees and members which resulted in my leading and/or advising approximately ten 'Demystifying Sharia' workshops for Imaan members in London, Birmingham, and Manchester between 2012 and 2015.

These workshops consisted of sessions that began with one that critically analysed specific Qur'anic verses on 'homosexuality'. This opening session would establish that the term 'homosexuality' or any equivalent does not exist in the Qur'an. Instead, the Qur'an contains short passages on divine punishment for the followers of the Prophet Lut (the equivalent of the Biblical Lot) in Qur'an 54:33–40, 37:133–8, 50:13, 26:160–75, 15:58–77, 38:13–4, 21:74–5, 27:55–8, 11:70, 11:74 and 11:77–83, 29:26 and 29:28–35, 7:80–84, 6:86, 22:43–44, and 66:10. The Arabic term for sodomy – *liwat* – does not appear in the Qur'an and was coined by subsequent Islamic commentators. These nuances in Qur'anic content and exegesis were then built upon in the following sessions on the formulation of relevant *hadith* (exemplary sayings and conduct of the Prophet Muhammad) and rulings in *fiqh* (jurisprudence). The workshop content drew upon material from my doctoral research at the time as well as the work of Islamic feminist scholars and activists, notably the Malaysian organisation, Sisters in Islam (2004). The workshops received overwhelmingly positive feedback from participants who often said that they offered them a fresh space to integrate their supposedly incompatible Islamic and LGBT identities. Some credited the workshops with giving them the confidence and religious literacy to engage more meaningfully with other Muslim organisations. In fact, the Muslim organisations that were keen to engage with Imaan were also already receptive to the nascent body of progressive and feminist Islamic scholarship and activism.[13]

Imaan and the Muslim organisations that now engage with it are, therefore, part of the same progressive milieu of Muslim networks in Britain and around the world. The difference is that Imaan, as an organisation is non-conformist by design while many of the Muslim activists, community leaders and scholars who engage with it now have gradually turned towards more inclusive views of Islam in the last decade or so. At the same time, several LGBT Muslim individuals who turn to Imaan were previously part of other Muslim social movements that are often stereotyped as 'extremist' or 'fundamentalist', such as Hizbut Tahrir, Tablighi Jamaat, and various Salafi groups. This is also true of the various individuals who are now turning to the more 'progressive' Muslim groups such as the Muslim Institute, the Inclusive Mosque Initiative, and New Horizons in British Islam.[14] Thus, the so-called 'progressive' milieu of Muslim activists and scholars is also permeated by individuals who were once active in the so-called 'radical' or 'fundamentalist' milieu.

I observed similar dynamics during my ethnographic fieldwork in Malaysia – several of the LGBT Muslims I met gravitated towards directly or indirectly supporting more 'progressive' Muslim groups such as Sisters in Islam (SIS) and the Islamic Renaissance Front (IRF). Many of them, as well as other supporters of SIS and IRF, were also once part of the more 'conservative' or 'fundamentalist' milieu of Muslim groups and networks there. However, the only difference in Malaysia at the time was that there was no direct equivalent to Imaan, that is, an explicitly LGBT Muslim organisation.[15] This is largely because homosexuality remains illegal in Malaysia under both civil and Islamic laws and political homophobia remains rife.[16] Islam is also tightly regulated by the state and 'deviant' expressions of Islam are often demonised and prosecuted in the *sharia* courts. The range of Islamic groups that state authorities consider 'deviant' includes the Islamic feminist SIS, Shi'as and certain groups associated with Sufism (mystical expressions of Islam).

Given the politicised nature of Islam and sexuality in Malaysia, I also encountered LGBT Muslims who personally held that groups such as Imaan were in fact 'deviant' if they upheld pro-LGBT interpretations of Islam. Examples of such responses are

> I don't want gay rights rallies .... To me, when you are a Muslim you are a Muslim. You cannot oppose what is enshrined in Islam. ('Ayie', lesbian in her early 30s – my own translation from the original Malay)

> If something is wrong [in Islam], it's still wrong. [If you want to] have gay rights, it's fine, but then again if you want to get married [to a partner of the same sex], it's not right, it's something wrong. To address homophobia is a different thing if you are gay. But if I am in Malaysia, if really I want to learn [about my religion], then I don't have to join a gay Muslim group, I can just go to a masjid (mosque) and go to the normal [religious authorities]. ('Sulaiman', gay man in his early 30s)

Sulaiman, Ayie, and several other Malaysian LGBT Muslims I met were critical of political and/or violent homophobia but still accepted conventional Islamic teachings forbidding homosexuality. To them, even suggesting that there are LGBT-friendly interpretations of Islam is tantamount to heresy. Their reactions suggest that if an organisation like Imaan were to exist in Malaysia, it would be considered 'deviant' and treated with as much, if not more, hostility as several NRMs in the West. I encountered fewer views like this during the British phase of my ethnographic fieldwork and these were largely among the LGBT Muslims who were not part of Imaan and other 'mainstream' Muslims.

The theological innovations within Imaan are thus part and parcel of its organisational development as well as particular politicised trends in relation to Islam and sexuality in Britain. I do not wish to advocate defining Imaan as an NRM or not an NRM but rather to explore how NRM analysis can help us understand Imaan as an archetype of contemporary LGBT Muslim activism.

Imaan and NRM analysis

From the above accounts of Imaan's organisational development and theological innovation over the years, it is possible to evaluate it against some basic sociological characteristics of NRMs. These include the predominance of a first-generation membership which is atypical from the rest of the population; the presence of a charismatic leader; the promotion of an alternative set of beliefs and practices in tension with the rest of society; and fundamental changes within a short time of the movement's founding (Barker 2013: 2). There would also be an element of 'serendipitous experimentation' that characterises many NRMs (Bromley 2013: 247).

Imaan's members are first generation by default – they consist of individuals who are coming (or have already come) to terms with their

Muslim and LGBT identities who proceed to join the organisation. Because of the deeply personal and sometimes uncomfortable nature of these individual journeys, membership criteria remain ambiguous. In practice, during my research, 'members' could consist of LGBT Muslims who simply turned up at an Imaan event or registered on its online forum or Facebook group. Despite the inclusive intentions of this definition of membership, its ambiguity resulted in serious tensions in the past, especially when members' votes were taken on potentially divisive decisions at AGMs.

Membership is also atypical from the rest of the population by default – people who identify as LGBT and Muslim are a minority within a minority in Britain. This also lends a sense of inevitability in Imaan members' experimentation with alternative, pro-LGBT interpretations of Islam which are in tension with those accepted by mainstream Muslim communities. However, Imaan's insistence upon claiming an *Islamic* identity has also placed it at odds with some militantly secular LGBT activists and does sometimes turn it into an oddity amongst the wider non-Muslim population, for example, in its 'rainbow hijabs' effort at London Pride. Yet, as I elaborate below, key changes in British society have enabled Imaan to reduce tensions or even forge alliances with a few Muslim groups as well as Jewish, Christian, and/or secular LGBT groups.

There were also fundamental internal changes within a short time of the organisation's founding, e.g., the name change from Al-Fatiha UK, the schism with Safra Project, and various electoral power struggles. The volatile nature of some of these changes can be traced back to the ambiguous membership structure – on one hand, Imaan seeks to formalise membership criteria and institute democratic governance, but on the other hand 'membership' remains loose, informal and leaves the door open to vicious personality clashes. Thus, although Imaan has never had a charismatic leader, there is an ongoing struggle between some members pushing to institutionalise rational-bureaucratic authority and some individuals attempting to take on a quasi-charismatic authority.

In terms of the organisation's changing vision, Imaan first 'envisioned' (Bromley 2013: 247) itself as explicitly Muslim *and* LGBT (mostly through its choice of title, subtitle and logo). This vision has remained largely unchanged over the years, but the style of Muslim and LGBT activism it pursues has been affected by some key internal and external drivers. Internally, Imaan's membership was traditionally London-based and largely British Pakistani. In recent years, there has been a rise of a younger membership from outside London (mostly in Greater Manchester but also in the West Midlands of England) and of non-Pakistanis (including British Bengalis, Indians, Arabs, Iranians, and converts).

Externally, Imaan members – like many other LGBT Muslims in Britain – have found themselves caught between a pervasive political and ideological spotlight on Islam and terrorism, on one hand, and increasingly liberal state policies on sexual diversity on the other hand. At the same time, the passage of the Equality Acts of 2006 and then 2010 has enabled many established activists from LGBT and Muslim circles to cooperate meaningfully to uphold the rights of sexual *and* religious minorities. These external and internal drivers are partly what have led to the 'revisioning' of Imaan amongst some sections of its leadership and membership. For example, as explained above, they have opened up avenues of collaboration between Imaan and other Muslim organisations that are equally critical of anti-LGBT and anti-Muslim attitudes.

In terms of the 'concentration' (Bromley 2013: 251) of Imaan's membership, the organisation has always predominantly attracted LGBT Muslims actively seeking a like-minded community and/or a means of resolving their internal sexual and religious conflicts. Yet, there is now a distinction in the attitudes of particular cohorts of recruits. The founding/ first generation of Imaan members were pioneers in articulating a public stance against anti-LGBT attitudes among Muslims *and* anti-Muslim attitudes in certain sectors of British society. Their approach to activism was therefore largely aggressive, confrontational and defensive towards various external threats. The newer cohorts of members were no longer pioneers in this sense but could experiment with emerging opportunities to build nascent alliances with various Muslim and LGBT organisations. Thus, although the newer cohorts still took a principled stance against anti-LGBT and anti-Muslim attitudes, their style of activism was much more about broad-based alliance building. This was also reflected in the increasing 'horizontal diversification' (Barker 2013, 5) of Imaan's membership with the growth of greater ethnic/national, theological, linguistic, and regional diversity. In terms of 'vertical diversification' (Barker 2013, 5), the newer cohorts also tried more actively to avoid the creation of an 'inner circle of elites' by registering officially with the Charity Commission and adhering to its criteria regarding transparent and accountable governance. This was, however, met with some resistance among earlier cohorts who saw it as a dilution of the organisation's earlier, more organic vision of activism.

Applying an NRM analysis to the development of an organisation such as Imaan thus does not mean that we need to *classify* it as an NRM. Imaan does not straightforwardly exhibit the common characteristics found in NRMs which consist of a first-generation membership, e.g. the presence of a 'charismatic leader'.[17] At the same, this does not mean that Imaan is decidedly not an NRM – as discussed above, it does exhibit other characteristics commonly associated with NRMs. My aim in this chapter is not to define Imaan one way or another. Rather, I propose that an NRM framework allows us to look at how particular individuals – LGBT Muslims in this case – draw upon their beliefs and identities collectively to pursue aspirations that are constrained by existing social conditions. It also allows us to see how their efforts intersect with those of other Muslims who are also navigating politicised debates on Islam through a host of different movements and groups. An NRM analysis therefore enables us to discern such fluid dynamics which are so often obscured by simplistic, black-and-white media portrayals of 'radical' versus 'moderate' Islam, or a clash of 'Islamic' and 'Western' values.

Concluding remarks

The attitudes of Muslims towards LGBT issues form a significant part of current public debates on 'radicalisation', 'extremism', or the 'integration' of Muslims in the West. However, as I have argued, it is too limiting to deploy labels such as 'extremist' and 'fundamentalist' or 'moderate' and 'liberal' to Muslims simply based on their attitudes towards LGBT people. Rather, by analysing the experiences of an organisation such as Imaan, we get to see how LGBT Muslims themselves negotiate their marginality and belonging within the wider Muslim community and wider society more generally.

In particular, I have argued that employing an NRM framework to an LGBT Muslim organisation such as Imaan allows for more nuanced analysis of the group's inter-related organisational development and theological innovation. I have also demonstrated that in addition to its internal revisionism and diversification, Imaan has contributed and responded to the revisionism and diversification of other Muslim groups in Britain. Yet, while it is true that Imaan and these organisations are part of the growing progressive milieu of Muslim activism, Imaan has experimented and innovated on Islamic interpretations of sexual diversity almost by default. This is because the *raison d'être* of its founding members and subsequent leadership has always been to reconcile sexual identities which they feel they have little choice over with their highly politicised religious identities. The growing number of Muslim organisations interested in collaborating with Imaan, however, have significantly but only gradually revised their original theological and political positions on LGBT issues.

By applying an NRM framework, I am not arguing for us to classify any of these organisations as NRMs. Instead, I am suggesting that this framework allows us to investigate their complex interactions and shifts over time instead of merely labelling them as 'extremist'/'fundamentalist' or 'moderate'/'liberal'. This chapter has thus shown how a focus on the experiences of Imaan tells a new story of inter-related revisionism and diversification within the wider landscape of Islam in Britain. The narrative arc of Imaan's story demonstrates that it and the other Muslim groups that interact with it do not exist as static 'liberal', 'radical' or other ideological types. Rather, these groups undergo their own internal revisionism and diversification within a wider political landscape which can push or pull them into competing pathways – including liberalisation, pluralisation, and radicalisation.

Notes

1 Founded in 1997 by Faisal Alam, Al-Fatiha was dissolved in 2011 after Alam stepped down.
2 The *Pink Paper* began publishing in 1987 and switched to internet-only publishing in 2009 (Pink News 2009).
3 Al-Fatiha, literally 'The Opening', is the first chapter in the Qur'an while Imaan means 'faith' in Arabic.
4 Personal communication with Imaan members who participated in the 'rainbow hijabs' march.
5 Personal communication with a former Imaan chair.
6 Personal communication with several former Imaan chairs.
7 The organisation was only formally registered with the Charity Commission in 2014, explained below.
8 Personal observations and communication with several Imaan members and former chairs; elections for new Board of Trustees were usually called every three years.
9 Personal communication with several Muslim activists from the Muslim Institute, the Islamic Society of Britain and the City Circle.
10 Personal observation and participation.
11 Personal observation and communication with Imaan ex-members and founders of Hidayah.
12 The ninth month of the Islamic calendar in which Muslims are ordained to fast, that is, to refrain from food, drink and sex between sunrise and sunset.
13 E.g. amina wadud has spoken at events organised by New Horizons in British Islam and her writings have been republished or promoted by the Muslim Institute (Wadud 2005; Lynch 2016)
14 Personal communication with leaders and members of these groups.
15 There are, however, secular and multicultural groups that advocate LGBT rights such as Seksualiti Merdeka (literally, 'Independent Sexuality'). There are also signs of small, informal LGBT Muslim collectives emerging recently in Malaysia - some years after the period of my ethnographic fieldwork which this chapter is based on.
16 This has been the case ever since former Deputy Prime Minister Anwar Ibrahim was sacked in 1998 and jailed on charges of corruption and sodomy.
17 Besides, there are other analytical frameworks that could yield different types of insights regarding the emergence of groups such as Imaan, e.g. social movement theory.

Bibliography

All URLs were accessed on 4 June 2020.
Barker, Eileen. 2013. "Revision and Diversification in New Religious Movements: An Introduction" in *Revisionism and Diversification in New Religious Movements*, Eileen Barker (ed.). Farnham, UK: Ashgate, pp. 1–14.
BBC. 2005. "Woman Leads US Muslims to Prayer." *BBC News*. (18 March). Available at: http://news.bbc.co.uk/1/hi/world/americas/4361931.stm.
Bromley, David G. 2013. "Changing Vision, Changing Course: En-Visioning/Re-Visioning and Concentration/Diversification in NRMs" in *Revisionism and Diversification in New Religious Movements*, Eileen Barker (ed.). Farnham, UK: Ashgate, pp. 247–260.

Carlile, Jennifer. 2006. "Gay and 'Passionate about Islam.'" *NBC News.* (7 June). Available at: http://www.nbcnews.com/id/13712248/ns/world_news-islam_in_europe/t/homosexual-passionate-about-islam/#.V0mv3fkrKUl.

Charity Commission. 2020. "Charity Framework." *UK Charity Commission.* Available at: http://apps.charitycommission.gov.uk/Showcharity/RegisterOfCharities/CharityFramework.aspx?RegisteredCharityNumber=1158977&SubsidiaryNumber=0.

Decolonizing Sexualities Network. 2020. "Safra Project Archive (2001–2005)." University of Kent. Available at: https://research.kent.ac.uk/decolonizing-sexualities-network/safra-project-archive2001-2005/#.

Firestone, Reuven. 2012. "'Jihadism' as a New Religious Movement" in *The Cambridge Companion to New Religious Movements*, Olav Hammer and Mikael Rothstein (eds.). Cambridge: Cambridge University Press, pp. 263–285.

Guardian, The. 2001. "An Islamic Revolutionary." *The Guardian.* (30 August). Available at: http://www.theguardian.com/g2/story/0,3604,544059,00.html.

Hidayana, Irwan Martua. 2015. "Does the Fatwa on Homosexuals in Indonesia Matter?" *The Conversation.* (2 April). Available at: http://theconversation.com/does-the-fatwa-on-homosexuals-in-indonesia-matter-39531.

Hunt, Stephen. 2010. "Introduction" in *New Religions and Spiritualities*, Stephen Hunt (ed.). The Library of Essays on Sexuality and Religion. Farnham: Ashgate, pp. xi–xxv.

Imaan. 2020. "About." *Imaan.* Available at: https://imaanlondon.wordpress.com/about/.

Kamal, Shazwan Mustafa. 2015. "LGBT Community Will Never Have Equal Rights in Malaysia, Tourism Minister Says." *Malay Mail Online.* (11 September). Available at: http://www.themalaymailonline.com/malaysia/article/lgbt-community-will-never-have-equal-rights-in-malaysia-tourism-minister-sa.

Lubin, Rhian. 2016. "Saudi Arabia 'Pushes for Homosexuals to Be Executed' amid Fears Social Media Is 'Turning People Gay.'" *The Mirror.* (1 April). Available at: http://www.mirror.co.uk/news/world-news/saudi-arabia-pushes-homosexuals-executed-7672283.

Lynch, Lucy. 2016. "Islam Conference in Coventry Will Debate Thorny Issues such as Donald Trump's Anti-Muslim Rants." *Coventry Telegraph.* (18 March). Available at: http://www.coventrytelegraph.net/news/coventry-news/islam-conference-coventry-debate-thorny-11055584.

Mahmood, Shabnam. 2009. "Gay Muslim Story for EastEnders." *BBC News.* (28 May). Available at: http://news.bbc.co.uk/1/hi/8072720.stm.

Mirza, Hassan. 2007. "Adnan Ali Speaks." *Hassan!.* (30 May). Available at: https://shnoobert.blogspot.com/2007/05/adnan-ali-speaks.html.

Mosbergen, Dominique. 2015. "Brunei's LGBT Community Faces Terrifying Future." *The Huffington Post.* (15 October). Available at: http://www.huffingtonpost.com/entry/lgbt-brunei_us_561501f9e4b0fad1591a1167.

Moyer, Justin Wm. 2014. "Don't Forget: The Islamic State Is Also Homophobic." *The Washington Post.* (19 September). Available at: https://www.washingtonpost.com/news/morning-mix/wp/2014/09/19/dont-forget-the-islamic-state-is-also-homophobic/.

Muslim Institute, The, and Imaan. 2014. "'Diversity: The Gift of Islam': Joint Conference Held by Muslim Institute and Imaan." *The Muslim Institute.* Available at: http://musliminstitute.org/events/diversity-gift-islam-joint-conference-held-muslim-institute-and-imaan.

Perraudin, Frances. 2016. "Half of All British Muslims Think Homosexuality Should Be Illegal, Poll Finds." *The Guardian*. (11 April). Available at: http://www.theguardian.com/uk-news/2016/apr/11/british-muslims-strong-sense-of-belonging-poll-homosexuality-sharia-law.

Pink News. 2009. "Pink Paper Suspends Printing." *Pink News*. (24 June). Available at: http://www.pinknews.co.uk/2009/06/24/pink-paper-suspends-printing/.

Regan, Daniel. 1989. "Islam as a New Religious Movement in Malaysia" in *The Changing Face of Religion*, James A. Beckford and Thomas Luckmann (eds.). London: SAGE Publications, pp. 124–146.

Rory, McKeown. 2015. "Former Islamic Extremist Was on the Verge of Bombing Britain, Then He Came out as Gay." *Daily Star*. (1 September). Available at: http://www.dailystar.co.uk/news/latest-news/461777/Gay-Islamic-extremist-sexuality-radicalised-Britain.

Sedgwick, Mark. 2012. "Neo-Sufism" in *The Cambridge Companion to New Religious Movements*, Olav Hammer and Mikael Rothstein (eds.). Cambridge: Cambridge University Press, pp. 198–214.

Shah, Shanon. 2012. "Muslims Building Bridges: Sexuality, Diversity and Faith." *The Muslim Institute*. Available at: https://musliminstitute.org/freethinking/culture/muslims-building-bridges-sexuality-diversity-and-faith.

Shterin, Marat, and Akhmet Yarlykapov. 2011. "Reconsidering Radicalisation and Terrorism: The New Muslims Movement in Kabardino-Balkaria and Its Path to Violence" in *Religion, State and Society* 39(2/3): 303–325.

Sisters in Islam. 2004. "A Framework for Understanding How Syariah 'Laws' Are Constructed." Training seminar. Sisters in Islam.

Tatchell, Peter. 2007. "Their Multiculturalism and Ours." *Dissent*. Available at: https://www.dissentmagazine.org/wp-content/files_mf/1389820114d8Tatchell.pdf.

Trayner, David. 2015. "Children Who Hold Homophobic Views More Likely to Become Extremists, Warns Nicky Morgan." *The Independent*. (30 June). Available at: http://www.independent.co.uk/news/uk/politics/education-secretary-nicky-morgan-at-risk-of-becoming-extremist-10355850.html.

UK Prime Minister's Office. 2011. "PM's Speech at Munich Security Conference." *GOV.UK*. (5 February). Available at: https://www.gov.uk/government/speeches/pms-speech-at-munich-security-conference.

Wadud, Amina. 2005. "Amina Wadud on Justice, Gender and Islam." *Critical Muslim*. Available at: https://criticalmuslim.com/upfront/religion/amina-wadud-justice-gender-and-islam.

Wyke, Tom. 2015. "Thrown from a Roof, Stoned to Death and Crucified: While the World Reacts with Horror to Terror in Europe, New ISIS Executions Show the Medieval Brutality Jihadists Would Bring to the West." *Mail Online*. (16 January). Available at: http://www.dailymail.co.uk/news/article-2913733/Thrown-roof-stoned-death-crucified-world-reacts-horror-terror-Europe-new-ISIS-executions-medieval-brutality-jihadists-bring-West.html.

Part IV

New prophecies or revelations

14 Digital revisionism: the aftermath of The Family International's Reboot

Claire Borowik

The Family International's history spans five decades of continuous transformation, from its emergence on the countercultural fringe of the Jesus People Movement in the 1960s to its evolution as a communalist new religious movement with a global presence, culminating in its reinvention as a digital community. In 2010, the movement experienced a profound redirection in the form of a comprehensive organisational overhaul known as the 'Reboot', which repositioned its theological beliefs and religious practice in closer alliance to Christian orthodoxy, while marginalising the majority of its unconventional doctrines and practices and relinquishing exclusivist claims. Simultaneously, the Reboot systematically deconstructed historic pillars of the Family International's culture, notably its communal society structure, leadership, and oversight committees organised at the grassroots level and lifestyle practices that had served to maintain boundaries of separation between the movement and the surrounding sociocultural environment.

The Reboot's intentional revisionism of the Family International's radical interpretations of Christian discipleship and countercultural practice, coupled with the dismantling of the communal household structure, engendered unprecedented cultural upheaval, eventuating a process of 'identity renegotiation' for members in their reintegration into conventional society (Smith 1998: 100). The lack of organisational framework post-Reboot consequentially led to the movement's metamorphosis from a communitarian movement with a transnational structure and a membership extending three generations to an amorphous networked community with little formal structure, cohesion, or visibility beyond its online presence. Ten years after the introduction of the Reboot, the movement remains largely unstructured, and the contemporary virtual community has faced numerous challenges in fostering movement vitality, membership retention, collective identity, and cohesion.

In a previous volume of this series, a chapter was devoted to an analysis of the changes in doctrine, practice, and lifestyle introduced at the Reboot (Borowik 2013). This second chapter, drafted ten years post-Reboot, will explore the outcomes, both intended and unintended, of the Reboot, its impact on the movement's culture, practice, and subsequent evolution as a

DOI: 10.4324/9781315226804-14

virtual networked community. The Family International's introduction of sweeping revisions of doctrine and practice, and the subsequent struggle to reconceptualise its community and identity, offer insights into the challenges faced by new religious movements in their quest to accommodate dynamics of change, both internal and external, while retaining cultural vitality, membership engagement, and unique identity.

Backdrop of TFI's Reboot

From its early beginnings in the late 1960s as the Children of God, the history of the Family International (TFI) has been punctuated by alternating periods of innovation and adaptation in the form of internal upheavals referred to as 'revolutions', and controversy and opposition originating from external sources, including numerous government raids and legal cases in the early 1990s. (For analyses of raids and legal cases, see Borowik 2015: 3–23; Wright and Palmer 2016: 73–98.) TFI's founder, David Berg (1919–94), constructed the movement's ideology and doctrine around anti-establishment themes, radical Christian discipleship, sexually liberal practices, and an imminent apocalypse, referred to as 'the Endtime'. Within this context, Berg excoriated established religion and societal institutions, and developed a communalised movement devoted to evangelism, with an engrained sense of responsibility to impart the Gospel message before the arrival of the Endtime (Figure 14.1).[1]

Throughout the movement's early lifetime until the end of the 1970s, it experienced a period of rapid growth and dispersion from its starting point in the United States, expanding its presence into over 90 countries and nearly 10,000 members. Organisationally, the movement was characterised

Figure 14.1 Children of God in a Sackcloth Vigil, carrying signs calling for repentance of sins, salvation in Jesus, and warning of future apocalyptic events. Austin, Texas, 1971 (Courtesy of The Family International)

by cycles of authoritarian leadership and institutional regimentation, and an emphasis on local autonomy and organisation. In 1979, Berg dismantled the previous organisational structure at the 'RNR' (Reorganization Nationalization Revolution) in response to the excessively authoritarian approach of the leadership hierarchy and resultant lack of autonomy for rank and file members (Chancellor 2000: 10–1). Subsequently, in the early 1980s, the movement was reorganised in a 'Fellowship Revolution' that created a loosely-knit structure for community with democratically elected leadership at local, regional, and national levels (Melton 1997: 22–6). This new structure gradually evolved once more into a close regimentation of the communal homes, as Berg aged and his wife and successor, Karen Zerby (known within the movement as Maria Fontaine), began to assert leadership of TFI, and sought to institutionalise the belief system and practices.

After Berg's death, consistent steps were taken under the direction of Peter Amsterdam, who became co-director of TFI in 1994, to democratise the movement. These included: the drafting of a Charter of members' rights and responsibilities in 1995; the development of a board structure in 2001 that provided a venue for grassroots participation in the movement's direction; an international leadership body with decision-making authority (known as the Family Policy Council); and a democratised communal household structure to promote a higher degree of autonomy and member participation. During this period, a 'culture of prophecy' evolved under Maria's leadership, which both democratised prophecy within the homes and established an authoritarian context in the use of corporate prophecy for direction of the membership (Shepherd and Shepherd 2008: 50–1).

Despite the global dispersion of TFI's membership and its lack of formal meeting places or administrative centres, the movement proved singularly adept at creating its own vibrant culture, separate from institutional Christianity and the surrounding sociocultural environment in which it was embedded for purposes of evangelisation (Bainbridge 2002: 29). Through Berg's (and later, Maria's) writings, the leadership effectively indoctrinated its members in its unorthodox belief system, socialised its members into its world-rejecting culture, and perpetuated its evangelistic purpose. The movement was prolific in its in-house creation of evangelistic publications, musical and audio-visual productions, children's books, and original artwork. The advent of the Internet further facilitated the dissemination of TFI writings and culture, as the movement rapidly embraced this new technology to foster community in its widely dispersed membership, and for evangelisation and reputation management in the public forum (Borowik 2018: 66–8).

By the mid-1990s, the percentage of second-generation children and young adults had become substantial, representing two-thirds of the membership (Amsterdam 2002). Berg contended that the second generation would be purer than the first generation that gave birth to the movement, due to their upbringing in a radical Christian utopian lifestyle, free from individualistic, materialistic values prevalent in Western society (Berg 1983). Consequentially, the indoctrination and socialisation of the second generation into TFI's belief system rapidly took precedence over the recruitment of new members, a natural progression considering that recruitment rates had already declined due to TFI's isolationist and high-demand lifestyle (Richardson 2013: 254).

Throughout TFI's history, varying degrees of tension have existed between attempts to regiment movement purity and maintain boundaries of separateness, and efforts to adapt and accommodate to contemporary expediencies and external pressures (Borowik 2013: 19). This dialectical tension was exacerbated upon the coming of age of the second generation, many of whom chafed at the narrow restrictions of the TFI worldview and insular boundaries of the communal homes. As digital technology became widely integrated into the communal homes by the late 1990s, the second generation became more inclined to engage in boundary-permeating forays into previously forbidden territory on the Internet, where secular worldviews proliferated and they could freely interact with their former-member peers (Barker 2005: 73–4). Previously incontrovertible truths and lifestyle practices likewise met with resistance from the younger generation, which led to numerous accommodations and attempts to modernise the culture to appeal to the youth (Chancellor 2000: 244–5). The literature became increasingly populated with spiritual heroes and villains reminiscent of the superhero fiction genre revitalised in contemporary entertainment media, as well as magical powers and miracle-working incantations, not unlike those popularised in *The Lord of the Rings* and *Harry Potter* fantasy series (Figure 14.2).

TFI's liberal sexual practices, albeit largely domesticated by the early 1990s, provided a counterpoint to contemporary society's hook-up and party culture for the second generation. Accommodations notwithstanding, lingering assumptions that each child born into TFI was predestined to serve God as part of 'His Endtime Army' (van Eck Duymaer van Twist 2015: 29) rendered the movement ill-equipped to respond to the inevitability of children opting for a secular lifestyle (Fontaine and Amsterdam 2009b).

The widespread use of corporate prophecy from the mid-1990s served to reinforce centralised authoritarian leadership and isolationist cultural practices, as well as to advance new revelation and exclusive truth claims. Increasingly, prophecy was channelled to address internal problems and to reinforce boundaries, as the leadership grappled with concerns that the youth would be drawn away by corrupting influences (Borowik 2013: 19). Prophecies were alternately channelled to reaffirm TFI's destiny and unique calling and place in Christendom, and to demand heightened levels of commitment and compliance to regulations and cultural expectations (Fontaine 2010c). Prophetic pronouncements detailed how the movement would bridge the daunting limitations it faced due to its legacy of controversy to become accepted and popularised and eventually assume a

Figure 14.2 XN09 – TFI Publication (Courtesy of The Family International)

leadership role in Christianity (Fontaine 2006). Progressive revelation throughout 2006–08 postulated that TFI's membership and circle of influence were poised to expand exponentially in the near future. In anticipation of this prophetic occurrence, a protracted review process was undertaken to identify aspects of TFI's theology, lifestyle, and practice potentially incongruent with future evangelistic expansion and membership growth, culminating in the Reboot (Fontaine and Amsterdam 2009a).

The convergence of numerous factors has been identified as underpinning the sweeping reorganisation and revisionism introduced at the Reboot, principally: demands for change and modernisation by the second generation (Shepherd and Shepherd 2013: 92–3); increasing numbers of second-generation members abandoning the movement (Borowik 2013: 19); the ageing of the first generation and the delay in millennial expectations of an imminent Endtime (Barker 2011: 8–10); the collective weight of stigma and controversy that hindered the evangelistic work and growth of the movement (Richardson 2013: 254); and the lack of appeal of TFI's exclusivist truth claims and communalist lifestyle for potential converts (Amsterdam 2010a). In addition, the divergent, and at times clashing, streams of direction issued in prophecy produced a potentially irreconcilable chasm between charismatic truth claims issued by the leadership regarding envisioned expansion and public acceptance, and previous writings that demanded separation from the world, excoriated institutional Christianity, and maintained a highly regimented interpretation of discipleship.

The realities of the limitations the movement faced as a result of the intense stigmatisation of its public identity due to legacy issues and Berg's polemical writings, coupled with the departure such accommodation would represent from its foundational beliefs and identity, proved to be formidable barriers to successful reinvention of the movement. In the absence of an organisational structure to foster community post-Reboot, the movement morphed organically into a virtually networked community centred in website services with minimal formal community interaction.

Rewriting the script

The rationale for the monumental changes introduced at the Reboot was mapped out in 18 comprehensive documents, inclusive of a 'manifesto' articulating the ideological underpinnings of the Reboot (Amsterdam 2010), a document analysing TFI's history and Berg's impact and model (Amsterdam 2010a), a four-part series addressing doctrinal revisions (Fontaine 2010b), and twelve documents repositioning lifestyle and organisational practices. TFI's gradual transition to Internet-based forms of communication from 2000 onwards was central to the implementation of the Reboot, enabling its exclusive adoption of websites for disseminating its writings. Numerous websites were created in conjunction with the implementation of the Reboot to transition TFI communications online and phase out paper publications. These included two websites for the dissemination of devotional and directional publications: *Directors' Corner*[2] for post-Reboot writings by TFI directors Peter Amsterdam and Maria, and *Anchor*,[3] a venue for publishing edited versions of pre-Reboot TFI writings, as well as resources by other Christians.

The theological modifications introduced at the Reboot represented an intentional approximation of TFI doctrine to Christian orthodoxy and lessening of tension with the surrounding sociocultural environment, rationalised as essential to future evangelisation objectives and membership expansion. This radical repositioning pivoted on the affirmation of the supremacy of the Bible over new revelation and extra-biblical teachings, which were consequently relegated to the category of 'additional teachings'.

Corporate prophecy, a hallmark of Maria's leadership that had previously been accorded an authoritative role in defining doctrine, religious practice, and the direction of the movement, was recast and heavily deemphasised (Fontaine 2010c). The majority of previously published prophecies would prove unsustainable in the post-Reboot context, necessitating their redefinition as time-contextual and no longer applicable (Borowik 2013b: 21–2).

The use of corporate prophecy has in practice greatly diminished since the Reboot; while brief prophecies have been incorporated into nearly a third of the 310 posts published by Maria since the Reboot, the vast majority reference personal situational contexts rather than corporate instruction. As a notable exception, corporate prophecies providing spiritual instruction and encouragement were published in 2020 in response to the COVID-19 pandemic (Fontaine 2020a). Maria also published rare corporate instruction in response to questions from members as to whether the COVID-19 pandemic could be interpreted as a sign of the immanence of the Endtime (Fontaine 2020b). Ongoing revelation, however, while not discounted at the Reboot as a possibility for the future, has in fact not eventuated. Prophecy and new revelation have clearly been eclipsed by the contemporary motivational, and minimally directional, approach adopted post-Reboot. The theological innovations introduced in prophecy prior to the Reboot are rarely visible; extra-biblical teachings removed from circulation at the Reboot have not been reinstated or recontextualised. Post-Reboot writings published by Peter Amsterdam indicate a definitive shift to Christian orthodoxy, the majority of which have been devoted to teachings aligned with mainstream Evangelical theology. His 50-part 'The Heart of It All: Foundations of Christian Theology' series summarises the teachings of contemporary Protestant theologians, while not attempting to reconcile these with previous novel interpretations published in TFI writings.[4]

Subsequent to the implementation of the Reboot, a review process was initiated to examine TFI writings to determine whether these were in alignment with the doctrinal revisions introduced, and thus would be reaffirmed, or would be excerpted or discarded. Standards were crafted to ensure that the writings preserved would be amenable to the organisation's contemporary objectives of alignment to biblical doctrine and relevancy to a wider audience beyond the limited circle of its membership (Fontaine 2010b). The majority of Maria's writings from 1996 onwards were of the prophetic and revelatory genre and were not reintegrated into TFI's official library. Berg's writings likewise underwent a lengthy review process, resulting in the preservation of excerpts of 385 of his nearly 2,900 published letters. Excerpts of nearly 200 of the 900 missives published by Maria from 1995 to 2010 have been adapted and subsequently republished on *Anchor*. *Anchor* editors have been granted editorial license to edit and adapt pre-Reboot TFI writings, thus providing a venue to recontextualise previous prophecies to align with post-Reboot doctrine and culture.

The Law of Love

As a distinct departure from the Reboot's realignment of TFI doctrine to mainstream Christian theology, Berg's antinomian 'Law of Love' doctrine and associated liberal sexual practices were ratified at the Reboot in a document entitled 'Applying the Lord's Law of Love' (Fontaine 2010a). According to this doctrine, members had been freed from the strictures of the Mosaic Law, inclusive of biblical prohibitions of adultery and sexual immorality, through faith in Christ. David Berg's most polemical statements and theological speculations on the topic, published from 1978 to 1985, had challenged traditional moral boundaries for sexual relations, including those relating to minors, which ultimately led to incidences of inappropriate adult/minor sexual interaction and exposure of children to harm (Fontaine and Amsterdam 2008). In response to complaints raised by several teenagers in 1986, measures were taken from the mid-1980s onwards to eradicate practices that placed minors at risk, including the drafting of child-protection policies with denunciations of child abuse and exploitation, the renouncement of previously published literature at variance with this position, and the issuance of official apologies to the second generation. Berg's polemical writings and the liberal sexual practices promoted by his Law of Love doctrine had placed children at risk and positioned the movement in high tension with the surrounding sociocultural environment, ultimately resulting in highly publicised raids and court cases in the early 1990s and much of the controversy and stigmatisation associated with the movement. The court-appointed investigations conducted in the early 1990s in several countries, in which nearly 500 children were taken into state custody, attested to the institutionalisation of the child protection measures introduced from the mid-1980s onwards. No signs of abuse were evidenced in the children examined, and all children were remanded to the custody of their parents (Melton 1997: 38).

In a landmark case in 1992, the mother of a Family member filed a case with Lord Justice Ward in England, requesting the custody of her daughter's unborn child based on perceived risk to the child due to her daughter's membership in the movement. In 1995, after three years of intensive investigation, Justice Ward emitted a lengthy ruling, in which he levelled harsh criticisms of past eras of the movement's history, requiring assurances of changes made in years past, while also concluding that the Family International had undergone reformative changes (Ward 1995). Prior to publishing his final ruling, Family leadership were required to publish an acknowledgement that David Berg and his teachings were responsible for cases of children having been subjected to sexually inappropriate and harmful behaviour prior to the institution of child protection policies from 1989 onwards (Amsterdam 1995). Justice Ward concluded that he was satisfied that "the wrongs of the past had been stamped out" and the movement provided a safe environment for children raised within the group and awarded the mother care and control of her infant child (Bradney 1999: 217–8). (See also Barker's chapter in this volume and Borowik 2015: 5–7.)

Although the validity of the Law of Love doctrine and its allowance for sexual relations between adults (regardless of marital status) was ratified at the Reboot, liberal sexual practices were significantly de-emphasised and recast from doctrine to personal lifestyle choice (Fontaine 201a). No mention has been made in post-Reboot writings of previous unorthodox sexual practices, and in 2019 Peter Amsterdam published a series of theological posts on the Ten Commandments affirmative of biblical teachings on sexuality.[5] In 2019, the 'Applying the Law of Love' document was redacted and retitled 'Marriage, Divorce and Child Support', and previous affirmations of liberal sexual practices therein were removed from circulation. While the extent to which members or former members may continue these practices is unknown, evidently these have no place in the contemporary digital religious world of TFI.

Reimagining community, virtually

Although the main rationalisation presented for the Reboot was the need to modernise the movement to position it to accommodate growth and an expanded community, a secondary, if not equally prominent theme, was the shift to personal autonomy and individualism. In light of these dual objectives, a light-weight structure for community-building was presented at the Reboot that designated four quasi-leadership positions, referenced as 'facilitators', who would represent the pillars of TFI's evangelistic mission, community-building, public affairs, and mission works (The Family International 2010a).

These facilitators would jointly form a national facilitator counsel, analogous to Berg's reorganisation of the movement in 1981 at the Fellowship Revolution. Prior to the implementation of the Fellowship Revolution, Berg had likewise dismantled the leadership structure at the Reorganization Nationalization Revolution (RNR), claimed sole authority for the movement, and proclaimed an era of personal autonomy and liberty (Berg 1978). Numerous parallels between the Reboot and the RNR may be drawn in their proclamations of liberty from rules and regulations, affirmation of personal autonomy, and minimal membership requirements limited to the submission of a monthly report, tithe or offering, and commitment to TFI's mission purpose. Here the parallel ends, however, as the RNR did not intentionally disband the communal society model as did the Reboot, which represented a significant departure from the collectivist ideology central to TFI's definition of Christian discipleship. Unlike the post-RNR Fellowship Revolution, where a vibrant community was recreated through a re-envisioned communal home model, the post-Reboot TFI lacked a structure to reconstruct its community on the ground, ultimately relegating community to virtual spaces (Figure 14.3).

Figure 14.3 The Family International's public website, which links to its TFI Online community website (portal.tfionline.com) and numerous other websites created for evangelistic purposes (Website screenshot published with permission from The Family International)

Prior to the Reboot, Maria and Peter had conceded that 'building a strong sense of community will be crucial to the future of the Family' (Fontaine and Amsterdam 2009a), thus the lack of implementation of new mechanisms for community proved to be a contested point, periodically addressed by the directors in their missives to the membership. In a poll conducted in 2011 that elicited 2,740 responses (representing 67 per cent of the adult population of TFI at the time), 94 per cent of participants affirmed that 'it was important to them to be in community with likeminded TFI members'. Fifty-six per cent further indicated that 'they would be willing to invest time and funds in making TFI community events happen' (Amsterdam 2011). Nonetheless, the new framework for community, anticipated to be instituted in 2011, did not eventuate.

The issue of community was revisited more comprehensively in 2013 via a series of 16 webcasts produced by Amsterdam to address members' concerns regarding the loss of community cohesion and collective identity, and requests that new agencies for community be developed. Amsterdam enumerated therein several challenges to developing community, in particular members' aversion to previous authoritarian models of leadership and lifestyle differences that had evolved with the dissolution of the communal households that previously set the pace for TFI culture. He concluded that a new organisational structure would not be implemented in the foreseeable future. Amsterdam further indicated that the coordination of fellowship and mission works would rest in the court of individuals to mobilise and enact, in cooperation with other local members or through virtual media such as Skype and Facebook. He also suggested that members consider joining local churches in cases where local or online community-building proved insufficient (Amsterdam 2013a).

Although members welcomed the greater freedom and autonomy introduced at the Reboot, many struggled with the loss of collectivist values and lifestyle and questioned this institutional shift, as interviews with members conducted in late 2015 indicated:

> As a movement, in the form and format as it was, [the Reboot] ended it. The whole idea is that it would resurrect, that it would reboot in another fashion. I think it has, but just not what we expected. We expected it to still be a cohesive movement, and I feel like it's not.

> I think what was lost was the collective will ... [W]e couldn't convert what the structure was of the past into an ongoing structure that was going to work. I think that meant that we really didn't convert the positive of the Reboot into something that made us a stronger group. (Borowik 2018: 71)

The distribution of members in over 80 countries posed unique challenges in rebuilding community and coordinating evangelistic efforts, underscoring the central role communalism played in the cultural life and identity of members. The virtual movement's inability to effectively foster a revitalised sense of community, collective identity and purpose since the Reboot is evidenced in the decline in membership and finances. According to membership statistics disclosed annually since 2011, TFI membership has declined from 5,400 adult members in 2010 to its current numbers of approximately 1,500, representing an average decline of nearly eleven per cent annually. The generational composition has also shifted significantly. Whereas prior to the Reboot approximately two-thirds of the adult membership were second-generation members, currently the trend has reversed, with over two-thirds of the membership comprising first-generation members. Income to the organisation through tithes and offerings has likewise diminished at a rate of nearly seven per cent per year on average, necessitating the annual discontinuation of various services (Amsterdam 2019).

In a bid to compensate for the loss of pre-Reboot frameworks and TFI's unexpected evolution to online community, measures were taken to strengthen its virtual community through the creation in 2013 of a community website, *TFI Online*, which features both a 'members only' community space, and a public interface.[6] Efforts have also been made to preserve and archive online cultural and nostalgic artifacts of TFI's history, including thousands of photographs and musical productions from the Children of God era,[7] as well as David Berg's unique interpretations of biblical apocalyptic doctrine and references.[8] The majority of TFI's prolific collection of nearly 150 original music albums have been reinstituted,[9] whereas little of TFI's signature artwork, previously featured in evangelistic posters and TFI publications were preserved.

Recreating TFI's identity

Throughout its nearly five decades of existence, The Family International's narrative has been characterised by controversy and adversity, and the stereotyping and stigmatisation of the movement and, consequently, its members (Bainbridge 2002: ix). The movement's ability to reinvent itself as a contemporary Christian movement that has shed controversial doctrines and practices of the past and reintegrated into the mainstream has been hindered by contemporary digital information dynamics that facilitate the indiscriminate flow of information on the Web and its permanence in cyberspace. Stigmatising narratives and profiles highlighting negative legacy issues have been perpetuated through former-member narratives in media articles, blogs and books, a damaging profile on Wikipedia created by a counter-cult administrator with editorial authority, and old documentaries and expurgated writings that have become permanently resituated on the Internet.

In the early 2000s, the movement's struggle for legitimacy and tolerance intensified due to the emergence of a large network of disaffected second-generation former members, who, availing themselves of digital community-building tools, coalesced on the *Moving On* community website to share their grievances and lobby for the movement's demise (van Eck Duymaer van Twist 2015: 170).[10] Two additional adversarial former-member websites came to the fore,[11] further polarising the debate. The ensuing contest for ownership of the defining narrative of TFI, featuring intense rhetoric on both sides, culminated in the murder of former member Angela Smith, perpetrated by Maria's son, Ricky Rodriguez, who subsequently committed suicide. This incident once again placed the movement at the centre of negative media coverage, revived old controversies long addressed, and provided a platform for new counter-narratives (Shepherd and Shepherd 2010: 144). In the aftermath of this tragic incident, TFI adopted a conciliatory approach vis-à-vis the former member community, with the intent of lessening hostilities and promoting reconciliation. Official apologies from leadership were issued to second-generation members, validating their grievances and accepting responsibility for previous policies that had disadvantaged the second generation in their transition to secular society (Fontaine and Amsterdam 2009b).

The permanence of counter-narratives on the Internet has indubitably hindered the ability of new religious movements such as TFI to distance themselves from past controversies, achieve legitimacy in the religious marketplace, and successfully reinvent themselves as contemporary world-engaging movements (Cowan 2004: 268). Although TFI had consistently weathered the storms of adversity and accommodated as needed to survive and propagate its message, it became evident that for the Reboot's objectives of evangelistic success to prosper, new strategies for identity management would be in order, including the lessening of its historic tension with the greater society. Upon recognition of the likelihood that legacy issues would potentially continue to trouble members as they reconstructed their lives and identities post-Reboot, it was determined that members need no longer affiliate their mission works or personally identify themselves with TFI (The Family International 2010b). As a result, the majority of mission works previously affiliated with TFI opted to disaffiliate in order to protect their works from detractor campaigns or official scrutiny. Concerted efforts to promote and legitimise TFI's public identity thus increasingly lacked a context as TFI transitioned to a virtual network with no brick-and-mortar presence. The reinvention of TFI's public persona has proved to be a contested endeavour, indicative of the fragmentation of TFI's collective identity post-Reboot and the formidable obstacles to renegotiating its identity (Borowik 2018: 68–71).

In spite of the challenges the movement has faced in the public arena, strides of progress have been made toward developing a transparent and relevant public identity. TFI's writings, previously restricted to 'members only' due to their betimes controversial and exclusivist truth claims, have been made largely available to the public in their revised format. The movement's signature evangelistic publication, *Activated Magazine*, is available online in 13 languages and is widely accessed by a global audience, as are TFI's other evangelistic websites.[12] Notwithstanding efforts to modernise and construct a world-engaging contemporary identity conducive to new member recruitment, the movement has lacked a mechanism for growth in the absence of a structure to receive new members or build tangible forms of community. Paradoxically, while the Reboot was predicated on church growth and new member recruitment, this lack of visible community and collective identity has largely undermined congregation-building objectives and membership retention. As legacy membership has continued to decline, the anticipated recruitment of new members has not eventuated, nor have new strategies to address this trend been introduced.

Conclusions

TFI's evolution from its early beginnings as a countercultural new religious movement to its current metamorphosis as a virtual networked community attests to the innovative and dynamic nature of new religions, and their ability to adapt and accommodate in response to internal and external expediencies and prophetic revelation (Barker 2013: 3). In the case of TFI's 'reboot', the successful interjection of new truth claims necessitated a decisive departure from doctrines central to the movement's formation and worldview, as well as the disassociation from previous prophetic direction inharmonious with the movement's new identity and purpose. The systematic revision of the movement's writings, lifestyle practices, and culture proved to be a protracted process, requiring adjustments to the original intents and anticipated outcomes of the Reboot to harmonise with actual outcomes, resulting in further distancing from TFI's radical roots and identity.

The Reboot's disassembling of TFI's foundational discipleship model and communal lifestyle had an unprecedented impact on TFI culture and practice, precipitating a challenging process of identity renegotiation for its members in their reintegration into a world they had abandoned decades earlier. Although TFI has periodically weathered and innovatively adapted to significant change throughout its history, the cultural reversals of the Reboot and departure from TFI's communalist roots and world-rejecting philosophy had the unintended consequence of calling into question the core identity and purpose of the movement.

The assumption woven throughout Berg and Fontaine's writings was that their prophetic writings (accorded equal status with the Bible) and unique doctrines were the main 'glue' that provided cohesiveness and identity (Berg 1981), thus allowing for innovation to be introduced without destabilising the movement. However, the disruption occasioned by the dismantling of the communal society model underscores the central role communalism played in the cultural life and identity of members. Although World Services, TFI's previous upper management structure, had provided spiritual and administrative direction for the movement, the rank and file membership rarely had the opportunity to meet Berg, his successors, or World Services' representatives in person. Conversely, the grassroots membership lived under the same roof and shared common experiences and narratives, which fostered camaraderie, galvanised commitment, and empowered members to develop mission works in over 90 countries with little formal training, visible organisational backing, or funding. Within the shared life experiences in the communes, meaning and identity were co-constructed and reinforced in everyday life, which served to forge a vibrant culture and strong bonds based on shared experiences, worldview, and lifestyle practices that transcended nationality and location.

The movement's inability to effectively restructure its community and shared identity have inevitably contributed to the ongoing decline in TFI membership and revenues. A decade after the introduction of the Reboot in 2010, the movement lacks mechanisms for growth and adaptation; no new organisational structure has been introduced to replace the grassroots board structure and leadership councils dismissed in 2010 (Amsterdam 2013c). Membership statistics and anecdotal evidence indicate that members have by and large effectively reintegrated into society and moved on in new directions for their lives (Borowik 2018: 79–80). A segment of the membership continue to sustain vibrant mission works, while others limit their participation in TFI to the online community and engage in evangelistic pursuits to a lesser extent. Previous barriers between members and former members virtually disintegrated post-Reboot, and sporadic informal gatherings are often inclusive of current and former members alike, with little significance accorded to membership standing. Cultural ties and shared experiences often form the common denominator at such events, rather than commitment to TFI's belief system. In the absence of a structured community, members have created their own community places through Facebook, blogs, Skype groups, and chat forums. Two closed Facebook groups, one for English speakers and one for Spanish, have provided a virtual space for interactive engagement for over 1,500 users and a sense of community built on pre-existing relationships and cultural cues (Borowik 2018: 62–3).

As the Reboot recedes further into the past in TFI's narrative and the life journeys of members continue to lead them in diverse directions, it appears increasingly unlikely that future attempts by TFI to restructure the movement would be met with membership's characteristic accommodation to reorganisation. Likewise, new models for informal community appear unlikely to emerge organically with the passage of time, as the first generation ages and membership declines. In response to queries and speculations from members regarding the movement's future, Amsterdam addressed the issue in a webcast entitled, 'Is TFI a Dying Movement' (2013b):

> Something I've heard quite a bit lately, and I'm pretty sure you've heard it too, is that the Family is a dying movement or it's dead or it's on its last leg.

Amsterdam proposed that TFI's future and legacy lie in its individual members and their personal influence and Christian testimony, as opposed to previous conceptualisations of community, congregation-building or organisational structure:

> The Family is not dead, the Family's not dying. It's alive in you, it's alive in your family... The things that really make the Family alive, God's Spirit, His movement, His desire to win souls, His inspiration, His word, the life that He gives us, that's not dead at all. (2013b)

The revisionism introduced at the Reboot ultimately ushered in the deradicalisation of the movement and its transformation from a worldrejecting new religious movement to an amorphous networked community that has effectively distanced itself from many of the beliefs and practices that formed its core identity and the *raison d'être* of the movement. The Reboot's radical departure from TFI's previous belief system and countercultural worldview, coupled with the virtually insuperable stigmatisation of the movement in the modern digital public square, have presented formidable obstacles to the successful accommodation of the array of revisionist changes introduced at the Reboot. In the absence of new strategies, and agencies to reverse ongoing trends of declining membership and loss of community and unique identity, the sustainability of the movement beyond its first generation and its future vitality remain uncertain. Contemporary challenges notwithstanding, TFI members continue to share the movement's unique brand of Christianity in over 80 countries through the dissemination of its Gospel message in 20 languages, scores of multilingual websites, and charitable and humanitarian programmes around the world.

Notes

1 Berg's advocacy of an imminent fulfilment of the apocalyptic events prophesied in the Bible, and his belief that the Second Coming would occur within the lifetime of the movement's first-generation weighed heavily in the early organisational strategies of the movement.
2 http://directors.tfionline.com.
3 http://anchor.tfionline.com.
4 https://portal.tfionline.com/en/pages/the-heart-of-it-all/.
5 https://portal.tfionline.com/en/pages/living-christianity/.
6 https://portal.tfionline.com/.
7 https://childrenofgod.com/.
8 https://countdown.org/.
9 See https://www.nubeat.org/, an unofficial archive of TFI music.
10 The *Moving On* website was withdrawn in 2013.
11 https://www.xfamily.org and http://www.exfamily.org/index.htm.
12 See https://activated.org/en/.

Bibliography

All URLs were accessed on 18 June 2020.
Amsterdam, Peter. 2019. *Renewing Our Commitments*. The Family International.
Amsterdam, Peter. 2013a. *Community and Structure*. [Video file]. The Family International. Available at: www.youtube.com/watch?v=haDuXp37nTY.
Amsterdam, Peter. 2013b. *Is TFI a Dying Movement?* [Video file]. The Family International. Available at: https://www.youtube.com/watch?v=bpF65y7nAgo.
Amsterdam, Peter. 2013c. *The Reboot in Hindsight* [Video file]. The Family International. Available at: www.youtube.com/watch?v=4-ZTN7aiCIs.
Amsterdam, Peter. 2011. *A Snapshot of the TFI Member Poll*. The Family International.
Amsterdam, Peter. 2010a. *Backtracking Through TFI History*. The Family International.
Amsterdam, Peter. 2010b. *Change Journey Manifesto*. The Family International.
Amsterdam, Peter. 2002. *2003, Here We Come!* The Family International.
Amsterdam, Peter. 1995. *World Service's Response to Mr Justice Ward*. September.
Bainbridge, William S. 2002. *The Endtime Family: Children of God*. Albany, New York: SUNY Press.
Barker, Eileen. 2013. *Revisionism and Diversification in New Religious Movements*. Burlington, VT: Ashgate.
Barker, Eileen. 2011. "Ageing in New Religions: The Varieties of Later Experiences" in *Diskus*, 12: 1–23. Available at: http://jbasr.com/basr/diskus/diskus12/index.html.

Barker, Eileen. 2005. "Crossing the Boundary: New Challenges to Religious Authority and Control as a Consequence of Access to the Internet" in Morten T. Højsgaard and Margit Warburg (eds). *Religion and Cyberspace*. London, UK: Routledge. Pp. 67–85.

Berg, David. 1983. *Thank God for the Children*. The Family International.

Berg, David. 1981. *The Fellowship Revolution*. The Family International.

Berg, David. 1978. *Proclaim Liberty!* The Family International.

Borowik, Claire. 2018. "From Radical Communalism to Virtual Community: The Digital Transformation of the Family International" in *Nova Religio* 22(1): 59–86.

Borowik, Claire. 2015. "Courts, Crusaders and the Media: The Family International" in James T. Richardson and François Bellanger (eds). *Legal Cases, New Religious Movements, and Minority Faiths*. Burlington, VT: Ashgate. Pp. 3–23.

Borowik, Claire. 2013. "The Family International: Rebooting for the Future" in Eileen Barker (ed.). *Revisionism and Diversification in New Religious Movements*. Burlington, VT: Ashgate. Pp. 15–30.

Bradney, Anthony. 1999. "Children of a Newer God" in Susan Palmer and Charlotte Hardman (eds.). *Children in New Religions*. New Brunswick, NJ: Rutgers University Press. Pp. 210–223.

Chancellor, James D. 2000. *Life in the Family: An Oral History of the Children of God*. Syracuse, NY: Syracuse University Press.

Cowan, Douglas. 2004. "Contested Spaces: Movement, Countermovement, and E-space Propaganda" in Lorne Dawson and Douglas Cowan (eds.). *Religion Online: Finding Faith on the Internet*. New York: Routledge. Pp. 255–272.

Fontaine, Maria. 2020a. *Conquering Fear with Faith: A Response to the Coronavirus Crisis*. The Family International. Available at: https://anchor.tfionline.com/post/conquering-fear-with-faith/.

Fontaine, Maria. 2020b. *Endtime Specifics*. The Family International.

Fontaine, Maria. 2010a. *Applying God's Law of Love*. The Family International.

Fontaine, Maria. 2010b. *God's Words for Today: A Living Faith*. The Family International.

Fontaine, Maria. 2010c. *God's Words for Today: Prophecy and Revelation*. The Family International.

Fontaine, Maria. 2006. *Promises for the Future*. The Family International.

Fontaine, Maria, and Peter Amsterdam. 2009a. "The Future of The Family International: Establishing a Culture of Innovation and Progress." Paper presented at the annual Centre for Studies on New Religions (CESNUR) conference, Salt Lake City, Utah.

Fontaine, Maria, and Peter Amsterdam. 2009b. *Letter of Apology from Karen Zerby (Maria) and Steve Kelly (Peter Amsterdam) to Former Members of the Family International*. The Family International. Available at: https://www.myconclusion.com/apology-to-former-members.html#more-1796.

Fontaine, Maria, and Peter Amsterdam. 2008. *An Open Letter of Apology to Current and Former Second Generation Family Members from Maria and Peter*. The Family International. Available at: https://www.myconclusion.com/apology-to-second-generation.html#more-1785

Melton, J. Gordon. 1997. *The Children of God: 'The Family'*. Salt Lake City, UT: Signature Books.

Richardson, James T. 2013. "Changing Vision, Changing Course: Envisioning/ Re-visioning and Concentration/Diversification in NRMs" in Eileen Barker (ed.). *Revisionism and Diversification in New Religious Movements*. Burlington, VT: Ashgate. Pp. 247–260.

Shepherd, Gary, and Gordon Shepherd. 2013. "Reboot of The Family International" in *Nova Religio*, 17(2): 74–98.

Shepherd Gordon, and Gary Shepherd. 2010. *Talking with the Children of God*. Chicago: University of Illinois Press.

Shepherd, Gary, and Gordon Shepherd. 2008. "Evolution of the Family International/Children of God in the direction of a responsive communitarian religion." *Communal Societies*, 28(1): 27–53.

Smith, Christian. 1998. *American Evangelicalism: Embattled and Thriving*. Chicago, IL: University of Chicago Press.

The Family International. 2010a. *Structure and Services*. The Family International.

The Family International. 2010b. *TFI Member Works*. The Family International.

van Eck Duymaer van Twist, Amanda. 2015. *Perfect Children: Growing Up on the Religious Fringe*. New York: Oxford University Press.

Ward, The Rt. Hon. Lord Justice Alan. 1995 (November). W42 in the High Court of Justice, Family Division: Principal Registry in the Matter of ST (a Minor) and in the Matter of the Supreme Court Act 1991.

Wright, Stuart A., and Susan J. Palmer. 2016. *Storming Zion: Government Raids on Religious Communities*. New York: Oxford University Press.

15 The Mexican *Santa Muerte* from Tepito to Tultitlán: tradition, innovation, and syncretism at Enriqueta Vargas' temple

Stefano Bigliardi, Fabrizio Lorusso, and Stefano Morrone

Specialists in new religious phenomena and of Mexican history are acquainted with the fast growth of the folk devotion for *la Santa Muerte,* who is mostly worshipped by the marginal classes of Mexican society. Devotees show disillusionment both with governmental and Catholic institutions that have in turn stigmatised the saint of death. In Tepito, an old Mexico City neighbourhood, the first public altar appeared in October 2001 and its warden, Enriqueta Romero (b. 1945), always refused any kind of institutionalisation, while elsewhere there have been attempts to establish rules, associations, and hierarchies. Correspondingly, *la Santa* is represented and venerated with significant differences from place to place, notwithstanding shared beliefs and iconographic traits. Among such attempts at establishing rules was the foundation of the *Templo de la Santa Muerte Internacional* in Tultitlán (State of Mexico) by Jonathan Legaria Vargas (1982–2008), also known as *Comandante Pantera*. The official inauguration took place on 27 January 2008. At the moment of writing, the Temple is run by Jonathan Legaria Vargas' mother, Enriqueta Vargas Ortiz (1959–2018), who took up her religious role as *Madrina* (Godmother) after her son's death: Jonathan was shot dead in his car, under mysterious circumstances, on 31 July 2008. This essay reconstructs the specific traits and differences of the devotion as it is expressed at Tepito and at Tultitlán and considers change in the movements through these examples.[1]

Our fundamental assumption is that Tepito and its surroundings, comprising the districts of Candelaria and Morelos, are to be considered the 'Golden Triangle' of *Santa Muerte,* namely the area where the devotion first emerged in the 2000s and where the standards for the successors were set. In other words, the devotion in Tepito is taken as the *traditional* one, whereas the Temple of Tultitlán represents a case of *innovation*. Further, such innovation came in two successive waves. First, the Temple's foundation was the result of the specific creative and entrepreneurial initiatives of Jonathan; from the outset it displayed a marked, highly personalised distinction from the shrines in Tepito in terms of rituals and symbols. Such initiatives were abruptly interrupted by Jonathan's violent death. Enriqueta Vargas became the new leader and had to respond to the situation both as a

DOI: 10.4324/9781315226804-15

bereaved mother coping with a personal tragedy and as a spiritual entrepreneur assuming a religious role with which she was unfamiliar, all during the context of a deep institutional crisis. The result has been the emergence of special narratives and rituals, as well as a new, specific theology: a second wave of innovation. This chapter focuses on notable and visible manifestations of the devotion and on the attempt at institutionalizing the discourse and rituals of *Santa Muerte*. We bear in mind that these innovations should be regarded as the exception, not the rule; most devotees entertain a direct relationship with *la Santa* through domestic and street altars.

Our methodological approach is twofold. First, while being based in Mexico City, we have personally approached the shrines in Tepito and the Temple of Tultitlán, interviewing *la Madrina* and the devotees, and participating in Sunday rituals on five different occasions, thus embracing an ethnographic, descriptive approach. Second, as scholars, respectively, trained in philosophy, Mexican history, and sociology, we have analysed the social context of the devotion as well as *el Comandante*'s and *la Madrina*'s self-narratives (as contained in printed material and orally conveyed during ceremonies) in order to describe reasons for the success of Vargas Ortiz' narrative and practice. The result is an analytical reconstruction of the theological evolution of the devotion as it is practiced and preached at the Temple, in contrast with the first devotional spaces in Mexico City.

La Santa Muerte: representations and reputation

La Santa Muerte (*Saint* or *Holy Death*) or *Santísima Muerte* is also referred to with appellatives such as *Niña Blanca* (the White Girl); *Flaca/Flaquita* (the Skinny/the Little Skinny One); *Hermana Blanca* (the White Sister); and *Patrona* (the Patron). She is represented in print; in statues of diverse dimensions and of various materials; in jewellery; in painting and graffiti; and in tattoos. She frequently appears as a skeleton draped in a tunic or a cape, similar to medieval representations of death. Items attributed to her include arches and/or arrows; axes; books; candles; crosses; crowns a globe in her hands or under her feet; a halo; a hat; an hourglass; a lantern; a lock; an owl; a rose; balancing scales; a sceptre; a scythe; a skull; a sword; a torch; and angelic or bat wings. The number and dimensions of such associated items vary considerably. Noteworthy is the image of *la Santa* sitting on a throne; in this position she can be represented as *piadosa,* that is, holding an emaciated corpse, or even Jesus Christ himself. Further representations include her riding a horse or a motorcycle, flying over graves with the rising dead, and appearing pregnant (For further examples of devotional statues see Figures 15.1 and 15.2) (Thompson 1998).

Santa-Muerte merchandise comprises candles; devotional books; perfumes; soap; incense; oils; powder; and sprays. Votive candles (*veladoras*) are produced in different colours, corresponding to different areas of

Figure 15.1 The biggest *Santa Muerte's* statue in the world (Photograph by Stefano Morrone).

intervention: black (death and power); brown (communication with the dead); blue (success in studies); golden (business and money); green (legal issues); purple (health); red or pink (love and friendship); and (bone) white (bodily purification), A version in seven colours, integrating all the respective powers, exists as well. Typically, the effigies are placed in a public or private altar,[2] often with more than one exemplar. The versions are prayed to, individually or collectively, and honoured with offerings such as alcoholic drinks; balloons; candles; cigarettes and cigars (often lit and placed in her mouth or hands); cigar smoke (in a *pureo* or purification ritual); cocaine stripes; food; heroin (contained in a syringe); incense; jewellery; joints; money; necklaces; rosary beads; seeds; and toys. Other forms of worship for *la Santa* include chants and cheers (*porras*); dance; musical performances (by *mariachis* or *norteño* big bands); songs; and firecrackers (Perdigón Castañeda 2008). *La Santa Muerte's* interventions in human affairs are rather down-to-earth, concrete, and useful: she mainly helps devotees in finding a job; success in business; getting out of jail; purging addictions; getting a lover back; protecting health; and in finding a good defence attorney or a just judge (Bigliardi 2016).

The popularity of *la Santa Muerte* has exploded since TV shows, such as *Breaking Bad* (season 3, 2010) and *Dexter* (season 5, 2010), represented the devotion and associated it with criminality. However, the imaginary of *Santa Muerte* as a *Narco Saint* really began to spread in Mexico during the 1990s, due to press releases that linked her to kidnappers and drug lords.

Figure 15.2 A devotee in Tultitlán (Photograph by Fabrizio Lorusso).

The *Santa* has now become part of the drug-trade mythology, together with another folk saint, Jesús Malverde, a criminal regarded by the people as a local 'Robin Hood', who probably lived in the first years of the 20th century in the State of Sinaloa (Gerardo et al. 2014).

The Golden Triangle in Tepito and the origins of the Holy Death

Tepito is a neighbourhood in the historic centre of the capital that represents in the collective imaginary several features, including stereotyped ones, of Mexican popular culture and the 'art of getting by' (Mejía Madrid 2008: 21). Tepito, and the neighbouring Merced and Morelos, are districts hosting permanent indoor and outdoor markets; these areas are known as being particularly affected by multiple forms of criminality (Ramírez 2016).

Walking from one area to another is like covering the sides of a triangle: the 'Golden Triangle of the *Santa Muerte*'. This name is also due to the presence of three important shrines, as well as to the density of effigies and other public evidence of the devotion. Over the past decade, particularly in Mexico and in the USA, new rituals have developed through imitation and innovation, syncretism, and re-elaboration, mostly inspired by the Triangle and its media propagation.

The historical roots of the devotion are somewhat mysterious. The popular view is that the Holy Death secretly emerged as a popular Mexican icon during the colonial era. Wooden or painted images of skeletons and skulls, representing death and reproducing the medieval iconography of *Memento mori*, *Justo Juez* and the Death Carts,[3] had been imported by missionaries, brotherhoods and colonisers, and were adopted by indigenous people who used them to perform 'pagan rituals', until they were eventually opposed and banned by the Catholic Church (Gil Olmos 2010: 41–21). A more complete list of iconographic motifs related to death in the arts includes *Ars moriendi*; *Memento mori*; *Et in Arcadia ego;* Three ages; *Vanitas*; Death nature; Skulls and Skeletons; Self-portrait with the Death; Symbols of Death; and *Homo Bulla* (De Pascale 2007: 20–7; see also Malvido 2005).

After a period of clandestinity, the devotion re-emerged in August 2001 in Tepito, in *calle* (street) *Alfarería* 12 when *señora* Enriqueta Romero set up an altar that included a life-size *Santa Muerte* that had been donated to her by one of her sons (Baena Crespo and Morales Nava 2014). After some months, this initiative was followed by the opening of *señora* Blanca's oratory of *Santa Esperanza*, at *calle Alarcón* 38. Then, a few blocks away, the ISCAT Mex-USA Church (Holy Catholic and Apostolic Mex-USA Church) in *calle Nicolás Bravo* 35 was founded, by the self-declared archbishop (*arzobispo*) David Romo (b. 1959). This founding was also the first attempt at institutionalising the devotion. Romo's church was recognised by the Ministry of Internal Affairs from 2003 to 2005 and generated remarkable controversy. Romo not only celebrated masses but also ordained 'deacons' and created new churches in order to establish a network. Such initiatives came to an abrupt end in 2011 when he was charged with theft, kidnapping, and extortion, and sentenced to 66 years in prison (Lorusso 2013: 110–20). The sanctuary, however, is still open and managed by Romo's family and ISCAT deacons, who celebrate Sunday masses while dressed in a black cassock that makes them indistinguishable from Catholic priests. *Calle Alfarería* 12 is still the most popular and most visited shrine of the nation (and of the world), with thousands of visitors the first day of each month attending for the rosary, according to the Mexican press (Escalada Medrano 2013). On 7 June 2016, Enriqueta Romero's partner, Raymundo Romero 'don Ray', was shot to death by a couple of *sicarios* in front of her altar. As a consequence, from that date the monthly rosary has been temporarily suspended but many devotees still visit (Gilet 2016). The oratory-shop at *calle Alarcón* 38, after a temporary and unsuccessful collaboration with ISCAT in 2002, is now autonomous. Small groups of people gather there for the rosary (very similar to the one in *calle Alfarería*) every first Sunday of the month (Mossetti 2008: 70–2).

The ritual models marking the beginning of the public devotion in the Triangle can be considered the 'traditional' ones. The public rosaries in the streets, guided by a master of ceremonies holding a megaphone, generate a *horizontal* model of engagement; they call for an active participation of the community. A mass such as the one celebrated by Romo and his successors corresponds to a more conservative and *vertical* model; the engagement of the community is passive and limited. A private yard, an oratory-like institution, open to the public certain hours of the day, with a shop or a specific space to make purchases and to recite rosaries and prayers, is perhaps halfway between the two models. Also popular are the itinerant altars, the 'Saint Pilgrims' or semi-mobile statues, carried during the religious processions or in on-demand altars, as well as 'on demand ceremonies' (Fragoso 2011: 5–16). Syncretism with different religions and religious beliefs are common; a significant influence is exerted both by Catholicism and by the Afro-Antillean *santería* and *palo mayombe*. Today, the global success of *Santa Muerte* is due to migration, the dramatic increase in mass media exposure, and dissemination on the internet. This is a scenario very different to the context just 15 years ago (Lorusso 2011: 59–70).

The Temple in Tultitlán

The Temple in Tultitlán can be reached in a ten-minute car-ride from the central station, half an hour from the capital in a metropolitan train. It is a plot of land with a two-storey building and a rectangular yard (approximately 50×20 m^2) that can be accessed through a large gate or through the building itself. In the first storey is a shop selling *Santa Muerte*-related items. The second storey hosts Enriqueta Vargas' personal offices. The building's, as well as the shop's, walls are decorated with colourful *murales* showing *el Comandante*, his mother, and the Aztec god of the dead. In the yard, on one of the long sides, is located an effigy of *la Santa* represented as a caped skeleton stretching her arms, made of asphalt panels on a metal structure, and standing 22.17m high. Originally white, Enriqueta had the effigy painted black after her son's death. During the ceremonies, the devotees sit on chairs placed under a plastic roofing right in front of *Pantera*'s templet, which is a golden kiosk just next to the giant effigy. Sometimes a life-size figure of Jonathan, *el Comandante Pantera,* is placed next to the kiosk as well (Figures 15.3).

Tables are located in front of the chairs where the devotees place their own images of *la Santa* so that they can be blessed during the ceremonies. Baptisms and marriages (including same-sex ones) are performed (Santa Muerte Internacional 2010). Jonathan had believed that any time an image

Figure 15.3 Comandante Pantera's own statue (Photograph by Stefano Bigliardi).

of *la Santa* was accidentally broken, it absorbed a negative event that would have otherwise hit its owner, so the devotees bring the broken statuettes to another templet on the giant effigy's right side, where they are first left some days to 'discharge' and eventually buried beneath it. This tradition has been kept by his mother. The press calls Enriqueta Vargas '*Lideresa*', (female leader). However, she dislikes this form of address and she prefers to be called *Madrina* or *La Mom*.[4]

In an autobiographic booklet, co-written in 2007 with a Mexican journalist, *el Comandante* is described as a criminal, albeit a noble-hearted one, with political connections (Demier and Legaria Vargas 2007: 122), and a series of archetypes have been conflated in his profile: youngster criminal in Tepito; inmate; wrestler; biker; drug dealer; policeman; illegal migrant; entrepreneur; and pimp. He also talks about his good relationship, at least at the beginning, with David Romo (Demier and Legaria Vargas 2007: 130). The booklet is not strictly autobiographical; it reads more like an advertisement for the opening of the Temple, which is announced in the conclusion (Demier and Legaria Vargas 2007: 156). Whether its contents are true or (partly) invented, the pamphlet emphasises a connection between the movement and criminality and violence. Such a connection was also emphasised by the Mexican press after Jonathan's murder, while pointing out, somewhat sarcastically, that the Holy Death had this time failed to protect him.[5]

The account of Jonathan published by his mother, Enriqueta Vargas, is different and perhaps tempered by their relationship. According to her, Jonathan was extremely brilliant as a child and he received a Catholic education. She claimed that the nickname *Pantera* (panther) referred to a tattoo he sported on his left arm, and that *Comandante* (commander) was his role in a bikers' group (Vargas 2011: 23). In an interview, she confirmed Jonathan's expensive lifestyle, but she also claimed that he was not a delinquent: his money came from a mechanic's workshop and other unspecified 'business' (Vargas 2011: 19, 21–2).[6]

Using social networks and engaging in frequent travels to celebrate weddings and baptisms, and to take part in inauguration ceremonies of temples, Enriqueta Vargas has succeeded in creating and strengthening devotee communities in different Mexican states, in the USA, and in Colombia. On 24 April 2016, while being interviewed at her altar, the *Madrina* claimed that she manages three Facebook pages, one in memory of the *Comandante*, and two in honour of the International *Santa Muerte*. Videos of their ceremonies are also posted on such pages.

Rituals at the Temple are remindful of TV shows and teleshopping programs. The *Madrina* speaks on the microphone while walking among the *hermanos devotos* (devotee brothers), distributing words and caresses, smiles, and motherly advice. She alternates prayers with sermons that, according to her, were written by *el Pantera* before his death, and to which the worshippers listen in silence. They cry and laugh when they are told to do so by the *Madrina*. During the ceremonies, Enriqueta often glances at the devotees' smartphones, to make sure that they record and upload the videos on Facebook and she reads the prayers and requests of the online audience following her live on social media. The devotees cross themselves 'In the name of the Father, of the Son, and of *Pantera*'s spirit' and *la Santa* is invoked in a prayer mimicking the Lord's Prayer that begins with the words 'Our mother in earth ...', while Enriqueta's daughter, who wears Jonathan's colourful necklaces, imparts the final aspersion as well as the individual blessing, once again in the name of *Pantera*'s spirit.

Talking about the differences with traditional altars, Enriqueta pointed out in our interview with her that:

> We recite the Lord's prayer for God, our Lord, because, in actual facts, we all have one God, right? But we do not recite the Ave Maria or the First and Second Mystery, as they do in other altars [...] other altars have even adopted commandments on the example of the Catholic tradition.

Rituals include heterosexual and homosexual weddings and baptisms. The idea is not completely new, since in Romo's church gay marriage and baptisms were already introduced and advertised. Such ceremonies are, however, a powerful identity marker creating a distinction from the Catholic Church. Enriqueta Vargas maintains that:

> If I were to write a book, I would rather focus on the fact that the cult of the Saint is a thousand-year old and ancestral. What is modern worship? Nowadays, many people join the modern worship. It is certainly beautiful because it does not have a definite form nor a structure, so everybody keeps it as they want, but devotees are confused, because some people dress as priests and it is not a good thing. I'd never dress as a nun, by any means. Some people dress as priests and they imitate rituals of the Catholic Church. I think many individuals are still afraid to profess their faith in the *Santa Muerte*. They are afraid of people's judgement, but I think it should not be like this in Mexico. There is freedom of worship here, and we can worship whoever we want [...] why do people imitate Catholic prayers? If you join my ceremony, you will see that it is different. Why should it be as in the Catholic Church?

Moreover, Enriqueta criticises Romo's ISCAT Church and the traditional rosaries adapted for the *Santa Muerte* while she talks fondly about her itinerant services in many regions of Mexico. Such ceremonies usually take place at night, are personalised and show innovation and diversification. In our interview, Vargas described one of the itinerant rituals, a wedding including a baptism in a cave with a stretch of water, a *cenote* of the Yucatan peninsula:

> First of all, we enter the underworld, a cave-like space with a *cenote*. [...] I want the ceremony to happen at night, so we will enter the forest and walk through it [...] we will then reach the cave. What a wonderful place! We will enter the cave, everything will be dark, and then one of

my 'children', Carlos Ríos, the Scorpion, will hold a stone skull representing the Goddess. We will build a bonfire and then people in front of the Saint, with their hands tied up with a rope, will turn around the fire reciting their vows [...], the bride will be accompanied by witnesses holding torches, the groom by witnesses holding incense [...] when they will be in front of each other, the groom will cense the bride, and then she will do the same with the groom. [...] We will immerse in the water of the *cenote* which will be freezing! [...] We will celebrate the baptism there, and we will invite the couples to enter in the water [...] we will be joined by the majority of the group leaders.

Inspired by the ethno-nationalistic vision of 'discovering the origins', Vargas has also included some elements of pre-Columbian Mexico in the ceremonies – among others, shells and drums; natural elements, such as water and fire; and some statues of deities from Maya and Aztec cultures. The *Madrina* said:

I believe that our roots are good [...] I think I'm trying to go back to our roots, gradually. [...] I feel this is good, we don't want to be like the others.

When remembering the death of her son the Commander, Enriqueta Vargas told us:

He was killed on July 31 at 2.10 a.m., and every year, here, we remember this anniversary. We always do different things, and this year some followers want to organize a night procession carrying their Saints to the temple. Many altars want to join this initiative.

Pilgrimages and processions represent a variation in the devotion of the Saint, since they are not present in Tepito. They are not totally new, however, since similar initiatives were promoted in the past by ISCAT (*El Economista* 2009), by the associations of altars and the masters of ceremonies, such as Martín George from Tepatepec (state of Hidalgo) (Chávez 2014: 18).

Mother, daughter, mourner, and influencer: the complexity of Enriqueta Vargas

Numerous interviews with national and international media and researchers portray Enriqueta Vargas as a kind, accommodating and sweet woman, with a sparkling wit and management skills. She truly believes in her mission, telling us that:

I dedicate myself exclusively to the worship of *Santa Muerte* and God. I do not believe in other Saints nor in the Devil [...] I abandoned the Catholic faith for *Santa Muerte*.

She also claims that, since her son died, she has accepted the loss in the name of a higher good, Peace, and, in a country torn by violence:

I want to launch a message of love and peace. *La Santa Muerte* wants to go to the border, to Michoacán, Zacatecas, Guerrero, and Tamaulipas. I want the International *Santa Muerte* to go there, in these areas torn apart by the highest rates of criminality and violence.

By accepting to be the *Madrina* of the devotion, Enriqueta Vargas embodies two contrasting roles at the same time: on the one hand, on earth, she is Jonathan's mother; on the other hand, she is his *sister*, since they both became children of *la Santa* when Enriqueta decided to convert to Jonathan's creed after his murder. Such a double role is constantly stressed during the ceremonies, especially when the sentence '*todos somos hermanos*' (we are all brothers) is shouted and when the brother-devotees shake their hands. Enriqueta herself stated in our interview:

I want them to feel as if they are talking to their brothers. As their mother, I try to give them advice as if they were my children.

La Santa herself is often described by devotees as having human characteristics, such as jealousy, or as being *cabrona* ('stubborn' or 'tough'). She is perceived as one of 'them'. However, she lacks a main narrative, a hagiography, with which a devotee can emotionally and biographically identify. She is not a human being who has been sanctified, she did not appear for the first time anywhere, and there is no principal, original miracle for believers to connect with. In Tultitlán, the absence of such events is compensated by Enriqueta's biographical narrative: she has built her persona as a *Madrina* who is a suffering mother (a clear symbolic overlapping with Mary) but also a convert. Enriqueta thus synthesises in herself the two elements that characterise most devotees' experiences: pain and conversion. For the devotees this allows for a powerful self-identification and creates in the movement a special charisma. This self-narrative also neutralises a trait that otherwise might distance Enriqueta from the devotees: being a middle-class entrepreneur, married to an *abogado* (lawyer/attorney) with important political ties (a point she nevertheless proudly stresses in her biography, as we found while speaking with her).

Legaria based his own narrative and the construction of his religious authority on claims that he had received an esoteric apprenticeship around the world, as well as his 'tough' criminal image. In the account of his life produced by his mother, the focus shifts from this criminality to his early spiritual vocation. He is described as endowed with extraordinary qualities, including honesty and innocence, in order to contradict the malignant rumours that followed his assassination. Narratively and visually he has become a 'Santo de la Santa' (saint of the Saint). He now plays an advocate's role similar to that of Mary (*advocata nostra*) in Catholic doctrine. In other words, he can either perform extraordinary deeds in person or intercede with *la Santa* for devotees (Demier and Legaria Vargas 2007). Such a 'new trinity' (*Santa Muerte-Padrino-Madrina*) definitely overshadows Catholic figures, despite the devotees' (and Enriqueta's) insistence that they still believe in God.

La Santa Muerte is a more difficult religious figure: she can avoid death, *because* she *is* death, but she saves you every time except the *last* time (Gaytán Alcalá 2008: 40–51). Enriqueta, symbolically and psychologically, dealt with this deep-seated ambiguity (as well as the overwhelming, terrible *fact* that her son was killed) through the creation of a narrative in which Jonathan's atrocious assassination turns into a *success story*. Enriqueta Vargas took upon herself the role of *hija de la Santa Muerte* (a 'daughter of Santa Muerte'), while also presenting herself as a tireless leader who courageously endures pain and enemies' threats. Mary is traditionally described as 'daughter of her own son' and Enriqueta is now the 'sister of her own son'. Jonathan had already described death as a 'mother' but now *La Santa Muerte is* the mother to the two of them: Jonathan's death was his mother's second birth through *la Santa Muerte*. His plans can be accomplished through Enriqueta. His death is exorcised by claiming that death did come but, through the intervention of *la Santa*, it came 'without pain'.

Each challenge she suffers in life adds to Enriqueta's charisma as a leader who can understand the devotees' pains and problems. And each success reinforces the message that *la Santa*'s power, as well as her son's, is present and efficacious. *La Madrina* also presents herself as a 'political' hero who fights for freedom of expression and against corruption both in Mexican politics and in the Church.

Comparative remarks on the two locations

We argue that the Tepito and Tultitlán altars are the most important and emblematic to explain tradition, innovation, and syncretism in *Santa Muerte*'s devotion. Here we will sum up their differences and similarities, focussing in particular on comparison with other female warden-run shrines in Tepito. The comparison with David Romo's temple is, as we have observed, already an explicit part of the narrative promoted by Jonathan and, later, by his mother.

At the altar in *calle Alfarería*, *doña* Queta Romero does not define herself as a *Madrina* or as a leader of the devotees. She does not have plans for its future even though she has been the first person to run a public altar, and the most recognised and popular altar keeper in Mexico and, indeed, the world. Analogous observations hold for the less visible and vocal *doña* Blanca at the aforementioned oratory of *Santa Esperanza*. Whereas, as we have seen, Enriqueta Vargas from Tultitlán is building an international reputation and has a clear plan to unify devotees, altars, and associations under her *Santa Muerte Internacional* organisation, which entails the creation of some kind of hierarchies and institutionalisation. When we asked about her plans for *Santa Muerte Internacional*, Enriqueta Vargas with no hesitation answered:

> You know, everything I say usually happens for real! I've the feeling that the worship will grow stronger and stronger because I have many plans in mind. It will turn into the biggest cult in the world and I will have a group of *Santa Muerte* in every corner of the country. You'll see.

Moreover, *doña* Queta is the keeper of the Tepito altar, not a master of ceremonies, while Enriqueta Vargas is a leader and a preacher who celebrates rituals, weddings, and baptisms. Enriqueta Vargas' desire for innovation and differentiation is also manifest and relates to her ambition she wants Tultitlán ceremonies to be the best ones:

> It is obvious that I'd like people to say that they like to come to my altar because of my way of reciting prayers [...] I always try to give the best, to gain devotees' appreciation.

Tepito's altar has, however, still played a pioneering role and the devotion there developed as a spontaneous practice and as part of an evolution of previous social dynamics that eventually consolidated a community and a collective identity (Lewis 1964: 638–40). The sense of belonging and the creation of social connections are fundamental in Tepito. At Enriqueta Vargas' temple in Tultitlán, people feel identified and accepted by the *Madrina* and the other habitués; however, the flow of devotees is considerably smaller than in Tepito. Thus, the *Madrina* efficiently complements rituals and ceremonies held at her shrine with a presence on social networks and in the press, thereby compensating the lack of geographical centrality and the scarce participation in Sundays' *oraciones* (prayers). The *guardiana* in Tepito, albeit criticising the Catholic Church and its corruption, still defines herself a Catholic. Enriqueta Vargas does not. Instead, she emphasises the novelty of Tultitlán ceremonies against the tradition of established religions (Roman Catholicism, Protestantism and Neo-Pentecostalism) and other *Santa Muerte* altars (Figures 15.4).

Nowadays, in Tultitlán, some influences from *santería* or *brujería* (sorcery) rituals have been totally banished from the ceremonies, although Jonathan claimed in his books that he was deeply influenced by them. The exchange of gifts and small objects and simulacra, a fundamental moment

Figure 15.4 Pantera's shrine in Tultitlán (Photograph by Fabrizio Lorusso).

in the worship in Tepito, are almost non-existent. However, the *limpia*, or spiritual purification, that is also reminiscent of *santería*, is commonly practised because, as Enriqueta Vargas stated, in our interview, 'it is an ancient practice dating back to our ancestors'. Recently, in Tultitlán, the idea of a direct relationship between death and nature has become more and more popular, and there are many attempts to embellish the figure of the Saint with natural elements. All this fulfils a symbolic function strictly related to the specific vicissitudes of the Temple in Tultitlán: by bringing back the pre-Hispanic origins of the devotion, and by associating it with natural elements, the *Madrina* cleanses the black clothes of the Saint from all impurities.

Other innovations fostered by Enriqueta Vargas are the insertion of (alleged) pre-Hispanic elements in the iconography and the rituals of *Santa Muerte* as well as face-to-face dialogue between her and the devotees, to whom she explains directly 'the message' of the *Santa*. She also promotes her narrative in writing, whereas Enriqueta Romero never wrote a book about her story. The shop in Tepito is actually the entrance hall to Enriqueta Romero's home and very modest. Tepito sellers form a dynamic and disseminated informal market. In Tultitlán people can only find Vargas' shop and another small store nearby. The ceremonial space in Tultitlán is also private and this allows *la Madrina* to enforce rules, such as the prohibition of drugs, that wouldn't be (and are not) fully respected at Tepito.

Conclusion

We propose that flexibility is the secret of the devotion's success (Flores-Martos 2008). What is happening in Mexico can be considered part of a 'religious mutation' taking place throughout Latin America, in which major shifts in traditional social structures and the multiplication of new religious movements are intertwined (Bastian, Jean-Pierre 1997: 7–18). It is common to find Mexicans who call themselves Catholic praying at the altars of popular saints opposed by the Church, such as Malverde; *Niño* Fidencio; Juan Soldado; San Pancho Villa; and Santa de Cabora (Gil Olmos 2010: 153–82) or lining up to receive the *limpia* (spiritual purification) by a *brujo* (warlock). Antagonism and cooperation among different altars generated innovation, imitation, and syncretism; together with media attention and word-of-mouth information, it has all contributed to the diffusion of the devotion.

Most elements in Tultitlán seem to conform to the general attributes of the devotion: the syncretism, the symbolism of colours, the typology of miracles attributed to *la Santa Muerte*, the kind of people who attend the Temple, and their needs and wishes. However, some creative variations that marked its specific identity were introduced by the founder, such as the aforementioned ritual of bringing in and burying the 'broken *Santas*' statuettes.

Jonathan's assassination was unexpected and devastating: the hierarchy was beheaded, the reputation of the leader was tainted, and the community was shaken by an event that seemingly demonstrated *la Santa*'s non-existence, or at least her powerlessness. Showing unusual fortitude and entrepreneurial skills, Enriqueta Vargas has managed to produce a powerful counter-narrative and to perform efficacious actions that have turned a seemingly ineluctable decline into a renewal of the devotion that has acquired an even more distinct identity in Tultitlán.

[Update. The present chapter was completed in 2016. On 19 December 2018 Mexican media outlets, soon followed by international ones, broke the news of Enriqueta Vargas Ortiz's death the day before because of pneumonia after having suffered from cancer for a few years].

Notes

1 The authors are grateful to Enriqueta Vargas Ortiz, for her interviews and the warm welcome at the Temple; we also wish to thank *doña* Enriqueta Romero and *señora* Blanca.
2 Researchers have recorded the existence of at least 300 altars in all of Mexico (see Ruiz 2011).
3 One of them is conserved at the Brooklyn Museum of New York: https://www.brooklynmuseum.org/opencollection/objects/156928
4 Interview with Enriqueta Vargas, 24 April 2016.
5 See for instance: Barrera Aguirre and Juan Manuel (2008).
6 The unspecified 'business' was also mentioned in our personal interview.

Bibliography

All URLs were accessed on 5 June 2020.

Aguirre, Barrera and Juan Manuel. 2008. "Falla *Niña Blanca* al *Comandante Pantera*," *El Universal*, 31 July. Available at: http://archivo.eluniversal.com.mx/notas/526728.html

Baena Crespo, Erick and Celeste Morales Nava. 2014. "La guardiana de la Santa Muerte," *Milenio*, 20 July. Available at: http://www.milenio.com/df/Santa_Muerte-Santa_Muerte_en_Tepito-milenio_dominical-dona_queta_0_337766359.html

Bastian, Jean-Pierre. 1997. *La mutación religiosa en América Latina*, Mexico: FCE, 1 (2003, first reprint), pp 7–18.

Bigliardi, Stefano. 2016. "*La Santa Muerte* and Her Interventions in Human Affairs: a Theological Discussion," *Sophia*, 55(3): 303–23.

Chávez, Edgar. 2014. "Piden operativo en Tepatepec por peregrinaciones a la Santa Muerte,"*Quadratín Hidalgo*, 18 August. Available at: https://hidalgo.quadra-tin.com.mx/principal/Piden-operativo-en-Tepatepec-por-peregrinaciones-la-Santa-Muerte/

Demier, Carlos Marín and Jonathan Legaria Vargas (eds). 2007. *El hijo de la Santa Muerte. Una vida sin límites*. Mexico: Self-Published.

De Pascale, Enrico. 2007. *I Dizionari dell'Arte: Morte e Resurrezione*. Milan, Italy: Electa Mondadori.

El Economista. 2009. "Seguidores de la Santa Muerte salen a las calles a exigir libre culto," 6 April. Available at: https://ecodiario.eleconomista.es/espana/noticias/1148382/04/09/Seguidores-de-la-Santa-Muerte-salen-a-las-calles-de-Mexico-a-exigir-el-libre-culto.html

Escalada Medrano, Paula. 2013. "Miles de mexicanos dan gracias a la Santa Muerte por un año más de vida," *La información*, Mexico, 2 November. Available at: https://www.lainformacion.com/mundo/miles-de-mexicanos-dan-gracias-a-la-santa-muerte-por-un-ano-mas-de-vida_cdqkso2vefvshchdjwerr/

Flores Martos, Juan Antonio. 2008. "Transformismo y transculturación de un culto novomestizo emergente: la Santa Muerte Mexicana," *Teorías y prácticas emergentes en antropología de la religión*, M. Cornejo, M. Cantón and R. Llera (eds). *Ankulegi*: 55–76. Available at: http://www.ankulegi.org/wp-content/uploads/2012/03/1004Flores-Martos.pdf

Fragoso, Perla. 2011. "De la 'calavera domada' a la subversión santificada. La Santa Muerte, un nuevo imaginario religioso en México," *El Cotidiano*, 169, September–October, pp 5–16.

Gaytán Alcalá, Felipe. 2008. "Santa entre los malditos. Culto a la Santa Muerte en el México del siglo XXI," *Liminar* VI (1 January–June): 40–51.

Gerardo, Gómez, Michel Gerardo and Jungwon Park. 2014. "The Cult of Jesús Malverde. Crime and Sanctity as Elements of a Heterogeneous Modernity," *Latin American Perspectives*, 41(2): 202–214.

Gil Olmos, José. 2010. *La Santa Muerte. La Virgen de los olvidados*. Mexico City: Random House.

Gilet, Eliana. 2016. "Los 15 años de la Santa Muerte de Tepito y el fin de la misa de media noche," *Vice*, 1 November. Available at: http://www.vice.com/es_mx/read/los-15-anos-de-la-santa-muerte-de-tepito

Lewis, Oscar. 1964. *Los hijos de Sánchez* (1st ed. in Spanish). Mexico: FCE.

Lorusso, Fabrizio. 2013. *Santa Muerte Patrona dell'Umanità*. Viterbo: Stampa Alternativa/Nuovi Equilibri.

Lorusso, Fabrizio. 2011. "La Santa Muerte y la prensa italiana: una reseña crítica desde méxico," *El Cotidiano*, 169 (September–October): 59–70.

Malvido, Elsa. 2005. "Crónicas de la Buena Muerte a la Santa Muerte en México," in *Arqueomex*, 76 XIII (November–December): 20–27.

Mejía Madrid, Fabrizio. 2008. "Tepito: los combates de la sonrisa", *Tepito. Bravo el barrio*. Francisco Mata et al. (eds). Mexico City: Trilce.

Mossetti, Paolo. Economia informale e sub-cultura religiosa: la devozione alla Santa Muerte, Master's Degree Thesis, Master's Degree in Economics and Management for the Arts, Culture and Communication, L. Bocconi University, Milan, Italy, 2008.

Perdigón Castañeda, J. Katia. 2008, *La Santa Muerte protectora de los hombres*. Mexico City: INAH.

Ramírez, Bertha Teresa. 2016. "Cuauhtémoc y Benito Juárez, con mayor incidencia delictiva," *La Jornada*, 13 June. Available at: https://www.animalpolitico.com/2 017/06/cuauhtemoc-benito-juarez-homicidios-robos-cdmx/

Ruiz, Claudia Reyes. 2011. "Historia y actualidad del culto a la Santa Muerte," *El Cotidiano*, 169(September–October): 51–54.

Santa Muerte Internacional. 2010, *Santa Muerte. Siguiendo un legado*. Mexico: Self-produced documentary. Available at: https://www.youtube.com/watch?v= y9WZbjIWn90

Thompson, John. 1998. "Santísima Muerte: Origin and Development of a Mexican Occult Image," *Journal of the Southwest*, 40(4): 405–436.

Vargas, Enriqueta. 2011. *¿Quien mató al Comandante Pantera?* Mexico: Self-published.

16 From the Church of Satan to the Temple of Set: revisionism in the Satanic Milieu

Eugene V. Gallagher

Those who want to change the direction, practice, doctrine, or some other element of a religious tradition need to articulate their reasons and ground them in some sort of claim to authority. Claims that entail any kind of interaction with a realm beyond the human can be especially powerful. Max Weber famously used Jesus' statement that "it is written, but I say unto you" as an indelible example of such an appeal to transformative charismatic authority (Weber 1968a: 24; see 1968b: 51). New and minority religions are particularly fertile grounds for examining how charismatically authorised attempts at revision of existing traditions are made, evaluated, and acted upon. By no means do all attempts at revision succeed as revisions; some fail, and the status quo remains; others succeed and the tradition remains intact but changed; others fail as revisions but lead to greater changes, even the founding of new groups within a broader tradition.

The Seventh-day Adventist tradition provides an apposite example. The early visions of Ellen White gave substance to a millennial movement that developed among some of the disappointed followers of William Miller's prophecy that the end of the world would occur in the mid-19th century. Because the Adventists espoused a doctrine of 'present truth', which led them to expect prophetic guidance in any generation, they were particularly open to bouts of divinely authorised revisionism. In the 20th century, for example, a series of leaders of the Davidian and Branch Davidian sectarian movements that intended to purify the Adventist church claimed divine approval of their ideas, culminating in David Koresh's assertion that he was the 'Lamb of God' mentioned in the book of Revelation as being the only one capable of opening the book sealed with seven seals (see Revelation 5; Gallagher 2014: 41–51). Many other examples could be cited from new and minority religions (as this volume and Barker 2013 show). In this chapter, I will focus first on an example where an appeal to charismatic authority as the rationale for revision of an existing tradition might not be readily expected: the Church of Satan.

DOI: 10.4324/9781315226804-16

Anton Szandor LaVey and the Church of Satan

When Anton Szandor LaVey founded the Church of Satan in 1966, he made no appeal to experiences with the supernatural. Whatever authority LaVey claimed was founded on the insights he had achieved, not on inspiration from any superhuman figure. In The Satanic Bible, the central text of his form of Satanism, he asserted that 'no creed must be accepted upon authority of a 'divine' nature. Religions must be put to the question' (LaVey 1969: 31). LaVey's preference for insight over inspiration cast him as first among equals, but only that. He claimed no privileged contact with a realm beyond the human, no prophetic call, and no particular charisma in the sense of a 'divine gift'. Instead, he claimed simply to see things as they really were. He counselled would-be Satanists to follow his example, 'you must be perceptive enough to see things as they really are, not how you might have been taught by others who stand to gain from your ignorance' (LaVey 1992b: 67). In LaVey's view, Satanists must constantly make the intellectual effort to see through the multiple obfuscations that can cloud their vision of how the world really works. He can serve as a guide, but individuals must strive to be the authors of their own enlightenment. That entails applying systematic doubt especially to the doctrines of established religions. In characteristic fashion, LaVey argued that 'The truth alone has never set anyone free. It is only DOUBT which will bring mental emancipation' (LaVey 1969: 39).

On the positive side, LaVey was convinced that the Satanic principles that he had discovered would themselves survive the application of even the most corrosive forms of doubt. He assures the reader in the third book of The Satanic Bible, 'Probe no further. Here is bedrock!' (LaVey 1969: 109). That confident tone permeates The Satanic Bible and the rest of LaVey's writings. His magisterial authority is founded on what he presents as his unprecedented insight into human nature and his concomitant unmasking of the pervasive hypocrisy and self-delusion that have kept humans from recognising their true nature. LaVey makes no reference to visions or any of the other trappings of supernaturally legitimated charismatic authority because he is confident that the only proof that matters will be evident in the lives of himself and other Satanists. In one of his strongest characterisations of what someone can achieve by following his example, LaVey roars in the distinctive typography of The Satanic Bible, 'I AM A SATANIST! BOW DOWN, FOR I AM THE HIGHEST EMBODIMENT OF HUMAN LIFE!' (LaVey 1969: 45).

While LaVey could be viewed as a charismatic or even prophetic figure (see Dyrendal et al. 2016: 95–100), the ways in which he claimed, legitimated, and defended his authority in the Church of Satan were decidedly this worldly. LaVey presented himself as an exemplar, but he also emphasised that others could achieve the same kind of insight that he had, especially since LaVey offered them guidance in The Satanic Bible and his other writings.

Although LaVey was pessimistic about the abilities of most of his fellow humans to achieve full Satanic insight, he did not believe that such insight was exclusively his in the way that, for example, David Koresh claimed that he alone could perform the task of the Lamb of God in revealing the message of the book sealed with seven seals. LaVey was comparatively more democratic in insisting that any clear-thinking and hard-headed individual could achieve the same insight that he did.

LaVey's relatively democratic approach to the possession of truth also influenced his stewardship of the Church of Satan as an institution. Throughout his career he displayed a marked ambivalence towards exercising organisational control over the Church of Satan. In addition, exerting tight control ran counter to his persistent emphasis that individuals themselves needed to seek after the truth rather than accept it on the authority of someone else, even including LaVey himself. LaVey employed the pervasive stereotype of 'cults' as highly regimented organisations that effaced all signs of individuality among their members. In the last interview that he gave, LaVey asserted that 'the 'Satanic Army' is composed of individuals, not cultists" (Bugbee and Bugbee 1999: 1). For LaVey, the Church of Satan constituted:

> the ultimate conscious alternative to the herd mentality and institutionalised thought. It is a studied and contrived set of principles and exercises designed to liberate individuals from a contagion of mindlessness that destroys innovation. (LaVey 1992a: 9)

Despite intermittent efforts to impose a comprehensive structure on the Church of Satan, including an attempt to establish a system of affiliated 'grottoes' (see Dyrendal et al. 2016: 60–3), LaVey provided much more intellectual leadership than organisational control over the Church of Satan throughout his career as its titular head. Consequently, the Church of Satan oscillated between being a distinct group and a more diffuse movement inspired by LaVey's teachings. In fact, the very ways in which LaVey constructed his own authority impeded his ability to maintain and extend it. By basing his authority on insight rather than revelation and by portraying himself as the first among equals, LaVey left wide open the possibility that someone would claim equal if not superior authority. Just such a claim animated the first major schism within the Church of Satan.

Michael Aquino, revisionism, and the Temple of Set

By his own account, Michael Aquino had been an influential member of the early Church of Satan. He contributed to the Church's newsletter, The Cloven Hoof, and maintained a close friendship with LaVey. But when LaVey decided to raise cash by offering initiation into the Church's priesthood in exchange for money or property, Aquino concluded that

LaVey had betrayed his own principles. When he proved unsuccessful in getting LaVey to change his mind, Aquino resolved to leave the Church. He decisively did not, however, intend to leave Satanism behind. Like many other would-be reformers, Aquino intended to purify the Church of Satan by returning it to its roots, this time under his own authority, a not un-familiar pattern for change and schism. Aquino resigned from the Church in a 10 June 1975 letter to Anton and his partner, Diane LaVey. The formal diction of the letter signals its solemn intent and indicates some of Aquino's differences with LaVey. Aquino wrote

> I reaffirm my degree as Magister Templi, and I reaffirm the degrees of all those who have won them and honored them according to the standards Satan himself has upheld since the`` dawn of human civilization. Since you—Satan's High Priest and High Priestess—have presumed to destroy those standards and replace the true Church of Satan with a "Church of Anton," the Infernal Mandate is hereby withdrawn from the organization known as the "Church of Satan, Inc." and you are no longer empowered to execute your offices. (Aquino 2013a: 1109)

Aquino's letter indicates that he took his own priesthood very seriously; rather than seeing it as something to be purchased, it was something that was to be achieved through dedicated service and even study. Aquino also intimates that he understood Satan rather differently to LaVey's portrayal of him in The Satanic Bible. In that text LaVey asserted that 'most Satanists do not accept Satan as an anthropomorphic being with cloven hooves, a barbed tail, and horns. He merely represents a force of nature...' (LaVey 1969: 62). Aquino, on the other hand, seems to have something more an-thropomorphic in mind, viewing Satan as a male being who has set stan-dards for the Church and who empowers humans to act in certain ways. Also noteworthy is Aquino's implicit claim that he has the authority to remove 'the Infernal Mandate', or the approval and endorsement of Satan himself, from Anton and Diane LaVey. While it may have been an attempt to purify the Church of Satan and return it to its pristine origins under new leadership, in retrospect Aquino's letter can be seen as the first step in the process of a failed attempt at reformation that, at the same time, led to the successful founding of a new group (see Dyrendal et al. 2016: 68).

The fault lines that divided LaVey from Aquino and, subsequently, LaVey's Church of Satan from the organisation that Aquino would found as the Temple of Set are evident in the letter and also have strong ties to Aquino's other experiences in the Satanic milieu (Dyrendal et al. 2016: 47, 65). Of particular importance for an understanding of the processes of revisionism and diversification is the particular claim to authority that Aquino made. Unlike LaVey and more in alignment with his different understanding of Satan as a real, anthropomorphic being, Aquino did not base his claim to authority solely in his own insight into the ways things actually are. As he hints at in the letter, Aquino claimed a real and continuing intimacy with the being he identified as Satan.

In fact, around five years before his resignation from the Church of Satan in 1975, Aquino had an uncanny experience that he came to understand as an encounter with Satan himself. While serving in the US Army in Viet Nam, Aquino undertook to re-read Milton's Paradise Lost as a statement of the Satanic point of view. Deciding that Milton did not quite have it right, Aquino began to compose his own treatise during his free time. He soon found that 'what flowed from my pen began to assume a dignity beyond what I had anticipated' (Aquino 2010: 152). Like his letter, Aquino's Diabolicon has a somewhat stilted, archaic diction whose impact is re-inforced by it being printed in a calligraphic script rather than a standard typescript. The text itself is less circumspect about its origins than Aquino was in his autobiographical account. The voice in the text is that of Satan himself, who declares that 'I, Satan, who first brought thee into the light, shall again reveal my power, that man may witness the dawn of the Satanic Age' (Aquino 2013: 694). Thus, well before his break with LaVey and the Church of Satan, Aquino was developing an understanding of the source of his inspiration that differed substantially from LaVey's depiction of Satan. The anthropomorphic being Satan had been behind Aquino's participation in LaVey's Church of Satan all along; it simply took some time for Aquino fully to realise that fact, deepen the relationship, and act upon its im-plications. Although the doctrinal formulations of the Diabolicon fit easily enough with those of The Satanic Bible, the first text that Aquino received expresses a markedly different understanding of the source of the power of the true Magus.

Despite his diligent efforts to produce it, it was around four years before Aquino would have a similar experience to receiving the Diabolicon. In 1974, however, Aquino received The Ninth Solstice Message, which explicitly presented itself as a continuation and further clarification of the message of the Diabolicon. That Aquino at this point still considered himself as working within the confines of LaVey's Church of Satan is indicated by a passage that directly addresses LaVey himself. But, in another sign of Aquino's developing heterodoxy within the context of the Church of Satan, the Satan of The Ninth Solstice Message makes an extraordinary claim about the status of LaVey—one that LaVey himself would likely resolutely refuse. Satan declares that 'by my Will, Anton Szandor LaVey, you are divest of your human substance and become in your Self a Daimon' (Aquino 2013: 1047). The Ninth Solstice Message shows that in the year before his split with LaVey and the Church of Satan Aquino had definitely arrived at both a different un-derstanding of Satan and a different understanding of LaVey himself. Aquino's intermittent experiences of revelation were leading him ever further away from the Satanism of the Church and The Satanic Bible even before his formal split with the organisation and its leader. The Ninth Solstice Message implicitly challenges LaVey's understanding of his own authority at the same time that it increases Aquino's status as a favoured recipient of Satan's direct messages. Aquino's formal departure from the Church of Satan thus ratifies through action the theological ideas that he had already come to accept. Even if the Church's exchange of priesthoods for money was the precipitating event for Aquino's departure, a theological trajectory that would lead him well beyond the confines of the Church of Satan had already been initiated in 1970 with the Diabolicon and confirmed and extended in 1974 with The Ninth Solstice Message.

That trajectory was absolutely confirmed less than two weeks after Aquino submitted his resignation. Although Aquino recalls that after his departure he had been thinking about a replacement for LaVey's Church that would be something like a 'reformed Church of Satan' or a 'Second Church of Satan', everything changed on the evening of 21–22 June 1975, just a year after Aquino had received The Ninth Solstice Message (see Aquino 2010: 11). For a third time in five years, Aquino received a revelation from beyond this world. That experience transformed Aquino from a would-be reformer of the Church of Satan into the founder of a new religious movement within the Satanic milieu, one with a very different understanding of the figure of Satan, a different form of organisation, and a much more elaborate initiatory practice.

As with the other two texts he received, Aquino is elusive about the exact circumstances in which he received The Book of Coming Forth by Night, though he does assert that 'something beyond Michael Aquino was generating it' (Aquino 2010: 15). Distinctive to the new text was its attribution to Set, not Satan. That connection to an ancient Egyptian deity purchases for Aquino's teachings a particular kind of antiquity that distinguishes it from the counter-Christianity that LaVey emphasises at multiple points in The Satanic Bible. Set even explicitly rejects any association with Satan in The Book of Coming Forth by Night, asserting that 'No longer will I accept the bastard title of a Hebrew fiend' (Aquino 2010: 173). The text also explicitly abandons any attempts at reformation of the Church of Satan; it confidently declares that 'the work of Anton Szandor LaVey is done' and 'a new Aeon is now to begin' (Aquino 2010: 172). In less than two weeks between his resignation and his reception of a new revelation, Aquino made the transit from a reformer aiming to return the Church of Satan to its original purity to a founder of a new religious movement that would remain within the Satanic milieu but would take a very different path from the organisation with which Aquino had previously been associated.

The religious system of the Temple of Set has constantly been in development, especially during its early years, but its outlines can be glimpsed in The Book of Coming Forth by Night. The text explicitly sets itself within the Satanic milieu, but with a twist. Unlike the Church of Satan, Aquino's new system is founded on the 'actual existence of "Satan" (as Set—the original pre-Judaeo-Christian entity)' (Aquino 2010: 63). The historical priority given to Set over Satan anchors the Temple of Set more firmly in an authoritative antiquity, one that by assertion predates Judaism and Christianity and hence their concepts of Satan. The text identifies Aquino as Set's chosen Magus for the new age that is coming about through Set's self-revelation through Aquino. The core of Set's message is expressed in a single Egyptian term, Xeper, pronounced 'khefer' and translated as the imperative 'become!'. Although the emphasis on individual self-realisation recalls the message of The Satanic Bible, Aquino quickly developed a much more elaborate initiatory system than anything in the Church of Satan. For Aquino advancement in the Temple of Set is founded on intellectual effort; he lists more than a hundred pages of recommended readings and films that the aspiring Setian should view. Affiliation with his Temple is not a casual matter; rather, it demands a deep and continuing dedication to self-betterment.

Aquino clearly constructs his authority very differently from the way LaVey did. Aquino is the sole recipient of Set's revelations and Set's chosen representative in this world. His experiences of revelation are exclusive to him and not available to others, unlike LaVey's achievements in doubting established truths and discerning the true nature of human beings, which were theoretically open to anyone with similar courage and insight. Just as Set is positioned at the top of a hierarchy of superhuman beings, so is Aquino located at the top of a hierarchy of Set's acolytes in this world. The distinctiveness of Aquino's position is underscored by how he dealt with dissent within the Temple of Set.

When LaVey urged the rigorous application of doubt to all dogmatic statements, including his own, he opened up the possibility that his own authority could be challenged. But when his position as 'the Black Pope' was assailed, the challenge was founded not on the basis of rational questioning but on the basis of a privileged revelation. A similar challenge was posed to Aquino almost four years after he received The Book of Coming Forth by Night. Ronald Keith Barrett had become the High Priest of the Temple of Set on 24 March 1979. Around that time Barrett had come to understand that he, like Aquino, had been inspired to deliver his own message, which he documented in his own Setian text, The Book of Opening the Way. Barrett claimed that he, too, had a 'Word' to deliver, Xem, pronounced 'khem'. Just as Aquino's letter of resignation propounded a basis for the revision and repristination of the Church of Satan, so Barrett's new message was presented as a reformation of the Temple of Set. As with Aquino's critique of LaVey, Barret's claimed revelation also involved an elevation in status for him, one that would implicitly put him on a level equal to Aquino as someone favoured by Set with a revelatory experience. The way that Barrett lays out the relation between his revelation and that received by Aquino makes his claims clear. He proposes that:

Xeper is initiating, causing change, Becoming for its own sake. Xem then gives direction to the changes that are willed, and that is why Xem is always higher, more specific, and causes balance between being and potential being. Xem is that which is recognised, realised, and understood by the Elect being, perceiving higher being. Xem is the self ahead of itself. (Aquino 2010: 590)

Were Aquino and the Temple of Set to accept Barrett's claims as authentic and authoritative, then Aquino's status as the sole representative of Set on earth would be decisively compromised. Simply put, Aquino could not be who he claimed to be if Barrett were who he claimed to be. Something would have to give.

Aquino's response to Barrett was more subtle than an outright denial of Barrett's inspiration. Aquino acknowledged that Barrett's new 'Word' initially served as a helpful focusing lens for many Setians. Where Barrett went astray, according to Aquino, was when he insisted that acceptance of the Xem utterance had to be a necessary part of the process of becoming for any Setian. Aquino rejected Barrett's claim to exclusivity in favour of seeing members of the Temple as 'free agents with a common field of interests and specialties' (Aquino 2010: 592–3). In countering Barrett's claim to elevated status Aquino appealed to the prior example of LaVey. Arguing that 'Anton screwed up the Church of Satan when he took his Word to a personal and selfish extreme, and the same could be said of RKB' (Aquino 2010: 593). While Aquino's statements could be read as allowing some degree of plural sources of authority within the Temple of Set, knowing precisely how that would have played out in the case of Barrett was forestalled when Barrett himself resigned from the Temple of Set.

Significantly, Barrett's attempt to wrest the role of 'primus Magus' away from Aquino was couched in the same type of reformist logic that Aquino had used against LaVey. In each instance an appeal to an experience of revelation was designed to provide leverage for a reform of an existing group. In neither case did it succeed on those terms, however. Aquino's independent career as a reformer of the Church of Satan lasted less than two weeks. Once he received The Book of Coming Forth by Night, he abandoned, at the urging of his new supernatural patron Set, any attempts at reform in favour of the establishment of a new religious group. Revisionism in his case was short lived. The conflict between different perceptions of the ground of authority, divergent images of the ideal (Satanic) religious community, and incommensurate understandings of the responsibilities of the dedicated follower of Satan provided too many obstacles to finding common ground between LaVey and Aquino.

Aquino's conflict with Barrett was fought on different grounds. Both accepted the idea that the supernatural figure of Set could communicate with human beings. Aquino even tolerated the diversification of the recipients of such revelation by granting the temporary and limited utility of Barrett's new Xem utterance. In responding to Barrett, Aquino appealed to the principle of individualism that has played such a prominent role in

LaVeyan Satanism. When push came to shove, Aquino appeared to despise authoritarianism more than he prized exclusivity of revelation. His envisaging of the members of the Temple of Set as free agents recalls the insistent emphasis on individualism throughout The Satanic Bible. By encouraging individuals to follow their own paths within the field of Setianism, just as LaVey did for would-be Satanists in The Satanic Bible, Aquino implicitly opened up space for others, like Barrett, to claim that they, too, were inspired by Set, or even some other figure. Barrett resolved the tension between his claims and Aquino's counter-claims in the same way that Aquino settled his conflict with LaVey, by resigning from the parent group to begin his own alternative organisation. In each case attempts at reform resolved into the foundation of new groups; where revision failed, diversification within the broad Satanic milieu increased.

Change in the Satanic Milieu

As Weber underscored in his original anatomy of charisma, such authority can be highly volatile. By attributing their authority to a source beyond the human, individuals can wield substantial power among those who are inclined to accept such claims. In his critique of LaVey, Aquino's appeal to his inspiration by Satan in the Diabolican and The Ninth Solstice Message gave him the type of authority that, in his eyes at least, effectively trumped LaVey's reliance on merely human insight. Fresh revelation necessarily entailed revision of existing doctrine. The focus of their mutual attention, Satan, had spoken and, in Aquino's eyes, LaVey could only obey. When Aquino's self-assured proclamation of revelation was met by LaVey's intransigent refusal to accept it, schism resulted. The gap between what Aquino believed was necessary and what LaVey could tolerate was too great to bridge. Aquino's departure from the Church of Satan very quickly turned into a schism, suggesting that there are limits to how much revision a system, organisation, or individual leader can tolerate. Identifying and analysing those limits is a topic for further research.

Aquino's assessment of Barrett's attempt to establish his Xem utterance as an essential element of the doctrine of the Temple of Set shows a religious leader in the process of negotiating tolerable levels of revisionism. Rather than rejecting it out of hand, Aquino attempted in effect to domesticate Barrett's new message by incorporating it into the theological system constructed around his own Xeper utterance. Aquino proved willing to tolerate even a revision that relativised his own status as the sole recipient of Set's revelations. Crucial to Aquino's response was the attempt to subordinate the Xem utterance to his own Word by assigning it a clarificatory but definitely secondary role. But such subordination was intolerable to Barrett who viewed the revelation he received as 'higher, more specific', and generally an advance over Aquino's previous rendering of Set's teachings. Thus, even though Aquino displayed much more doctrinal flexibility and willingness to change than LaVey had, Barrett ended up taking the same route of withdrawal from the parent body that Aquino had.

Both incidents within the broader Satanic milieu underscore the dynamic and interactive nature of revisionism and diversification. Proposed revisions to the direction, practice, doctrine, or other elements of a religious group necessarily can appear as challenges to those who are invested in the status quo. But it is possible for religious groups to metabolise such challenges effectively and to incorporate changes without courting schism. It is important to identify and analyse the conditions that facilitate such assimilation of change and control the disruptive potential of proposed revisions. It is equally important to identify the conditions that make it difficult for groups and leaders to respond positively to proposed changes and incorporate them without dividing the group in any way. The examples examined in this chapter show that the fundamental conception of authority within a religious group is a significant variable. LaVey's insistence that individuals discover things for themselves left him open to challenges from anyone who would claim to do just that. When Aquino appealed to his own intimate connection to Satan through his revelatory experiences, he not only challenged LaVey's authority but appealed to a superior source. In his critique of LaVey, Aquino appealed to a source of authority that was initially exclusive to him. But Barrett's challenge to Aquino was founded on the implicit contention that if Set could communicate with Aquino, he could communicate with anyone. The mere assertion of charismatic authority does not render the claimant immune to challenges that have a similar basis. Ultimately, all forms to authority are sufficiently fragile that they are open to challenges that can produce revision if not schism.

Another factor that the examples point to is the predominant conception of the religious community. As the history of the Church of Satan shows, LaVey exercised only a loose hold over the membership, due as much to his insistence on individuals discovering the truth for themselves as to his inattentive and lackadaisical organisational oversight. Aquino's characterisation of the ideal members of the Temple of Set as 'free agents' applies even more so to the members of the Church of Satan. Groups with such a loose hold on their members may well be especially prone to continuing bouts of revisionism, some of which may give rise to diversification through schism (see Lewis and Lewis 2009). Getting such free agents to agree on the same doctrine, adopt the same practices, or even remain in the same group is not an easy task. The ways in which both LaVey and Aquino conceived the communities they led made challenges to their authority more likely than not. LaVey's resistance to Aquino's pleas for change effectively hastened the formation of a schismatic group, even though Aquino gave all the credit to Set. Aquino's willingness to accept the validity of the Xem message, even in a limited fashion, had the potential to contain Barrett's new message within the theology of the Temple of Set, but Barrett did not match Aquino's accommodating stance with his own. As a free agent, Barrett left the Temple, reducing the challenge to Aquino's authority at the same time that he initiated a schism.

In their short histories both the Church of Satan and the Temple of Set have experienced multiple attempts at revision as well as episodes of schism that increased the diversity of the Satanic milieu. Some efforts at revision were initiated by the leaders themselves, as with LaVey's institution and then abandonment of the grotto system and Aquino's multiple revisions of his history of the Church of Satan and his treatise on the Temple of Set. Other efforts at revision were initiated either as requests or direct challenges to established leaders, as with Aquino's attempt to get LaVey to abandon the selling of priesthoods and Barrett's proclamation of a new Setian message. When challenged, both LaVey and Aquino attempted to preserve their positions as leaders. LaVey completely denied Aquino's entreaties for change and Aquino attempted a more subtle manoeuvre to incorporate Barrett's message into the theology of the Temple while simultaneously blunting its claims to superiority. Both leaders strived to manage the process of revision, one by a strategy of rejection and the other by a strategy of containment. Rejection makes schism all the more likely; frustrated reformers who remain true to their convictions are propelled by rejection to establish new groups. Containment has the capacity to forestall schism to the extent that all involved parties are willing to moderate any claims to exclusive authority or wisdom and adjust their initial positions in the direction of compromise. When compromise fails, schism can ensue.

Successful revisionism, which is not evident in either of the cases considered here, primarily diversifies a religious group diachronically; positions that were held at one time appear to differ from positions held at another time even when they are asserted to be in substantial continuity. But such assertions are frequently in the eye of the beholder. Another example would be the Davidian and Branch Davidian groups mentioned in the introduction. At the outset, Victor Houteff believed that his 'Shepherd's Rod' message was in substantial continuity with the earliest teachings of the Seventh-day Adventist Church, from which the Church in the early 20th century had unfortunately departed. The hierarchy of the SDA Church disagreed and eventually excommunicated Houteff. Those who followed Houteff as leaders of Davidian and, later, Branch Davidian sectarian opposition to the mainline SDA church, including his wife Florence, Ben and Lois Roden, and eventually David Koresh, saw themselves in substantial continuity both with the early teachings of Ellen White and also with the teachings of their Adventist sectarian predecessors, even when outside observers can observe marked differences between their teachings. From the outside, distinctive teachings can be associated with the historical period under each leader, but from the inside, looking backward, continuity eclipses diversity. From the insider's perspective, revision continually refines a core message that has remained essentially unchanged. The truth is preserved despite variations. What David Koresh taught, for example, subsumes, clarifies, and extends what Lois Roden, Ben Roden, Florence

Houteff, Victor Houteff, and Ellen White herself taught (see Gallagher 2013). That is the position that Aquino took in relation to LaVey, but LaVey resisted Aquino's attempt to change the Church of Satan.

Conclusion

Failed revisionism, as in the cases of both Aquino and Barrett, sometimes just leads frustration, disaffection and eventual disgruntled departure, but it can also lead to principled defection and intentional schism. In that case, it diversifies a religious tradition primarily synchronically rather than dia-chronically, increasing the forms of a broad tradition or broader milieu in existence at any one time and expanding the array of options available within a given religious economy. Thus, the Temple of Set increased the number of identifiable groups within the Satanic milieu in the 1970s and beyond. Had Barrett's distinctive message gained sufficient traction, he also would have contributed to the diversity of groups both within the broad Satanic milieu and the narrower sector of Setian groups. Some forms of revision, then, present a double aspect. They may fail in the stated objective of getting the parent body to change, as with Aquino's short-lived effort to bring to life a 'Reformed Church of Satan'. But they may nonetheless succeed when the merely reformist impulse mutates into the more radical desire to constitute a new, separate group, either because of rejection by the original audience or when further innovation comes to seem necessary to the reformer. As Aquino's experience with Barrett shows, schismatic groups themselves are hardly immune to further efforts at revision. Thus, the examples considered here suggest that the cycle of revisionism and diversification within a specific religious tradition, milieu, or economy is open ended and constantly in flux. Revisionism and diversification are the rule, rather than the exception.

Bibliography

All URLs were accessed on 11 June 2020.

Aquino, Michael. 2013. *The Church of Satan*, 8th ed. San Francisco: Self-published.

Aquino, Michael. 2010. *The Temple of Set*, 11th ed. (draft). San Francisco: Self-published. (Both of Aquino's books are works in progress that are occasionally revised; the basic documents that they contain, however, remain unchanged.)

Barker, Eileen (ed.). 2013. *Revision and Diversification in New Religious Movements*. London: Ashgate

Bugbee, Shane, and Amy Bugbee, 1999. "The Doctor Is in…" Available at: http://www.churchofsatan.com/interview-mf-magazine.php.

Dyrendal, Asbjørn, James R. Lewis, and Jesper Aa. Petersen, 2016. *The Invention of Satanism*. New York: Oxford University Press.

Gallagher, Eugene V. 2014. *Reading and Writing Scripture in New Religious Movements: New Bibles and New Revelations*. New York: Palgrave.

Gallagher, Eugene V. 2013. "'Present Truth' and Revisionism among the Branch Davidians" in *Revision and Diversification in New Religious Movements*. Eileen Barker (ed.). London: Ashgate. Pp. 115–126.

LaVey, Anton Szandor. 1992a. "Foreword" in *The Devil's Notebook*. Venice, CA: Feral House.

LaVey, Anton Szandor. 1992b. "How to Be God (or the Devil)" in *The Devil's Notebook*. Venice, CA: Feral House. Pp. 66–67.

LaVey, Anton Szandor. 1969. *The Satanic Bible*. New York: Avon Books.

Lewis, James R., and Sarah M. Lewis (eds.). 2009. *Sacred Schisms: How Religions Divide*. Cambridge, UK: Cambridge University Press.

Weber, Max 1968a. "The Sociology of Charismatic Authority" in *Max Weber on Charisma and Institution Building*. S. N. Eisendstadt (ed.). Chicago: University of Chicago Press. Pp. 18–27.

Weber, Max 1968b. "The Nature of Charismatic Authority and its Routinization" in *Max Weber on Charisma and Institution Building*. S. N. Eisendstadt (ed.). Chicago: University of Chicago Press. Pp. 48–65.

17 The 'messenger' as source of both stabilisation and revisionism in Church Universal and Triumphant and related groups

Erin Prophet

Belief systems with roots in Theosophical and New Thought traditions, which emphasise personal inspiration, are prone to crises of charismatic legitimacy brought on by claims and counter-claims of authority (see Campbell 1980; Satter 1999). However, during the 1930s, the concept of exclusive *messengership* emerged in an American group known as the I AM Religious Activity, which drew on both Theosophy and New Thought. This leadership innovation seemed for a time to stabilise the tradition, and the group attracted thousands of followers with an authoritarian leadership style and pithy self-help message.[1] However, rival messengers soon arose and thus the concept of the 'messenger' has served as both a source of stabilization and revisionism in groups tracing their roots to the I AM Activity. Messengers, and their revelations known as *dictations,* had a significant impact on the new age movement in both its strict and wide senses, as defined by Hanegraaff (1998).

This chapter begins with a historical review of the concept of *messenger* in the I AM and its defunct spinoff The Bridge to Freedom (founded in 1952), before moving to a more detailed evaluation of its use in three current groups: First, The Summit Lighthouse (TSL), founded in 1958, and later transformed into Church Universal and Triumphant (CUT), referred to as TSL-CUT after the 1975 founding of CUT; second, The Temple of the Presence (founded in 1995); and, third, the Hearts Center (founded in 2004). Both the Hearts Center and Temple of the Presence drew their core initial membership from TSL-CUT. The focus of the evaluation is on legitimacy, charismatic authority, and response to internal and external pressures.

As author of the chapter, I write from personal experience; the TSL-CUT founders Mark and Elizabeth Prophet were my parents and I was in training to become a 'messenger' under Elizabeth for six years, beginning in 1986 until I rejected the role in 1992, as I describe in *Prophet's Daughter* (2009). Both Mark and Elizabeth were revered by their followers as messengers, with sole authority to receive group inspiration from 'Ascended Masters'. This chapter focuses on how the three groups have used 'messengership' to legitimate themselves, and how the construct functioned during transitions of

DOI: 10.4324/9781315226804-17

authority. It will demonstrate that shifts in doctrine can sometimes be correlated with internal and external challenges to authority, suggesting that revisionism in these traditions is at least partly driven by the challenge of maintaining legitimacy. Some of the primary areas of doctrinal tension and revision, which were justified by the concept of 'progressive revelation', involved evil and sexuality, as well as adjustments to the soteriology. The concept of messenger can be seen as an attempt to stabilize leadership in the Theosophical and New Thought traditions, and it did lead to large and popular groups – the I AM and TSL-CUT.

Historical development of the concept of messenger – from Blavatsky to Prophet

Groups in the Theosophical tradition base their legitimacy on contact with beings that have been known variously as Mahatmas, masters and ascended masters as the tradition has developed since the Theosophical Society was founded in 1875 by the Russian mystic Helena Blavatsky and the American writer Henry Steel Olcott. Since the early days of Theosophy, as pointed out by Olav Hammer (2001: 374), 'heresiological' arguments have been used to distinguish true from false visionary experience.

The *Mahatma Letters*, founding texts of the tradition written between 1880 and 1884, claimed that differences in the teachings of various mystics were caused by distortions that could occur when 'pure Spirits', trying to communicate truth, had to contend with the 'physical, moral and intellectual idiosyncrasies' of the individual, who is subject to myriad 'kosmical influences', as well as 'direct hostility of the Brethren of the shadow' (quoted in Hammer 2001: 375). The Mahatmas claimed that Stainton Moses, a competitor of Theosophy's founder, Helena Blavatsky, has been veiled from the truth by his habits of drinking alcohol and eating meat.[2] This narrative sets up the structure of competing legitimacy claims surrounding movements claiming to speak with *adepts* (later *masters*) in the Theosophical tradition.

Theosophical masters become ascended

Unlike the direct descendants of the Theosophical Society, the groups reviewed here all subscribe to the theological innovation of ascension as a universal goal. They base their claims to authority on contact with ascended masters, believed to be enlightened souls who once lived on earth, and have achieved liberation from their karma through ascension, described as union with God either before or after death. Jesus Christ is revered and considered an exemplary ascended master, though many others are considered to have ascended before and after him; however, he does retain a position of special importance, particularly in TSL-CUT. Portraits of Jesus and the ascended master Saint Germain flank a 'Chart of the Divine Self' in the Church's official iconography. It was Guy and Edna Ballard, founders of the I AM

Religious Activity in 1930s Chicago, who transformed the 'masters' of the Theosophical tradition into 'ascended' masters, building upon ideas from New Thought (Melton 1994; Rudbøg 2013: 156–60).[3]

Although ascended master traditions encourage individuals to connect directly with the *higher self,* also known as the I AM Presence, and with the masters themselves for personal guidance and inspiration, only designated messengers have authority to give inspiration to an entire group. In the I AM as well as TSL-CUT, numerous members were expelled or disciplined for promoting their own messages from ascended masters. Conflicts surrounding authority and inspiration are the most important catalysts for revisionism in this tradition. Among the groups studied here, the Hearts Center is experimenting with a more diffuse model of inspiration.

The I AM Activity and the concept of messenger

In founding the I AM Activity, Guy and Edna Ballard developed important innovations in the concept of divine inspiration. Where Blavatsky and previous teachers in the Theosophical tradition had communicated through written materials, the Ballards produced both spoken and written messages. Their spoken messages were more along the lines of tent revival sermons in that they delivered them live before audiences, either extemporaneously or by reading from written text. In addition, there was a markedly religious component to the events, which included ritual, prayer, and sacred music.

The official title adopted by the Ballards for themselves, beginning in 1934, was 'Accredited Messengers' (Braden 1949: 270). In their early work, a dictation consisted of them reading aloud messages from Saint Germain (the master believed to have founded their group), which they had previously typed or written. They also wrote decrees – repetitive, rhythmic prayers and positive affirmations – which were also said to have been *dictated* by ascended masters. Later, Guy took 'dictation' by speaking in real time rather than reading the messages. After his death in 1939, Edna later also produced both kinds of messages.

In addition to *accredited* messengers, of whom there were only two – a possible third being the Ballards' son, Donald, who was accredited but did not give messages – there were also *appointed* messengers (Braden 1949: 270). These messengers were primarily meant to function as group leaders, but they later took on greater authority, sometimes in rebellion against headquarters. 'Psychic activity' of any sort was forbidden, which meant in practice that no one else could claim to have received messages from masters without the sanction of the accredited messengers (see Saint Germain 1935: 255). Messages through accredited messengers were seen as coming from a purer or higher level than 'psychic' messages, which were said to be subject to error and deception.

Bridge to Freedom

The Bridge to Freedom was a religious group founded in 1952, based upon messages received by I AM member Geraldine Innocente, who had begun receiving them as early as 1945. As a loyal member, she reported one of her early messages to Frances Ekey, a strong Ballard supporter who had used her metaphysical group in Philadelphia to promote the I AM. Ekey reported Innocente to Ballard, who responded by conducting an exorcism which, however, did not stop the messages. Innocente continued to receive and circulate her messages privately to I AM members under the pseudonym Thomas Printz. Eventually, Ballard dismissed her, but Innocente took Ekey with her. Ekey assisted Innocente in incorporating her own group, the Bridge to Freedom, in 1954. One of Innocente's primary disagreements with the I AM was with Ballard's refusal to translate the I AM teachings into languages other than English.

In the Bridge, Innocente was known as the 'Ascended Masters' Representative', as well as 'the contact'. Ekey, who had been an appointed messenger in the I AM tradition, took an active role in the Bridge. She was considered a 'messenger' there as well, in the sense that she was permitted to publicly read transcripts of Innocente's messages. Ekey also edited the messages prepared by Innocente. The Bridge continued many of the practices and doctrines of the I AM but developed additional teachings. Although most of the doctrinal changes were cosmetic, the group's emphasis on greater autonomy led to splinter groups and competing claims to authority.

By April 1958, tensions had developed between Innocente and Ekey. A letter from Innocente accuses Ekey of 'tantrums' and declares she is no longer a messenger. In May 1958, Mark Prophet, who was already taking messages of his own in the I AM-Bridge tradition, sent Ekey letters from El Morya, which invited her to help start a new group (TSL Research Dept. 1994a). The Bridge ceased issuing dictations as of 1961 and ended its activities in 1979 (Ascended Master Teaching Foundation 2020).

The Summit Lighthouse (TSL) and the Lighthouse of Freedom 1958–1960

Mark Prophet, a native of Wisconsin, was a salesman with spiritual inclinations. A Methodist who had also been exposed to Pentecostalism, Mark developed esoteric interests during the 1930s and both taught and participated in spiritual groups during the 1940s. Around 1951, Mark encountered the 'Thomas Printz' dictations by Innocente. In 1952, he began distributing his own letters from El Morya, a master known in Theosophical and other circles. In August 1956, Mark met Ekey and visited the Bridge headquarters in Flourtown, Pennsylvania. Later that year, he read the Ballard books and probably also joined the Bridge as a 'reader', a basic level of membership.

Two years later, in August 1958, in Philadelphia, Mark took seven 'live' (extemporaneous) dictations during a meeting with Ekey and other former Bridge or I AM members. The messages inaugurated both the Lighthouse of Freedom, which ran conferences and published a magazine, and The Summit Lighthouse, the original purpose of which was simply to publish and distribute dictations.

Before long, Ekey and Prophet fell out over tensions concerning leadership and inspiration. Ekey did not reveal Mark, who lived in Washington, DC, and worked for the postal service, as the source of the Lighthouse dictations. Between 1958 and 1959, she held conferences in Philadelphia at which she read Mark's dictations and stated that they were from 'the contact'. Due to her extensive editing, the dictations can be seen as a joint project between Mark and Ekey. This process led to friction.

In August 1959, Mark (writing as the master El Morya) asked Ekey to stop editing the dictations, reserving the right for 'our beloved Messenger'. Frances bridled at the use of the title 'Messenger'. She asked, 'May I also know, please, when the "contact" was made a Messenger?' In September 1959, Morya-Mark sent a message directing that the Lighthouse of Freedom be dissolved over the 'grievous assaults and untrue accusations' levelled by Ekey against Mark (TSL Research Dept. 1994b). Ekey continued to run the Lighthouse of Freedom until her death in 1968.

The Summit Lighthouse (TSL) and Church Universal and Triumphant (CUT)

As of Autumn 1959, Mark Prophet was running TSL independently, acknowledged as its sole messenger. Almost all of his early followers were former I AM or Bridge members, which made it important for him to uphold in general the teachings of those organizations. However, he introduced a few important innovations. First, he liberalised lifestyle restrictions on meat consumption and sexual activity. He also created a new variation on the I AM's depiction of the individual 'Divine Self'. None of these changes occasioned much, if any, opposition from former I AM members. In fact, his expansion of the use of decrees with new rhyming and rhythmic repetitive prayers and chants was one of the most popular and widely accepted of his innovations.

Mark justified his innovations, as well as the need for a new organization, through the concept of progressive revelation, articulated in a new age way, as seen in a 1962 dictation by Jesus Christ through Mark:

> Progress as progressive revelation is the law of spiritual evolution. For with each new level of attainment, even after the ascension, vistas of knowledge transcending the old open before the soul. And some of this knowledge will even seem to contradict one's former understanding or prophetic insights, even as a child grows into new truths and discards the outworn mode of expression. (Jesus Christ 1986 [1962]: 230)

This doctrine was not enough to prevent ongoing challenges to the authority of the messengers, especially after Mark met Elizabeth Clare Wulf Ytreberg[4] in 1961 and married her in 1963. Mark and Elizabeth developed several narratives for why a new 'activity' was needed. Although they did not often directly address differences with other groups, they did claim that the leaders of previous groups had 'failed' in their mission or had mixed 'psychic' with genuine teachings or had fallen victim to pride (see El Morya 1976: 122). The Bridge was seen as more suspect than the I AM. Both Prophets supported the major I AM revelations and promoted the Ballard books, while elaborating upon their teachings.

When Elizabeth began working with Mark in the fall of 1961, the older I AM members were sceptical of her role. Mark began training her to be a messenger in secret but she did not take her first public dictation until 1964. From then until Mark's untimely death of a stroke in 1973, Elizabeth's dictations were in the minority and most TSL members saw Mark as their leader. After his death, Elizabeth was able to legitimate her message through dictations she gave from Mark as the Ascended Master Lanello.

Elizabeth Clare Prophet as messenger

Upon Mark's death, TSL was nominally governed by a board of directors, of whom Elizabeth was a member, the rest consisting of TSL staff members, including at least two ministers ordained by Mark. Previous academic work has not dwelt on the transition of power, and focused instead on Elizabeth's subsequent expansion (e.g. Whitsel 2003: 37–8), but in fact there were attempts to curb her authority. After a transition period between 1974 and 1981, Elizabeth removed most of the board members appointed by Mark. Monroe Shearer, a minister ordained by Mark who questioned some of her decisions, was dismissed from the staff and board in 1980. Randall King, another of Mark's appointees, became her third husband in 1973. After divorcing Randall in 1980, Elizabeth married Edward Francis, who became her fourth husband in 1981 (see Erin Prophet 2017).

As the movement grew rapidly, the proportion of followers who had known Mark dwindled. Elizabeth's innovations included the use of astrology (forbidden in the I AM), as well as a complex theory of evil and hybrid humanity based on interpretations of the apocryphal Book of Enoch (discussed in greater detail below). One of her major innovations was to incorporate Church Universal and Triumphant (CUT) in 1975, which became the primary identity of the group, with The Summit Lighthouse called the 'publishing arm' (until 2000, when it once more became dominant). The Church offered sacraments but also introduced behavioural requirements, discussed in greater detail below. Church members were required to tithe, confess a variety of sins, and attend prescribed services. Some of these innovations could be seen as a natural progression from Mark's work, while others ran counter to his less restrictive approach to behaviour.

Elizabeth did continue to maintain the Keepers of the Flame Fraternity, an organization with no lifestyle restrictions, founded by Mark in 1962 along the lines of a Rosicrucian order. 'Keepers' agreed to a minimal financial commitment of dues only. Another of Elizabeth's innovations was to strengthen and codify requirements for joining the TSL-CUT staff, which had numbered about a hundred during Mark's life, but swelled to as many as seven hundred by the late 1980s. The staff agreed to a restrictive code of conduct and the elite 'permanent staff' committed to share all of their assets with the Church. See Chart 1: TSL-CUT Membership Categories (Figures 17.1).

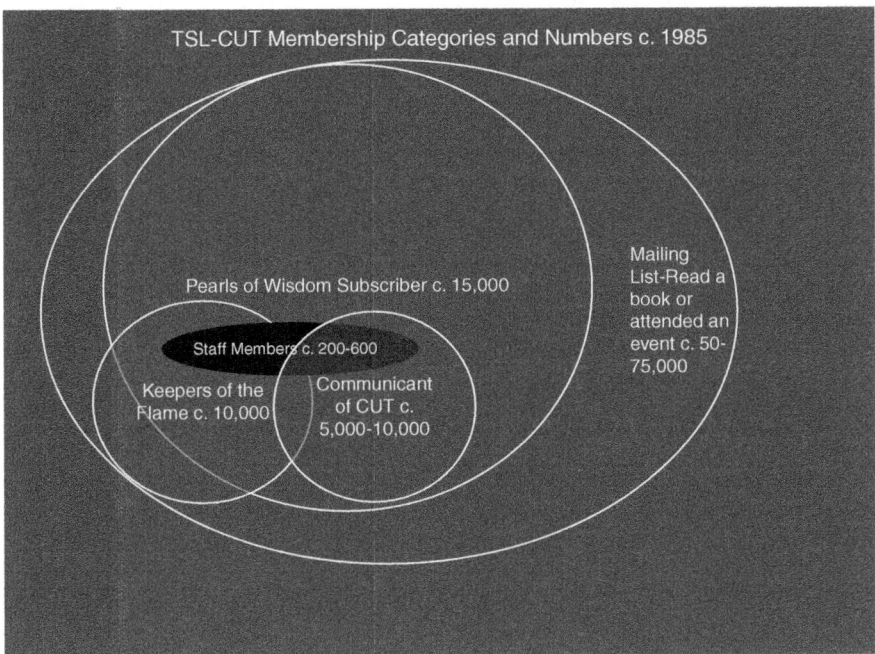

Figure 17.1 Approximate membership in different categories of affiliation with TSL-CUT c. 1985. Communicants of Church Universal and Triumphant were required to tithe and adhere to a specific lifestyle. Members of the Keepers of the Flame Fraternity had no lifestyle restrictions, received monthly lessons, paid annual dues and could attend most events. All staff were members of the fraternity and subscribers to the Pearls of Wisdom, the Church's weekly digest of ascended master teachings. Summit University was a three-month retreat and training programme. The mailing list included individuals who had attended an event or otherwise expressed interest. Not to scale.

Elizabeth Clare Prophet: prophecy and revisionism

Prophet is best known for the predictions that led to the 'shelter episode' of 1989 and 1990, which brought her and the Church to worldwide attention. Her warnings of a 'ride of the Four Horsemen' manifesting as economic collapse, nuclear war and subsequent natural disaster led several thousand people to Montana where they built and stocked bomb shelters. But these prophecies cannot be seen as an entirely new development. While the extreme response of building the shelters was new, prophecies of war and disaster were not. As far back as 1965, the Prophets had warned of both cataclysm and nuclear war (TSL Research Dept. 1992b). Concerns about both types of events were one catalyst for the move of TSL headquarters from Virginia to Colorado in 1966.

War and cataclysm were a part of the complex equation of 'planetary karma', which was a frequent subject of dictations. Much of the decree (prayer) work of the group was intent on dissolving this karma (and eradicating the evil forces believed to be using it for nefarious ends) and to prevent or turn back predicted events. There were several periods, including just after Mark's death, when actual physical preparations were made, but it was not until 1987 that Elizabeth Prophet named specific dates and directed an extensive programme of preparation, linking the prophecy to ongoing evil acts in the world, including sexual perversions, abortion, and the failure to 'heed' the word of the masters through their messengers.

Each of these elements may have been present in Mark's work in embryo, but they were developed and refined during the 1980s in both Elizabeth's dictations and her other published writings. In *Prophet's Daughter* (2009), I suggest a connection between the prophecies and the challenges to Elizabeth Prophet's authority which surrounded the Church's loss of a lawsuit in 1986 (*CUT v. Mull*) (see also Prophet 2019 for a complete review of the trial). Further work remains to be done in tracing correlations between external challenges and doctrinal shifts in ascended master traditions.

In *Prophet's Daughter* (Prophet, E. L. 2009), I also covered the revisionism that occurred after what I call the 'shelter episode,' the period from 1989 to 1990 when shelters were built and briefly occupied. After the episode, as many as one-third of the members left the group, but many of those who stayed spiritualised the prophecies, believing that their prayers had mitigated the karma. Others accepted a prophecy 'update' given in 1990, which suggested the karma would descend during a 12-year period and not all at once (see Prophet 1990). In spite of the defections, the group might have returned to its former strength if Prophet had not begun to exhibit symptoms of memory loss, which by 1998 were diagnosed as Alzheimer's disease.

Although beyond the scope of this article, and covered well by Palmer and Abravanel (2009), Prophet's illness led to schism and fragmentation in TSL-CUT. Prophet's refusal to appoint a spiritual successor prior to her formal retirement in 2000 and death in 2009 left the way open to further schism. However, current leadership has been attempting to repair the schisms, focuses on simple, positive messages, and has reasserted TSL as the group's primary identity (TSL 2020).

Temple of the Presence: Monroe and Carolyn Shearer

Challenges to Elizabeth Prophet's authority had already been underway as her abilities weakened during the early 1990s. The first group to claim new inspiration was the Temple of the Presence, founded by Monroe Shearer, former CUT minister and board member. He and his second wife, Carolyn Yost Shearer, who had been a music teacher and choir member in CUT, began to take dictations and gather a following in the mid-1990s.

The Temple of the Presence, currently headquartered in Tucson, Arizona, legitimates itself with a declaration of a 'new dispensation' from the masters El Morya and Saint Germain (Temple of the Presence 2013). The Shearers take their primary inspiration from the I AM but have introduced their own innovations, drawing from Neoplatonism and placing less emphasis on the Bible than did TSL-CUT. While revering Mark Prophet as an ascended master, the Temple of the Presence has no formal position on Elizabeth's status since her death in 2009 (Anon 2015). Both Shearers proclaim themselves messengers in the I AM-TSL tradition, though they call themselves 'Anointed Representatives' of the 'Brotherhood of Light', rather than the 'Great White Brotherhood', a term derived from Theosophy and used in TSL-CUT.[5] Only one set of 'ordained Messengers' are said to be active on earth at a particular time (Shearer 1999).

The Temple of the Presence bears many similarities to TSL-CUT and the I AM, particularly with its order of 'Torch-Bearers', which recalls the Keepers of the Flame, and new decrees and songs written in the I AM and TSL-CUT tradition. The Temple of the Presence distinguishes itself theologically from TSL-CUT by refining the concept of the Presence as more personalized and self-created. The Shearers have replaced the TSL-CUT Holy Christ Self with the 'Holy Christ Presence.'

One of the Temple of the Presence's most serious disagreements with TSL-CUT concerns Elizabeth Prophet's use of astrology. It also disagrees with the practice of decreeing against evil forces, stating that such practices will only result in the lowering of one's 'energy'. The Shearers have stated that they prefer to send out light rather than trying to dissolve sources of negativity, which had been a key part of both Mark and Elizabeth's teaching on decrees (Anon 2015).

Unlike either the I AM or TSL-CUT, the Temple of the Presence has avoided setting forth rules for behaviour. Nevertheless, in online forums, vestiges of the high-handed tone of earlier messengers can be seen. A representative of the Temple (Shepherd Templar) threatened 'far-reaching karmic consequences' for those who question the validity or accuracy of any detail of the Ballards' work (L. F., Shepherd Templar, 2012). The Temple of the Presence maintains a small but loyal following in the hundreds.

David Lewis – Hearts Center

In 2004, David Christopher Lewis (b. 1956), who had recently resigned from his position as manager of the Keepers of the Flame fraternity at TSL-CUT, received a series of what he calls 'direct transmissions' from Lanello (the ascended name of Mark Prophet). Lewis had joined the TSL-CUT at age 18, and the church staff at age 20. He shared the 'transmissions' with members of Church leadership. The messages from El Morya asked them to consider him as the next messenger, which was provided for in the CUT bylaws. The leadership was not receptive and, according to Lewis, sent out an e-mail calling him a 'false hierarchy messenger' (Lewis 2015: 2).

Like the Shearers, Lewis generally supports the I AM and TSL work, but thinks that Prophet took a wrong turn in transforming TSL into CUT. He stated, 'In retrospect, transforming the Summit into the Church was fraught with problems. The organization became too entrenched with certain rituals and codified its own "new age" doctrines with too many do's and don'ts' (2020). According to him, Elizabeth Prophet is ascended and is known as the ascended master *Clare de Lis*. He has taken messages from her which, like other messages he receives, he calls 'Heart Streams', rather than 'dictations' (see The Hearts Center 2019).

In addition to rejecting an organised institutional Church, Lewis has embraced a more diffuse leadership model than either TSL-CUT or the Temple of the Presence. In a 2015 interview, he said that *anyone* could be a messenger. 'God doesn't stop. God has never stopped. We are all messengers, everyone' (Lewis 2015:2). He has sanctioned messages that have come through a number of other people, saying that he trusts them, and that even nonmembers such as Vietnamese Buddhist monk Thich Nhat Hanh or self-help author Wayne Dyer are 'messengers of a sort' (Lewis 2015:2). However, he said that he does occasionally exercise his power as gatekeeper of Hearts Center teachings, mentioning that he had to 'just put my foot down' on doctrinal questions (Lewis 2015: 3).

Hearts Center, currently headquartered in Livingston, Montana, does not offer sacraments, though it legally functions as a church. Lewis feels it should not have a Christian bent because it transcends religious boundaries, and actually does not use a chart of the Divine Self like TSL, the I AM or Temple of the Presence. This appears to be a demonstration of what Hammer calls a 'shift [in the Esoteric Tradition] from an exclusive, privileged, prophetic experience to a democratic ideal' (Hammer 2001: 417). Lewis has attracted new members from outside the TSL-CUT milieu and some Hearts Center videos have thousands of hits on YouTube

Exclusivity

Although they initially took a nonexclusivist stance towards membership in other movements, in response to competition the Prophets eventually came down more on the side of exclusivity. At first, there was no sense that one had to belong only to TSL. In 1960, Mark wrote to a man who was currently involved in the Unity school of Christianity that he disagreed with the Christian church's exclusivist attitude.

> I have never felt that this attitude was proper as pertains to Spiritual progress. And I believe in a free and open mind and heart. However, I think that that free mind and heart should include our own activity as well as all others. (TSL Research Dept. 1992b)

However, this position was not without tension. Also in 1960, Mark suggested that it would be preferable if people could make a choice, remarking on the 'benefits' that could accrue when people devoted all their support to 'a particular channel,' though he himself 'personally would not attempt to indicate to individuals that they were bound in any way to do as we do' (TSL Research Dept. 1992b). By 1975, Elizabeth Prophet had made disaffiliation from other groups a requirement of Church membership, though members of the Church's less-restrictive Keepers of the Flame Fraternity could always maintain other affiliations.

One boundary of exclusivity that was maintained even for members of the fraternity was the prohibition on anyone except official messengers transmitting messages from masters as 'psychic' dictations. In 1970, the Prophets gave an ultimatum to a woman named Erma Jean Lee to 'give up the taking of dictations or give up membership in Saint Germain's Keepers of the Flame Fraternity' (TSL Research Dept. 1992b). This was one of numerous threatened and actual expulsions based on 'psychic activity'.

Prophet explained why it was important to make a choice. In 1975, a dictation from El Morya declared that 'false teachers' and 'false gurus', particularly from India, were 'unappointed, or self-appointed, messengers' trying to usurp the office of the true messengers, and engaging in psychic activity. A 'true messenger' did not commune with the (unascended) dead, which was seen as the practice of 'necromancy or spiritism.' Students were encouraged to 'test the spirits', according to the Biblical formula in 1 John 4:1, indicating their freedom of choice as to teacher (El Morya 1976: 115–8).

By 1995, however, in light of the challenges to her legitimacy following the shelter episode, Elizabeth did temporarily reverse her long-standing rule against communication with the deceased by church members. TSL published a booklet with a note penned by Elizabeth from El Morya stating that 'a special dispensation' had been created to permit an unascended and recently deceased 'brother' to communicate, because 'too many have not heeded our warnings [of] serious challenges to the nations,' i.e. prophecies concerning the period between 1990 and 2002.

What this meant in practical terms was that a female member of TSL-CUT claimed to have received a message from her recently deceased father which, though he was not ascended, Elizabeth believed was sanctioned by El Morya. Her note from El Morya introducing the work stated,

This is a *special dispensation* and should not be used as an excuse to seek communication from or with those who have gone on to their rightful place of service in the heaven-world. To do so would be to place yourself outside the protection of the Ascended Masters. (El Morya 1995: 1)

The 'Special Dispensation' is largely supportive of Elizabeth Prophet as messenger and blames problems in the Church on middle management. It also supports her prophecy of a period of upheaval between 1990 and 2002, which was a revision of her earlier prophecies (Prophet 1990).

As the Temple of the Presence began to gather members, spiritual con-demnations were tossed back and forth between Elizabeth Prophet and the Shearers. Prophet warned her students against attending the Shearers' meetings. And an undated Declaration from El Morya published by the Temple of the Presence in the late 1990s, claiming to be an updated version of one written by Geraldine Innocente, declares, in a clear criticism of Prophet, that 'One who professes to represent Us has been so bold as to canonize by innuendo and by use of Our Name the tenet that the Ascension can come only through her and her personal intercession as Guru' (El Morya, n.d.). In the 2000s, the leadership of TSL-CUT expelled numerous individuals for participating in the Temple of the Presence and Hearts Center groups. According to Lewis, the TSL-CUT leadership also threa-tened that anyone who joined his group could forfeit their ascensions (Lewis 2015). In the 2010s, the leadership of TSL-CUT made amends with some of the expelled and sought to reduce tensions. Neither the Temple of the Presence nor Hearts Center requires exclusive membership.

Correlation of outside pressure with shifts in theology of evil

After Mark's death, Elizabeth greatly expanded the theology regarding in-visible evil forces, called 'shadow forces' in Theosophy, and 'black magicians' in the I AM. She connected them with evil forces mentioned in the Bible, such as the angels 'cast out' of heaven in Revelation 12, whom she termed 'fallen angels'. In 1980, Elizabeth also incorporated the apocryphal Book of Enoch and the work of Zechariah Sitchin (1975) into an elaborate theory of human-divine miscegenation based on Genesis 6:2–4. She speculated that the biblical sons of God who mated with the 'daughters of men' were really fallen angels or evil Sumerian gods who were really aliens. These gods were called *Nephilim* by Sitchin, meaning 'fallen ones', or 'those who fell', though this translation has been disputed by at least one Hebrew expert, who states that the word means simply *giant* (See Flaherty 2012: 89–90).

Elizabeth retro-fitted her new theology of evil into Mark's work as she edited it for publication. Some of these dictations had already been published by him prior to her editing, and so it is possible to compare them. For example, in 1961 Mark had taken a dictation on sacrifice from Jesus Christ, whose central message is that neither animal sacrifice nor the blood sacrifice of the son of God are required for remission of sins, i.e., balancing karma (Jesus Christ: 1961). Elizabeth added an interpolation on the topic of sacrifice, describing Canaanite child sacrifice as an abomination 'of Nephilim origin' (Jesus Christ 1986: 179). Although Mark never used the term *Nephilim*, this was her own 'progressive revelation' a claim that he was dictating to her the complete message of his earlier work.

Crucial to Elizabeth's new theology about 'godless' Nephilim hybrid races was that some human beings were not fully human and did not possess a 'divine spark' and therefore were not eligible for the ascension, although at times dictations implied that even the godless could earn a divine spark if given enough lifetimes. The development of theology regarding Nephilim coincided temporally with a period of increased media scrutiny of TSL-CUT, the kidnapping and deprogramming of numerous members by the anti-cult movement and the emergence of high-ranking apostates.

The Nephilim theology also supported the 1989–1990 'shelter episode' and attendant separation from society by heightening group boundary tensions and an insider-outsider mentality. This pessimistic outlook on salvation persisted until the early 1990s, when a more optimistic period began. Neither the Temple of the Presence nor Hearts Center adopted the theology about Nephilim; both take the attitude, also promoted in the I AM and TSL, that *all* humans can ascend.

Changing positions on personal behaviour

The I AM Activity had taken a strong stand against eating meat and engaging in sexual activity, stating that both would interfere with the ascension. If the ascension were not 'earned' in the current life, reincarnation would be required. According to Davies Anderson, a former I AM member, even sex for procreation was recommended against, since the golden age would arrive soon and procreation would be unnecessary. As the group codified membership requirements, the rules around sex led to the breakup of marriages and drove many people out of the I AM (Anderson 1999).

Mark Prophet began TSL with the goal of being less strict than the I AM. In a 1965 lecture, Mark stated that group leaders should not direct the lifestyle of members with regard to food (Prophet 1965). TSL-CUT never adopted dietary requirements, though the leaders promoted health-food regimes and generally supported vegetarian diets as being more spiritual. During the early 1960s, Mark and the rest of the TSL staff ate meat, but they became vegetarian by 1970. In the 1980s, various diets were experimented with, some of which included animal products.

In terms of sexual activity, Mark stated that procreation was a good thing, needed for the continuance of the group. Elizabeth later taught that sex was not just for procreation but for the balancing of masculine and feminine energies, and therefore also supported contraception (see Erin Prophet 2017). These shifts away from I AM doctrine do not seem to have cost TSL-CUT members; rather, they attracted former I AM students and young hippies.

However, as the sexual revolution progressed, Elizabeth Prophet eventually decided that some restrictions on sexuality were necessary, at least for staff and formal Church members. She made pronouncements on the spiritual risks of oral sex, homosexuality, and masturbation, warning they could lead to reincarnation rather than ascension (Prophet 1974, 1978). After the United States Supreme Court legalized abortion in 1973, Prophet took a dramatic public stance with dictations directly linking sexual perversion and abortion with prophecy of destruction. For example, in 1982: 'that nation and that people who will tolerate the murder of the Almighty in his own – that nation shall suffer cataclysm' (Archangel Uriel, 1982). In spite of the warnings surrounding sexual infractions and abortions, Elizabeth Prophet did not penalize them with the same severity as psychic activity. Usually sexual infractions could be expiated by penance or demotion, rather than expulsion.

The Temple of the Presence and Hearts Center do not pay the same kind of attention to their members' private lives as did the I AM, Bridge and TSL-CUT. However, the former do maintain a stance against abortion, echoing the sentiments of the Prophets. Both the Temple of the Presence and Hearts Center have affirmed the TSL-CUT stance that abortion constitutes murder. Lewis stated that he sees it as exposing the nation to returning karma through cataclysm or war (Lewis 2015).

As of 2020, TSL-CUT does not have a messenger but does have a spiritual director. It continues to function at the Montana ranch, governed by a council of ministers and a board, although its numbers are greatly diminished from the peak in the early 1990s. It adheres to the most conservative of Elizabeth Prophet's teachings on abortion, which appears to be one area, at least, not subject to further revisionism in any of the extant groups. However, according to some sources, debate has taken place in all of the groups concerning teachings against homosexuality, given rapid changes in attitude among the target membership audience.

Conclusion

This brief history demonstrates how the concept of 'messenger' has served both to unify and to divide groups in the I AM tradition. It contains clear examples of the correlation of revision of doctrines with internal and external challenges to authority. It also shows both the strengths and weaknesses of 'messengership' in a time of the increasing appeal of diffuse notions of authority. Finally, it demonstrates the limit to revisions made to accommodate declining membership. If the core group remains faithful to principles which are out-of-step with the times, its leaders may prefer decline over revision.

The history of ascended master activities is one of continued schism, doctrinal controversy and ongoing 'progressive revelation'. Given the inherent tension between individual inspiration and centralized authority, there is no reason to expect this will change. However, it remains to be seen whether any of the three groups evaluated here – TSL-CUT, Temple of the Presence, and the Hearts Center – will succeed in attracting the kind of large audience that TSL-CUT did in the 1980s and, if so, whether members will coalesce around new messengers or around less exclusive models of inspiration and leadership.

Notes

1 Although the figure of a million members has often been used concerning the I AM Activity's size at its peak, a more likely number is fifty thousand members or interested individuals. I AM meetings filled the Shrine Auditorium in Los Angeles for weeks at a time during the 1930s (capacity c.7,000) but its footprint in other cities militates against a larger figure.
2 Barker, ed. 1923, Letter 9, 39; not an adept, 43; "flesh-eating," Letter 68, 276–7.
3 New Thought is a system of mental and physical healing in the tradition of Mary Baker Eddy's Christian Science, founded in 1879. Many of its early teachers had been Christian Scientists, but they also drew from the work of Warren Felt Evans, who had studied with Eddy's teacher Phineas Quimby. New Thought was most prominent in the United States from the 1880s through the 1930s.
4 Elizabeth Prophet's middle name was "Clare." She used it in her formal publications but not in informal speech. It was not a formal title or modifier of her last name. *Prophet* is Mark's family surname, inherited from Scots emigrants to Canada.
5 These masters are said to belong to a secret and both physical and ethereal group known as a 'brotherhood' – variously of Luxor, a 'Great White Brotherhood', or a Brotherhood of Light. These brotherhoods also include sisters and do not consider 'white' to refer to race.

Bibliography

All URLs were accessed on 22 June 2020.

Anderson, Davies. 1999. Erin Prophet Interviews Davies Anderson re I AM Activity. Audio recording in person with notes, 26 January. Pray: Montana.

Anon. 2015. Former Temple of the Presence Member. Temple of the Presence Doctrines Questions from Erin Prophet, e-mail, 3 July.

Anon. 1995. *A Special Dispensation from the Darjeeling Council of the Great White Brotherhood*. Edited by Elizabeth Clare Prophet. Livingston, MT: The Summit Lighthouse.

Archangel Uriel [through Elizabeth Clare Prophet]. 1982. Published on 1997 CD-ROM as *Pearls of Wisdom* 33(12). Livingston, MT: Summit University Press.

Ascended Master Teaching Foundation. 2020. 'AMTF History.' Available at: https://ascendedmaster.org/about-amtf/history/

Barker, A. Trevor, ed. (1923) 1975. *The Mahatma Letters to A.P. Sinnett*. Pasadena, CA: Theosophical University Press.

Braden, Charles S. 1949. *These Also Believe: A Study of Modern American Cults & Minority Religious Movements*. New York: Macmillan.

Campbell, Bruce F. 1980. *Ancient Wisdom Revived: A History of the Theosophical Movement*. Berkeley: University of California Press.

El Morya [through Monroe and Carolyn Shearer]. n.d.c. 1996. I Come Bearing New Wine. Redlands, CA: Temple of the Presence.

El Morya [through Elizabeth Clare Prophet]. 1995. "A Special Dispensation" in *A Special Dispensation from the Darjeeling Council of the Great White Brotherhood*. Livingston, MT: The Summit Lighthouse.

El Morya [through Elizabeth Clare Prophet]. 1976. *The Chela and The Path*. Livingston, MT: Summit University Press.

Flaherty, Robert Pearson. 2012. "'These Are They': ET-Human Hybridization and the New Daemonology" in *Nova Religio* 14(2): 84–105.

Hammer, Olaf. 2001. *Claiming Knowledge: Strategies of Epistemology from Theosophy to the New Age*. Vol. XC. Numen Book Series. Leiden: Brill.

Hanegraaff, Wouter J. *New Age Religion and Western Culture: Esotericism in the Mirror of Secular Thought*. SUNY Series, Western Esoteric Traditions. Albany, NY: State University of New York Press, 1998.

Jesus Christ [through Mark Prophet, edited by Elizabeth Prophet]. 1986 [first published 1961]. "Corona Class Lesson 22 – Sacrifice" in Jesus Christ and Kuthumi, *Corona Class Lessons*. Livingston, MT: Summit University Press, pp. 177–184, 225–233.

Jesus Christ [through Mark Prophet]. 1961. "Corona Class–22" in *Pearls of Wisdom 4(49): 68–69* . Washington, DC: The Summit Lighthouse.

L.F., Shepherd Templar, Temple of the Presence. 2012. Comment. *Facebook* (closed group), 6 November.

Lewis, David. 2015. 'Erin Prophet Interviews David Lewis re: Hearts Center.' Via telephone with notes, 9 June.

Lewis, David. 2020. Personal communication via email to Erin Prophet 22 June.

Melton, J. Gordon. 1994. "The Church Universal and Triumphant: Its Heritage and Thoughtworld" in James Lewis and J. Gordon Melton (eds) *Church Universal and Triumphant in Scholarly Perspective*. Stanford: Center for Academic Publication, pp. 1–20.

Palmer, Susan, and Michael Abravanel. 2009. "Church Universal and Triumphant: Shelter, Succession and Schism" in James Lewis and Sarah Lewis (eds) *Sacred Schisms: How Religions Divide*. Cambridge, UK: Cambridge University Press, pp. 171–195.

Prophet, Elizabeth Clare. 1990. "The Four Horsemen: A 2,000-Year Ride" in *Pearls of Wisdom 33(6)*. Livingston, MT: Summit University Press.

Prophet, Elizabeth Clare. 1978. Lecture in Dallas, TX, 18 February.

Prophet, Elizabeth Clare. 1974. Lecture at Summit University. Santa Barbara, CA, 24 January.

Prophet, Erin. 2019. *Coercion or Conversion: A Case Study in Religion and the Law, Church Universal and Triumphant v. Gregory Mull v. Elizabeth Clare Prophet*. Gainesville, FL: Linden Books. Available at: https://www.eprophet.info/publications

Prophet, Erin. 2017. "Elizabeth Clare Prophet: Gender, Sexuality and the Divine Feminine" in Inga Bårdsen Tøllefsen and Christian Giudice (eds) *Female Leaders of New Religious Movements*. London, UK: Palgrave Macmillan, pp. 51–77.

Prophet, Erin. 2016. "Charisma and Authority in New Religious Movements'" in James Lewis and Inga Bårdsen Tøllefsen (eds) *The Oxford Handbook of New Religious Movements*, vol. 2. Oxford, UK: Oxford University Press, pp. 36–49.

Prophet, Erin 2009. *Prophet's Daughter: My Life with Elizabeth Clare Prophet Inside the Church Universal and Triumphant*. Guilford, CT: Lyons Press.

Prophet, Mark. 1965. Lecture. Unpublished, 24 October.

Rudbøg, Tim. 2013. "The I AM Activity" in Olav Hammer and Mikael Rothstein (eds), *Handbook of the Theosophical Current*. Leiden: Brill, pp. 151–172.

Satter, Beryl. 1999. *Each Mind a Kingdom: American Women, Sexual Purity, and the New Thought Movement, 1875-1920*. Berkeley, CA: University of California Press.

Saint Germain. 1935. *The "I AM" Discourses*. Edited by Guy W. Ballard [Godfré Ray King]. Chicago, IL: Saint Germain Press.

Shearer, Carolyn. 1999. In-person interview with Erin Prophet regarding Temple of the Presence. Tape recording and notes. 3 June. Bozeman, MT.

Sitchin, Zecharia. 1975. *Twelfth Planet: Book I of the Earth Chronicles*. New York: Avon.

Temple of The Presence. 2013. 'The New Dispensation – A Dawning New Day from the Great Central Sun! The Temple of The Presence'. Available at: http://templeofthepresence.org/temple.aspx

The Hearts Center. 2019. Lady Master Clare de Lis. Available at: https://www.heartscenter.org/TeachingsBlogs/AscendedMasters/MessengersNowAscended/ElizabethClareProphet-GuruMa/tabid/1159/Default.aspx

The Summit Lighthouse. 2020. 'Teachings of the Ascended Masters.' Available at: https://www.summitlighthouse.org/

TSL Research Dept. 1992a. "The Summit Lighthouse Early History from Split with Frances Ekey through 1961". Unpublished.

TSL Research Dept. 1992b. "Summit Lighthouse Chronology of Events", July 1961 through February 1973. Unpublished.

TSL Research Dept. 1994a. Frances K. Ekey Biographical Research. Unpublished.

TSL Research Dept. 1994b. Lighthouse of Freedom-The Summit Lighthouse Correspondence Involving Frances Ekey, 1952–1959. Unpublished.

Whitsel, Bradley C. 2003. *The Church Universal and Triumphant: Elizabeth Clare Prophet's Apocalyptic Movement. Religion and Politics*. Syracuse, NY: Syracuse University Press.

Index

NB Some of the Icelandic names have their first names before their last names on purpose